WITH US AND AGAINST US

COLUMBIA STUDIES IN TERRORISM AND IRREGULAR WARFARE

COLUMBIA STUDIES IN TERRORISM AND IRREGULAR WARFARE

Bruce Hoffman, Series Editor

This series seeks to fill a conspicuous gap in the burgeoning literature on terrorism, guerrilla warfare, and insurgency. The series adheres to the highest standards of scholarship and discourse and publishes books that elucidate the strategy, operations, means, motivations, and effects posed by terrorist, guerrilla, and insurgent organizations and movements. It thereby provides a solid and increasingly expanding foundation of knowledge on these subjects for students, established scholars, and informed reading audiences alike.

Ami Pedahzur, *The Israeli Secret Services and the Struggle Against Terrorism*
Ami Pedahzur and Arie Perliger, *Jewish Terrorism in Israel*
Lorenzo Vidino, *The New Muslim Brotherhood in the West*
Erica Chenoweth and Maria J. Stephan, *Why Civil Resistance Works: The Strategic Logic of Nonviolent Conflict*
William C. Banks, editor, *New Battlefields/Old Laws: Critical Debates on Asymmetric Warfare*
Blake W. Mobley, *Terrorism and Counterintelligence: How Terrorist Groups Elude Detection*
Jennifer Morrison Taw, *Mission Revolution: The U.S. Military and Stability Operations*
Guido W. Steinberg, *German Jihad: On the Internationalization of Islamist Terrorism*

For a complete list of title, see page 411.

STEPHEN TANKEL

WITH US AND AGAINST US

How America's Partners Help and Hinder the War on Terror

Columbia University Press / New York

Columbia University Press
Publishers Since 1893
New York Chichester, West Sussex
cup.columbia.edu

Library of Congress Cataloging-in-Publication Data
Names: Tankel, Stephen, author.
Title: With us and against us : how America's partners help and hinder the war on terror / Stephen Tankel.
Description: New York ; Chichester, West Sussex : Columbia University Press, [2018] | Includes bibliographical references and index.
Identifiers: LCCN 2017044061| ISBN 9780231168106 (cloth : alk. paper) | ISBN 9780231168113 (pbk. : alk. paper) | ISBN 9780231547345 (e-book)
Subjects: LCSH: Terrorism—Government policy—United States. | Terrorism—United States—Prevention. | United States—Foreign relations—2009–2017.
Classification: LCC HV6432 .T39 2018 | DDC 363.325/170973—dc23
LC record available at https://lccn.loc.gov/2017044061

Columbia University Press books are printed on permanent and durable acid-free paper.

Printed in the United States of America

Cover design: Mary Ann Smith

For Stephanie.

CONTENTS

PREFACE AND ACKNOWLEDGMENTS

SOMETIME DURING MY FIRST WEEK at the Department of Defense, where I served as a senior advisor for Asian and Pacific Security Affairs in 2014, I was asked to review a pretty routine set of talking points for a briefing to Congress. I noticed a minor inaccuracy and pointed it out to my colleagues. "How wrong is it?" one of them asked. I wasn't used to this type of question. The talking point was pretty inconsequential—a throwaway line of background—but it was also incorrect. I pointed out that it would not take long to change and offered to make the tweak if someone sent me the file. It was not that simple, my colleague explained. The language had been cleared, and changing it could require rerunning the clearance process. If something were seriously wrong with the points, then our office would run them back up the chain. Otherwise, my colleagues would just as soon avoid a fire drill, considering the briefing was the next day and we had other work to do. So, the same colleague asked again, "How wrong is it?" "Not wrong enough," I replied. The talking points remained as is.

I've since recounted this story to numerous students as just one example of how the perfect can become the enemy of the good when it comes to governing. Policy makers face myriad constraints. Some are bureaucratic and self-imposed. Others are political, structural, or resource driven. The overwhelming majority of them require tradeoffs that are far more consequential than the ones that rested on my brief quest to tweak a talking point. Constraints and the tradeoffs they entail are especially prevalent when working with and through other countries to realize U.S. interests—something that is impossible to avoid in today's interconnected world. I encountered these constraints regularly at the Department of Defense. I worked mainly on U.S. defense policy in South and Central Asia, which is a region where the United States has no treaty allies and must cooperate with a host of challenging partners. The experience not only gave me a much greater appreciation for how policy gets made and implemented. It also led me to rethink the book I was working on before entering government service.

I originally envisioned this book as an investigation of how the relationship between jihadist groups and the states where they originated or operated (the two are not always synonymous) influenced these groups' development and behavior. I left government captivated by the challenges of working with partner nations to realize U.S. national security objectives. Working by, with, and through other countries had become a cornerstone of the U.S. counterterrorism approach by this time.

These partnerships are often frustrating, rarely satisfying, and never perfect. Measuring success is difficult precisely because many partners simultaneously enable and constrain U.S. efforts. This raises numerous questions, including: How can America gain or exert more leverage to get more out these relationships? Should the United States act more unilaterally? And, are there reforms that could be instituted to build partners' capacity *and* political will? My purpose in writing this book is to present an unbiased, evidence-based assessment that addresses these questions and others through the prism of a single, overarching inquiry: What can the United States reasonably expect from its counterterrorism partners? Only by answering this question can we identify the trade space where U.S. policy makers could increase the rate of return on these relationships and the areas where mitigation is necessary because limitations are immutable.

* * *

Unpacking jihadist-state relations, which was the nucleus of the book I initially set out to write, is a critical piece of the puzzle. But it is not the whole story. Widening the aperture to focus on how partner nations both enable and constrain U.S. counterterrorism efforts forced me to explore the extent and limits of American influence, the utility of instruments of statecraft, and the changing nature of counterterrorism and alliances themselves. My lodestar during this exploration has been the idea that we must know our partners as well as we know the enemy and know ourselves.

The shift from writing a book where jihadist groups were the main players to exploring what the United States can expect from its counterterrorism partners was hardly seamless. I owe a great debt of gratitude to friends and colleagues who helped me make this transition. The School of International Service at American University sponsored a book incubator for me that proved invaluable. I walked in with a manuscript that was really still two books—the one I had set out to write before heading into government and the one I ended up wanting to write once I'd left. Miles Kahler expertly moderated a marathon session with Tricia Bacon, Jake Shapiro, Clint Watts, Joe Young, and Aaron Zelin. Together, they helped me navigate the necessary structural changes and sharpen the main arguments. Thanks also to Laura Bosco and Jessica Herring, who volunteered as notetakers and managed to capture all the participants' useful critiques.

Jim Goldgeier, who is one of the most astute analysts of U.S. foreign policy, was an incredibly supportive dean and carved out time to review the first half of the book after I revised it. Tricia Bacon, Nora Bensahel, Josh Geltzer, Luke Hartig, Andrew Lebovich, Dan Markey, Clint Watts, and Joe Young all made time to act as sounding boards and review parts of the manuscript at various times during the writing process. I'm also thankful to the two anonymous reviewers who read the manuscript. They provided me with useful suggestions on where to make adjustments to the manuscript and with the confidence not to mess with the rest. Ryan Evans tore himself away from running War on the Rocks to review the near-final product and offer recommendations on how to make it more readable. I was blessed with two great research assistants, Yumna Fatima and Joseph Marcus, and a dedicated cadre of current and former students who helped with fact checking and the formatting of citations. Laura Tyler deserves special mention—she assisted with multiple versions of the manuscript and was as indefatigable as she was precise. I'm also thankful to Jessica Herring, Rathna Muralidharan, and Pavan Rajgopal for their valuable support on this front.

I conducted interviews with numerous current and former U.S. officials, intelligence officers, and counterterrorism practitioners. This was in addition to the hundreds of interviews conducted in the Middle East, Africa, South

Asia, and Europe for other projects. Some of these interviews appear directly. Data gathered from others has appeared in assorted writings I published and subsequently drew on here. Still other interviews informed how I thought about the issues in this book, even if they did not always make it into the text. My experience in Egypt and discussions with numerous experts and activists while living there also informed that case study. I am deeply grateful to all those who graciously offered me their knowledge and insights and spoke to me about their experiences.

My thinking on security assistance, which is a critical instrument of statecraft, benefited substantially from collaboration with Dafna Rand, Alice Hunt Friend, Loren Dejonge Schulman, and Ilan Goldenberg at the Center for a New American Security (CNAS). I also benefited from conversations with Melissa Dalton at the Center for Strategic and International Studies and Rose Jackson at the Open Society Foundation. Participation in a CNAS Study Group on the Islamic State of Iraq and al-Sham yielded important insights about the organization and provided food for thought about broader U.S. counterterrorism efforts.

Columbia University Press lived up to its reputation as an incredibly rigorous press that puts its authors first. Bruce Hoffman is the editor of the Terrorism and Irregular Warfare series, the doyen of terrorism studies, and a mensch. He remained supportive of this project throughout the process, even when I told him I wanted to scrap my original book idea for a new one. Anne Routon, who was my original editor, moved on from Columbia before this manuscript was finalized but was a source of steadiness and patience while there. Miriam Grossman stepped in after Anne left to ensure a seamless transition, and Caelyn Cobb shepherded the book across the finish line. Rob Fellman was a precise and patient copy editor. Marisa Lastres deftly and patiently managed the production process.

Many friends provided encouragement and exhibited great degrees of understanding when I would suddenly disappear for marathon writing sessions. My parents' seemingly endless capacity for support helped sustain me and remains a source of inspiration. Finally, as with all things in life, my wife, Stephanie, was there every step of the way, celebrating the highs, suffering the lows, and helping me keep both in context. She is a partner in the truest sense of the word and has always been with me 100 percent.

INTRODUCTION

This is the world's fight. This is civilization's fight. This is the fight of all who believe in progress and pluralism, tolerance and freedom. We ask every nation to join us.

—PRESIDENT GEORGE W. BUSH, SEPTEMBER 20, 2001

"BE PREPARED TO be bombed. Be prepared to go back to the Stone Age." Pakistan's former president, General Pervez Musharraf, claims this was the threat then-U.S. deputy secretary of state Dick Armitage leveled if Pakistan did not cooperate in the War on Terror. Armitage has denied using this language when speaking to Pakistan's intelligence director days after the 9/11 attacks.[1] But there is no disputing that Pakistani leaders were made to understand the grave consequences for their country if help was not forthcoming. In the immediate aftermath of September 11, this meant supporting the U.S. invasion of Afghanistan to destroy al-Qaeda and topple the Taliban regime. Pervez Musharraf, the Pakistani general who had taken power in yet another military coup and later appointed himself president, got the message. Despite the domestic and foreign policy costs of helping the United States overthrow the Taliban, a movement and regime that Pakistan had supported for years by this time, Musharraf's government agreed to most U.S. demands.

This was not an auspicious renewal of a relationship that had atrophied after the Cold War ended. Nevertheless, Pakistan provided vital counterterrorism cooperation—helping hunt down al-Qaeda members in the early years after 9/11 and allowing the United States ongoing access through its territory to supply coalition forces in Afghanistan. At the same time, Pakistan remained a state sponsor of terrorism, supporting multiple militant organizations, some of which now have American blood on their hands. Viewed through one prism, Pakistan was a critical counterterrorism partner. Looked at through another prism, it was a hostile state. Pakistan is an extreme case, but this dichotomy is hardly unique to it. Alignments between two countries are often characterized by cooperation in some areas and competition in others. This dynamic is magnified when it comes to counterterrorism, which often requires working with countries where terrorist groups are based because their governments are often weak or prone to engaging in problematic behavior.[2] Yet the need for cooperation is typically unavoidable. As the National Commission on Terrorist Attacks Upon the United States (hereafter, 9/11 Commission) observed, "Practically every aspect of U.S. counterterrorism strategy relies on international cooperation."[3]

Because combating terrorism was not a defining feature of U.S. foreign policy before 9/11, the paradox of counterterrorism partnerships was not as big a challenge for the United States. That all changed on September 11. Defeating al-Qaeda and associated movements became one of the defining national security challenges under President George W. Bush, and he pursued partnerships to accomplish this objective. Al-Qaeda had expanded by the time President Barack Obama took office. He aimed to degrade and defeat terrorist groups threatening the United States, while simultaneously rebalancing American foreign policy and making U.S. counterterrorism efforts more sustainable. Obama sought greater burden sharing and made working with and through partner nations the cornerstone of U.S. counterterrorism strategy.[4] The rise and expansion of the Islamic State of Iraq and Syria (ISIS) posed a new set of challenges, most of which still required cooperation from other countries.

Seventeen years after 9/11, the United States faced far-flung threats from ISIS, al-Qaeda, their respective affiliates, and assorted other jihadist groups. International terrorism has consistently topped the list of threats that Americans worry about most.[5] Even if these concerns were overblown, policy makers nevertheless must respond to them. President Donald Trump had failed to outline a coherent foreign policy by the time this book went to press, but his emphasis on counterterrorism was clear. Whatever policies Trump ultimately settles on and whoever succeeds him after four or eight years, counterterrorism will remain a top national priority for years to come. The jihadist movement, especially al-Qaeda and ISIS and people inspired by them, is likely to pose a significant terrorist threat to the United States for the foreseeable future.[6]

Fighting the War on Terror has required the United States to adapt longstanding relationships with other countries and forge new ones.[7] This was especially true in the Middle East, South Asia, and Africa, where jihadists have the most robust presence. During the Cold War, if a country aligned with America, it opposed the Soviets. Combating jihadists or other rogue nonstate actors is fundamentally different. When President Bush drew a line in the sand, saying, "Either you are with us or you are with the terrorists," no government other than the Taliban-led regime in Afghanistan seriously entertained siding with al-Qaeda.[8] But reality has not been so black and white.

The fundamental premise underlying this book is that it is incorrect to ask whether partner nations are "with or against" America. The reality is often "both." Viewing counterterrorism partnerships as binary obscures the complex dynamics that characterize them. Most U.S. counterterrorism partners help and hinder Washington's efforts to some degree. A core challenge is to consolidate cooperation where it is good, mitigate risks where it is bad, and concentrate on getting the most out of the trade space in between. Putting this into practice requires determining what the United States can reasonably expect from its partners.

To solve this puzzle, we must first be clear about what the United States wants from its partners and who these partners are. I explore counterterrorism cooperation with countries located in the Middle East, Africa, and South Asia that had active jihadist movements before and after 9/11. I identify five aspects of counterterrorism cooperation: domestic counterterrorism operations that target terrorists or curtail illegal activities that support them; efforts to keep people from radicalizing; tactical cooperation, which is an umbrella term for the provision of access, intelligence cooperation, and coordination on detainees; contributions to military coalitions, stabilization operations, and diplomatic initiatives or other regional efforts that have bearing on terrorists; and the traditional steps necessary to monitor ports, airports, and borders. My focus in this book will be mainly on the first four elements—domestic operations, countering radicalization, aspects of tactical cooperation, and military or diplomatic coalitions.

If one examines the totality of U.S. counterterrorism objectives since 9/11, America was asking for more than it had in the past. This was true in terms of counterterrorism cooperation writ large, which had expanded considerably. It was also the case that the United States was seeking more from the countries in the aforementioned regions than ever before. In some cases, attaining U.S. objectives would have required a partner to change its foreign or domestic policies. Yet, although 9/11 transformed the U.S. security paradigm, the security paradigms of many partner nations in the Middle East, Africa, and South Asia did not change as dramatically. I use the term "security paradigm" to encompass a state's national interests, relevant domestic politics, strategic culture, and perceptions of its environment.

In the cases covered in this book, the United States was seeking cooperation against terrorists who were external to it but internal for its partners. When it comes to counterterrorism partnerships, the dynamics of traditional state-state alliances interact with those that exist between states and nonstate armed groups. Many states that became critical partners after 9/11 had preexisting relations—sometimes positive, other times negative—with the jihadists that were the target of cooperation. Often, the same factors that informed a partner's overall security paradigm also shaped its relationship with these actors. These counterterrorism partners therefore have to balance two relationships: one with the United States, including whether and how to cooperate with it; and a second with the terrorist group that is the target of cooperation.

With these ideas in mind, it is possible to offer four propositions about what the United States can expect from its partners. These propositions focus primarily on a partner's political will but also account for their capacity. The two are often, although not always, interconnected.

First, a partner's relationship with a terrorist group or infrastructure is the most critical factor in determining that partner's willingness to undertake domestic counterterrorism operations against it. The nature of this relationship depends on a partner's threat perceptions and the utility it ascribes to the terrorist group or infrastructure in question. Incentives, coercion, and the strength of the U.S. bilateral relationship with a partner can facilitate limited actions but cannot overcome the dynamics related to terrorist-state relations.

Second, instruments of statecraft are more helpful in securing tactical cooperation, in areas such as intelligence, military access, and detainees. This is true even in cases where terrorist-state relations preclude domestic counterterrorism operations.

Third, a partner's threat perceptions inform whether it cooperates with the United States on regional counterterrorism-related initiatives. Traditional alliance dynamics are also relevant and may help facilitate limited actions.

Fourth, defining the field of counter violent extremism (CVE), much less evaluating cooperation on it, is incredibly difficult. It appears that where partners are willing to make efforts in this area, they are considerably more willing to pursue direct, targeted CVE initiatives than they are to undertake broader political or economic reforms. However, it is important to note that the latter take considerably longer to bear fruit and can be more difficult to observe.

I flesh out these propositions at the end of the chapter after discussing the universe of partners this books considers, expanding on the nature of counterterrorism cooperation, and unpacking the importance of threat perceptions and terrorist-state relations.

THE UNIVERSE OF PARTNERS

There is no agreement in the literature on a common definition of alliances, which is a term that has been used to describe relationships ranging from informal military alignments to highly institutionalized relationships like NATO. The nature and degree of commitment necessary for a relationship to be considered an alliance is a major point of contention. Many scholars argue for a narrow definition of alliances as "formal associations of states for the use (or nonuse) of military force, in specified circumstances, against states outside their own membership."[9] These associations are typically reached in advance of the onset of hostilities rather than after they have erupted and are often codified in a treaty or other written agreement.[10] Other scholars, including prominent figures like Stephen Walt, have argued for defining alliances more broadly to include any interstate alignments built on specific areas of security cooperation.[11]

There is greater consensus on the idea that alliances are formed primarily for interstate war rather than for opposing nonstate actors. But the threat environment has clearly changed since the Cold War ended. The September 11 attacks highlighted the need to apply longstanding concepts about alliances to the new challenges presented by actors like al-Qaeda, ISIS, and associated movements. I do this in chapter 1. My purpose here is to define and categorize the nature of relationships with other countries from which the United States sought counterterrorism cooperation. First, in keeping with the narrow definition of alliances, I differentiate treaty allies from partners. The former refers to countries that have collective defense treaties obligating participants to intervene militarily if one of them is attacked. Partners, on the other hand, may cooperate closely on a variety of issues but do not have formal agreements committing them to collective defense. I use "alignments," which may or may not be formalized commitments, as an umbrella term for alliances and partnerships. Second, I subdivide partners into two categories: countries where the United States had multidimensional relationships before 9/11, with counterterrorism being one of several important security issues, and countries with which the United States established security relationships after 9/11, expressly or primarily for the purposes of counterterrorism.

Treaty allies have provided critical counterterrorism cooperation. On September 11, 2001, members of NATO invoked, for the first time in the alliance's history, Article 5 of its treaty. This commits each member to take necessary actions, including the use of armed force, to respond to an attack on another member. The Australian government invoked Article 4 of the 1951 ANZUS Treaty (a security treaty among Australia, New Zealand, and the United States), also for the first time. ANZUS and NATO countries have worked closely with the United States on various aspects of counterterrorism, including contributing forces to the missions in Iraq and Afghanistan. Cooperation has been closest among the Anglo countries (the United States, United Kingdom, Australia, Canada, and, to a lesser degree, New Zealand). France and Spain have also been important partners. Eastern European countries, including Poland, Romania, Bulgaria, and the Czech Republic, proved eager to cooperate after 9/11.[12] Outside Europe, a treaty alliance with the Philippines, which experienced its own jihadist insurgency, facilitated closer cooperation on counterterrorism than otherwise would have been the case.

The main theater in the War on Terror has been defined by where jihadist organizations—especially al-Qaeda and, later, ISIS—have a significant presence: the Middle East, Africa, and South Asia. The United States does not have formal treaty arrangements with any countries in these regions.[13] However, it did have enduring relationships with a number of states before 9/11, including with Egypt, Israel, Jordan, Morocco, Saudi Arabia and the other Gulf Cooperation Council (GCC) members, Kenya, and Ethiopia.[14] Although the U.S. relationship with Pakistan atrophied in the 1990s and needed to be rebuilt after September 11, early counterterrorism cooperation benefited from the two countries' past experience working together during the Cold War. Counterterrorism is not the only security issue of consequence in U.S. relations with any of these partners, but it gained immense importance with all of them after 9/11. On the one hand, the longstanding nature of U.S. relations with these countries made cooperation easier in certain areas. On the other hand, the fact that the United States sometimes pursued multiple objectives created complications and conflicts between different goals.

Counterterrorism became the main and sometimes sole driver of partnerships formed or fast-tracked by the September 11 attacks. Afghanistan and Iraq were adversaries until the United States overthrew their governments after 9/11. Libya seized on the attacks to improve its relations with America and the international community, at least until the Arab uprisings. The United States had only begun building relations with countries such as Algeria and the Central Asian states, all of which were in the Soviet sphere, albeit to varying degrees, during the Cold War. Yemen was just reemerging from the isolation imposed on it after its government sided with Saddam Hussein during the Gulf War. Somalia was a failed state and one that America largely avoided after eighteen servicemen were killed during the 1993 Battle of Mogadishu. Other countries, including Mali, Mauritania, and Djibouti, simply did not matter much to the United States when it came to security matters before 9/11. Although the United States had diplomatic relations with these countries, it needed to build stronger partnerships with them, sometimes from scratch, to prosecute the War on Terror.

In this book, I focus squarely on bilateral cooperation between the United States and other countries. Partnerships with both international and irregular forces are discussed tangentially but excluded as case studies. I zero in on counterterrorism cooperation with six Muslim-majority countries in the Middle East, South Asia, and Africa where jihadist movements were active at one time or another both before and after 9/11: Algeria, Egypt, Mali, Pakistan, Saudi Arabia, and Yemen. I chose these countries for three reasons. First, they are geographically spread across the regions that collectively constitute the main theater in the War on Terror. Second, they are evenly split between established and newly acquired partners. Third, all six countries not only provide a good mix when it comes to their relationships with the United States but also with the jihadist movements active on their soil. The existence of active jihadist movements—defined by the presence of proper organizations or at least robust networks supported by a wider infrastructure—not only made the countries I selected important partners. It also meant the factors contributing to their cooperation or lack thereof were often more acute.

I discuss U.S. engagement in Iraq and Afghanistan and touch on cooperation with U.S. allies and other partners throughout the book. However, I eschewed Iraq and Afghanistan as case studies because the United States had a major troop presence in both. Thus, U.S. experiences in these countries made them more analogous to South Vietnam during the Vietnam War than to the case studies selected. Focusing on the six countries selected also excludes treaty allies and other partners that did not have active jihadist movements on their territory. Many of these countries are critical to American counterterrorism efforts, and their omission from this book should not suggest otherwise. Yet countries where terrorists are based will always be some of the most difficult but most critical partners for the United States. At the time of writing, the countries studied in this book were likely to remain crucial to U.S. counterterrorism objectives for the foreseeable future. Moreover, cooperation with these countries holds lessons for dealing with other states, especially when it comes to the importance of threat perceptions and the utility of instruments of statecraft. Similarly, although I focus on counterterrorism against jihadist groups, many of my findings could be extrapolated to other types of terrorist organizations and movements.

COUNTERTERRORISM DECONSTRUCTED

The United States had plenty of counterterrorism instruments at its disposal on 9/11. Military force and covert action, although rarely used against terrorists before 9/11, were among them. Law enforcement was frequently called on to investigate, detain, arrest, prosecute, and incarcerate individuals in the United States and to coordinate with partners overseas to do the same. Rudimentary financial controls were in place to deny terrorists access to funding. Technical tools were already being used to help protect critical infrastructure and interdict terrorists at airports and borders.[15] America expanded its toolkit substantially after 9/11, improving existing instruments, especially in the areas of intelligence and surveillance, and adding new ones, such as the use of drones to launch missile strikes. Yet despite the notable advances the United States made in counterterrorism, these instruments are typically insufficient by themselves. In the fight against al-Qaeda, ISIS, and other jihadist groups, partner nations often must take the lead or at the very least carry much of the burden.

It is possible to disaggregate bilateral counterterrorism cooperation into five categories (see table I.1). The elements outlined in the table are not exhaustive, and, as noted above, cooperation would sometimes look different with treaty allies or countries where terrorist groups are not present. Nevertheless, these elements are indicative of the breadth of areas in which the United States seeks cooperation.[16] They also reflect a more expansive view of counterterrorism than traditionally has been the case. For example, counterterrorism before 9/11 typically did not include major military actions or stabilization operations. Diplomatic initiatives were also more limited, as was cooperation on detainees. Countering violent extremism is a relatively new field and one that some might argue should exist alongside—rather than under—the umbrella of counterterrorism. Taking a broad view is not an argument for designating every policy or program that might touch on counterterrorism as an element of it. However, if we look at the totality of requests that the United States makes of its partners, then we cannot discount the relevance to U.S. counterterrorism objectives of the elements listed in table I.1.

Domestic counterterrorism operations include both enemy-centric actions, such as dismantling terrorist organizations and killing or capturing their members, and infrastructure-centric ones focused on curtailing illegal activities by members of society who may or may not be part of an organized terrorist movement. Because America cannot and should not invade every country where terrorist groups are based, it has looked to partner nations to act as the tip of the spear in terms of degrading and defeating them. Local governments are also essential for preventing the emergence of an infrastructure that can support terrorist activities and dismantling one if it exists.

Tactical cooperation is an umbrella term for the provision of access, intelligence cooperation, and coordination on detainees. These are some of the most important aspects of tactical cooperation but, as with counterterrorism elements overall, do not reflect an exhaustive list of all the efforts that occur under this umbrella. Tactical cooperation is typically insufficient to defeat a terrorist group, but the activities it includes are often critical to disrupting terrorist attacks. They also may be necessary to enable the United States to support another country's counterterrorism operations or to conduct its own in order to degrade a terrorist group.

"Access" refers to another country's permission to use its territory, including for basing, transit, U.S. airstrikes by manned or unmanned aircraft, and raids by special operations forces. Despite the fact that airstrikes and raids are often described as "unilateral" when conducted solely by the United States, they typically involve permission from the host nation. Whether they "require" permission as matter of international law is more complicated, but these actions traditionally have been conducted on this basis.[17] Access may be geographically limited to parts of the country, time limited, or granted on a contingent basis, for example, the requirement to brief a partner nation's government before particular operations may proceed. Access, as I define it here, does not include entrée to foreign officials or influence over them. This latter type of access is necessary for securing cooperation, not a feature of it. Intelligence cooperation includes activities such as intelligence sharing, the joint collection of information, and the

TABLE I.1 ELEMENTS OF BILATERAL COUNTERTERRORISM COOPERATION

DOMESTIC CT OPERATIONS		TACTICAL COOPERATION			REGIONAL COOPERATION	DOMESTIC CVE		HOMELAND SECURITY
ENEMY-CENTRIC	INFRASTRUCTURE-CENTRIC	INTELLIGENCE	ACCESS	DETAINEES		DIRECT	INDIRECT	
Dismantle terrorist organizations and deny terrorists safe haven	Interdict would-be foreign fighters	Share and act on intelligence	Provide access for basing, overflight and/or transit specifically for counterterrorism	Detention and interrogation of enemy combatants	Participate in or coordinate regional counterterrorism initiatives, including capacity building for other countries.	Counter terrorist ideology / narrative in various mediums	Implement governance reforms	Secure borders, airports, and ports
Kill and/or capture and incarcerate terrorists	Counter terrorist financing and recruitment	Provide access for U.S. intelligence officers, infrastructure	Allow United States to engage in lethal action on host nation soil	Participate in renditions	Contribute to military coalitions and/or reconstruction and stabilization of conflict zones	Run counter-radicalization or de-radicalization programs	Address socio-economic issues	Protect U.S. persons and infrastructure in country
Disrupt terrorist operations	Dismantle or preclude the establishment of safe houses or other physical infrastructure intended to enable terrorist activities.	Cooperate to collect intelligence or infiltrate / disrupt terrorist groups	Allow U.S. forces in country for capacity building	Host black sites /accept detainees from Guantanamo Bay	Help reach political settlements to armed conflicts			

provision of access to intelligence officers. Coordination on detainees includes handing over suspected terrorists to the United States, taking custody of them, allowing American officials access to detainees or interrogating them on Washington's behalf, and otherwise supporting U.S. detention and interrogation programs.

Since 9/11, the United States has sometimes attempted to convince partner governments to take counterterrorism-related actions outside their borders, including by contributing to military coalitions, regional counterterrorism initiatives, capacity building for weaker neighbors, stabilization operations, or diplomatic efforts to reach a political settlement to a conflict. These types of activities constitute regional cooperation.

The field of countering violent extremism still lacks a clear definition and has evolved into a catch-all for various direct and indirect initiatives intended to reduce the number of people who join, support, or act on behalf of terrorist groups through noncoercive means.[18] Because CVE lacks boundaries, programs conducted abroad have often spilled over into more well-established fields, including development, governance, and democracy promotion.[19] Senior counterterrorism advisors in the Obama White House focused mainly on countering extremist messaging and ideology online and through other mediums and on targeted economic assistance to address perceived risk factors for radicalization.[20] However, the State Department and USAID took a wider view that included promoting governance and rule of law, strengthening civil societies, and supporting various community-based initiatives such as youth-empowerment programs.[21] This broader menu is reflective of the range of U.S. policies that fall under CVE. Whether defined narrowly or broadly, buy-in from partner nations is critical to the implementation of CVE initiatives on their soil.

Finally, there are the traditional defensive steps that a country takes to protect American citizens living abroad, insulate physical infrastructure including U.S. property, secure borders and ports of entry and exit, and keep civil aviation safe. This book touches on cooperation in this area for some partners but primarily focuses on the first four categories.

It is important to differentiate the counterterrorism instruments listed above from the tools of statecraft available to secure and optimize cooperation. The latter include public and private diplomacy, coercive measures used to compel action or cooperation, and security and economic assistance to build partner nations' counterterrorism capacity, help them address potential risk factors, and incentivize them to take desired actions.

THREAT PERCEPTIONS AND TERRORIST-STATE RELATIONS

How a partner perceives threats to itself and the extent to which its threat perceptions are congruent with U.S. threat perceptions are critical factors in determining the potential for counterterrorism cooperation. At their most basic level, threats are a function of a current or potential adversary's offensive capacity and aggressive intentions. On the surface, this seems pretty straightforward. Dig deeper, however, and it becomes apparent we must also account for other factors, beginning with where a partner ranks the pertinent terrorist threat relative to other threats. Other things being equal, countries are most willing to commit blood and treasure when a terrorist group threatens them directly. Of course, other things are not always equal. Countries may share a specific terrorist threat with the United States but face other, greater threats from a variety of sources, including regional competitors, domestic opposition movements, or separatist movements.

As other scholars have observed when writing about conventional conflicts, allies sometimes face dissimilar levels of danger from the same or different sources or perceive the same threats differently. These countries may pursue divergent objectives or the same goal with different degrees of intensity as a result.[22] The same fundamental challenge applies to counterterrorism partnerships.[23] Thus, focusing on how a partner qualifies the terrorist threat relative to other threats helps explain variations in behavior among states that face the same terrorist threat. It also helps explain variation within states where more than one terrorist group exists or where other nonstate actors threatening to the state are present.

Even if a partner government does not confront any other specific threats, it may be concerned about general threats from instability or to its hold on power. As a result, these governments must weigh how subsets of the population will respond to counterterrorism action against a terrorist group or to other forms of cooperation with the United States. Thus, in some cases the partner government may share U.S. concerns about a terrorist threat but be more worried about the domestic consequences of cooperation. A state's perception of the nature and cause of a terrorist threat matters as well. Leaders who believe a terrorist group's objectives are fueled mainly by poverty or lack of opportunity will respond differently from those who view religious extremism as the motivating factor. If a partner believes that terrorists are acting as a stalking horse for a political opposition movement or receiving support from foreign forces, this may warp its response.

Geography and identity also inform threat assessments. Governments tend to worry more about proximate threats than distant ones and may be reluctant to conduct counterterrorism operations outside their country's borders.[24] Even domestically, governments do not always view all territory equally and thus may not perceive threats uniformly. Territory can be more or less valuable depending on the presence or absence of natural resources and economic infrastructure. When considering these internal dynamics, it is often necessary to factor in the sectarian, ethno-national, and tribal identities of a terrorist group's members and the segments of the population it threatens. A terrorist group whose members come from the same ethnic or tribal cohort as state elites may be viewed and treated differently than one whose members do not. Geography and identity are sometimes related.[25] For example, in countries with diverse populations, the composition of people living in a certain area may heighten or reduce the perceived threat from terrorists operating there.

In each of the case-study chapters that make up the second half of this book, I depict how the United States and its partner perceived threats in the partner's country or region (see figure I.1). In the top two quadrants I also include other, nonterrorist threats to the partner where appropriate. The potential for cooperation is higher when the United States and its partner share a common terrorist threat (the upper-right quadrant). Indeed, U.S. counterterrorism strategies emphasize cooperation against shared threats.[26] But sharing a terrorist threat does not guarantee cooperation. It is possible for the United States and its partner to have asymmetric priorities regarding a common threat. This is more likely if a partner faces competing threats and especially problematic if the United States does not share these other threats (upper-left quadrant). Where asymmetric threat perceptions

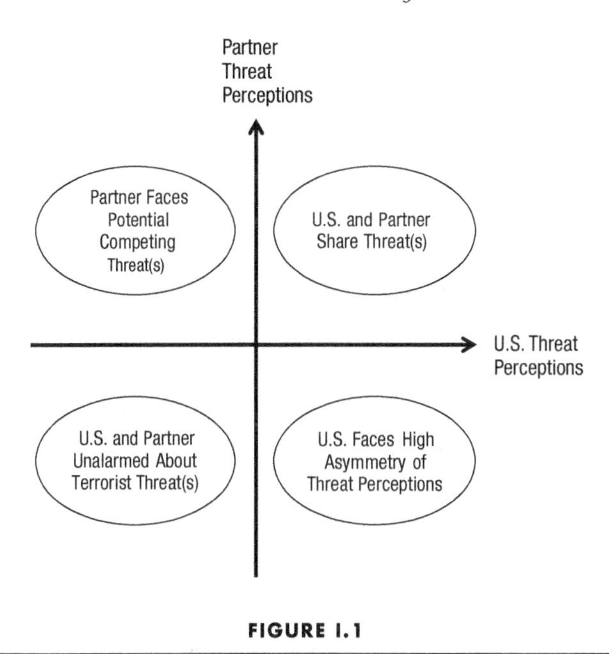

FIGURE I.1

U.S. and Partner Threat Perceptions

regarding a terrorist group exist because the United States ranks it highly and a partner nation does not (lower-right quadrant), it can be very difficult to convince the partner to treat the group like a threat. Instances where both the United States and another state are both unalarmed about a terrorist threat (lower-left quadrant) are uncommon and less pertinent to counterterrorism cooperation.

Threat perceptions alone do not determine a state's relationship with a terrorist group or its position toward terrorist infrastructure on its territory. It is also critical to account for the utility the group or infrastructure provides to the state. States may perceive a terrorist group to be useful for various reasons, including to destabilize or weaken a regional rival, project power abroad, export a certain ideology, assist kin in another country, supplement the coercive power of the state against domestic enemies, or boost legitimacy among a domestic population that strongly supports a certain cause.[27] These rationales are not mutually exclusive. Often multiple motives will apply and reinforce one another. Moreover, they may also apply to elements of a terrorist infrastructure.

Even a terrorist group that directly threatens a partner may still have utility to that partner either against other threats or as an instrument to extract security assistance from a patron like the United States. In this latter case, the partner has a perverse incentive to combat but not decisively defeat the terrorist group because doing so could lead to reductions in aid. It is also possible for a state to oppose a terrorist organization but perceive the infrastructure that supports it to have value. In these instances, the state might target specific terrorists without dismantling their supportive infrastructure.

I pair the depiction of U.S. and partner threat perceptions with a second figure that illustrates the nature of terrorist-state relations based on the partner's perception of the utility a terrorist group (or infrastructure) provides and the threat it poses relative to other threats (figure I.2). As this figure indicates, it is possible to posit four types of relationships that states may have with a terrorist group or infrastructure on their soil: collaboration, belligerence, indifference, and cooperative competition. When contemplating both figures in the case-study chapters that follow, it is

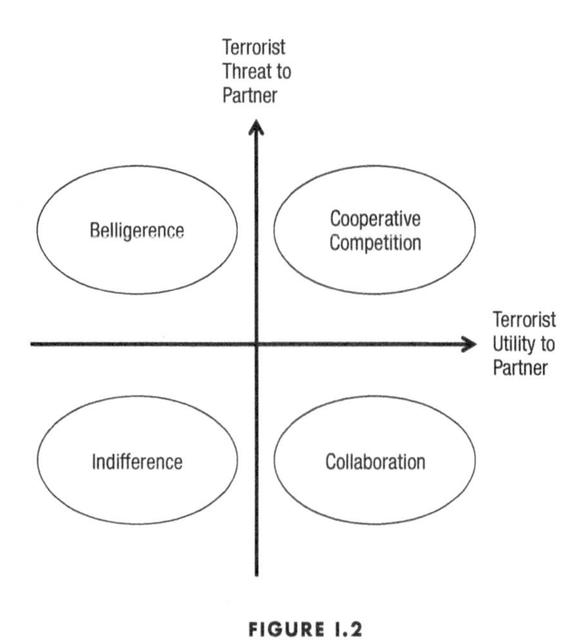

FIGURE I.2

Terrorist Threat and Utility to Partner

important to keep in mind that these are notional representations intended to illustrate the relational nature of threats and the utility of terrorist groups, not precise depictions of either. I update the two figures over the course of each case-study chapter to indicate how U.S. and partner assessments evolved.

Collaboration involves coordination to achieve a common objective and occurs when a government considers a terrorist group to pose a low threat and have high utility based on sufficient alignment of objectives. At the high-end of the collaboration spectrum, states actively support a terrorist organization. Active support includes the provision of some combination of sanctuary, money, weapons or other material, training, and assistance with operations or logistics.[28] Countries also sometimes use various tools of statecraft, such as diplomacy and intelligence sharing, to protect a terrorist group and preserve its safe haven. States providing active support may continue doing so partly because they fear blowback (in the form of terrorist attacks) if they stopped. A key point regarding active support is that the state deliberately uses government resources to provide direct assistance.

Enabling is at the lower end of the collaboration spectrum. It extends beyond knowingly turning a blind eye to terrorist activities but falls short of active support. I define enabling as pursuing policies that foster a supportive environment for terrorist activities such as fundraising, recruitment, or propagandizing, but without channeling government resources directly to terrorists or deliberatively providing them with sanctuary.[29] For example, various governments considered in this book promoted jihad campaigns fought on so-called open fronts, including in Iraq after the U.S. invasion; championed charitable giving for jihadist causes; or promoted the ideology underpinning them. States may take a belligerent position toward a terrorist organization but still pursue policies that create an enabling infrastructure.

The more reliant a terrorist group is on a state for support, the more influence that state is likely to have on the group in question. Terrorist organizations receiving active support will typically refrain from launching attacks against the state sponsor, coordinate at least some of their activities with it, and may submit to varying degrees of state direction. This can extend to undertaking specific operations at a state's request or to practicing strategic restraint, for example by refraining from certain activities that could harm the relationship.

Belligerence describes an oppositional relationship that occurs when a government believes a terrorist group is threatening and not useful. Even in these cases, numerous factors will inform how a government responds. For example, a state's capacity, assessment of a terrorist group's power and the appeal of that group's cause to the local population, perceptions about the drivers of the terrorist threat, and the presence or absence of other threats can all contribute to a state's approach to counterterrorism. Thus, states may take seriously a terrorist threat but refrain from executing a heavily resourced campaign because of capacity shortfalls or greater concerns about other threats. Simply because a state adopts a stridently belligerent approach toward a terrorist group, prioritizes action against it, and commits considerable resources to counterterrorism does not mean the organization won't flourish if the state fails to execute an effective campaign. Moreover, episodes of appeasement and collusion between state and terrorist forces may occur within a conflict, even one where the government is putting forth a high level of effort and resources.[30] Individuals in the government or security services may also collaborate with a terrorist organization for personal gain.

Indifference occurs when a government does not consider a terrorist group to pose a threat or have utility in terms of realizing national or regime interests. Although the security forces may occasionally harass the group in question, indifference is typically characterized by a live-and-let-live approach in which a government does not take any aggressive actions against terrorists based in its territory. This is analytically different from a government that considers a terrorist group a threat but that appeases it because of a lack of capacity, fear of blowback, or preoccupation with other threats. Taking a live-and-let-live approach is also distinct from providing direct support to a terrorist group or purposefully creating a beneficial opportunity structure for terrorism. In short, indifference amounts to a policy of turning a blind eye to terrorist activities. When terrorists and the state where they are based both refrain from targeting the other, this constitutes a tacit nonaggression accord. However, indifference may also occur in instances where terrorists are in engaged in violence on a state's territory but the territory in question or targets of terrorist violence have little value to the government.

When a state considers terrorists to pose a threat and have utility, it may treat them as "frenemies," to use the portmanteau that describes an entity that combines the characteristics of a friend and an enemy. This dynamic of cooperative competition can play out in one of several ways. A state may take more than one of position toward a group at the same time, simultaneously targeting it in some areas and enabling it in others. Or the state might rapidly oscillate between positions. In this case, a snapshot of the relationship on any given day might look like belligerence, enabling, or neglect, but the trend over time is toward a mixed approach. Alternatively, a state might target a group but hold back from doing so as vigorously as possible because the group's ongoing existence is useful for extracting assistance from the United States. In addition to these various forms of cooperative competition with a specific group, a government might pursue a similarly contradictory approach toward various elements of a terrorist infrastructure.

MANAGING EXPECTATIONS

The main argument I make in this book is that most partner nations both help and hinder U.S. counterterrorism efforts. This has always been true to some degree, but the dichotomy became starker after 9/11. Since then, the United States has asked more of its counterterrorism partners, especially Muslim-majority countries in the Middle East, Africa, and South Asia. The sheer breadth of counterterrorism elements on which America seeks cooperation is expansive, and Washington has pushed its partners to take types of actions that it never asked for in the past.

In the day-to-day focus on tactics, tools, and capacity building, it is possible to lose sight of the fact that counterterrorism cooperation is a fundamentally political activity. Cooperation is contingent on various factors, including the parties' geopolitical positions, domestic politics, and the other security threats they face. Many of the challenges of managing partner relationships are intensified when one of the parties is pushing the other to take actions that otherwise run counter to its core interests. As U.S. counterterrorism objectives expanded, this is precisely what the United States was seeking in a growing number of cases. Cooperation might require a partner nation to wage war against a subset of its own population or allow the United States to take lethal action against its citizens, clamp down on its population's support to coreligionists, or undertake domestic reforms that would disadvantage elites in power.

The elevation and expansion of counterterrorism cooperation is partly a result of the nature of the terrorist threat but also of the fact that the U.S. security paradigm was transformed by the September 11 attacks. The security paradigms of many partner nations in the Middle East, Africa, and South Asia did not change nearly as dramatically. To be sure, the global framework in which they operated was different, but governments in these countries still confronted the same sorts of security threats that had consumed them for decades. Most of these states were led by small coteries of elites or heavily influenced by their militaries, both of which had static interests and ingrained approaches to pursuing them. Many of these regimes also had preexisting positive or negative relationships with jihadists that informed how they responded to the U.S. War on Terror.

When assessing what to expect from partner nations, it is important to recognize that the United States does not pursue its counterterrorism objectives uniformly. Not every country with terrorist groups operating on its soil is of equal importance to the United States. Nor do all terrorist groups share the same intentions and capabilities, and hence not all pose an equal threat to U.S. citizens and interests. Just as U.S. objectives vary from country to country, so do the instruments that American policy makers are prepared to use to achieve them. In addition to this lack of uniformity, some forms of cooperation, like providing access, are more easily measured than others, such as addressing risk factors for terrorism. It is also the case that cooperation and outcomes do not always align. Some countries may rebuff assorted U.S. appeals and still manage a terrorist challenge effectively. Others might prove cooperative and still struggle to contain a terrorist threat. For these reasons, it is imprudent to propose a single iron law for predicting counterterrorism cooperation. It is possible to posit propositions regarding what the United States could expect from counterterrorism partners like the ones this book considers.

First, the nature of terrorist-state relations is the most important factor when it comes to whether a partner undertakes domestic operations and to the extent and consistency of these operations. This aspect of cooperation is obviously most pronounced in states where terrorist groups or infrastructure are extant, although it is also relevant for countries at risk of a growing terrorist presence.

On balance, governments that have a belligerent relationship with terrorists are most likely to carry out domestic operations against them. There is no guarantee that these partners will take a comprehensive or resource-intensive approach. The level of commitment and nature of counterterrorism operations will depend on range of factors, including the presence or absence of other threats, perceptions of the relevant terrorist threat, state capacity and strategic culture, and popularity of the terrorists' cause. As noted earlier, compromises and bargains may also occur between state and nonstate forces. Where the United States and its partner share the same threat perceptions and treat a terrorist group as a belligerent, strong bilateral relations and the provision of security assistance can augment or improve the partners' counterterrorism operations. In some cases, the United States may provide assistance to a country for these operations purely to combat a terrorist group. In others, the U.S. government may be seeking some other form of cooperation, such as military access, in return.

States that take a collaborative or indifferent position toward terrorists are by definition not predisposed to conduct domestic counterterrorism operations targeting them. It may seem like a stretch to use the term "partner" when talking about states that actively support terrorist groups. Yet it is equally hard to avoid the fact that Pakistan, which is a state sponsor of terrorism by any objective definition, has been an important partner since 9/11. Saudi Arabia has been a critical partner as well, despite nurturing an enabling infrastructure for many years. Mali was also considered a counterterrorism partner in spite of taking a live-and-let-live approach to the terrorists on its soil for almost a decade after 9/11.

In these types of cases, incentives such as foreign assistance are unlikely to change a partner's calculation. A good relationship with the United States or the lure of better a one is also typically insufficient. It may be possible to incentivize a partner to conduct limited operations. Similarly, states might also launch occasional face-saving raids in response to U.S. or international pressure. However, these types of operations are unlikely to be sufficient to degrade or defeat a terrorist group or destroy a supportive infrastructure. Put simply, it is difficult to incentivize a partner to conduct comprehensive counterterrorism operations if it does not consider the target of these operations to be a threat. It is even harder when the partner considers a terrorist group or infrastructure useful.

Coercion can be more effective than assistance or generic pressure, such as public pronouncements that a country should "do more" about terrorism, if the threats levied are sufficient and credible. The United States was able to use the threat of international isolation and military force to coerce some recalcitrant states, most notably Pakistan and Yemen, into conducting limited domestic counterterrorism operations after 9/11. However, this was a unique moment in time, and the United States also matched these threats with the use of incentives. Credibly sustaining a coercive posture becomes difficult, especially once a partner begins cooperating. Even nonmilitary forms of coercion, such as threats to impose economic sanctions or cut off security assistance, is more complicated once a partner is providing some level of cooperation. As a result, domestic counterterrorism operations undertaken in response to coercion will generally decline over time. This is true even when they are complimented with incentives. One possible exception is when coercion triggers blowback in the form of terrorist attacks against a state, thereby altering its threat perceptions. Yet rather than escalating a domestic counterterrorism campaign, some states may respond by reverting to coexistence, enabling, or support for terrorism in an attempt to reduce the terrorist threat.

Domestic counterterrorism operations conducted against frenemies can be harder to predict because of the nature of a relationship defined by cooperative competition. A government might conduct a highly resourced campaign against a group in one part of the country while simultaneously enabling it in another. Or the partner might shift back and forth between targeting the group and tolerating it. If the organization that is the target of cooperation is most useful as a mechanism for extracting assistance, then the partner government may calibrate its operations on this basis. These are just a few of the possible permutations. Similar inconsistency is likely to characterize operations against a supportive infrastructure that is simultaneously threatening and useful to a state. For example, a partner might target some elements, such as recruiting networks, while simultaneously pursuing policies that promote or tolerate terrorist financing. As is the case with terrorist-state relations that are defined by collaboration or disinterest, the efficacy of incentives and coercion is likely to be limited as long as the target of cooperation remains highly useful to the partner in question.

Outcomes in terms of domestic counterterrorism operations sometimes may look similar despite differences in terrorist-state relations. For example, a very weak state that considers a terrorist group as a threat might appease it, mimicking the type of neglect a stronger, disinterested state might practice. The cause of a partner's approach matters, or at least it should, when it comes to potential remedies. For example, if resource shortages are a genuine problem for a state that is sincerely committed to conducting counterterrorism operations, then capacity building might help. Capacity can be built, whereas political will is more difficult to manufacture. Thus, if a state does not consider the terrorist group in question to be a threat or, even worse, views its existence as a way to extract resources from the United States, then pouring in security assistance is unlikely to make the difference.

Second, traditional alignment dynamics and instruments of statecraft, such as foreign assistance, are most useful for securing counterterrorism elements that fall under the umbrella of tactical cooperation. These aspects of counterterrorism are also the most widespread. The U.S. government seeks access and cooperation on intelligence matters or detainees from partner nations around the world regardless of whether terrorists operate on or near their territory. If the United States and a partner share common threat perceptions regarding terrorism, this can enhance these forms of cooperation. However, the absence of shared threat perceptions does not preclude them. States may provide access or cooperate on intelligence or detainee issues even in cases where their position toward a terrorist group or infrastructure makes domestic counterterrorism efforts unlikely. The converse is also true. Simply because the United States and a partner nation both take a belligerent position toward a terrorist group, this does not guarantee tactical cooperation.

The provision of access is easiest to observe, and instruments of statecraft appear most useful in obtaining it. Cooperation on intelligence and detainees is more difficult to assess and the degree of alignment on threat perceptions can be more important. Where the United States and a partner nation both take a belligerent position toward a terrorist organization or infrastructure, strong bilateral relations with the United States or at least a healthy intel-intel relationship can enhance intelligence cooperation. It is also possible for two intelligence services to cooperate on certain issues or for states to agree on arrangements regarding detainees even if their overarching threat perceptions or security interests do not coincide as strongly.[31]

There are various explanations for why the United States can use diplomacy, soft power, or incentives to secure access, cooperation on detainees, and even limited intelligence cooperation in cases where terrorist-state relations preclude comprehensive domestic counterterrorism operations. Sometimes, this is because preexisting agreements with established partners help smooth the way. In other cases, providing various forms of tactical cooperation enables a partner to service its relationship with the United States (and perhaps keep assistance flowing) without committing to a domestic counterterrorism campaign that is likely to be more costly in terms of blood and treasure. Notably, fear of jeopardizing tactical cooperation can make U.S. officials more reluctant to press partners in other areas, such as domestic counterterrorism actions or reforms necessary to counter violent extremism. Most forms of tactical cooperation are also easier for a partner nation to conceal from its population or at least to deny if unpopular.

Third, a combination of threat perceptions and traditional alignment dynamics inform whether a partner engages in various forms of regional cooperation, including regional counterterrorism missions or programs, military coalitions, stabilization of conflict zones, and diplomatic initiatives to settle conflicts that enable terrorists to operate freely. Partner nations may agree to participate in one or more of these types of regional efforts because the United States asks them too, but whether they deliver will depend heavily on their threat perceptions and capabilities. States may also "free ride" in cases where they perceive a threat but believe they can sit back and allow the United States or other countries to do the heavy lifting. Or partner nations might calibrate contributions to a regional initiative based on whether they believe robust participation will help or hinder the ability to compete with a regional rival. Other variables also matter when it comes to regional initiatives. For example, some states have a stronger history of joining coalitions, deploying forces to foreign lands, or meddling in their neighbors' affairs. Other countries, such as Algeria, have a strategic culture that prizes diplomacy but eschews out-of-area military operations. It is also worth noting that when states are active regionally, they sometimes pursue agendas at odds with U.S. objectives.

Finally, CVE's ill-defined nature and long-term focus combined with the absence of publicly available evaluations makes assessment difficult. This is on top of the challenges of measuring a negative outcome, that is, whether a person does not join or support a terrorist group because of a certain CVE initiative. The U.S. government has also failed to develop a standard set of uniform methods for measurement, and data from foreign governments are even harder to find. On balance, partners appear more willing to pursue targeted initiatives intended to counter radicalization and recruitment directly than they are to undertake political or economic reforms. However, progress on targeted CVE, although more realistic, also may be insufficient in many cases.

All the countries considered in this book suffer from poor governance, corruption, and inadequate rule of law. They are also plagued by some combination of civil-military or other intragovernmental tensions, economic underperformance, and underinvestment in education and infrastructure. These structural deficiencies often reinforce one another and are sometimes exacerbated by demographic pressures; religious, ethnic, and tribal schisms; or regional competition. Although one cannot always draw a straight line between these conditions and the decision by an individual to join a terrorist group, they create an environment in which terrorism can flourish. Yet adequately addressing these conditions often requires major political and economic reforms that many partners, especially the ones this book considers, are unwilling to undertake. American policy makers generally favor shorter-term and more concrete objectives over the pursuit of longer-term reforms. The American political system encourages a focus on the near term, whereas convincing partners to address their immense inadequacies in these areas is a long-term endeavor with no guaranteed payoff. The United States cannot kill its way out of this problem, so abandoning efforts to promote reform should not be an option. However, the United States should have moderate expectations for CVE and will need to practice strategic patience in many instances.

SCOPE OF THE BOOK

With Us and Against Us explores U.S. counterterrorism policies and cooperation with partner nations in order to assess what the United States can expect from these countries. It focuses mainly on the 2001–2016 time period but also discusses key trends and developments before 9/11. In cases where new information emerged after 2016 that reinforced or altered major trends, I include it sparingly. This includes accounting for Donald Trump's approach to counterterrorism partnerships, which was still taking shape when the book went to press.

The book consists of two parts.

Part I examines U.S. counterterrorism policies and partnerships through theoretical, historical, and functional prisms.

Chapter 1 situates U.S. counterterrorism policies within the broader framework of the U.S. security paradigm, and puts counterterrorism partnerships within the wider context of alignments. As part of this discussion, I outline the changing nature of the terrorist threat to the United States from the Cold War to 9/11, apply some of the major theoretical works about alliances to counterterrorism partnerships, and highlight pre-9/11 attempts at cooperation with some of the countries selected as case studies.

Chapter 2 charts the major inflection points of U.S. counterterrorism policy and the jihadist movement after 9/11 and illustrates how they affected the evolving U.S. approach to cooperation with partner nations.

I turn in chapter 3 to an in-depth exploration of the counterterrorism elements introduced earlier: domestic counterterrorism operations, tactical cooperation, countering violent extremism, and regional cooperation. In addition to discussing how counterterrorism elements expanded and evolved, I also use this chapter to flesh out the utility of different instruments of statecraft to obtain cooperation.

After exploring counterterrorism policy and partnerships from the U.S. perspective, the second half of the book consists of case studies of cooperation with U.S. partners. The countries selected cover a range of relationships with the United States and jihadists on their soil.

Chapter 4 focuses on Pakistan, both a state sponsor and a victim of terrorism. The Pakistani security establishment has had all manner of relationships with jihadist groups. It has pursued collaborative relations with some groups that served geopolitical or domestic interests, treated others as belligerents, tolerated a third cohort, and viewed a fourth set as frenemies.

Saudi Arabia is the subject of chapter 5. It was a reluctant partner in the War on Terror until al-Qaeda launched a terrorism campaign in the kingdom in 2003. The Saudi government adopted a belligerent stance toward jihadist groups on its soil thereafter and became a critical partner in terms of intelligence cooperation. However, the Saudi government never fully dismantled the robust enabling infrastructure that exists on its territory. The malignant nature of this infrastructure is sufficiently noteworthy that I treat it as distinct from the terrorists it enables.

Chapter 6 explores counterterrorism cooperation from Yemen, which was a weaker state than Pakistan and Saudi Arabia and lacked their geopolitical compulsions. A mixture of coercion and incentives led the government to conduct counterterrorism operations against al-Qaeda networks on its soil after 9/11. U.S. instruments of statecraft proved less useful when al-Qaeda reemerged several years later. By then, the government faced new indigenous challenges that posed bigger threats than al-Qaeda, which also had potential utility as a mechanism for keeping U.S. assistance flowing. As a result, al-Qaeda was treated as either a third-tier belligerent or a frenemy.

Mali is the focus of chapter 7. It provides a useful contrast with other countries because the United States did not consider the jihadist group there a major threat. This theoretically could have provided time to build Mali's counterterrorism capacity and to address some of the risk factors that made the country a terrorist safe haven. However, U.S. policies failed to address the Malian government's lack of political will or preoccupation with other indigenous threats. The government pursued a tacit peace accord with foreign jihadists on its territory and never addressed the risk factors that enabled them to take root.

Chapter 8 considers cooperation with Algeria and Egypt. Both faced jihadist insurgencies during the 1990s and were quick to endorse the U.S.-led War on Terror after 9/11. This made them natural partners in some areas, but they also hindered U.S. efforts in others. Because they had dissimilar relationships with the United States—Egypt was a longstanding partner whereas Algeria was not—comparing them is also useful for teasing out how threat perceptions and terrorist-state relations on the one hand and bilateral relations on the other inform different types of cooperation.

The conclusion summarizes this book's findings and reiterates the challenges of the types of counterterrorism partnerships discussed in the preceding chapters. Rather than simply highlighting some of the seemingly immovable obstacles the United States faces, I attempt to identify steps that policy makers could take to optimize cooperation with difficult partners.

No book, especially one this broad, can capture all the nuances and nitty-gritty of either the terrorist threat or U.S. and partner responses. My hope is that by taking a step back and looking at some of the bigger-picture issues, this book will serve as a helpful guide for thinking about how to work with and through partner nations to combat terrorism. Understanding why partner nations make the decisions they do when it comes to cooperation enables U.S. policy makers to recognize not only when it is possible to influence these decisions and how they might do so but also where they must devise mitigation strategies when cooperation is unlikely.

1

COUNTERTERRORISM PARTNERSHIPS IN CONTEXT

Decisions about how to survive and ultimately prevail in the Cold War shaped U.S. foreign policy and relations with other countries from the end of World War II until the demise of the Soviet Union in December 1991. The United States' aspiration for an open and free international order led it to recruit and support allies and partners for two overarching purposes: to augment American military power in a potential conflict with the Soviet bloc and to keep countries from tilting toward the Soviet Union. The principal challenge facing the United States came from other countries. The end of the Cold War liberated America, at least temporarily, from the type of great-power security competition that had been the geopolitical norm. In search of a new paradigm to replace the security competition with the Soviets that had defined foreign and defense policies for almost fifty years, U.S. leaders embraced the promotion of democracy and protection of human rights. The U.S. government also began paying greater attention to nonstate threats emanating from weak states rather than to the traditional challenges posed by strong countries. These threats included criminal networks, refugee flows, and terrorism. American foreign policy shifted accordingly. It focused less on what other governments did beyond their borders and more on how they behaved within them.[1]

The 9/11 attacks provided another organizing principle for U.S. foreign policy, one that reinforced the preoccupation with nonstate actors and the internal dynamics of weak countries, especially ones with Muslim-majority populations. Burden sharing by these countries was important during the Cold War but not essential. The United States was often as concerned with wooing client states as it was with what they delivered. When it comes to counterterrorism, especially as practiced after 9/11, the United States simply cannot accomplish many if not most of its objectives without cooperation from its partners. As a result, burden sharing has become more important for the United States. It has also become more complicated for many U.S. partners, especially when the target of cooperation is external to the United States but internal for them. The United States has sometimes pressed these countries to wage war against a subset of their own populations, clamp down on popular support for terrorist causes, deemphasize longstanding internal or regional security priorities, and pursue reforms intended to transform aspects of their polities.

This chapter explores the transformation of U.S. security interests from the Cold War to the War on Terror, contextualizing changes in the nature of terrorism, U.S. counterterrorism policies, and the U.S. approach to alignments along the way. The first section discusses how competition with the Soviet Union informed America's approach to alignments with countries in the Middle East, Africa, and South Asia during the Cold War. It also demonstrates where terrorism and counterterrorism fit within U.S. foreign policy and the degree to which they were influenced by Cold War dynamics. The next section looks at how the end of the Cold War affected the United States in terms of its security priorities and approach to allies and partners. This section also discusses the growing jihadist threat and nascent attempts at counterterrorism cooperation with states that became critical partners in the wake of 9/11. The final section discusses in broad terms how the U.S. security paradigm changed in response to the September 11 attacks, paying special attention to the United States' adaptation of old relationships and creation of new ones for the purposes of counterterrorism. Although these partnerships were different from earlier alignments, the foundational theories that explained alignment formation remain relevant for how we think about them.

A "SIMPLER" TIME

The complexity of the post-9/11 world and multiplicity of threats facing the United States can evoke a misplaced nostalgia for the apparent simplicity of the Cold War, as this nostalgia forgets the ever-present danger of nuclear Armageddon during that time. The single overarching U.S. objective was to defeat the Soviet Union, and containment was the strategy for doing so. George Kennan, the American chargé d'affaires in Moscow, first outlined the strategy of containment in his "Long Telegram" and developed it in subsequent speeches and writings. At its core, containment argued for keeping the Soviet Union from spreading its influence to Western Europe and other core areas of the globe, including Northeast Asia and the Middle East. In due time, Kennan predicted, the Soviet Union would mellow, as he put it, because of its own internal contradictions.[2] Containment guided U.S. foreign policy for four decades, though American efforts to check Soviet expansion were more robust and military focused than Kennan thought necessary. In the 1980s, Mikhail Gorbachev began pursuing domestic political and economic reforms that he believed would strengthen the USSR in the long run. Instead, they hastened the Soviet Union's collapse, which occurred in under a decade.

The simple premise of containment obscures the many complex decisions that implementing it entailed. U.S.-Soviet competition for influence naturally fueled a corresponding bipolar competition for client states and participation in proxy conflicts involving them. The United States not only opposed direct Soviet influence but also leftist and Marxist movements in various countries, based on the premise that ideological solidarity would make them loyal clients of the Soviet Union.[3] As a result, the United States was repeatedly forced to determine whether, when, and how to intervene in different countries around the world. There were instances in which the United States accepted victories achieved by communist and leftist forces. Nevertheless, the fear that if one country fell to communism then others in its region might follow—the "domino theory"—still had currency from the 1950s until the end of the Cold War. Efforts to keep countries in the U.S. column reached their apotheosis with the Vietnam War, where America expended considerable blood and treasure supporting the noncommunist regime in South Vietnam. The country was one of nearly fifty treaty allies the United States pledged to defend in the event of an attack. In addition to these formal security guarantees, the United States formalized other types of security arrangements with many more countries.[4]

Europe was the most important theater in the Cold War. The countries of Western Europe welcomed U.S. protection. Indeed, the first secretary general of the North Atlantic Treaty Organization (NATO) famously described the purpose of the alliance as being "to keep the Russians out, the Americans in, and the Germans down."[5] East Asia was a secondary front but a vital one. Foreign troop deployments were overwhelmingly concentrated in these two regions during the second half of the twentieth century. U.S. forces fought two wars in East Asia—the Korean War in northeastern Asia and then the Vietnam War in Southeast Asia. And U.S. strategists and planners worked hand in glove with their counterparts in NATO member states and with Australia, Japan, and South Korea to build integrated military responses to counter the conventional Soviet and Chinese military threats. In some cases, such as South Korea, the United States essentially rebuilt its allies' militaries from the ground up.

In addition to forging treaty alliances with countries on the front lines of the Cold War, America also aligned with a host of other states, which one observer termed the "extended family."[6] Many of them were located in the Middle East, North Africa, and South Asia.[7] Relations with these countries were notable in several important respects. First, unlike in Europe and East and Southeast Asia, where the United States had permanent allies and adversaries, the portfolio of American partners in these regions was not static. A considerable number of countries were either "nonaligned" or moved back and forth between the NATO and Soviet blocs. This contributed to the U.S. propensity to focus more on forging alignments with some of these countries than on the security cooperation they provided. Second, the United States did not deploy troops or involve itself militarily in the wars fought in these places, for the most part. Instead, the American government adopted an "offshore balancing" approach that entailed a combination of diplomacy, foreign assistance, security cooperation, and arms sales to regional countries to check Soviet influence. Third, partners in the Middle East, North Africa, and South Asia were not committed to go to war in the event hostilities with the Soviets erupted.

Instead, they mainly cooperated with the United States to blunt the expansion of communist influences and provided it with military access, which although vital was not the same as committing to battle. Some countries, such as Saudi Arabia, also contributed financially to anticommunist movements around the world. In short, the states that have been on the front lines since 9/11 mainly played a supporting role during the Cold War.

Pursuing security cooperation with many of these countries was a way to prevent them from falling into the Soviet orbit. This effort often entailed working with anticommunist despots around the world. Most, but not all, of these autocracies were outside Europe.[8] Despite the fact that these regimes did not share America's political values, the United States never attempted to engineer the internal transformation of their countries.[9] Instead, American officials gritted their teeth and worked with these so-called friendly dictators. This sometimes included backing their efforts to crush Soviet- or Sino-supported insurgencies or other internal movements that were perceived to be susceptible to communist influence. In other words, with the exception of a potential communist takeover, the internal dimensions of an allied state's behavior were far less important to the United States than defeating the Soviet Union.

TERRORISM DURING THE COLD WAR

Cold War dynamics greatly influenced the nature of terrorism, which increased markedly after the late 1960s. Successful wars for self-determination waged against colonial powers after World War II spurred other ethnonationalist groups to wage their own "liberation" struggles. One of the most consequential struggles took place in South Vietnam, where the Viet Cong's fierce and effective resistance against the United States inspired many of the ethnonationalists and leftist groups activating at the time.[10] Although most of these terrorist organizations were focused primarily on parochial objectives, they often situated themselves within a wider revolutionary movement aligned against the U.S.-led forces of capitalism and imperialism.[11] Thus, while ethnonationalist organizations were most common in the Third World, the leftist revolutionary groups that predominated in the West tended to embrace their brethren's liberation struggles. Similarly, most ethnonationalist organizations were at least nominally leftist.

The Palestinian struggle for statehood became a prominent and popular cause, ultimately emerging as the heroic model once the Vietnam War ended.[12] Many other ethnonationalist and leftist groups supported the Palestinians' struggle. In addition to serving as a shared focal point for various terrorist organizations, the Palestinian struggle also led to the internationalization of modern terrorism. Several of the major Palestinian groups not only trained numerous terrorist organizations from other countries but also executed attacks across multiple continents and selected targets that had international dimensions. For example, the number of airline hijackings skyrocketed, with over one hundred occurring during the 1970s.[13]

During the Cold War, the causes for which most terrorists fought made defining terrorism a political issue. The Soviet Union and its client states argued that ethnonationalist or revolutionary groups were freedom fighters, not terrorists. Some Middle Eastern, African, and Asian states that were in the U.S. camp endorsed this distinction. After the Palestinian group Black September massacred eleven Israeli athletes at the 1972 Munich Olympics, Saudi Arabia, which was both a stalwart U.S. partner and a staunch advocate for the Palestinian cause, worked hard at the United Nations to avoid having violence committed in pursuit of "national liberation" labeled as "terrorist."[14] Because of the challenges related to defining terrorism, most UN counterterrorism conventions focused on the criminal acts committed, such as hijacking, rather than the nature of the perpetrators.

Most of the major terrorist groups active during the Cold War, along with many smaller ones, benefited from state support. The increase in state sponsorship was largely a function of U.S.-Soviet competition. Moscow sponsored and managed a small number of groups directly. More often, it outsourced these efforts either to other Soviet-bloc countries such as Bulgaria and East Germany or to client states like Libya, Syria, and South Yemen. In many cases, Soviet-bloc countries supported client states that in turn openly sponsored terrorist groups.[15] The growing prevalence of state support for terrorism was also a function of efforts by countries in the Arab world to exert more control over the major Palestinian groups.[16] After Shiite clerics seized power during the 1979 revolution, Iran became both a recipient of Soviet support and a prolific state sponsor of terrorism in its own right.

Although state sponsorship considerably increased the capacity of a number of terrorist organizations, it also served as a check on their lethality because the supporting countries were leery of triggering reprisals. Most organizations also had their own reasons for limiting the scope of their violence. Ethnonationalists sought to avoid alienating their constituencies. Left-wing terrorists viewed the minimization of violence as an ethical imperative, given their identification with the masses.[17] For the most part, this was an era when, as the terrorism expert Brian Jenkins famously observed, "Terrorists want[ed] a lot of people watching, not a lot of people dead."[18]

As terrorist attacks increased in number, if not necessarily lethality, the United States began developing a more comprehensive counterterrorism strategy. Two incidents catalyzed action. The Peoples' Front for the Liberation of Palestine hijacked four international flights in 1970 and then blew up three at a former British airfield in Jordan after releasing the passengers and crew. Two years later, Black September executed its operation at the Olympics in Munich. President Nixon established a cabinet-level committee to coordinate counterterrorism. It met only once, but the move set in motion an intergovernmental effort to combat terrorism more systematically.[19] Two streams of U.S. legal approaches emerged.[20] One gave the United States authority to prosecute terrorist crimes that occurred overseas. The other focused on unilateral actions the United States could take against state sponsors of terrorism. In 1976, Congress passed a law including a provision that cut off assistance to "any government which aids or abets, by providing sanctuary from prosecution, to any group or individual which has committed an act of international terrorism."[21] Three years later, the Export Administration Act authorized the State Department to designate governments that "provided support for actions of international terrorism."[22] This export-control list, which was initially intended to prevent the United States from exporting arms or other military equipment to states that supported terrorism, evolved into the list of state sponsors of terrorism.

Leftist and ethnonationalist terrorism ebbed in the 1980s. States that had been victimized at home, especially in Europe, which was a main theater for terrorist attacks, improved their domestic counterterrorism capabilities. Leftist revolutionaries consequently experienced one defeat after another. Israel's 1982 invasion of Lebanon seriously degraded the capability of Palestinian groups, most notably the Palestine Liberation Organization, to train other terrorist groups. International counterterrorism cooperation also improved, though it remained bedeviled by differences over longstanding issues such as how to define terrorism.[23] Cooperation was most effective with close Western allies but less so with partners in most of the Middle East, Africa, or Asia.

Although leftist and ethnonationalist terrorism declined, attacks overseas did not abate. The mad dog of the Middle East, Muammar Gaddafi, who seized power in Libya in 1969, was behind many of them. He saw himself as a bulwark against U.S. and Western interests in the Third World. Gaddafi viewed terrorism as a cheap and useful tool by which to counter the West and promote himself as a leader in the Arab world. He not only supported myriad groups but also dispatched state agents to carry out covert attacks against civilian targets.[24] Academics debate whether operations conducted by state agents should be considered terrorism or if this label only applies if nonstate actors are responsible. U.S. policy did not make this distinction.[25] In 1986, the United States launched Operation El Dorado Canyon. Fourteen A-6E Navy attack jets and eighteen FB-111 bombers pounded Libyan government and military targets in retaliation for a string of terrorist attacks against U.S. citizens and servicemen overseas. The air strikes marked the first time the United States used military force in retaliation for terrorist attacks, though it is notable that the target was still a state and not a terrorist group. El Dorado Canyon is also noteworthy because it illustrated how difficult counterterrorism cooperation can be. Political considerations led France, Spain, and Italy to deny permission for U.S. aircraft to fly over their territory.

The nature of terrorism was already changing by this time. The 1983 embassy and Marine barracks bombings by the Iranian-sponsored Hezbollah heralded the beginning of a new wave of terrorism by actors motivated more by religion than by secular ethnonationalism or Cold War dynamics. In response to the attacks, the United States changed its policy to characterize terrorism officially as a form of warfare, setting the stage for the strikes against Libya several years later. In 1989, the same year the Berlin Wall came down, the U.S. Congress passed the Antiterrorism and

Arms Export Amendments Act, which required sanctions on states designated as terrorism sponsors.[26] Cuba, Iran, Iraq, Libya, North Korea, and Syria were listed. Sudan, which hosted al-Qaeda and numerous other jihadist and nonjihadist terrorist organizations in the early 1990s, was added in 1993. Some of the men belonging to these organizations fought in the anti-Soviet jihad in Afghanistan during the 1980s, the last proxy conflict of the Cold War. Soviet forces completed their withdrawal from Afghanistan in February 1989. The Berlin Wall opened seven months later. In December 1991, the Soviet Union dissolved.

A HOLIDAY FROM HISTORY

While complicated and difficult to implement, containment provided American leaders with an overarching paradigm with which to guide foreign policy. After the Cold War ended, the United States lacked a lodestar around which to order its decision making. Foreign policy had gotten easier to the extent that the world was not poised on the brink of nuclear war, but it had also become messier. The democratic consolidation of Europe, the future of the NATO alliance, threats from rogue regimes, and the outbreak of ethnonational civil conflicts were the top items on the U.S. foreign policy agenda. Many of the debates that occurred touched on the questions of when, where, and how the United States should use its unrivaled power and influence. Two strands that were part of the patchwork of U.S. policy during the 1990s are notable.

The impetus to promote U.S. values, especially democracy, and to intervene to protect foreign populations where core American interests were not at stake constituted one strand. The UN Charter, signed in the aftermath of World War II, affirmed the principle of national sovereignty. This principle protects the territorial integrity of recognized states and holds that each state in the international system has total authority over behavior within its borders and the right to control movements across these borders.[27] Any state that attempted to infringe on another government's authority would be in violation of international law. Three years after the UN Charter was signed, the United Nations adopted a Universal

Declaration of Human Rights, which held that human rights should be protected by the rule of law.[28] There was a fundamental tension between the guarantee of sovereignty and the protection of human rights. The Cold War competition heavily tilted the field in favor of sovereignty, since most governments, including the ones led by ruthless tyrants, had a superpower patron. After the Soviet Union's demise in December 1991, the United States faced no ideological, economic, or military rival of equal status. In this new unipolar world, the United States was liberated to intervene in the domestic affairs of the world's nation-states.

America's first humanitarian intervention occurred not long after it fought in the last major interstate war of the twentieth century. In August 1990, Saddam Hussein's Iraqi military invaded and occupied Kuwait. The United States built a multinational coalition of thirty-four countries to confront Hussein. In January 1991, the United States and allied forces initiated a withering assault against the Iraqi military, routing Hussein's forces in little more than a month's time. The ground campaign, which followed a sustained aerial bombardment, lasted only four days. Toppling Hussein's regime was beyond the UN mandate, and the Bush administration feared that marching on Baghdad would splinter the coalition. Instead, the United States encouraged Iraq's Shiite and Kurdish populations, both of which Hussein had ruthlessly repressed for years, to rise up against him.[29] He launched a brutal crackdown against these internal opponents. The United States established "safe havens" for the Kurds in northern Iraq and subsequently imposed a "no-fly zone" to prevent Hussein from operating aircraft in the area. Intervening to prevent a foreign population from its own government not only set a precedent in terms of U.S. policy. It was also the first time that the United Nations, which supported these efforts, passed a resolution declaring internal repression to be a threat to the international order.[30]

Before he left office, President Bush committed the U.S. military to a second humanitarian mission, this time leading a UN-sanctioned multinational force to create a protected environment in Somalia. Whether Bush would have engaged in additional interventions had he been reelected is unknowable. A debate among his advisors over these types of engagements was already developing by the time Bush left office. President Clinton fulfilled the U.S. commitment in Somalia reluctantly and at considerable cost—eighteen servicemen were killed during the 1993 Battle of Mogadishu. He was more enthusiastic about subsequent interventions in Haiti, Bosnia-Herzegovina, and Kosovo. Clinton pursued an activist foreign policy that included using military force to resolve conflicts in countries where the United States had limited interests, though after Somalia the administration relied mainly on air power to avoid putting troops in harm's way.

The Clinton administration considered promoting U.S. values to be in America's interests even if the places where interventions occurred were not all that consequential. These humanitarian interventions were the most prominent examples of a wider foreign policy agenda that aimed to reinforce the liberal international order. American leaders believed that U.S. involvement was necessary to help solve an array of global problems, lest they be allowed to fester. Clinton and his advisors specifically viewed spreading democracy as a necessary antidote to the forces of instability unleashed by globalization and the Cold War's end. They also believed that globalization had contributed to the collapse of the Soviet Union and would pose growing challenges to the remaining authoritarian regimes. Where countries were embracing democracy, it was in the U.S. national interest to shepherd this process.[31] In states that continued to resist democratization in favor of dictatorship, the United States attempted to promote reforms. Yet the instruments of foreign policy—military might, economic power, foreign aid, and diplomacy—are far more effective when used to influence how other countries behave in the international system. These same instruments have considerably less utility when deployed to change a government's domestic behavior. This was a lesson the United States would learn at great cost after 9/11.

A second notable strand of U.S. policy during the 1990s had to do with the changing nature of security threats. America faced new sets of interconnected challenges from rogue nations, weak and failing states, and violent nonstate actors. The binary East-West divide had disappeared and been replaced by a division between states that were committed, at least in theory, to the international system and the "rogue states" that opposed that system. Iraq, Iran, and North Korea were in the latter camp. Each possessed or aspired to possess weapons of mass destruction, and all of them were designated state sponsors of terrorism. Deterring and defending against rogue states was one of the more traditional security objectives the United States pursued during the 1990s. While attempting to contain these countries and debating how hard to pursue regime change, the United States simultaneously had to contend with the fallout from weak and failing states. Ethnic conflicts and civil wars dominated the decade. Plenty of countries that avoided violence nevertheless struggled to contain the rising tide of nationalism or religious extremism.

Changing U.S. threat perceptions and the desire to advance American values intersected to influence decisions about the purpose and nature of formal alliances and more temporary coalitions. The collapse of the Soviet Union erased an existential threat to Western Europe and removed the primary mission of the NATO alliance. This naturally raised questions about NATO's utility. Rather than discard the alliance, the Clinton administration promoted NATO enlargement in Europe as a way to anchor former Soviet-bloc countries to the West. Outside Europe, there was less need to pursue partners because the need to contain the Soviet influence no longer existed. Instead, containing rogue nations like Iraq, ensuring stability in key regions, intervening to resolve civil wars or prop up failing states, limiting the proliferation of WMD, and countering transnational threats from terrorists and other violent nonstate actors created new demands from allies and partners.[32] President Clinton repeatedly stressed the need for global cooperation to address what he considered to be shared challenges.[33]

America's pursuit of international cooperation was predicated on the Clinton administration's assessment that globalization, combined with the end of the Cold War, had ended the zero-sum dynamics that had defined geopolitics since the dawn of the nation-state. Yet the United States was almost uniquely positioned to argue that gone were the days when one country's gains were another nation's losses. After all, America had just won an existential struggle and was the world's only superpower. Worrying primarily about the types of threats that occupied U.S. policy makers was a luxury many other governments still could not afford. It was not that other states were unaffected by these challenges. But many of them, especially in the developing world, still faced the same internal and external security challenges as they had before the Soviet Union collapsed. While America's need for formal alliances and informal partners had evolved, the threat perceptions, material interests, and other factors that led states to side with or against it during the Cold War often remained unchanged. As a result, the United States, despite all its power, was sometimes frustrated in its attempts to unify other countries against what American leaders viewed as common threats. As with the limitations of instruments of foreign policy to change a government's domestic behavior, the difficulty of corralling other states against shared threats was another challenge that would bedevil the United States after 9/11.

"Multilateral where possible, unilateral when necessary" became a U.S. mantra. One of the Bush administration's main objectives during the Gulf War had been to create a precedent for cooperation that would inform how the United States dealt with future crises.[34] Clinton and his team attempted to build on this model, securing the involvement of other countries before intervening in conflicts and getting their buy-in to address global challenges. But if other countries did not act—to staunch the bleeding in Bosnia-Herzegovina or to confront Saddam Hussein, for example—then the Clinton administration was prepared to go it alone. America no longer needed to compete for allies or partners like it had during the Cold War. As the only superpower on the planet, the United States enjoyed more flexibility than in the past to choose to work with countries based on their ideological affinity (favoring democracies, for example) or willingness to fall in line. In most cases, this amounted to pursuing a flexible form of multilateralism that leveraged traditional allies where possible while also relying on ad hoc coalitions when necessary.[35]

This approach had its limitations. U.S. power, including the application of military force, could deter rogue actors. Sometimes it could change the facts on the ground in a conflict zone and bring other nations on board as part of an intervention or to help keep the peace once hostilities ended. America could also work with like-minded countries to isolate states that sponsored terrorism. U.S. power could not transform societies, alter other states' threat perceptions, or stamp out ethnonational or religious extremism. When it came to securing sustained cooperation against terrorist groups, the states that mattered most typically did not share an ideological affinity or the same understanding of the threat with the United States. And they often were not willing to fall in line.

THE GATHERING STORM: TERRORISM AND COUNTERTERRORISM IN THE 1990s

The nature of terrorism continued to evolve after the decline of ethnonational and leftist terrorist groups. Religiously inspired organizations were proliferating by the 1990s. U.S. officials began the decade worried mainly about the Iranian-supported Shiite group Hezbollah. The 1993 World Trade Center bombing augured the growing jihadist threat to the United States. Jihadists are militant Sunni Islamists who view jihad primarily or exclusively as waging war, believe every able-bodied Muslim is obligated to contribute to the war effort, and eschew nonviolent participation in electoral politics.[36] Despite condemning nation-states in the Muslim world as artificial creations of the West and situating themselves within the *umma* (the worldwide community of Muslim believers), jihadists are influenced by their connections with their countries of origin. They disagree over issues such as which enemy to prioritize, where to fight, and whether it is appropriate to attack fellow Muslims. The two main currents in the jihadist movement before 9/11 were revolutionary and pan-Islamic. Simply because one current was paramount in a country did not mean that other currents were not present, but the lack of a major revolutionary challenge and predominance of a pan-Islamic current were often related. The relationship between the two is not dichotomous, however, and plenty of Muslim-majority countries avoided outbreaks of jihadist violence without promoting pan-Islamism.

Revolutionaries prioritized changing the political order in their own homelands by overthrowing the ruling powers.[37] A revolutionary current was strongest in North Africa, where states such as Egypt and Algeria had belligerent relationships with jihadist groups and faced jihadist insurgencies of varying duration and lethality during the 1990s.[38] Both countries were led by military-backed authoritarian regimes that pursued secular agendas and subverted the authority of their respective religious establishments. Their rulers were most concerned about regime preservation, prioritizing that above the national interest. These leaders viewed nonviolent Islamist movements and their jihadist analogues as major threats because both sets of actors sought to replace the regimes in power.

Islamists and other opposition movements were denied access to the institutionalized political system, including both formal institutions such as parliaments, ministries, and government agencies and the informal mechanisms through which elites sometimes governed. Powerful security services maintained public order through repression. The nature and timing of repressive measures is a particularly important factor that can curb or incite a violent movement.[39] Egyptian and Algerian rulers responded inconsistently to Islamist mobilization, but neither government ever truly opened up its political system. Instead, these regimes shifted from suppression to the provision of space for mobilization, only to reverse course and return to harsh repressive measures. This inconsistency helped catalyze a jihadist insurgency in Egypt and a civil war in Algeria, where jihadist groups emerged as the most lethal threats to the state.

Pan-Islamic jihadists were focused on defending the *umma* and liberating all occupied Muslim lands.[40] Those coming from Muslim-majority states typically had more positive relationships with their governments. A pan-Islamic current flowed more powerfully than a revolutionary one in Pakistan, Saudi Arabia, and Yemen before 9/11. When these countries did face internal challenges from Islamists or jihadists, calibrated responses were sometimes paired with efforts to reorient them externally. All three countries promoted Islam domestically, empowered their religious establishments, and provided Islamists with access to government institutions. They also cooperated with their respective Islamist movements and religious establishments to promote pan-Islamic jihads abroad. These policies—promoting pan-Islamic jihad and actively supporting or otherwise enabling jihadists—were implemented for different reasons, including to counter external threats, undermine geopolitical competitors, boost domestic legitimacy, and reorient internal challengers' focus to outside the country's borders. All three countries created or allowed the development of a supportive jihadist infrastructure. Pakistan went further, actively backing numerous jihadist groups and other militant organizations against its regional rival India and supporting the Taliban in Afghanistan.

Al-Qaeda was one of the few truly multinational jihadist groups that existed before 9/11. It developed its concept of global jihad while based in Sudan during the first half of the 1990s and then in Afghanistan for the latter half. Al-Qaeda's global jihadist ideology prioritized attacks against the United States as the first step in a larger plan to create the conditions for toppling apostate regimes in the Arab world. Bin Laden and his inner circle believed that as long as the United States could project power into the region, it would be able to pressure Muslim countries to bend to its will and keep jihadists from toppling local regimes.[41] Driving America out of the region would enable jihadists to confront local regimes directly and inspire the youth to rise up and join these revolutions. At that point, al-Qaeda leaders believed that regimes in the Middle East would collapse, beginning with the government in Saudi Arabia.[42] Al-Qaeda's global ideology remained at the fringes of the jihadist movement during most of the 1990s, but it became the dominant terrorist threat facing the United States by the end of the decade. By that time, the Clinton administration and Congress had already spent several years putting in place new measures to combat terrorism waged by transnational actors with tenuous ties to any one state.

In June 1995, Clinton issued Presidential Decision Directive (PDD) 39, which classified terrorism as a criminal act *and* as a potential threat to national security. It called for deterring all terrorist attacks against American citizens and infrastructure at home and abroad and for responding vigorously when attacks occurred.[43] The U.S. government crafted a range of measures targeting individuals and nonstate organizations. Clinton sent Congress proposals to extend the federal criminal jurisdiction, make it easier to deport terrorists, and act against terrorist fundraising.[44] Congress subsequently passed the Antiterrorism and Effective Death Penalty Act of 1996, which authorized the secretary of state to designate groups involved in international terrorism as Foreign Terrorist Organizations (FTOs) and block any of their assets that were in the possession of or under the control of U.S. financial institutions.[45] In 1997, Secretary of State Madeline Albright exercised this authority and designated thirty groups as FTOs.[46] The act also made it a crime for Americans knowingly to provide money or other material support to FTOs and amended the Immigration and Nationality Act to allow the secretary of state to put foreign groups on the Terrorist Exclusion List.[47]

While Washington put in place new measures to deal with superempowered nonstate actors, it also began working more closely with foreign governments on various elements of counterterrorism. These efforts presaged the more robust cooperation America would seek after 9/11. The impediments to cooperation that U.S. officials confronted were also a harbinger of things to come.

In Egypt and Algeria, where revolutionary jihadists sought to overthrow the ruling regimes, American leaders confronted the now familiar tension between attempting to address the underlying risk factors fueling conflict and more immediate concerns about security and stability. They were also forced to reckon with the limitations of U.S. influence when it came to the former. The Clinton administration urged both governments to improve governance, cease human-rights violations, reduce corruption, and address poor socioeconomic conditions. Egypt was a major recipient of U.S. assistance, and this theoretically provided Washington with leverage it could use to push Cairo into undertaking political and economic reforms. However, the United States also had other national interests that competed with its desire for these reforms and therefore curtailed its willingness to use the leverage it had to achieve them.

Bilateral relations with Algeria were far weaker, and American aid to that country was practically nonexistent. The United States had less leverage but also no national interests in Algeria, where violations in terms of governance and human rights were also more extreme. After canceling the country's first-ever competitive national elections when it looked like an Islamist party might win an absolute majority, the Algerian military declared a state of emergency and formed a caretaker government.[48] The authorities dissolved the Islamist party, incarcerated its leaders, and confined thousands of Islamist activists and sympathizers to detention facilities. These actions catalyzed a civil conflict in which war crimes and human-rights violations were routine.

Washington took a firmer line with Algeria than with Egypt, but it never really committed to promoting reform in either country. Subtle U.S. pressure on Egypt that began after the jihadist insurgency erupted in 1990 gave way to increased support for the regime by the middle of the decade.[49] Washington had conditioned its diplomatic support for Algeria on the regime's commitment to negotiate with the leaders of the Islamist party, hold elections, and cease gross violations of human rights.[50] When the regime refused, the American officials avoided high-level diplomatic contacts between 1993 and 1994. By 1995, Washington had resumed diplomatic relations and was softening its stance toward Algeria in other areas as well.[51]

The Clinton administration's evolving position was a function of its growing concerns about international terrorism and developments in both countries, where the security forces were gaining ground by the middle of the decade. As Egypt's counterterrorism efforts improved, American officials became more confident in the Mubarak government's ability to neutralize the threat. The Algerian security forces were also making progress by 1995, when the country held its first elections since the coup. The elections were not free or fair, but they still represented an important step.[52] As the jihadists lost ground in both countries, their violence became more indiscriminate.[53] Egyptian and Algerian jihadist groups also began attempting attacks abroad, reinforcing American concerns about the internationalization of jihadist terrorism. As the threat to the United States grew, intelligence cooperation with Egypt increased.[54]

The United States confronted a different set of challenges in Saudi Arabia and Yemen, where enabling infrastructures existed. The geopolitical and domestic compulsions that led both countries to create a beneficial environment for jihadist activities predated their support for the anti-Soviet jihad in Afghanistan. However, support for that cause kickstarted the process. Leaders in each country gave local tribes and the religious establishment a free hand to encourage citizens to participate in or financially support the anti-Soviet jihad. They also allowed foreign semistate and nonstate actors into their countries to recruit, propagandize, and raise money.[55] Unlike in countries such as Egypt and Algeria, where fighters returning from Afghanistan were heavily monitored or simply arrested, volunteers were lauded in Yemen and Saudi Arabia. Riyadh continued to support pan-Islamic jihads in Bosnia-Herzegovina, Chechnya, and elsewhere throughout the decade.[56] The Saudi authorities were aware of the potential for blowback, considered al-Qaeda an enemy of the kingdom, and did not allow any organized group to operate in the country. However, the regime still tolerated and sometimes promoted jihadist recruitment and fundraising for pan-Islamic causes. This likely was because of internal disagreements over the nature and magnitude of the problem, fears that dismantling the enabling infrastructure would provoke violent retaliation, and the geopolitical and domestic utility that such recruitment and fundraising provided. The supportive infrastructure was not as robust in Yemen, but al-Qaeda was allowed to use the country for recruitment and logistical support, provided it did not harm Yemeni interests.[57] The group ran multiple safe houses, and its members had ties to the security establishment.[58]

Washington had much stronger relations with the Saudi government than it did with Yemen's president Ali Abdullah Saleh. Counterterrorism became an increasingly important issue in the U.S.-Saudi relationship during the 1990s, but it still was not the top priority before 9/11. The United States sought more specific cooperation following a 1995 bombing outside a U.S.-administered National Guard training center in Riyadh and a 1998 attempted missile attack on the U.S. consulate in Jeddah. Saudi authorities were reluctant to provide access to militants involved in the plots or share much information gleaned from interrogating them.[59] The Saudi government also resisted cooperating on terrorist financing, although Washington had not made this issue a priority or provided the Saudis with actionable intelligence about it before 9/11.[60]

The U.S. government ostracized Yemen's president Saleh for siding with Iraq during the Gulf War, but relations were getting better by the end of the decade. Counterterrorism was not initially a priority. This changed after al-Qaeda bombed the USS *Cole* during a port visit in Aden in 2000. Yemeni authorities initially stonewalled American investigators, allowing some al-Qaeda operatives to escape. They belatedly detained some al-Qaeda members and implemented a limited crackdown on its activities. U.S. investigators were allowed to interrogate some of the detainees but refused access to others.[61] The al-Qaeda infrastructure remained intact. However, it paled in comparison to the sanctuary jihadists enjoyed in Afghanistan and Pakistan.

Some of the most notable jihadist groups operating in Afghanistan during the latter half of the decade migrated there from Sudan, which opened its doors to numerous jihadist and other terrorist organizations during the early 1990s. The United States designated Sudan as a state sponsor of terrorism in 1993, partly on the basis of Sudanese support for Egyptian jihadists.[62] This designation brought with it a raft of unilateral sanctions and carried a stigma that made attracting international investment more difficult. Arab countries also pressured Sudan to expel the jihadist groups on its soil. Sudanese leaders finally bowed to pressure and expelled these organizations between 1995 and 1996. Most of them resettled in Afghanistan, where the Taliban had seized power. Another jihadist sanctuary existed across the border in Pakistan, which oversaw the creation of a durable militant infrastructure to support terrorism against India. Islamabad's support for terrorism was a concern for the United States but not one that rose to the same level as the Taliban sanctuary because the groups in Pakistan were not focused on attacking U.S. targets at the time.[63]

Other works have explored why the United States succeeded in pressuring Sudan but failed to convince or compel the Taliban to expel bin Laden from Afghanistan.[64] Relevant here is that the United States was unable to secure cooperation for its diplomatic efforts from the three countries that recognized the Taliban government: Pakistan, Saudi Arabia, and the United Arab Emirates. All three considered the Taliban to be critical to their national interests. For Saudi Arabia and the United Arab Emirates, this meant counterbalancing against Iranian influence in the region. Their diplomatic recognition of the Taliban helped it raise money from private donors in the Gulf. In Pakistan's case, the Taliban's rise to power meant that for the first time in its history it was allied with a friendly government in Afghanistan. The Taliban did not maintain relations with India, Pakistan's regional rival, and it allowed Pakistani militants fighting against Indian forces in the disputed Kashmir region to train on territory under its control. Pakistan provided the Taliban with weapons, military advisors, intelligence, and money. Pakistani volunteers were encouraged to cross the border to fight alongside the Taliban against the Northern Alliance. Although Saudi Arabia and Pakistan both tried to use their influence with the Taliban to secure bin Laden's expulsion, neither ended its support for the movement when these efforts failed.[65] All three countries—Saudi Arabia, Pakistan, and the United Arab Emirates—refrained from enforcing sanctions on the Taliban. Pakistan also ignored a UN Security Council resolution that criminalized providing arms and military advisers to it.[66]

While pursuing diplomatic efforts, the United States considered options to capture or kill bin Laden. Proposals to use local proxies in Afghanistan never got the go-ahead for various reasons, including uncertainty about the reliability of tribal partners and questions about the legality of a capture mission versus a kill mission.[67] Plans to use direct military force were encumbered by political and logistical barriers. The deployment of Special Operations forces into Afghanistan to capture bin Laden would probably have required the support of at least two neighboring countries in a region with no reliable partners and many unsavory regimes.[68] The absence of nearby basing options may have helped scuttle plans to use AC-130 gunship aircraft. Taking off from ships in the Arabian Sea or from land bases in the Persian Gulf would require overflight of nations that "might not have been supportive" of the mission.[69] What's notable about these challenges is that they often stemmed from or were exacerbated by the absence of reliable partners in the region.

The most viable instrument, the cruise missile, was unreliable in the absence of actionable intelligence, as strikes—launched in response to the 1998 East Africa embassy bombings—illustrated when they failed to kill bin Laden or any other high-level al-Qaeda member. In that instance, Pakistan's military, which was alerted to the operation so that they would not think the missiles were coming from India, may have warned the Taliban or bin Laden.[70] Subsequent mooted cruise-missile strikes were never executed for a variety of reasons, including lack of good intelligence, fear of civilian casualties, and diplomatic considerations. In one case, U.S. officials pulled the plug because a UAE prince was believed to be with bin Laden. Emirati officials may have subsequently passed this information along to al-Qaeda, thereby alerting the group to U.S. intelligence about its camps. As the 9/11 Commission's report observed, the United Arab Emirates was both "a valued counterterrorism ally of the United States and a persistent counterterrorism problem."[71] This description could be applied to many countries after September 11.

COUNTERTERRORISM PARTNERSHIPS AFTER 9/11

The Clinton administration considered al-Qaeda to pose a major national security threat, but counterterrorism was not the organizing principle for U.S. foreign policy before 9/11. Other issues, including Iraq, the Israel-Palestinian peace process, humanitarian interventions, and democratization efforts in Eastern Europe dominated the U.S. agenda during the

1990s. Clinton was not prepared to compel other countries to provide the type of cooperation needed to destroy al-Qaeda's transnational networks. Absent a catalyzing event, it is questionable whether the president would have been able to mobilize the United States to take the type of action necessary to degrade or destroy the jihadist infrastructure in Afghanistan.

The September 11 attacks reshaped America's security paradigm. Terrorism replaced communism as the new threat facing America and thus shaped a new paradigm for the conduct of foreign policy. This created the need to reorient and rejuvenate old partnerships and build new ones but also reinforced the Bush administration's readiness to act unilaterally. The 2002 *National Security Strategy* articulated a policy of preemption in which America would seek international support where possible but act preemptively and alone when necessary.[72] This translated into a much more robust form of flexible multilateralism.[73] As Defense Secretary Donald Rumsfeld famously explained, "we will see evolving coalitions that will evolve and change over time, depending on the activity and the circumstance of the country and the mission needs to define the coalition and we ought not to think that a coalition should define the mission."[74] This approach was not only driven by the perceived exigencies following the 9/11 attacks. It was also shaped by the belief among senior Bush officials that the coalitions created to intervene in Kosovo and Iraq had imposed undue constraints on the United States.[75]

A coalition is, by definition, a temporary combination of states that will dissolve after achieving a specific objective.[76] Their ephemeral nature makes coalitions distinct from alliances like NATO. After 9/11, the United States announced the formation of a "coalition against terror." As Rumsfeld alluded to, multiple counterterrorism coalitions were formed to address different functional areas. These included military coalitions formed for the wars in Afghanistan and Iraq, a financial coalition created to counter terrorist financing, a law enforcement coalition that was intended to enable coordination among security forces across a host of countries, and a reconstruction coalition that focused on building or rebuilding weak states that al-Qaeda and associated organizations might exploit.[77] More recently, the Obama administration built a distinct coalition to degrade and defeat ISIS in Iraq and Syria. Various African countries have also formed coalitions that, with U.S. assistance, have fought against the jihadist groups al-Shabaab in Somalia and Boko Haram in West Africa. Coalitions are clearly necessary when it comes to confronting global challenges from nonstate actors like al-Qaeda and ISIL. Multilateral efforts also help establish broad principles for how to deal with security challenges. However, at the end of the day, most counterterrorism tasks are better approached bilaterally.[78] The United States adapted existing relationships and forged new ones after 9/11. Although these partnerships were different from earlier alignments, theories that explained alignments remain relevant.

The furious competition between the United States and Soviet Union during the Cold War contributed to a heavy emphasis on why countries might align with one or the other.[79] One book about how developing countries made decisions about alignments was simply titled *Choosing Sides*.[80] The U.S.-Soviet competition sparked debates over whether weaker countries bandwagon with or balance against stronger ones that could pose an external threat. Some states chose to bandwagon, often when they believed it was futile to resist or if the adversary in question could be appeased through accommodation.[81] Balancing proved more common.[82] Theorists initially posited that states aimed to balance against a stronger country or coalition of countries in order to prevent domination of the international system.[83] This explanation assumed that the strongest power would inevitably threaten weaker ones. In *The Origins of Alliance*, the international relations scholar Stephen Walt reformulated balance-of-power theory. He argued that states aligned in order to balance against threats rather than against power alone. A potential adversary's power was a critical component of the threats it might pose, but other factors, such as geographic proximity and perceived intentions, also mattered.[84] Thus, a state that was weaker but also closer and openly belligerent could be more threatening than a stronger state located halfway around the world.

The explanations for bandwagoning and balancing treated the state, rather than its leaders, as the principal actor and focused mainly on the presence of external threats from another state or collection of states.[85] Yet many leaders of Middle Eastern, African, and South Asian states cared more about maintaining power and enriching themselves (and sometimes their sect, tribe, ethnic group, or other cohort) than they did about the national interest.[86] Domestic politics in these countries could, and still can, be every bit as cutthroat as geopolitics, sometimes more so.[87] Losing power could be lethal. As a result, leaders in these countries commonly worried as much or more about internal threats to their power than about external ones to the state. Lacking in legitimacy with substantial portions of the population, they also sometimes used the power of the state to suppress internal dissent violently. Steven David used the concept of omnibalancing in his book *Choosing Sides* to account for the narrow self-interests of authoritarian elites, their focus on internal as well as external threats, and the need to treat these elites as the main unit of analysis when it came to alliance policies.[88]

Although Walt and David focus more on why states aligned than on what they delivered, the premises underlying the balance of threat and omnibalancing theories have important implications for how we think about many U.S. counterterrorism partners.

First, states make alignment decisions based largely on how they perceive different threats relative to one another. This same relational concept informs how partners make decisions about the cooperation they provide to the United States and against terrorist groups since 9/11. The presumption that the United States and its partners will have congruent threat perceptions regarding terrorists and that this will enable cooperation overlooks the fact that threats do not exist in a vacuum. Moreover, threat perceptions typically trumped incentives, such as foreign assistance, as a driver of alignment during the Cold War.[89] This remained true in most areas of counterterrorism cooperation after 9/11.

Second, omnibalancing highlights the importance of considering both internal and external dynamics, especially with Muslim-majority states where terrorist groups operate. The governments in these partner nations may confront external threats from foreign states, internal threats to their hold on power, or both. Because these threats are sometimes interconnected, a partner government may be fearful not only of external aggression by a rival but also anxious that its rival can stoke domestic instability.

The War on Terror stimulated the rethinking of old relationships and led to the creation of new ones. Although counterterrorism became a major facet of U.S. security cooperation with many of its treaty allies, these relationships were not reducible to the fight against jihadist groups. Moreover, the United States and its European allies clashed over various issues, including privacy rights, surveillance, and American detention and interrogation policies. At the same time, it is critical to recognize that the high degree of institutionalization that results from formal treaty alliances, combined with shared culture, has often facilitated closer cooperation on counterterrorism than might otherwise have been the case. Institutionalization and shared culture also make it easier to reconcile disagreements or at least find alternatives when disputes cannot be resolved. These countries are often more prone to share U.S. threat perceptions as well as cultural values. The United States and its treaty allies also have numerous, longstanding common interests that exist beyond any single issue. Thus there is a strong incentive to overcome disagreements in order to maintain strong and productive alliances.

Not surprisingly, after 9/11 the United States afforded increased value to relationships with countries that could serve its counterterrorism interests.[90] For evidence of this, one need look no further than the fact that the United States designated Afghanistan, Pakistan, and Tunisia as major non-NATO allies almost entirely on the basis of their cooperation against nonstate threats. Many of the most important countries were in the Middle East, Africa, and South and Southeast Asia. Their cultures, modes of governance, and security paradigms were almost always foreign to the United States. Some of these countries were established U.S. partners. In other cases, partnerships were created almost from scratch for counterterrorism purposes. One critical characteristic of many of these counterterrorism partnerships—whether with established or new partners—was that they were geared toward containing, degrading, or defeating an enemy that was chiefly external to America but internal for its partners.

Since the U.S.-led invasion of Afghanistan toppled the Taliban, no state has openly sided with a jihadist group. Even state sponsors of terrorism, like Pakistan, at least claim to be in America's camp. Yet this does not guarantee cooperation. Alliance reliability has historically been problematic, as countries often did not intervene when one or more of its allies became involved in a conflict.[91] Buck-passing, which is the term used when one state tries to get its ally to fight an aggressor while it remains on the sidelines, manifests differently in terms of counterterrorism, for several reasons. First, cooperation is more nuanced than simply whether to intervene in a conflict, and it has multiple elements, as we saw in the introduction. Second, although the two fought devastating proxy wars, the United States never actually went to war with the Soviet Union. America has been engaged in direct hostilities against al-Qaeda, ISIS, and various other jihadist groups for many years. Third, the enemy is more heterogeneous. It is true that the communist movement was hardly uniform, but the Soviet Union was still its undisputed leader. For all these reasons—the atomization of the jihadist movement, the multifaceted nature of counterterrorism cooperation, and the ongoing need for it since 9/11—partners have more opportunities to cooperate in some areas but pass the buck in others.

Shifting U.S. priorities since 9/11 can make securing consistent cooperation even more difficult. Although President Bush pledged to wage the War on Terror until every terrorist group of global reach was destroyed, in reality the United States initially focused mainly on al-Qaeda. As the group decentralized and the jihadist movement metastasized, the United States expanded its aperture to include other groups. Some jihadist organizations also transitioned from relying mainly on terrorism and guerrilla warfare to taking territory and administering social services, forcing the United States to adapt its counterterrorism strategy accordingly. America has inevitably asked even more from some of its partners as a result. U.S. officials understandably view such adaptations as necessary refinements and rightly seek to ensure that other countries carry their share of the burden. Nevertheless, partners may perceive such adaptations as America shifting the goalposts. This has led to the type of foot-dragging on counterterrorism that some analysts predicted not long after 9/11.[92]

Partners' concerns about U.S. reliability exacerbate the challenges of optimizing counterterrorism alliances. Some states shifted back and forth between the U.S. and Soviet camps during the Cold War, but the superpowers typically were not the ones ending these relationships. Treaty alliances promote a higher degree of trust because fears of abandonment are mitigated by formal agreements. Many of America's partnerships formed since 9/11 were forged explicitly for the purpose of countering jihadist groups. Others were regenerated or repurposed to focus on counterterrorism. It is not surprising that some partner nations fear the United States will abandon them once the jihadist threat dissipates. Such fears are not necessarily misplaced. This further reduces the likelihood that some counterterrorism partners will undertake difficult or unpopular actions against jihadists and sometimes even creates perverse incentives for them to prolong the terrorist threat.

During the Cold War, the United States, its allies, and partners could all agree that the Soviet Union was the enemy. Disagreements existed on numerous issues, including terrorism, but these were typically sublimated to America's overriding ambition to defeat the Soviet Union. After 9/11, Washington sometimes pressed for actions against jihadist groups or infrastructure that partner nations did not deem to be dangerous to them and actually considered useful against other internal or external threats. Even when the United States and its partners shared similar threat perceptions, Washington was commonly seeking more from these countries than in the past. In contrast to cooperation against godless communists led by another state, counterterrorism often requires partners to take lethal actions against their own citizens who share the same faith and claim to act in the name of causes that generate sympathy among the wider population. The United States also sought cooperation on other highly sensitive issues, including permission to launch drone strikes on a partner's soil when it is unable or unwilling to confront jihadists directly. And after decades spent working with friendly dictators, America began pressing certain partners to undertake political reforms that would effectively change the way they were governed. In short, the United States was asking for more in terms of counterterrorism cooperation than it had in the past and asking more of many of its partners in the Middle East, Africa, and South Asia than ever before. Before turning to how individual countries responded, the next two chapters explore the evolution of post-9/11 U.S. counterterrorism efforts chronologically and thematically.

2

AMERICA AND ITS PARTNERS IN THE WAR ON TERROR

One night in the summer of 2000, approximately two hundred jihadists came together for dinner in the main hall of Osama bin Laden's Afghan compound. Al-Qaeda's global jihad against America was still a controversial cause. Although the 1998 bombing of two American embassies in East Africa had fired the passions of some of the youth, many established jihadists feared launching terrorist attacks against the United States could result in disaster for their movement. At the meeting they urged bin Laden to reconsider his focus on the "Far Enemy."[1] The al-Qaeda leader was unmoved. America had not retreated from "all the lands of Islam" as the al-Qaeda-led World Islamic Front demanded.[2] Believing more and greater attacks were needed, bin Laden pushed ahead with his global jihad.

U.S. officials tracking al-Qaeda and the other anti-Western jihadists based in Afghanistan were growing increasingly alarmed. Within a year of bin Laden's conclave, "the system was blinking red," according to then CIA director George Tenet.[3] Richard Clarke, the Clinton administration's chief counterterrorism official who stayed on after the transition, repeatedly warned his new bosses about al-Qaeda.[4] The intelligence community issued multiple alerts, including the infamous memo included in the August 6 President's Daily Brief that bluntly stated, "Bin Laden determined to strike in U.S.."[5] It took almost another month before the Bush administration held its first cabinet-level meeting on al-Qaeda and Afghanistan. The meeting occurred on September 4, a week before the world changed.

Despite the many warnings, the Bush team simply was not focused on nonstate actors like al-Qaeda. President George W. Bush and his team came into office promising to end the practice of intervening in other countries for humanitarian reasons, strengthen relationships with allies that shared American values, focus more on Russia and China, and deal decisively with rogue regimes and other hostile states.[6] The Bush administration believed that the United States needed to leverage its flexibility as the sole superpower to confront state-based threats unilaterally when necessary.[7] Nontraditional threats like terrorism were second-tier concerns at most. Bush later admitted he did not feel a sense of urgency to confront al-Qaeda.[8] That changed on September 11.

America had been without a security paradigm since the Cold War ended. 9/11 provided a new organizing principle for U.S. foreign policy: winning the War on Terror. This new mission required "adapting old alliances and creating new partnerships."[9] Countries where the United States previously had few interests or with which it allowed relations to atrophy suddenly became critical to U.S. security. President George W. Bush drew a line in the sand, telling the rest of the world, "Either you are with us or you are with the terrorists."[10]

Chapter 1 situated U.S. counterterrorism polices and partnerships in the context of broader trends in American foreign policy and alignments. The next one explores the elements of U.S. counterterrorism cooperation after 9/11. This chapter provides a bridge between them by identifying major inflection points in the War on Terror and charting the macro shifts in U.S. counterterrorism policy that affected cooperation with partner nations. Jihadist adaptation and expansion influenced these shifts, as did the U.S. experiences in Afghanistan and Iraq. Broader changes in American foreign policy also were factors. There is considerable continuity between Bush's counterterrorism policies during his second term and Obama's policies throughout his presidency. Yet these similarities belie fundamental differences in how each president approached the War on Terror. Bush's apparent aim was to win it, although precisely what victory would look like was never defined. He demanded cooperation from other countries after

9/11 but also tended toward unilateralism. Obama was looking for a way to end the War on Terror while still keeping America safe and thereby enable the United States to focus more on other challenges. Building patterns of cooperation with partner nations was a way to increase burden sharing and make U.S. counterterrorism efforts more sustainable.

THE WAR ON TERROR BEGINS

Days after 9/11, Congress authorized the president to "Use all necessary and appropriate force against those nations, organizations, or persons he determines planned, authorized, committed, or aided the terrorist attacks that occurred on September 11, 2001, or harbored such organizations or persons, in order to prevent any future acts of international terrorism against the United States by such nations, organizations or persons."[11]

This was the first Authorization for the Use of Military Force (AUMF) that ever targeted "organizations and persons" rather than just nation-states. On October 7, 2001, the United States launched Operation Enduring Freedom (OEF), the official name used to describe the War on Terror. Although the AUMF was restricted to actors responsible in one way or another for 9/11, the ensuing U.S. counterterrorism effort was considerably broader. The number of places where the United States began pursuing counterterrorism objectives swelled, and the scope of these objectives was broader than in the past. This naturally created conflicts among overseas priorities, altered the nature of U.S. relations with many countries, and fueled an interagency competition for resources. It also spread the United States thin in terms of attention and resources that could be devoted to any one place.

Inflated threat perceptions and a poor understanding of al-Qaeda contributed to this overresponse. U.S. officials feared that the carnage inflicted on 9/11 augured a potentially greater onslaught.[12] Having been caught flat-footed, the administration focused not only on the actual al-Qaeda threat but also the possibility of emergent threats throughout a substantial portion of the world.[13] This included pursuing a counterhaven policy intended to eliminate extant terrorist sanctuaries and foreclose future access to territory. The United States consequently devoted substantial attention and resources to countries experiencing Muslim-led insurgencies and to failed or failing Muslim-majority states.[14] Knowledge of al-Qaeda as an organization was lacking throughout much of the government.[15] With no sense of the strength, scale, or uniformity of the enemy America faced, the Bush administration and the intelligence on which policy makers relied overestimated on all three counts.[16] They lumped al-Qaeda together with a host of other jihadist organizations, many of which were focused on local agendas and opposed attacking America, albeit mainly for strategic reasons. The War on Terror helped turn this faulty assessment into a self-fulfilling prophecy by creating conditions in which jihadists of various stripes rallied around one another to fight against America.

Bush outlined a mission that required a massive counterterrorism campaign and the type of hawkish action that would have been difficult to sell to the American people before September 11. The 2003 Counterterrorism Strategy called for simultaneous action on four fronts. First, defeating terrorist organizations of global reach by attacking their sanctuaries; leadership; command, control, and communications; material support; and finances. Second, denying terrorists sponsorship, support, and sanctuary, which included territory and physical structures such as training camps as well as "virtual" havens such as reliable financial networks. Third, diminishing the underlying conditions that created risk factors for terrorism. This included addressing structural issues such as governance and waging a "war of ideas" to delegitimize terrorism and promote freedom. Finally, defending the homeland and its citizens and interests abroad by improving homeland security and neutralizing threats before they were able to manifest.[17]

Theoretically, the Bush administration was prepared to pursue a holistic strategy in which enemy-centric operations would be accompanied by efforts to build partner nations' security forces and promote good governance, the rule of law, and respect for human rights.[18] This massive undertaking would require considerable buy-in and political will from many countries around the world. In reality, the counterterrorism campaign that the United States executed focused overwhelmingly on killing the enemy or thwarting plots. U.S. outreach to many key countries emphasized securing the cooperation necessary for these efforts. Attempting to spread democracy and rebuild Iraq after the U.S. invasion were the most important nonmartial elements of Bush's approach. In Afghanistan and Iraq, where America committed considerable military forces, the administration built coalitions and tried to obtain additional cooperation from neighboring states. In other countries, the United States sought to capture or kill al-Qaeda targets by proxy or to secure the right to send in small numbers of American forces to do the job.

BOOTS ON THE GROUND

After threats of military force failed to sway the Taliban's leader, Mullah Omar, to hand over bin Laden and other al-Qaeda leaders, the United States went to war.[19] A few hundred special operations forces and CIA operatives were inserted into Afghanistan, where they directed a massive air campaign. The Northern Alliance, which had been locked in a civil war with al-Qaeda's Taliban hosts since the mid-1990s, initially provided the bulk of the ground forces. Additional U.S. forces were subsequently deployed. NATO did not play an explicit role in the initial military operations, but special forces from Canada and a limited number of European countries helped hunt down al-Qaeda and Taliban members, gather intelligence, and advise the Northern Alliance.[20] The United Kingdom and Canada also contributed additional ground forces, as did France and Romania, albeit in smaller numbers.[21] NATO member states and numerous other countries provided various forms of assistance, including support aircraft, maritime patrols, access to basing, airspace and fueling stations, logistical assistance, and intelligence cooperation. The Taliban government was toppled within months of the U.S. invasion, and the entire jihadist infrastructure it hosted was destroyed. Most al-Qaeda members fled to Pakistan. A small number absconded to Iran, and others escaped to the Middle East and Horn of Africa. Many Taliban leaders, including Mullah Omar, migrated to Pakistan.

In December 2001, the United Nations authorized the International Security Assistance Force (ISAF). Over forty countries ultimately contributed troops. The United States relied on ISAF for stabilization operations, including attempts to rebuild the Afghan army and a national police force. ISAF's mission was originally limited to Kabul and only expanded to cover Afghanistan's whole territory after NATO took command of it in 2003. Also in December 2001, Afghan political factions gathered in Bonn, Germany, under UN auspices and signed an agreement establishing a provisional government. After the interim government's six-month term expired, a *loya jirga*, or "grand council," elected Hamid Karzai as interim president. He was subsequently elected president of the Islamic Republic of Afghanistan in 2004. Parliamentary elections were held the following year. Afghanistan was once again a sovereign nation, yet it remained heavily dependent on foreign troops to maintain a modicum of security and on financial assistance from the international community to stay afloat. There were approximately 5,000 ISAF troops in Afghanistan when NATO took over the mission in 2003. The number grew incrementally until 2006, when it doubled from about 10,000 to roughly 20,000 troops.[22]

The number of U.S. troops grew to approximately 5,000 by the end of 2002. Their mission was to hunt terrorists, not secure the country, but they were chasing ghosts. Al-Qaeda and most of the Taliban leadership had already fled. Taliban who remained in Afghanistan were attempting to return to civilian life. In exchange, they promised to disarm and recognize the new Afghanistan government.[23] The idea of any type of reconciliation was anathema to American officials, who continued pushing the fight long after the Taliban had collapsed. U.S. forces sought intelligence from established and would-be warlords who seized the opportunity to settle scores, arrogate power, and enrich themselves. Local strongmen served up tribal or business rivals as "terrorists" and created "actionable intelligence" out of thin air for profit. American troops lacked knowledge of the complex tribal dynamics and became unwitting enforcers for competing power brokers. Fabricated intelligence led U.S. forces to execute overly aggressive raids to capture or kill Taliban members and tribal leaders who had switched sides to support the government. These operations angered the local population.[24]

Karzai's government compounded the problem. The United States and other outside powers had promoted a centralized system of government that simultaneously contradicted the Afghan tradition of decentralization *and* lacked the resources to govern the country. Karzai was forced to rely on many of the same warlords with whom the United States was working while simultaneously competing with them for power and funds.[25] This dynamic played a part in the endemic corruption that further ripened conditions for the Taliban's return. It also contributed to a growing schism between Kabul and Washington, leading each side to cozy up even closer to local power brokers.

The Taliban were initially in disarray, but its leaders took advantage of the growing anger among local Afghans and sanctuary in Pakistan to launch an insurgency that still rages at the time of writing. Chapter 4 discusses Pakistani support for the Taliban insurgency. Here, it is enough to note that during the first several years after 9/11 the Bush administration's engagements with the Pakistani government were overwhelmingly focused on rounding up al-Qaeda militants who had fled across the border. U.S. officials did not begin pressing Pakistan to end its support for the Taliban until the insurgency in Afghanistan was already in full bloom. By that time, Washington was focused on Iraq, which consumed the attention of American policy makers, staffers, and intelligence officers and absorbed U.S. resources that could have been used to help stabilize Afghanistan.

Bush and his team viewed the invasion as a way of preempting the potential threat that Saddam Hussein might develop nuclear weapons and supply them to terrorists.[26] Removing him would also send an unambiguous warning to other governments considering the acquisition of nuclear weapons, potential sponsors of terrorism, and all terrorist groups about the perils of threatening the United States.[27] Simultaneously, replacing Hussein's authoritarian regime with a democratic form of government would be the first step toward changing the political conditions in the Arab world that were seen as responsible for al-Qaeda's emergence. Instead, the invasion created a power vacuum in the Middle East and triggered a civil war that inflamed sectarian and ethnic tensions throughout the region.

Iraq became the central front in the War on Terror. Quelling the violence there and rebuilding the country displaced defeating al-Qaeda as the most critical mission for the United States. In contrast to Afghanistan, where the international community was mainly responsible for stabilization and reconstruction, the United States embarked on a costly reconstruction effort in Iraq. L. Paul Bremer, the U.S. envoy, established the Coalition Provisional Authority (CPA), which governed Iraq from May 2003 until June 2004. The CPA was responsible for establishing new political and legal systems, drafting a constitution, reforming the Iraqi economy, and rebuilding the country's infrastructure. Mounting violence led the United States to return sovereignty to Baghdad sooner than anticipated. However, U.S. officials retained considerable political influence thanks to the large American military presence (100,000 to 150,000 U.S. troops through the end of the decade) and substantial contributions of economic and security assistance.

The Iraq war alienated U.S. allies and strained relations with key counterterrorism partners. NATO members, including Belgium, France, Germany, and Turkey, opposed the invasion. Increased tensions between the United States and some of its European partners over Iraq undermined the trend toward greater transatlantic cooperation on counterterrorism.[28] The invasion angered Sunni Arab states, whose leaders surmised that it would inflame sectarian and ethnic tensions. Because Iraq's Sunni minority had ruled over a Shiite majority during Hussein's reign, they rightly worried that Iran would benefit from his overthrow.[29] In addition to these concerns, Sunni Arab countries opposed one of the key rationales for the war: promoting democratization throughout the region. The United States was asking monarchies and autocracies to support a war intended to create conditions that would encourage the end of their undemocratic political systems.

Invading Iraq also heightened tensions with U.S. adversaries. 9/11 created opportunities to improve relations with Iran and Syria, both of which engaged in limited counterterrorism cooperation with the United States thereafter.[30] Bush's 2002 State of the Union speech listing Iran along with Iraq and North Korea as part of an axis of evil chilled enthusiasm in Tehran for any attempts at closer coordination.[31] Later that year, then undersecretary of state John Bolton added Syria to the list.[32] In an illustration of the dichotomous nature of some U.S. counterterrorism relationships, the United States continued to send men to Syria via rendition even after it declared the country a target for regime change.[33] Fears that the United States might attempt to topple their governments after it was finished in Iraq led Syria and Iran to increase security cooperation with each other in order to balance against America.[34] They also began abetting different insurgent factions in Iraq partly to bog down the United States and keep it from pressuring them militarily.[35]

PROXY WARS

In the wake of 9/11, then CIA director George Tenet provided President Bush with a global counterterrorism campaign plan. It included a worldwide attack matrix detailing operations against terrorists in eighty countries and highlighting states where al-Qaeda leaders might flee during the U.S. invasion of Afghanistan.[36] Putting large numbers of U.S. forces on the ground in all these places was impractical, unwise, and often unwelcome by the host nation. Instead, the United States worked with and through partner nations to capture or kill al-Qaeda members. Theoretically, the administration also aimed to prevent new jihadist sanctuaries from emerging. In reality, U.S. efforts to work with and through other countries amounted to a large manhunting effort.

Pakistan and Yemen—states that previously had supported or enabled jihadists and topped Tenet's list—became critical battlefields.[37] Washington used a mix of incentives and coercion to secure cooperation from both countries. Saudi Arabia, which also had enabled jihadists before 9/11, was initially a reluctant partner. It belatedly welcomed U.S. and UK security cooperation after al-Qaeda launched a terrorist campaign in the kingdom in 2003. Many other countries were much more eager to cooperate with the United States to combat local jihadist groups. Egypt and Algeria, which had experienced revolutionary challenges before September 11, were especially keen to connect their local challenges to America's global counterterrorism campaign.

Southeast Asia was another theater where the United States supported local partners to combat endogenous jihadist groups. The Philippines, which was a longstanding American treaty ally, had been confronting local jihadist and Islamist militant groups for years. Efforts to advise and assist the armed forces of the Philippines on internal defense increased after 9/11.[38] The most dangerous group in Southeast Asia, Jemaah Islamiyah (JI), originated in Indonesia but had expanded its footprint to the Philippines and Malaysia. Although creating an Islamic state in Southeast Asia was JI's top priority, a faction of the group was more globally oriented. Some of the men belonging to this faction exploded two bombs on the Indonesian tourist island of Bali in October 2002, killing over two hundred people. The United States and Australia cooperated to support counterterrorism efforts by Indonesia and other regional countries against JI.[39]

American forces executed a different type of proxy war in Somalia, where there was no functional government to partner with. A small al-Qaeda network, including members involved in the 1998 U.S. embassy bombings, was present in the Horn of Africa before September 11. Additional midlevel members headed for Somalia after the U.S. invasion of Afghanistan.[40] CIA agents and a small number of operators from the military's Joint Special Operations Command (JSOC) began conducting missions in the war-torn country soon thereafter. They relied heavily on local partners, including Somali warlords, to help carry out a capture-or-kill campaign.[41] Like the warlords in Afghanistan, these men exploited the Americans' paucity of local knowledge and handed over local Islamists and Arab immigrants along with actual al-Qaeda operatives in order to collect additional rewards.[42]

The U.S.-sponsored campaign may have helped foil terrorist attacks, but it also contributed to fostering the conditions in which al-Shabaab could emerge.[43] Veterans of the anti-Soviet jihad and Islamist sympathizers who converged to retaliate against the warlords targeting them formed its nucleus.[44] Al-Shabaab became the militant wing of the Islamic Courts Union, an Islamist movement that Somalis embraced as a way to rid their country of warlords and the foreigners backing them.[45] After outsourcing a covert war to Somalian warlords, the United States backed Ethiopia in its decision to launch a conventional one. According to one American official stationed in Ababa, Ethiopia, "The idea was to get the Ethiopians to fight our war." The invasion also provided cover for U.S. special operations forces to launch covert missions into Somalia.[46] Al-Shabaab leveraged nationalist outrage at the Ethiopian invasion to grow into a full-fledged jihadist organization that ultimately seized control of large swaths of territory.[47] After years of coordinating with al-Shabaab, al-Qaeda formally announced in 2012 that the group had become one of its affiliates.[48] This extended al-Qaeda's organizational reach, which had been growing since 2004.

AL-QAEDA EXPANDS

Jihadists can be malleable about the causes they fight for when new opportunities appear or circumstances demand. Numerous groups expanded their enemy hierarchies after 9/11. While jihadists who were previously pan-Islamic or sectarian began pursuing revolutionary action, some revolutionary groups grafted pan-Islamic or global jihad onto their preexisting local agendas. The formation of new U.S. counterterrorism partnerships heavily influenced these developments. States that were historically supportive of or neutral toward jihadists suffered blowback once they began cooperating with the United States. Similarly, U.S. cooperation with countries where a revolutionary current predominated sometimes led local jihadists to add America to their list of enemies. The invasions of Afghanistan and Iraq contributed to this phenomenon, muddying the waters between pan-Islamic jihad against non-Muslim invaders and global jihad against the United States specifically. Both conflicts also attracted revolutionary and sectarian jihadists.[49] Afghanistan was a focal point for every major jihadist group in Pakistan.[50] Iraq became a rallying cry for the jihadist movement and triggered a surge in recruitment across the Middle East and North Africa.[51]

Like other jihadist groups, al-Qaeda hybridized after 9/11. Its leaders refined and expanded their organization's rationale for action, blending takfiri thought, which justifies attacking apostate Muslim regimes, with the requirement to fight the United States and its Western allies as part of a defensive jihad.[52] Al-Qaeda's promotion of revolutionary jihad was a natural step, since this was always intended to follow the defeat of the United States. The decision to let its revolutionary flag fly was partly the result of the onslaught al-Qaeda faced in various Muslim countries, especially Pakistan. Being more overt about its revolutionary tendencies also helped al-Qaeda reduce the barriers to alliances with other organizations. Once groups began to merge with al-Qaeda and add its global agenda to their own parochial ones, al-Qaeda reciprocated. As a result, although bin Laden continued to prioritize the United States, al-Qaeda increasingly boasted an agenda that made less of a distinction between local and global enemies. As the late Abu Yahya al-Libi, once the top ideologue in al-Qaeda, explained:

> So the Mujahideen today are in the situation of repelling the enemy and stopping his fierce attack on the Muslim lands, and thus the option of beginning fighting with this enemy or that doesn't really have much

> meaning now. And even the one who wants to begin by fighting the apostate regimes dominating the Muslim lands will find himself after a little while—if not from day one—confronting in one way or another the Crusader forces, foremost among them America. . . . So with our enemies today, their near is near and their far is near.[53]

Al-Qaeda added its first affiliate after Abu Musab al-Zarqawi published a statement swearing allegiance to bin Laden in October 2004. Two months later, bin Laden accepted Zarqawi's oath and anointed the latter's organization al-Qaeda in the Land of Two Rivers (hereafter al-Qaeda in Iraq or AQI). Zarqawi had transited to Iraq after the U.S. invasion of Afghanistan. He correctly anticipated America would invade Iraq and established a network to bring men, money, and material into the country. This advance planning enabled Zarqawi to become the main outlet for foreign fighters trying to access the Iraq front. He made a name for himself via high-profile bombings, gruesome beheadings, and savvy use of the Internet. Before long, Zarqawi was the rising star of the jihadist movement. Meanwhile, al-Qaeda had no way to access the battlefield and thus was absent from what had quickly become the main front in the fight against the Zionist-Crusader alliance.

Affiliation was a marriage of convenience for both two organizations. By accepting Zarqawi's oath of fealty, al-Qaeda gained entrée to the Iraq front. Because he was theoretically subservient to al-Qaeda senior leaders, they also viewed the arrangement as a way to co-opt a potential rival. Zarqawi benefited from the al-Qaeda label, which had become a powerful symbol. This enabled him to attract additional money and manpower. Moreover, the geographical distance between Iraq and Pakistan meant Zarqawi could do so without sacrificing too much autonomy. He was viciously sectarian and even at the height of the Iraq war still viewed the Shi'a as a greater enemy than the United States.[54] This put Zarqawi at odds with al-Qaeda senior leaders, who wanted him to focus on fighting U.S. forces but struggled to exert authority over their new charge. The United States killed Zarqawi in the summer of 2006. Before his death, he helped to midwife not only the Sunni-Shi'a civil war in Iraq but also to bring the Algerian Salafist Group for Preaching and Combat (GSPC) into the al-Qaeda family in September 2006. The GSPC formally rebranded as al-Qaeda in the Islamic Maghreb (AQIM) in January 2007. While AQIM continued to fight against the Algerian regime, it also began attacking Western targets in Algeria and the Sahel.

In addition to gaining new affiliates, al-Qaeda also regenerated in Pakistan and Yemen during the five years after 9/11. Dozens of compounds connected to al-Qaeda and other militant groups, some of which enjoyed state support, sprang up in Pakistan's Federally Administered Tribal Areas.[55] The number of terrorist plots traced back to al-Qaeda in Pakistan grew markedly.[56] In the summer of 2005, four British men who trained with the group executed a series of simultaneous suicide bombings in London.[57] This was the first successful al-Qaeda-directed attack in a Western country since 9/11. Al-Qaeda's branch in Saudi Arabia was decimated by 2006, but its members across the border reorganized to form Al-Qaeda in Yemen (AQY) and began launching attacks against local and global targets.[58]

As a result of these developments, experts began to distinguish between the core al-Qaeda organization (or al-Qaeda Central, AQC), al-Qaeda affiliates that had pledged bay'a (an oath of allegiance) to bin Laden, independent groups with varying degrees of association to al-Qaeda and one another, and inspired individuals who may or may not have ties to any established organization. The remnants of the al-Qaeda organization based in Pakistan constituted the core of AQC, which also included a small number Pakistanis who formally joined the group and a smattering of transnational operatives and cells. Affiliates fixated primarily on regional objectives and had varying degrees of autonomy from AQC. Independent organizations and jihadist networks in the Middle East, Africa, and South Asia had different levels of connection to al-Qaeda. Most were locally focused but sometimes attacked global targets too. A 2006 U.S. intelligence assessment warned that organizations affiliated and associated with al-Qaeda were "likely to expand their reach and become more capable of multiple and/or mass-casualty attacks outside their traditional areas of operation" if left unchecked.[59]

AMERICA ADAPTS

When the Bush administration launched the War on Terror, it envisioned working with partner nations to degrade and disperse terrorist groups of global reach and then contain them locally, at which point capacity building would enable partner nations to finish the job.[60] By five years after 9/11, it was clear this approach had not played out as planned. The absence of a clear understanding of the human terrain or set of objectives for Afghanistan allowed the war effort there to drift and opened the door for the Taliban's return. Taking a military-centric manhunt approach to counterterrorism, which some senior Bush officials considered "the silver bullet against terrorism," successfully degraded al-Qaeda in Pakistan and Yemen.[61] However, as future chapters detail, the lack of a comprehensive approach to either country contributed to al-Qaeda's ability to regenerate in both and led the United States to overlook Pakistan's ongoing support for the Taliban.

Decisions to lump disparate jihadists together rhetorically and operationally and to invade Iraq created conditions for al-Qaeda to expand. These decisions and others, including using torture as an interrogation technique and imprisoning captured militants without trial at the Guantanamo Bay Naval Base and other secret facilities around the world, tarnished America's reputation and contributed to the perception that it was at war with Islam. These developments not only fueled jihadist recruitment. They also made gaining counterterrorism cooperation more difficult. Negotiation between states is a "two-level game" in which policy makers must strike bargains that are satisfactory to the opposing side's leadership *and* to domestic audiences on both sides.[62] Increasing distrust of U.S. intentions among Muslims across the world raised the costs of cooperation for many American partners.[63]

Some Bush administration officials responded to al-Qaeda's expansion by pushing to disaggregate the threat rather than continuing to lump together disparate jihadists. The aim was to sever the connections between al-Qaeda, its affiliates, and other jihadist groups connected to them. This would isolate core al-Qaeda and reduce its ability to work through affiliates or associated movements to attack the United States.[64] A parallel effort by officials at the Department of Defense aimed to shift the emphasis from manhunts to focusing more on the things al-Qaeda appeared to value highly: operational success and support from the wider Muslim population. This "new deterrence" approach, as some practitioners called it, focused more on denying al-Qaeda the opportunity to launch major attacks, targeting logistical nodes, disrupting al-Qaeda's cyber operations to mute its messaging, interdicting financial flows, and calling attention to the group's mistakes.[65] Together, these two approaches represented an attempt to isolate al-Qaeda from its affiliates, puncture the myth that it was a global movement, and counter the narrative of a U.S.-led war on Islam.[66] They coincided with a push to get key countries in the Middle East and Africa respectively to cooperate more closely with the United States and with one another.[67]

As al-Qaeda expanded, U.S. officials in the executive and legislative branches put greater emphasis on building the capacity of partner forces to help them combat al-Qaeda franchises and other jihadist threats.[68] The Bush administration also began to temper its calls for democratization, which had alienated critical partners, and to experiment with development programs intended to address some of the socioeconomic conditions believed to be fueling jihadism. While the United States put more energy into building partner forces' capacity, it simultaneously looked for ways to reduce dependence on problematic partners. These steps included an increased reliance on drone strikes in Pakistan and efforts to build parallel intelligence networks there and in other states where reliable intelligence cooperation was lacking.

Even as the Bush administration adapted its global counterterrorism strategy, stabilizing Iraq remained the top priority. In contrast to the anemic U.S. troop levels in Afghanistan, deployments to Iraq were robust. The situation looked bleak by 2006, when the number of troops grew to 143,800.[69] Civil war threatened to rend Iraq beyond repair. Al-Qaeda appeared poised to transform part of Iraq into a jihadist protostate that could become a launching pad for transnational attacks.[70] In January 2007, President Bush authorized a surge of another 30,000 troops into Iraq to help stabilize the country. The total number of U.S. forces peaked at a little over 170,000.[71] The additional troops were critical in enabling the United States to capitalize on the Sunni Awakening, in which Sunni tribesmen involved in the insurgency realigned to fight al-Qaeda in Iraq. While Sunni tribes and additional American troops rolled back AQI, U.S. special operations forces decimated its leadership. The torrent of sectarian violence unleashed by the invasion was temporarily quelled, although it would burst forth once again after the Arab uprisings. Around 145,000 U.S. troops remained in Iraq as Bush prepared to leave office.[72] When it came time to negotiate a new Status of Forces Agreement (SOFA) in December 2008, the United States hoped to keep a residual force that would draw down when conditions on the ground allowed. Iraq's prime minister Nouri al-Maliki insisted on a full withdrawal within three years.[73] President Bush signed an agreement that declared all U.S. forces would withdraw no later than December 31, 2011.[74]

Stability in Afghanistan, where the war effort still suffered in comparison to Iraq, continued to decline. Core al-Qaeda had regenerated in Pakistan and added affiliates in the Middle East and North Africa, and jihadist groups were multiplying around the world. The Bush administration adapted its counterterrorism strategy to account for these developments, putting in place some of the policies that Obama would later champion. These changes were welcome but did not come fast enough. For example, the Bush administration did not begin escalating drone strikes in Pakistan until the summer of 2008. Once changes were implemented, they took time to bear fruit. One former counterterrorism practitioner lamented, "Even at the end [of the Bush administration] we were not focused enough on the actual problem—core al-Qaeda. It was still Iraq. People were really frustrated."[75] U.S. relations with key partners also remained fraught. Moreover, Bush's decisions to make counterterrorism the main pillar of his foreign policy and to invade Iraq had reduced the administration's capacity to confront other challenges.

REBALANCING AND REFOCUSING

President Obama came into office in January 2009 seeking to situate counterterrorism within a more balanced U.S. national security framework. Terrorism was a major threat, but it was not the only one. In addition to the growing jihadist threat, Obama inherited wars in Iraq and Afghanistan, a severe economic recession, a growing challenge from China in the Asia-Pacific, and an Iran poised to become a nuclear power. The new administration considered the greatest immediate threats facing America to be nuclear weapons proliferating to additional states (Iran) or falling into terrorists' hands.[76] Administration officials also believed the United States was overweighted in the Middle East and needed to turn its attention toward the Asia-Pacific and China's rapidly growing influence there. To address these challenges, Obama aimed to develop a more balanced and sustainable political-military strategy that aligned U.S. interests, overseas commitments, and available resources.

The incoming president also sought to bring greater clarity to how the United States understood the jihadist threat and to define the counterterrorism mission more narrowly. Obama's first National Security Strategy, published less than eighteen months after he took office, explicitly stated, "We will always seek to delegitimize the use of terrorism and to isolate those who carry it out. Yet this is not a global war against a tactic—terrorism—or a religion—Islam. We are at war with a specific network, al-Qaeda, and its terrorist affiliates who support efforts to attack the United States, our allies, and partners."[77]

This language was a direct refutation of Bush's expansive rhetoric. Where Bush had spoken about an endless "War on Terror," the Obama administration pursued a global campaign to disrupt, dismantle, and eventually defeat al-Qaeda and its affiliates and adherents.[78] In reality, the Bush team was more targeted in deed than in word, and new challenges ultimately made it difficult for the Obama administration to narrow the aperture as much as it might have liked. Nevertheless, Obama clearly prioritized defeating core al-Qaeda.

AfPAK: OBAMA'S WAR

During his campaign, Obama promised that the very first step he would take in the fight against terrorism if elected would be "getting off the wrong battlefield in Iraq and taking the fight to the terrorists in Afghanistan and Pakistan."[79] In remarks at the State Department two days after his inauguration, the president reaffirmed that he saw Afghanistan and

Pakistan as "the central front in our enduring struggle against terrorism and extremism."[80] In the spring of 2009, Obama announced a new strategy whose key aim was "to disrupt, dismantle, and defeat al-Qaeda and its safe havens in Pakistan, and to prevent their return to Pakistan or Afghanistan."[81]

A central characteristic of this strategy was its treatment of Afghanistan and Pakistan as one interlinked entity: AfPak. Focusing on the two countries separately had created a strategic disconnect in terms of how U.S. officials thought about the war in Afghanistan and the issue of Taliban sanctuaries in Pakistan. This bifurcated view also exacerbated bureaucratic stovepipes in the U.S. government. The AfPak concept explicitly recognized that any success in Afghanistan would have to be directly linked to a reduction in Pakistan's robust support for the Taliban-led insurgency. This made sense given that insurgent movements are especially difficult to degrade if they have access to a foreign sanctuary. Connecting the two countries also exposed two difficult tradeoffs facing the United States. First, reliance on Pakistan for access into Afghanistan to supply troops reduced Washington's ability to pressure the Pakistani security establishment to end its support for the Taliban-led insurgency. Second, the Obama administration needed to balance both these objectives for Afghanistan with the need for counterterrorism cooperation against core al-Qaeda in Pakistan.[82]

The United States offered Pakistan a "strategic relationship" combined with ever-larger assistance packages in an attempt to alter its strategic calculus when it came to supporting the Taliban-led insurgency and other terrorist groups. This initiative failed to bear fruit, as we will see in chapter 4. Meanwhile, the situation in Afghanistan was bleak. The Taliban were expanding their presence and control throughout the country.[83] Governance remained incredibly poor, and corruption, extortion, and nepotism were rampant. Hamid Karzai turned out to be a tempestuous and deeply flawed leader. He was also dealt an incredibly poor hand partly as a result of the U.S. approach to Afghanistan. Although Bush and Karzai had spoken weekly, the partnership between their respective governments became increasingly strained.[84] The bilateral relationship between Washington and Kabul was on a downward trajectory by the time Obama took office.[85] The United States had fewer than 40,000 troops in Afghanistan, augmented by another 29,000 from NATO and other countries.[86] These forces were dispersed across the country, limiting their impact. Under-resourcing went beyond troop numbers. Admiral Mullen, the chairman of the Joint Chiefs at the time, ruefully observed that the war effort was intellectually and strategically under-resourced as well.[87] Inattention and a consequent lack of strategic direction contributed to shifting objectives. Outgoing members of the Bush administration told their successors that the United States still lacked a clearly defined objective in Afghanistan.[88]

Soon after taking office, Obama announced plans to deploy 17,000 more troops to Afghanistan. He also committed an additional 4,000 for the training mission, with the hopes of speeding the readiness of the Afghan National Security Forces to take ownership of the fight. This brought the total number of U.S. forces in Afghanistan to 68,000 by the end of 2009. To address the myriad governance and socioeconomic deficiencies in Afghanistan, Obama also planned to deploy American civilian workers, including agricultural specialists, educators, engineers, and lawyers.[89] The combined increase in military forces and civilian experts was intended to help stabilize Afghanistan by connecting security, governance, and development initiatives. In reality, the number of civilians never grew beyond approximately 1,000 at any one time.[90] Coordinating their efforts and achieving the stated objectives in the time period allotted proved challenging.[91] One report by civilians who were on the front lines found that the civilian surge achieved small but significant progress in confined areas but not the systemic changes needed or envisioned in terms of governance, economic growth, or social development.[92]

While the numbers of civilian and military personnel grew during Obama's first year in office, a bruising bureaucratic battle occurred over whether to pursue a more robust counterinsurgency (COIN) effort in Afghanistan.[93] The military presented three options for three different missions: 80,000 additional troops for a robust COIN campaign throughout the country, 40,000 troops to reinforce the southern and eastern areas where the Taliban were strongest, or 10,000 to 15,000 troops who would focus mainly on training Afghan forces.

President Obama ultimately decided to deploy an additional 30,000 troops. When he announced the troop surge in December 2009, Obama also set a date—July 2011—when U.S. forces would begin drawing down.[94] Conditions on the ground would determine the pace and endpoint of the withdrawal, but by setting a date for it to begin, the president signaled that the U.S. military presence in Afghanistan would be finite.[95] Domestic politics factored in this decision—Obama aimed to begin bringing the troops home before his first term ended. Two strategic rationales also informed the deadline. First, Obama was prepared to support a temporary surge that might change conditions on the ground in Afghanistan.[96] But he did not consider an open-ended large-footprint deployment to be financially or militarily sustainable and believed it could constrain the pursuit of other vital interests. Second, setting a deadline was intended to pressure Karzai to govern better. This gambit failed. Moreover, Obama's declaration inadvertently signaled to the Taliban, its allies, and supporters in the Pakistan military that they could wait out the U.S.-led coalition presence in Afghanistan. Once it became clear the surge had failed, U.S. strategy became to use drone strikes to decimate al-Qaeda in Pakistan and do enough keep the Taliban from overthrowing the government in Afghanistan.[97]

FROM PROXY WARS TO SUSTAINABLE PARTNERSHIPS

The growth of al-Qaeda affiliates, proliferation of jihadist fronts, and mainstreaming of global jihadism during the decade after 9/11 meant that the "operational dismantlement" of al-Qaeda in Pakistan would not eliminate the threat to the United States.[98] Days after Obama's inauguration, Yemeni al-Qaeda members officially united with their Saudi counterparts who had fled to Yemen. Together, they formed al-Qaeda in the Arabian Peninsula (AQAP). The intelligence community ranked the group as the second biggest jihadist threat after core al-Qaeda in Pakistan.[99] AQI and AQIM were not immediate threats to the U.S. homeland, but they also could not be ignored. Other jihadist groups that had varying degrees of association with al-Qaeda were active as well. Opting for a heavy U.S. presence in every region where al-Qaeda or other jihadist groups operated was neither sustainable nor prudent. In addition to the high costs associated with large-scale military interventions and their potential for blowback, experts increasingly recognized the importance of host-nation legitimacy.[100] Obama was especially skeptical about what the United States could achieve through major military interventions in foreign lands it often did not understand.[101]

Faced with these challenges, the president explicitly made working by, with, and through partner nations a cornerstone of his counterterrorism strategy.[102] By getting other countries to carry more of the burden when it came to the costs and risks of counterterrorism, the United States could expand its reach while conserving resources and military strength.[103] Relying more heavily on local partners to fight terrorist groups on the ground was also intended to make gains more sustainable by giving local actors "ownership" over the aftermath of military operations. To this end, Obama repeatedly called for more security and economic assistance, civilian advisors, and, sometimes, small numbers of military trainers to boost the capacity of local forces.[104]

Obama's enthusiasm for building partnerships was motivated by more than their potential counterterrorism value. Before he even ran for president, Obama wrote about the importance of building partnerships and coalitions as a way to promote American legitimacy and reinforce the international system.[105] Eschewing unilateralism requires ceding control, which Obama was prepared to do. Toward the end of his presidency, Obama explained that he believed part of his mission was to spur other states to act on their own, rather than always relying on America.[106] Bush had pursued partnerships mainly to achieve counterterrorism objectives. Obama valued these objectives, but he also wanted to reduce both the perception of American unilateralism and the practice of free riding by other countries.

Relying more on partners required improving America's reputation, which was also a key objective of Obama's broader foreign policy. This effort included the aforementioned abandonment of a "War on Terror" in favor of a narrower mission that identified al-Qaeda, its affiliates, and associated organizations as the enemy. On his second day in office, Obama pledged to shutter Guantanamo Bay and end the practice of using enhanced interrogation techniques. These actions were also intended to restore important American norms and strengthen the rule of law at home. Because Bush's emphasis on spreading democracy had strained relations with many partners, especially Muslim countries, Obama deemphasized democratization. During a speech in Cairo intended to reset relations with the Muslim world, Obama declared that while the United States remained committed to governments that reflect the will of their people, it would not attempt to impose a system of government on other nations.[107] Instead, the United States would push partner nations in a direction that advanced U.S. counterterrorism interests while setting an example through good governance and respect for human rights.[108]

Growing fears about the threat of homegrown terrorism led U.S. officials to focus more on keeping American citizens and residents from adopting a mindset that leads to political violence. Concerns about homegrown terrorism increased in 2007, when young members of the Somali diaspora living in the Minneapolis area began enlisting in al-Shabaab.[109] Two years later, in November 2009, Major Nidal Hasan, a U.S. Army psychiatrist, opened fire in at Fort Hood in Texas, where he was based. Hasan killed thirteen people. Intelligence intercepts revealed he had been in contact with Anwar al-Awlaki, a Yemeni-American cleric who was among the most popular English-speaking jihadist ideologues. Awlaki had fled to Yemen earlier in the decade and linked up with AQAP. The attack and Awalki's involvement caused a "rapid freakout," to quote one counterterrorism practitioner, about the need to move more quickly on developing a CVE strategy.[110] Muslim communities in America were the primary focus, but U.S. policy makers also began to internationalize CVE programming. In place of Bush's democratization agenda, the Obama administration focused more on rule of law, governance, and development to address some of the risk factors for jihadism. This was in addition to targeted efforts to counter jihadist narratives and promote community-based responses.

On Christmas Day 2009, a little over a month after Nidal Hassan opened fire in Texas, Umar Farouk Abdulmutallab attempted to detonate explosives hidden in his underwear midway through a transatlantic flight to the United States from Amsterdam. Anwar al-Awlaki had inspired Abdulmutallab to join the jihad and played an operational role in the plot. The explosive device AQAP's bomb maker constructed was sophisticated enough to avoid detection during preflight screening.[111] The Obama administration was already increasing civilian and military aid to Yemen and supporting a multilateral effort to stabilize the country.[112] Partner capacity-building efforts had been inconsistent up this point. It could be years before the security forces were up to the task of combating AQAP and even longer for economic and development assistance to have an effect. In exchange for additional assistance, Yemen's president Saleh granted the

United States permission to ramp up joint operations and allow unilateral air strikes against AQAP. Yemen thus became a laboratory for Obama's counterterrorism approach of working with and through indigenous security forces where possible but employing limited direct action when necessary. This approach was intended to protect the homeland, defeat the small number of groups that threatened it, and otherwise avoid crises that could derail efforts to focus on other challenges. The revolutions that swept the Arab world beginning in 2011 made this much more difficult and challenged the Obama administration's capacity to balance the pursuit of diverse interests with the need to manage crises.

THE ARAB WINTER

On December 17, 2010, Tarek al-Tayeb Mohamed Bouazizi, a Tunisian vegetable vendor, set himself on fire outside a municipal building to protest corruption. It would have been hard to predict that Bouazizi's self-immolation would catalyze the uprisings that followed first in Tunisia and then in Bahrain, Egypt, Iraq, Libya, Syria, and Yemen. However, the U.S. intelligence community missed or misread the evidence during the initial phase of the uprisings that pressures in the region were growing to dangerous levels.[113] There were several reasons for this. First, although the size of the analytical work force in the intelligence community grew after 9/11, analysts were increasingly tasked with looking at narrower slices of the problem. This had the potential to make identifying macro trends more difficult. Second, the intelligence community relied too heavily on classified intelligence and was not doing enough to mine social media or make use of open-source reporting.[114] Third, U.S. intelligence was overly dependent on Arab regimes and their intelligence services for information about events in their own countries. According to Mike Morell, then deputy director of the CIA, "We were lax in creating our own windows into what was happening, and the leadership we were relying on was isolated and unaware of the tidal wave that was about to hit them."[115] Counterterrorism requirements contributed to U.S. overreliance. James Clapper, then director of national intelligence, told Congress "we've learned that in our focus on counter-terrorism . . . we were in many of these countries engaged with local liaison services on that subject, and maybe weren't paying as much attention to the backyard that we were in at the time."[116]

Months before Bouazizi set himself on fire, Obama directed some of his top foreign policy officials to produce a report on unrest in the Arab world. It found that without major political reforms, a number of critical Arab partner nations were ripe for revolt. Obama requested country-by-country strategies for pursuing political reform in key countries led by autocratic rulers who were also important U.S. partners.[117] The Arab uprisings theoretically offered America an opportunity to promote these much-needed reforms.[118]

Many in the administration were initially bullish on prospect of success, but there was also concern about the risk of friendly governments falling.[119] Faced with the conundrum that bedeviled every modern American president over balancing U.S. interests and values, Obama tried to promote both. This required juggling competing objectives, including ushering in necessary political reforms and helping to midwife regime change in some countries while reassuring other longstanding but autocratic partners that the United States would not abandon them, optimizing opportunities to undermine the jihadist narrative, maintaining counterterrorism cooperation from key partners, and protecting vulnerable populations. The result was a policy that was both visionary and incoherent.[120]

Largely peaceful protests toppled regimes in Tunisia, Egypt, and Yemen. The Obama administration supported the democratic transitions in all three countries, though not with equal alacrity, and remained committed to supporting democratic transitions even when Islamist parties were elected in Tunisia and Egypt. Gaddafi's regime cracked down violently on demonstrations in Libya. The United States joined a UN- and Arab League–backed, NATO-led coalition that intervened to prevent the mass slaughter of Benghazi-based rebels.[121] The intervention took on a life of its own and morphed into an effort that toppled the government.[122] Gaddafi was captured and killed by rebels in October 2011. The National Transitional Council declared the civil war over and the country liberated later that month.[123] Violence escalated more slowly in Syria, where U.S. officials incorrectly assumed that Syria's president Basher al-Assad would fall just as President Mubarak had in Egypt.[124] After months of diplomacy, several rounds of sanctions against Syrian leaders, and a growing body count, Assad was still in power. Obama and European leaders issued a joint call in August 2011 for him to resign but ruled out a military intervention similar to the one in Libya.[125] As Syria descended into civil war the following year, the CIA began secretly training and arming some Syrian rebels.[126] Leery of being drawn into another Middle East quagmire, that was as far as the president was prepared to go.

In Iraq, the scene of the last Middle East quagmire, the Shiite prime minister Nouri al-Maliki also confronted popular unrest. He had been sidelining rivals since coming to office in 2006. When ethnic and sectarian dynamics combined with Maliki's consolidation of power to produce a nine-month electoral stalemate in 2010, he broke the political logjam by securing Iranian support.[127] Tehran pressured rival Shiite parties to accept Maliki as prime minister. In return, he reportedly agreed not to allow the United States to maintain a military presence after the Status of Forces Agreement the Bush administration had negotiated expired in December 2011.[128] The demonstrations that roiled Iraq earlier that year were not intended to overthrow Maliki's regime but rather to pressure him into undertaking political and economic reforms.[129] Maliki responded with a violent crackdown that evolved into a campaign targeting Sunni rivals. Fifty thousand U.S. troops were still in Iraq, but they were largely confined to bases and scheduled to depart. As the deadline for withdrawal approached, the Obama administration attempted to renegotiate the withdrawal and keep 5,000 to 10,000 U.S. combat troops in Iraq. Negotiations broke down over the issue of shielding remaining troops from criminal prosecution by Iraqi authorities. Maliki's pledge to Iran that he would not allow U.S. forces to stay in the country made finding a workable solution difficult. Yet critics, including some former members of the Obama administration, believed the White House did not press hard enough to resolve the impasse.[130]

Within days of the U.S. troop departure in December 2011, Maliki triggered a political crisis when he attempted to arrest senior Sunni government leaders.[131] Additional protests, which had taken on an increasingly sectarian hue, led to violent clashes, especially in former insurgent strongholds, portending a resurgence of armed Sunni resistance. Maliki had disbanded the Sunni militias that formed the backbone of the Awakening movement without integrating most of their members into the government as promised.[132] Al-Qaeda in Iraq, which was bowed but not beaten, recruited a sizeable number of them.[133] After the U.S. troop departure, the Iraqi security forces reduced their use of targeted counterinsurgency operations in favor of mass arrests. This shift spared AQI and helped swell its ranks.[134]

RETURN OF THE JIHADISTS

The year 2011 looked to be particularly bad for the jihadist movement. Drone strikes were degrading al-Qaeda in Pakistan. Operatives who were not killed had to prioritize their survival over the ability to move around, communicate, or execute transnational attacks.[135] As a result, core al-Qaeda was on the ropes by the time U.S. intelligence officers identified a compound in the upscale city of Abbottabad, Pakistan, as the place where Osama bin Laden might be hiding. Obama approved a high-risk raid by U.S. Navy SEALs, and they killed the al-Qaeda leader on May 2, 2011, shortly after 1:00 a.m. local time. Information gathered during the raid enabled the United States to target additional high-ranking leaders with subsequent drone strikes.[136] AQAP had emerged as the most dangerous al-Qaeda affiliate, but U.S. counterterrorism efforts and cooperation with partner nations were keeping the threat at bay. AQI appeared to be seriously damaged. Groups like al-Shabaab and AQIM were still operating, but they had not yet become more than a regional challenge. Meanwhile, successful transitions in Tunisia, Egypt, and Yemen seemingly undermined the jihadist narrative that violence was a necessary handmaiden for revolution or that the United States would prop up autocratic regimes. The NATO-led intervention in Libya showed that the West would intervene to protect Muslim civilians.

Yet, far from being a death knell, revolutions across the Arab world reinvigorated jihadists and enabled a level of activity unforeseen hitherto.[137] The weakening or outright removal of police states created space for mobilization in places where jihadists previously had little room for maneuver. While many experts initially focused on how the Arab uprisings affected the jihadist narrative, jihadist leaders recognized the opportunities the revolutions presented. A week before his death, bin

Laden referred to the uprisings as "a great and glorious event" and stressed the importance of winning new supporters through missionary outreach.[138] The deputy emir of AQAP encouraged jihadists to take advantage of the newly open environments to spread their ideas.[139] This is precisely what they did. Jihadists in Egypt and Tunisia seized on their newfound operational freedom to organize and enlist supporters. The environment was even more open in Yemen, which was not a police state in the first place. Autocratic regimes in Libya and Syria deliberately facilitated jihadist mobilization immediately after protests began in order to promote the narrative that they were fighting terrorism and to create conflict among various opposition groups.[140] This helped jihadists emerge as some of the most organized forces in post-Gaddafi Libya and in the escalating conflict in Syria.

Lasting democratic transitions and improved governance did not accompany the deterioration of police states. Tunisia was the only Sunni-majority Arab state where a democratic transition held.[141] And even there, the security situation deteriorated. Many Tunisians were left wondering whether life really changed for the better.[142] Egypt slipped back into autocracy when the military overthrew the democratically elected prime minister. The new military-backed regime was battling an escalating jihadist insurgency when this book went to press. Libya, Yemen, and Syria descended into civil war. The NATO-led coalition that toppled Gaddafi's regime failed to execute follow-up stabilization operations. After escalating factional violence in Libya tipped over into a second civil war, a mélange of militias, some of them Islamist or jihadist in character, took control of large parts of the country. Rival would-be regimes, one of which was in league with jihadist militias, claimed the right to govern. Yemen looked for several years like it might be a success story before collapsing into civil war in early 2015. The Syrian civil war spilled over into Iraq and claimed the lives of almost half a million people as of 2016.[143] These developments validated the jihadist narrative that the only way to take power was at the point of a gun. The civil wars that erupted created beneficial conditions for jihadists and drew an influx of foreign fighters. The overwhelming majority of them went to Syria and Iraq, which had attracted approximately 40,000 fighters from over 120 countries by 2017.[144]

As the Arab uprisings gained steam in 2011, Ayman al-Zawahiri, who took the reins of al-Qaeda after bin Laden was killed, directed AQI to form a group and deploy it across the border into Syria.[145] Abu Bakr al-Baghdadi, the leader of AQI, which since 2006 was officially known as the Islamic State of Iraq, sent a contingent of battle-hardened fighters to form Jabhat al-Nusra (JN).[146] It became one of the most effective rebel groups in the Syrian conflict.[147] In April 2013, Baghdadi issued a statement officially absorbing JN and renaming his organization the Islamic State of Iraq and al-Sham (ISIS).[148] The move both revealed and exacerbated a rift between ISIS and JN. Different objectives and approaches to the Syrian conflict, which informed the organizational power struggle, burst into the open. JN prioritized jihad against the Assad regime, was willing to cooperate with other rebel groups to realize this objective, and pursued a population-centric approach.[149] ISIS remained committed to the old AQI strategy of intimidation and sectarian provocation.[150] It also sought to use Syria as a launching pad for a renewed offensive in Iraq and was prepared to enter into a temporary peace accord with the Assad regime to achieve this objective.[151] Before long, ISIS controlled substantial territory in Syria. These battlefield successes, combined with a mastery of social media, helped ISIS poach thousands of Nusra members and attract the lion's share of foreign fighters in Syria.[152] On February 3, 2014, al-Qaeda formally dissociated itself from ISIS.[153]

In June, ISIS launched a major military offensive in Iraq that captured the country's second largest city, Mosul. The United States had spent billions over the previous ten years to build the capacity of the Iraqi Security Forces (ISF) so they could replace U.S. combat troops and lead counterterrorism operations across the country.[154] This enormous investment in security cooperation and assistance proved inadequate, in large part because Maliki oversaw the systematic degradation of the ISF in an effort to reduce the chances of a coup.[155] The rout at Mosul, where Iraqi forces dropped their weapons and fled, was a reminder of the limits of hardware and tactical training when political challenges undermine a partner security force's will to fight.[156] Afterward, Baghdadi announced the reestablishment of the caliphate—the Islamic State—and declared himself the leader of the *umma*.[157] Numerous jihadist groups—some of them previously loyal to al-Qaeda—offered their allegiance. ISIS controlled territory stretching across Iraq and Syria. Although primarily focused on building its protostate, it also used the territory as a base for launching international terrorist attacks.

ISIS and al-Qaeda became competing lodestars in the jihadist movement and forced U.S. policy makers to confront an increasingly complex threat matrix. There were notable differences between the two groups. ISIS wasted little time declaring a caliphate, whereas al-Qaeda leaders believed it was necessary to build public support and make sure that suitable conditions existed before an Islamic state could be created.[158] Unlike al-Qaeda, which was sensitive to alienating potential supporters through the use of wanton violence, ISIS practiced extreme brutality to intimidate local populations and stoke sectarian conflict. Yet ISIS also reflected important trends within the jihadist movement.

The first was a return of locally focused jihadist violence in the heart of the Arab world. The most robust revolutionary jihads since 9/11 had been waged against countries like Pakistan, Yemen, and Saudi Arabia, which had previously supported or enabled jihadist groups. After the Arab uprisings, Arab states that had avoided or put down revolutionary challenges before 9/11 were forced to reckon with them. Second, this renewed local emphasis was accented by the growing influence of sectarianism on jihadist agendas. ISIS inflamed and benefited from an increasingly bloody Sunni-Shi'a competition that infused other conflicts across the region. Third, jihadist organizations transformed into war-fighting militias that pursued state-building enterprises. ISIS was the most successful group in terms of holding and administering territory, but it was not the only one. Al-Qaeda affiliates temporarily seized territory and engaged in rebel governance in Yemen and Mali. Fourth, before ISIS burst on the scene, attacks against Western targets were either centrally directed, like 9/11, or inspired. AQAP, in particular, had used propaganda to try to inspire individuals with no organizational ties to the group to carry out their own attacks. ISIS's mastery of social media and its declaration of a caliphate not only enhanced its inspirational capabilities. These developments, combined with the growth in end-to-end encryption, also enabled it to pursue a "virtual-planner model," in which ISIS operatives used technology to guide lone attackers who were sometimes halfway across the world.[159]

A TEAM OF RIVALS

Doris Kearns Goodwin's book *Team of Rivals* paints a vivid portrait of Abraham Lincoln, the men who served in his cabinet, and his ability to reconcile their conflicting personalities and objectives in pursuit of abolition and victory in the Civil War. Barack Obama is said to have been such a fan of the book that he used Lincoln's approach as a model when constructing his own cabinet. This approach may work well when everyone is on the same team, although scholars of American politics will ultimately be the judges of that. It is a pretty safe bet that the president was not looking to create an international team of rivals when, in September 2014, he announced the formation of a global coalition to "degrade and ultimately defeat" ISIS.[160] However, this is more or less what he got.

The global coalition actually consisted of overlapping coalitions focused on military operations and capacity building in Iraq and Syria, stopping the flow of foreign fighters, cutting off ISIS's access to financing, providing humanitarian relief, and combating ISIS's ability to radicalize and recruit. On paper, the coalition was sixty-plus countries strong and dedicated to combating ISIS.[161] In reality, the coalition was beset by conflicting interests, especially between the United States and its Sunni Arab partners. Three interrelated issues that hampered cooperation within the coalition also affected bilateral relations between the United States and some of its Arab partners, including Saudi Arabia and Egypt, as we will see in future chapters.

The first was a total disconnect over the Arab uprisings themselves. Where the Obama team saw the opportunity to promote democracy and deal a blow to repressive autocracies, many of the United States' Arab partners perceived threats to their own regimes. The Obama administration's decision to call for the ouster of President Hosni Mubarak, a longstanding U.S. partner, was especially troubling: it suggested there were limits to American loyalty. This set a dangerous precedent in the eyes of other Arab partners, including Saudi Arabia, as we will see in chapter 6. Making matters worse, Mubarak was succeeded by a member of the Muslim Brotherhood, a group that key U.S. partners in the Middle East vehemently opposed.

Second, Obama's pursuit of a deal that would keep Iran from becoming a nuclear power was deeply unsettling to Sunni Arab states. Iran was on the precipice of becoming a nuclear-weapons state by the time Obama took office. Although air strikes would slow Iran's pursuit of nuclear weapons, they would not remove its capability to produce them. The Obama administration succeeded in imposing a new round of crippling international sanctions intended to coerce Iran into dismantling its nuclear program. In the summer of 2012, the UN Security Council's five permanent members—China, France, Russia, the United Kingdom, and the United States—plus Germany began secret talks with Iran. Talks were running openly by the fall of 2013 and resulted in an agreement signed in July 2015. Iran agreed to shut down many but not all of its centrifuges and to produce only a small stock of uranium for civilian use. Provided Iran abided by the deal, it would not be able to make a bomb's worth of weapons-grade uranium in less than a year for at least a decade. In return, major oil and financial sanctions put in place to pressure Iran were lifted.[162]

Obama wanted to halt the spread of nuclear weapons, keep a U.S. adversary from becoming more dangerous, and avert a potential nuclear arms race in an unstable region. Sunni states did not view it this way. The U.S. overthrow of the Taliban in Afghanistan and Saddam Hussein's regime in Iraq had already removed two governments that Sunni states historically relied on to check Iranian advances in the region. At the very least, the lifting of sanctions as mandated by the deal would provide Iran with greater financial resources to support its proxies and sow chaos across the Middle East. At worst, Iran might be able to develop a nuclear bomb down the road. Some Sunni states, especially Saudi Arabia, also feared the deal might be the beginning of an American-Iranian rapprochement that would leave them out in the cold. The Obama administration attempted to reassure anxious Gulf countries by selling them billions in advanced military hardware.[163] This failed to reassure America's partners of its commitment to their security.

Third, Sunni states were incredibly frustrated by Obama's reluctance to intervene directly in Syria against Assad's Iranian-supported Alawite regime or take more robust measures to help build up indigenous Sunni forces there. In their eyes, the U.S. response contrasted poorly with Iranian efforts. Tehran sent special forces operatives, weapons, and nonmilitary assistance for several years. The Iran-supported Lebanese Hezbollah dispatched advisers and then combat units to help Assad put down the rebellion.[164] Russia also intervened to prop up the Syrian regime. Sunni states could not help but notice that Iran and Russia were committed to the Syrian regime's survival in a way that the United States had not been to its partners in Egypt or Yemen.

If Sunni states were frustrated by U.S. inaction, then the United States was also exasperated by their support to various rebel organizations. Private citizens, especially in the Gulf, also donated large sums to help different rebel groups. The Arab states shipping weapons and supplies into Syria often showed little regard for where this material ended up. Much of the weaponry flowed through Turkey, where a jihadist infrastructure replete with safe houses, smuggling channels, and medical support sprang up.[165]

Despite the internal contradictions of the anti-ISIS coalition, the US-supported military effort slowly rolled back ISIS. This effort directly targeted the group with air strikes while simultaneously arming and advising local Iraqi and Kurdish forces and supporting them with air power to retake territory. Obama used the lure of military assistance to ease out Iraq's prime minister Maliki in favor of a more inclusive leader. By the end of 2017, ISIS had lost almost all the populated territory it had held in Iraq and Syria.[166] U.S. and coalition airstrikes combined with intense fighting on the ground by Iraqi and Kurdish forces killed thousands of ISIS fighters and some of its top leaders.[167] Yet these military gains were not matched by political progress. While efforts to negotiate a resolution of the Syrian civil war foundered, Assad strengthened his hold on power, and Russia and Iran solidified their influence. Iraq also remained in political crisis. Various factions competed for power, leaving open the question of whether Iraqi leaders and coalition partners would be able to build on the hard-fought military gains. As ISIS transitioned from a state building organization back to a clandestine militant group, many of the conditions that had allowed its meteoric rise remained.

After ISIS announced its caliphate in 2014, more than forty jihadist groups around the world pledged support to it. ISIS had formally recognized governorates in nine countries outside by 2016.[168] Most of these states were experiencing civil wars or jihadist insurgencies. Sectarian and geopolitical competition fueled or exacerbated these conflicts. ISIS expanded to

Afghanistan, where the Taliban was already going from strength to strength on the battlefield. In the summer of 2016, Obama announced plans to leave 8,400 troops in Afghanistan through the end of his term. Donald Trump subsequently announced plans to increase the number of U.S. forces there. A U.S.-backed Libyan campaign retook the main ISIS stronghold in Libya in December 2016. However, as in Iraq and Syria, political solutions lagged behind military successes. By the time ISIS's territorial caliphate began to crumble, the group was already increasing its use of international terrorism. ISIS directed, coordinated, and inspired operations in numerous countries across multiple continents. And while the United States and the international community focused heavily on ISIS, al-Qaeda and its affiliates had time to grow in the shadows.

* * *

America lacked a security paradigm when George W. Bush took office. After 9/11, Bush made winning the War on Terror the defining element of his foreign policy. This naturally led to shifts in terms of how the United States viewed relationships with other countries. The Bush administration adapted existing alliances and partnerships and forged new ones largely on the basis of counterterrorism objectives. This meant building coalitions for Afghanistan and Iraq, although the latter effort remained largely unilateral, and securing cooperation against al-Qaeda targets in other countries.

While he spoke of terrorism in existential terms, Bush was simultaneously optimistic about what the United States could achieve in the Middle East. Bush appears to have believed that if America projected strength and acted forcefully, it could transform the region. It is difficult to overstate the corrosive effect that the Iraq invasion had on America's political and military power and on its counterterrorism efforts. The war in Iraq not only complicated relations with numerous allies and partners. In tandem with the administration's decision soon after 9/11 to lump together various independent jihadist groups with al-Qaeda, the Iraq war also created conditions for bin Laden's organization to add affiliates across the Middle East and Africa. Bush course-corrected during his second term. His administration put more emphasis on nonmilitary aspects of counterterrorism, attempted to promote more regional cooperation, and worked with Congress to develop new authorities to build the capacity of partner forces. Yet Iraq continued to consume U.S. attention and resources while the core al-Qaeda organization regenerated and other challenges, such as Iran's pursuit of nuclear weapons, went unchecked.

Bush talked about winning the War on Terror. Obama came into office looking for a way to end it. Thus, although he adopted and built on aspects of Bush's counterterrorism approach, the paradigm in which Obama executed them was different. He was more much measured about what he thought America could achieve on its own but also more optimistic about the U.S. capacity to withstand jihadist threats. Obama believed that the fundamentals of the international system favored the United States. Thus, America needed to husband its power to address the greatest threats to the international system, which he considered to be a nuclear Iran, catastrophic climate change, and conflict with China.[169] This required situating counterterrorism within a more balanced U.S. foreign policy and building sustainable partnerships with other countries. Obama made working by, with, and through partner nations the centerpiece of his counterterrorism strategy. This included increasing the emphasis on nonmilitary assistance and the promotion of good governance and rule of law. However, Obama simultaneously looked for ways to work around dysfunctional partners through the use of unilateral direct action where necessary.

The Arab uprisings threw a wrench into Obama's attempts to reduce America's counterterrorism commitments because they created conditions in which jihadists could flourish. Ironically, while forcing the United States to devote more attention to immediate counterterrorism priorities, the Arab uprisings illustrated the consequences of decades spent prioritizing immediate security objectives at the expense of long-term reforms. The administration's response to the uprisings, combined with its pursuit of a nuclear deal with Iran, complicated U.S. relationships with critical counterterrorism partners. Dealing with the fallout from the revolutions in the Arab world and the rise of ISIS forced the United States to adapt its objectives for counterterrorism cooperation.

The evolution of counterterrorism polices under Bush and then Obama contributed to changes in U.S. counterterrorism elements on which the United States sought cooperation. It is to these elements that we now turn.

3

THE ELEMENTS OF COUNTERTERRORISM COOPERATION

ONE OF THE MOST MADDENING aspects of studying terrorism is trying to define it. Two scholars once painstakingly catalogued over 260 definitions. Even U.S. government agencies cannot agree on a single one. The ongoing definitional debate, which is decades old by now, led to one expert's pithy observation that terrorism is what the "bad guys" do.[1] So it is hardly surprising that an agreed-upon concept of counterterrorism has also proved elusive. Viewed through one lens, the U.S. approach to counterterrorism resembles a game of whack-a-mole. Cooperation means killing the "bad guys" or allowing U.S. forces access to do so. Yet if one looks at the counterterrorism architecture that already existed on 9/11 and the extensive additions made to it since then, it is clear there's much more to it than that. Indeed, viewed from another perspective, pursuing political or economic reforms became relevant to counterterrorism in cases where those reforms were intended to address underlying risk factors. And as we saw in the previous chapter, the United States sought military and other contributions from other countries as part of the anti-ISIS coalition.

Table 3.1 summarizes the various aspects of counterterrorism, which were put forward in the introduction. This chapter expands on all but the last element (homeland security) and illustrates how they evolved in line with shifting U.S. imperatives, partners' cooperation or lack thereof, and technological advancements.

TABLE 3.1 ELEMENTS OF BILATERAL COUNTERTERRORISM COOPERATION

DOMESTIC CT OPERATIONS		TACTICAL COOPERATION			REGIONAL COOPERATION	DOMESTIC CVE		HOMELAND SECURITY
ENEMY-CENTRIC	INFRASTRUCTURE-CENTRIC	INTELLIGENCE	ACCESS	DETAINEES		DIRECT	INDIRECT	
Dismantle terrorist organizations and deny terrorists safe haven	Interdict would-be foreign fighters	Share and act on intelligence	Provide access for basing, overflight and/or transit specifically for counterterrorism	Detention and interrogation of enemy combatants	Participate in or coordinate regional counterterrorism initiatives, including capacity building for other countries.	Counter terrorist ideology / narrative in various mediums	Implement governance reforms	Secure borders, airports, and ports
Kill and/or capture and incarcerate terrorists	Counter terrorist financing and recruitment	Provide access for U.S. intelligence officers, infrastructure	Allow United States to engage in lethal action on host nation soil	Participate in renditions	Contribute to military coalitions and/or reconstruction and stabilization of conflict zones	Run counter-radicalization or de-radicalization programs	Address socio-economic issues	Protect U.S. persons and infrastructure in country
Disrupt terrorist operations	Dismantle or preclude the establishment of safe houses or other physical infrastructure intended to enable terrorist activities.	Cooperate to collect intelligence or infiltrate / disrupt terrorist groups	Allow U.S. forces in country for capacity building	Host black sites / accept detainees from Guantanamo Bay	Help reach political settlements to armed conflicts			

The United States placed considerably more emphasis on counterterrorism after 9/11 than it had beforehand, and it has asked more of its partners since then. U.S. officials use various positive instruments to secure different types of cooperation. Public diplomacy is useful primarily as a mechanism for the United States to signal or reinforce certain messages, whereas private diplomacy may help broker arrangements or break logjams when they arise. Diplomatic efforts benefit from the fact that the United States wields a considerable degree of soft power as a result of its economic, political, and cultural clout. The term, coined by Joseph Nye, refers to the ability of one country to persuade others to do what it wants without force or coercion.[2]

Diplomatic backing or public statements of support are one way the United States can incentivize cooperation. For example, a partner may be more willing to cooperate on some counterterrorism elements than otherwise would be the case because it wants U.S. political support on a certain issue. Incentives also include tangible goods, such as security or economic assistance and arms sales. After 9/11, U.S. officials attempted to use security and economic assistance and the lure of arms sales to incentivize local partners to take concrete counterterrorism actions, adapt their militaries to focus on nonconventional threats, undertake reforms necessary to reduce some of the risk factors that can create conditions for violent nonstate actors to flourish, and provide various types of tactical cooperation.[3]

Incentives in the form of assistance and arms sales can make a partner force more committed or effective at doing something it was already doing. They can also have positive transactional value and lead partners to take or allow limited actions they otherwise would not. Incentives are rarely enough to change a partner's threat perceptions or strategic calculus. State actors seldom act against their own perceived interests simply because a patron tells them to, and this is especially true when these interests relate to their domestic political affairs or are imperiled by threats they considers existential. Instead, recipients often try to maximize the support they receive while making minimal concessions.[4] Moreover, the longer assistance flows, the higher the likelihood that partners will begin to view it as an entitlement rather than an incentive. Indeed, in some cases ongoing U.S. assistance or diplomatic support might make a partner more resistant to change because that assistance or support defrays the costs of staying the course.[5]

Coercive instruments include the threats of military force, designation as a state sponsor of terrorism, or international isolation. The consequences of these actions are severe, and this often makes U.S. leaders reluctant to use them. There are more limited coercive tools at the United States' disposal. For example, Washington can place conditions on assistance or threaten to end it entirely. Conditionality is intended to shape another country's behavior by making assistance contingent on its implementation of certain policies. Put another way, conditionality combines the rewards of assistance with the threat to withhold it. In addition to these various methods of coercion, the United States can also threaten to shame a partner publicly or pursue other diplomatic measures that might damage it politically or economically, such as siding with the partner's rival in diplomatic forums or withholding trade and investment or support with multilateral bodies like the International Monetary Fund. Coercion works in cases where U.S. threats are credible and the potential costs to be imposed are high enough to yield the desired outcome. A major limitation of coercion is that threats have a shelf life. They can only be made for a limited time before they must be carried out or else they lose their potency. The costs of coercion also rise for the United States once a country begins to play ball because carrying out ultimatums risks putting this cooperation at risk.

We will explore the utility of different instruments to obtain cooperation of various types in the sections and chapters that follow. While doing so, it is imperative to keep in mind that America sought different types of cooperation from different partners, who enabled U.S. counterterrorism efforts in some areas and constrained them in others. The increased importance of partner nations and the larger menu of items on which the United States wanted their cooperation after 9/11 increased the need for tradeoffs. Moreover, in addition to securing direct cooperation, both the Bush and Obama administrations attempted to influence partner nations to share the U.S. diagnosis of relevant terrorist threats and adapt accordingly.[6] Cooperation provided as a result of incentives or coercion can increase the terrorist threat to a partner nation, thereby altering its calculus either to favor greater cooperation or to reduce engagement with the United States. However, absent catalytic events, efforts to change partners' threat perception have not met with much success. Although 9/11 transformed the U.S. security paradigm, the security paradigms of most partner nations did not change nearly as dramatically. Many states that became critical partners had preexisting relations—sometimes positive, other times belligerent—with jihadists that were the target of cooperation. Often, the same factors that informed a partner's overall security paradigm also shaped its relationship with the jihadists on its soil. This relationship was a critical determinant in terms of a partner's willingness to provide various types of cooperation, and especially to engage in domestic counterterrorism operations.

TIP OF THE SPEAR

Because the United States cannot and should not put combat troops on the ground in every country where terrorists operate, it has looked to partner nations to act as the tip of the spear in terms of taking the fight to the enemy. Where possible, the U.S. government ideally wants its partners to arrest, prosecute, and incarcerate them. An approach that relies purely on law enforcement is not always possible. Sometimes the military is needed to retake territory under jihadists' control, mount incursions into areas where they enjoyed safe haven, or conduct search-and-destroy missions. In some countries, law enforcement simply has not been up to the task, especially where jihadist groups have considerable military capacity. However, it is also the case that the United States has reinforced partners' use of the military in place of law enforcement through its disproportionate focus on building military capacity.

Scholars have identified various types of counterterrorism and counterinsurgency (COIN) campaigns. One useful typology posits four ideal types.[7] The first, which emphasizes attrition and repression, deploys considerable effort and resources toward directly annihilating the enemy. In its military incarnation, this approach is heavy on firepower. When conducted chiefly by law enforcement, it relies on repression and mass arrests. Captured or arrested militants as well as potential sympathizers in the local population may be tortured and imprisoned without a fair trial. This approach is light on attempts to win over any members of the population who might be sympathetic to the enemy's cause. A population-centric approach that attempts to abide by the rule of law is a second approach. It focuses on both the supply side (the enemy) and the demand side (the population). This approach musters a high level of effort and resources not only to capture or kill the enemy but also to win over elements of the population that might be prone to recruitment or sympathetic to the enemy's cause. As one would expect, countries pursuing this path seek to avoid indiscriminate violence or repression. The military abides by the laws of war, and police or other internal security forces obey the rule of law.

Enfeeblement is a third approach. Although it overwhelmingly relies on hard power, like the first approach, enfeeblement is an economy-of-force approach that does not expend much in the way of effort or resources. The aim is not to crush the enemy but rather to disrupt and deter enemy activity periodically in order to keep attacks below a tolerable threshold. Finally, a mitigation approach is also designed to contain the threat, but it does not rely as much on the military or law enforcement. Instead, the government outsources containment to power brokers, for example, tribal leaders or warlords, who keep the enemy in check through collusion and/or coercion. Security forces may launch period raids, but the government is prepared to forfeit a degree of sovereignty in exchange for keeping insurgent violence below a tolerable level. In some cases, a government may pursue peace accords with the enemy as part of an enfeeblement or mitigation approach in order to conserve resources, limit losses, or contain attacks.

A partner's relationship with the terrorists on its soil is the paramount factor influencing whether it conducts domestic counterterrorism operations. Earlier, I described this relationship as a function of the utility a terrorist group provides and the threat it poses relative to other threats. I posited four types of relationships that can exist between states and terrorist movements or infrastructure on their soil: belligerence, neglect, collaboration, and cooperative competition, where terrorists are treated like frenemies. Before expanding on these, two points are worth noting. First, various other factors may influence whether a state is prepared to expend considerable effort and resources on counterterrorism campaigns. These include its strategic culture, its military and law enforcement capabilities, its bureaucratic capacity to execute a campaign that extends beyond directly targeting the enemy, and its political will to undertake necessary reforms or avoid ruthless repression and violence. Second, although a partner's calculations will be different depending on its position toward a terrorist group, the outcomes may look similar as a result of these or other factors. Nevertheless, comprehending the calculations behind a partner's approach to domestic counterterrorism operations is critical when it comes to formulating U.S. policies toward the partner and group in question.

Partners that take a belligerent position toward terrorists are most likely to carry out domestic operations against them. When this occurs, strong bilateral relations and the provision of U.S. assistance can augment or improve a partner's counterterrorism operations. In some cases, the United States may seek other forms of cooperation in return. In others, it will provide assistance simply on the basis of combating a shared threat. A partner nation's level of commitment and the nature of counterterrorism operations it conducts will also depend on other factors, including the presence or absence of other threats, perceptions of the relevant terrorist threat, and popularity of the terrorists' cause. Even in cases where a partner government commits sufficient effort and resources, it may adopt a repressive approach that violates the rule of law and leads to abuses of human rights. This can fuel terrorist recruitment and raises the costs of cooperation for the United States, in some cases to the point where U.S. laws require assistance be cut off.

Domestic counterterrorism operations conducted against frenemies are harder to predict because they occur in a relationship defined by cooperative competition. The partner might simultaneously target and enable a group or shift rapidly or repeatedly back and forth between targeting and tolerating it. The effectiveness of U.S. assistance is likely to be limited as long as the group in question remains useful to the recipient. In some cases, a terrorist organization that threatens a partner nation may also have utility precisely because its existence serves as a mechanism for keeping assistance flowing. When this occurs, the partner might calibrate its operations to ensure the group is never destroyed or perhaps even tacitly allow it to conduct some attacks.

Because of the expansive nature of counterterrorism cooperation and locations where terrorists operate, the United States has had to work with countries that support, enable, or tolerate terrorists on their soil. A partner is obviously unlikely to conduct domestic counterterrorism operations against a terrorist group that it has a collaborative relationship with. Even convincing states that turn a blind eye toward terrorists to take action against them can be difficult. Coercion and incentives are typically unlikely to change a partner's calculation if it has a positive relationship with a group, although they can have short-term utility. For example, a combination of coercion and incentives led Pakistan and Yemen to conduct domestic operations in cases where they otherwise would not have. However, this occurred immediately after 9/11, when the threat of U.S. military action against noncooperative states was at its peak. Maintaining a coercive posture becomes difficult especially if a partner is taking even limited actions or cooperating in other areas. Indeed, both Pakistan and Yemen refrained from committing a high level of resources or effort for a sustained period of time but still avoided major punitive action by the United States (that is, until the Trump administration announced plans in 2018 to cut all security assistance to Pakistan). Ongoing U.S. assistance or pressure may lead a partner to conduct occasional operations, but these are unlikely to be comprehensive and sometimes may be done mainly for show.

The existence of a supportive infrastructure does not always guarantee the presence of a terrorist group, but the two often go hand in hand. Such an infrastructure may include training camps, mosques, or madrassas that promote jihadist ideology, facilitate recruitment, or are used to enable operations, safe houses, and recruitment and funding networks. Some of these elements, especially recruitment or funding networks, may be found in countries where terrorists are not present. Many countries strengthened their counterterrorism laws after 9/11, theoretically enabling them to dismantle any existing infrastructure. However, not all countries implemented and enforced these laws or supported them with sufficient manpower and resources. Assessing partners' progress against terrorist infrastructure is more difficult than against a terrorist group because many of the activities associated with various infrastructure elements are harder to observe than the more straightforward types of actions related to enemy-centric operations.

A partner's commitment to conduct enemy-centric operations does not always ensure it will dismantle any support structure that exists. Just as a partner may collaborate with some terrorists and target others, it is possible for a state to treat terrorists as belligerents and still maintain a supportive infrastructure. The same factors that govern whether a partner conducts a domestic counterterrorism campaign against a specific set of terrorists also help determine its commitment to dismantling any supportive infrastructure that might exist. For example, partners may not view the supporting activities as threatening because they enable terrorists in other countries. Some governments that have a belligerent relationship toward terrorist groups may even see benefits in maintaining an infrastructure because it enables these governments to exert influence domestically or regionally. Cracking down on supportive activities, especially if the government previously encouraged them, can undermine the regime's legitimacy with the population. Other barriers to action also exist. Partners do not always share the United States' assessments of what constitutes a supportive infrastructure. Even if they do, comprehensive action requires bureaucratic and judicial capacity rather than simply strong security forces. Laws must be passed outlawing various types of activities that support terrorist operations or causes, prosecutors must be able to secure convictions, and judges have to be prepared to oversee fair trials. If madrassas or mosques are a problem, then the government must have not only the will but also the capacity to shut them down or implement reforms.

Terrorist financing became a particularly important issue after 9/11. Al-Qaeda and other jihadist groups historically raised money by appealing to donors, including "polyterror" supporters who gave to multiple causes.[8] Jihadists also siphoned money from charities, ran legitimate and illegitimate businesses, extorted money from local populations, and engaged in other forms of criminality. Stemming the flow of terrorist financing required going after banks, couriers, wire transfers, and hawala networks, which constitute an alternative remittance system that operates beyond Western banking or financial channels and is therefore difficult to trace.[9] In addition, not all terrorist-related funds derive from illicit sources. These funds were sometimes commingled with cash intended for legitimate causes.

The United States endeavored to cut off financing for al-Qaeda and other jihadist organizations and to gather financial intelligence in the process. This information was sometimes useful for disrupting operations and locating members and supporters of jihadist organizations.[10] The U.S. counter-threat-finance effort recognized the centrality of the banking sector and other private-sector interests that were the prime movers in international financial and commercial systems.[11] The USA Patriot Act gave the

Treasury Department the power to cut banks that were doing business with designated terrorists or terrorist financiers off from the U.S. financial system and to designate as terrorist financiers the companies or businesses that those banks own or control, as well as those "associated" with them. This made these entities subject to sanctions, asset freezes, and fines.[12] These policies have considerable bite because the U.S. dollar is the principal reserve and trading currency around the world.[13] The United Nations helped internationalize the process. UN Security Council Resolution 1373, which was adopted weeks after 9/11, called upon UN member states to keep any terrorist group from using their sovereign territory; suppress, freeze, and prohibit terrorist financing; and take steps to prevent the movement of terrorists.[14] Other international organizations, especially the Financial Action Task Force (FATF), which is devoted to combating money laundering and terrorist financing, established new measures to help track and freeze terrorist assets.

Cooperation from partners is still critical. The United States needs them to adopt common standards; otherwise terrorists can exploit countries where they are not in place. In particular, the United States sought assistance from Saudi Arabia and other Gulf countries after 9/11 because they were major sources of money for the jihadist movement. U.S. officials pressed these and other partner nations to act in accordance with UN conventions and adopt best practices in terms of financial transparency, information sharing, and due diligence when seeking to implement global anti-money-laundering regulations. This included applying reporting and information sharing to new sectors of the financial community, such as hawala networks.[15] The United States has also urged partners to crack down on actors operating outside the financial sector, especially private donors and financiers.

BUILDING PARTNERS' CAPACITY FOR BURDEN SHARING

The Bush administration initially took an overwhelmingly military-centric approach to counterterrorism, putting a heavy emphasis on manhunting. Security assistance was often used mainly as an incentive with countries where al-Qaeda operated; building capacity for counterterrorism was a secondary objective. The effort to build partner capacity really took off in Iraq, where the escalating insurgency led the Bush administration to devise a military plan that would train Iraqi forces to assume responsibility for security as quickly as possible.[16] U.S. officials harbored a similar ambition in Afghanistan. Building the capacity of partners outside Iraq and Afghanistan became increasingly important as al-Qaeda expanded.

Before September 11, the Antiterrorism Assistance (ATA) program was the principal mechanism used to enhance partner nations' counterterrorism capabilities. The State Department administers the program, which is intended to improve the ability of civilian security and law enforcement in the areas of border security, the protection of critical infrastructure, and the prevention, management, and resolution of terrorist attacks.[17] Congress and the executive branch worked together to design new programs focused mainly on training and equipping partners to enhance their capacity to conduct counterterrorism operations at home and contribute to international missions. Many of the new programs were housed at the Department of Defense and focused on partner nations' military forces. For example, Section 1206 of the 2006 National Defense Authorization Act (NDAA) authorized the secretary of defense to implement programs designed to train and equip foreign security forces to support U.S. counterterrorism missions. Other new programs were administered by multiple agencies. For instance, the Obama administration worked with Congress to create the Counterterrorism Partnerships Fund (CTPF), which allocated money to the Defense and State Departments.[18] In addition to state partners, nonstate actors, such as those in the Syrian resistance that opposed ISIS, were also eligible for CTPF. These are just two of many security-assistance programs created after 9/11. Building partner capacity (BPC) became the catchall term for the effort these programs were intended to support. (The appendix to this book identifies the major programs related to counterterrorism before and after 9/11.)

There are different types of military BPC missions. Most involve some combination of providing training and equipment to a partner military. In "train, advise, and assist" missions, the U.S. military not only provides training and equipment but also conducts noncombat activities in support of the host nation. For example, U.S. forces may assist with intelligence, surveillance, and reconnaissance in order to help partner forces locate and eliminate the enemy. U.S. troops sometimes remain on secure bases or embassy grounds for these missions. Increasingly, however, U.S. forces are participating in "advise, assist, and accompany" missions, which entail accompanying local forces on operations. This exposes American forces to greater risks. Troops are authorized to respond if they come under attack by the enemy. Every mission requires that the government grant specific "authorities" delineating the outer limit of what U.S. forces can do. Depending on the mission parameters and agreements with the host nations, the rules of engagement may be looser and allow U.S. forces to engage proactively in combat operations either on their own or alongside local forces.

Outside Afghanistan and Iraq, where the United States was building or rebuilding entire militaries, the main focus of BPC missions has generally been improving a partner force's ability to neutralize terrorist threats and monitor and control borders. U.S. special operations forces (SOF) have been primarily responsible for these efforts, which have often focused on a partner's special operations forces. The increase in multiactor conflict zones where jihadists were present after the Arab uprisings contributed to an expanded role for SOF geographically. Because the counter-ISIS coalition was so diverse and the nature of the missions were different in Iraq and Syria, the SOF counterterrorism mission also grew wider functionally. Special operations forces could find themselves involved in traditional counterterrorism activities that involved targeting ISIS fighters, helping Iraqi forces or militias with counterinsurgency, or engaging in unconventional warfare by aiding nonstate actors fighting in Syria.

To their detriment, military capacity-building efforts since 9/11 have overemphasized tactical skills. These efforts often fail to achieve stated objectives because they ignore the need for institutional and personnel reforms.[19] This is highly problematic considering that partner forces on the front lines against terrorist groups are often corrupt, poorly motivated and trained, burdened with mediocre or poor leadership, undereducated at all but the more senior levels, and lacking in legitimacy among the population. For training and assistance to be effective, it has to include a focus on the professionalization of partner forces and efforts to build strong institutions rather than just tactical improvements. Professionalization is also important because U.S. laws do not allow the provision of assistance to a partner force found to have committed gross human rights violations. Similarly, military aid must be withheld in the event of a coup.[20] Yet although the

United States theoretically may want its partners to protect the population and obey the rule of law, training efforts have still focused mainly on imparting the ability to target terrorists.[21] In countries where civil-military relations are already imbalanced, this has sometimes had the unintended consequence of reinforcing bad military behavior at the expense of civilian institutions. Indeed, a number of U.S. counterterrorism partners, including Egypt, Mali, Mauritania, and Niger have experienced military coups since 9/11.

BPC initiatives have also been slow to reflect the evolution of a U.S. counterterrorism policy focused overwhelmingly on military action toward one that became more comprehensive. Research has shown that poor governance, corruption, and inadequacies in terms of the rule of law can increase the risk of terrorism. BPC efforts are also more likely to have lasting success in countries that practice good governance and have stronger institutions and democratic norms.[22] Most of the countries where jihadist groups are based do not exhibit such characteristics, which is often what made these states fertile soil for jihadism in the first place. U.S. officials have recognized the importance of helping and encouraging countries to develop or reform their legal frameworks and prosecutorial and judicial capacity to ensure the rule of law. Yet their entreaties have not been backed up with proportionate resources. While the amount spent on security assistance skyrocketed after 9/11, the proportion of funding directed by the State Department declined. In contrast, the Department of Defense administered almost 60 percent of all security assistance funding by 2015, up from less than 20 percent in 2001.[23] Because the DoD administered most of the new programs and an increasing amount of security assistance, the focus was often narrowly on building partner nations' military capacity or meeting immediate U.S. defense needs, at the expense of security-sector reform. Furthermore, as many current and former officials lamented during interviews for this book, partner nations were typically much more interested in receiving military assistance. Policy makers and members of Congress were similarly more eager to provide it because killing militants rather than addressing systemic deficiencies was deemed the hallmark of effective counterterrorism.

President Obama tried to address this imbalance. While the Obama administration increased the focus on building partners' military capacity outside Iraq and Afghanistan, it simultaneously emphasized development and diplomacy to match the defense aspects of counterterrorism. In 2013, Obama issued Presidential Policy Directive 23 (PPD 23) to the national security agencies, instructing them to take a series of steps intended to help partner nations build their security capacity consistent with the principles of good governance and rule of law. This directive outlined the need for a coordinated effort across U.S. government agencies, including State, Defense, the Department of Justice, and the U.S. Agency for International Development.[24] Implementation of this guidance remained in its earliest stages at the end of Obama's term. As one former senior U.S. official observed, "Security sector reform is a major U.S. objective, and there are major parts of the bureaucracy dedicated to this. But it is a Sisyphean task getting them to work together, and that's before you even start talking about getting our partners on board."[25] Another former U.S. official also noted that although the administration recognized the need for security-sector reform and institution building, conditions on the ground sometimes tipped the scales further in favor of a military-centric focus.

Building capacity generally requires years of investment with no guaranteed payoff. The United States has spent over $250 billion building up foreign military and police forces since 9/11.[26] Research has shown that whether the United States is working with ideal or suboptimal partners, the efficacy of security assistance and cooperation intended to build partner capacity increases when U.S. and partner objectives for how that BPC will be used are in alignment.[27] In other words, BPC will be more effective when it is used to improve partners' capabilities for fights that America wants them to fight and that they are already fighting or are prepared to undertake. Even if this condition is met, there are other limits on what BPC efforts can accomplish. For example, convincing even dedicated partners to comply with U.S. prescriptions for how to fight or to address political and economic factors fueling insurrections historically has been difficult.[28] Furthermore, sometimes the United States exacerbates this problem or creates new ones because U.S. officials cannot agree on the objectives or parameters for capacity-building efforts.[29]

While the United States continued to search for the right approach to building partners' capacity, it simultaneously looked for ways to work around countries when necessary. Less than a week after 9/11, President Bush signed an order expanding the CIA's authority to conduct covert operations and use deadly force.[30] The Joint Special Operations Command (JSOC) was subsequently given the authority to go after al-Qaeda and its allies in a number of countries, although the precise rules under which it could do so in different places varied.[31] Obama continued his predecessor's practice of using JSOC for direct action. Its forces were not always operating with the host nation's knowledge or consent. In instances where this was the case, U.S. forces often operated under CIA sponsorship in order to enable covert operations.[32] These forces proved adept at finding, fixing, and "finishing" individual terrorists, but manhunts have proven not to be a silver bullet. Drone strikes are no panacea either, but they nevertheless became the Obama administration's primary means of compensating for partners' unwillingness or inability to prosecute effective counterterrorism campaigns. Executing drone strikes typically required host-nation approval and benefited from local intelligence. It is to these types of tactical cooperation that we now turn.

NUTS AND BOLTS

The United States has sought various forms of tactical cooperation from its partners, including the provision of access, intelligence cooperation, and help with detainees. Tactical cooperation in one or more of these areas is not guaranteed simply because the United States and a partner share a belligerent position toward a specific terrorist group, but this may increase the chances of it. Different aspects of tactical cooperation are still possible even in cases where a partner's threat perceptions or the utility of a terrorist group or infrastructure preclude domestic counterterrorism operations. Indeed, traditional alignment dynamics and instruments of statecraft appear more useful for securing tactical cooperation than other elements of counterterrorism. There are several possible reasons why this is the case.

To begin with, the United States may benefit from a longstanding relationship with a partner that has a history of providing military access or intelligence cooperation. It is also true that the costs of providing tactical cooperation are typically not as high as the costs of committing to a domestic counterterrorism campaign. In addition to the fact that they do not directly require the investment of blood and treasure or painful domestic reforms, intelligence cooperation, coordination on detainees, and even the provision of access are generally easier for a partner government to conceal from its population or at least to deny. Thus, contributing various forms of tactical cooperation can enable a partner to service its relationship with the United States without acting against its core interests. Indeed, the receipt of tactical cooperation that is considered critical to U.S. counterterrorism efforts can make American officials more reluctant to press partners in other areas, such as undertaking domestic counterterrorism actions or reforms necessary to counter violent extremism.

ACCESS

Instruments of statecraft appear most useful for obtaining access, and its provision is easier to observe. Access includes the willingness of a host nation to allow U.S. forces on its territory and in its airspace either on a semipermanent basis or for the purposes of transit. These forces may be based out of the U.S. embassy in a partner nation. In cases where the United States has or is building up a more permanent presence, it will construct or lease military bases. On the high end, there are main operating bases, which house a large force and are well defended. Forward operating bases have a smaller, permanent force. At the low end are "lily pads." These are facilities with little or no permanent U.S. personnel presence. They may contain prepositioned equipment to enable quick, flexible action and provide intelligence, supply, and transportation. The Obama administration's military strategy envisioned expanding the number of lily pads across parts of Middle East, Africa, and Asia to enable more small-footprint operations.[33] In addition to basing, the United States has also sought access for overflight or transit. The invasions of Afghanistan and Iraq required the short-term use of existing bases and overflight permissions by many countries. To keep forces supplied in Afghanistan and Iraq, the United States needed access for ground- and air-transit corridors.

Host nations also must approve access for U.S. forces conducting capacity building or advise-and-assist missions. If U.S. forces accompany their local counterparts and provide assistance, such as video feeds from drone surveillance or close air support, then the United States will require access for drones or other aircraft. In addition to operating alongside or otherwise enabling partner forces, U.S. forces may conduct unilateral raids. Sometimes the United States secures host-nation consent to conduct such operations. In other cases, these are covert operations conducted without the knowledge or consent of the host nation by U.S. forces already in the country with permission. U.S. forces responsible for these operations might be embedded with a larger training or civil-affairs mission.[34] Only rarely have U.S. forces clandestinely infiltrated into a country to execute an operation. The raid that killed bin Laden was the exception, not the rule, and required a carefully crafted legal strategy.[35]

The use of drone strikes has been arguably the most important military innovation of the War on Terror. Strategic necessity combined with technological innovation led to the expanded use of drones for targeted killing. Cruise missiles were an imperfect instrument for trying to kill bin Laden before 9/11 because the time to target was too long and the risk of collateral damage too great.[36] The U.S. Air Force had developed armed unmanned aerial vehicles. Pilotless aircraft armed with missiles provided a way to locate, identify, track, and eliminate a target via remote control. Clinton administration officials were uncomfortable with where the use of such a weapon might lead. The Bush administration shared these concerns, but 9/11 changed the U.S. calculus.[37]

Mohammed Atef, al-Qaeda's military chief, was among the first casualties of America's remote-killing campaign. An armed drone took him out in November 2001 during the U.S. invasion of Afghanistan. Drones continued to be used in Afghanistan and Iraq, but manned aircraft accounted for the majority of missile strikes while U.S. forces were engaged in combat operations. The United States launched its first drone strike outside an active war zone with a heavy U.S. troop presence in Yemen the following year, killing the top al-Qaeda commander in the country. Since then, the United States has executed over five hundred drone strikes in countries where large-footprint U.S. military operations were not ongoing. Almost all of them were launched against militants in Pakistan, Yemen, and Somalia.[38] Drone strikes increased in Afghanistan after the Obama administration ended U.S. combat operations there.[39] As ISIS spread, the map of places where drone strikes were employed expanded to include Syria and

Libya.[40] The increasing ubiquity of remote-controlled killing owes to several factors: drone strikes are highly effective, they are more precise than air strikes and thus reduce civilian casualties, and they do not risk the lives of U.S. pilots. Unmanned aerial vehicles are also cheaper to produce and operate than are manned aircraft. It is worth noting that beyond their use as remote killing machines, drones also continue to be used for surveillance missions over friendly countries and espionage over hostile ones.

The use of drone strikes altered relationships with a set of partners by simultaneously decreasing American reliance on them in some ways and increasing it in others. On the one hand, drone strikes offered a way to work around countries such as Pakistan and Yemen, where domestic counterterrorism efforts were lacking. On the other hand, the right to conduct these "unilateral" operations typically required consent from the host nation. Dropping explosive ordnance on a country's territory without government approval could be considered an act of war. Moreover, because drones hover in the air for hours, a host nation with antiaircraft capabilities could shoot them down if it chose. For drone strikes to be most effective, they also required human intelligence. The United States could and did build its own networks in some cases, but it still relied on partner intelligence services too. It is worth noting that both Pakistan and Yemen secretly allowed drone strikes while simultaneously denying these agreements and sometimes lambasting the United States for violating their sovereignty. In effect, these countries secretly ceded an element of their sovereignty, allowing the United States to kill their citizens in a targeted campaign that was theoretically covert but widely reported in the media.

In addition to access to airspace, the United States needed bases for its pilotless aircraft. Drones may be unmanned, but they require U.S. government personnel or private contractors to control them during takeoff and landing, perform maintenance, and load and unload munitions. Security personnel must be stationed on site to protect drones and the people maintaining them. Identifying the complete architecture of drone bases is difficult. One open-source report provided a representative sample that included twelve bases across Europe, the Middle East, South Asia, and Africa as of 2012.[41] Among the countries discussed in this book, Pakistan, Saudi Arabia, and Yemen allowed the United States to build new air bases for drones or to use existing ones. These arrangements are discussed in the chapters that follow. Notable here is that all three states, like others that hosted drone bases, attempted to keep these arrangements secret.

INTELLIGENCE COOPERATION

In 2010, the *Washington Post* unveiled an investigative project two years in the making. "Top Secret America" described the enormous national security buildup that occurred after 9/11. The intelligence community became a major hub of the counterterrorism effort and went on a hiring frenzy. The number of case officers and analysts working on terrorism and counterterrorism grew substantially. Constellations of new intelligence programs were spread across a vast, top-secret universe. According to then defense secretary Robert Gates, "There has been so much growth since 9/11 that getting your arms around that—not just for the CIA, for the secretary of defense—is a challenge."[42]

Most intelligence work focuses on gathering and analyzing information and presenting it to policy makers (often dubbed the "consumer" or "customer"). Counterterrorism intelligence is different. It entails identifying and thwarting threats before they eventuate.[43] Analysis and operations are interwoven to prevent an attack or neutralize a threat. Thus, elements of the intelligence community responsible for working with foreign agencies to disrupt plots and for unilateral covert action are sometimes both the "consumer" *and* the "producer" of terrorism-related intelligence.[44] The United States uses various methods to gather both standard and terrorism-related intelligence. These include intercepting phone calls, email, and other signals (SIGINT); using geospatial intelligence to collect imagery on terrorist activities (GEOINT); and recruiting human spies (HUMINT). The budgets for these areas grew considerably after 9/11, with much of the increase focused on counterterrorism.[45]

The United States already had a variety of intelligence relationships with most countries. Counterterrorism suddenly figured more prominently in these relationships, which took on an enhanced and more operational role in many places in the Middle East, South Asia, and Africa.[46] The CIA also scrambled to build relationships with some foreign intelligence services it had once considered hostile and others it had simply ignored. Intelligence cooperation is best understood not as simply "sharing" but rather as the exchange of intelligence for an equivalent good. Simple cooperation involves the exchange of intelligence, often on a common target. More complex forms of cooperation might entail bartering intelligence. For example, the United States has often used its robust technical collection capabilities to barter information gleaned from SIGINT or GEOINT for human-source reporting that is more difficult to acquire.[47] It is also possible to trade intelligence for economic, political, military, or operational goods. Intelligence cooperation sometimes extends beyond the exchange of information, either raw data or finished assessments, to include the conduct of joint operations.[48] To institutionalize cooperation, the United States established joint-operation centers in some partner nations to track, target, and capture or kill militants.[49]

As with alignments between countries, some intelligence relationships are deeper and more durable than others. Cooperation traditionally occurs bilaterally, since intelligence services tend to guard their sources and methods of collection closely.[50] The degree of alignment on threat perceptions can be an important factor in determining the extent and type of intelligence cooperation.[51] If the United States and a partner nation both take a belligerent position toward a terrorist organization, then a long-standing intel-intel relationship can enhance intelligence cooperation. Conversely, if the intelligence relationship is nascent or characterized by mistrust, this can complicate intelligence cooperation even if both countries prioritize a threat highly. Shared foreign policy objectives also matter, although it is possible for two intelligence services to cooperate closely on certain issues even if their overarching security interests do not coincide as strongly.[52] Because intelligence cooperation is conducted through a specialized channel, it can be insulated to some degree from the vagaries of broader bilateral relations if both sides are still benefitting from the exchange.

Despite the enhancements and improvements the United States made after 9/11, intelligence cooperation was an essential component of the War on Terror. Information collected via technical means can be frustratingly inconclusive and is often much more useful if paired with HUMINT.[53]

Partner nations are often better positioned to collect intelligence on their own soil and to act on that intelligence when necessary. This is partly a numbers game. Even after going on a hiring binge, the United States still did not have enough intelligence officers to cover all the ground necessary. It is also the case that partner services will know the local language, including various dialects; share ethnic and historical ties to intelligence targets; and understand the cultural terrain in ways that most U.S. intelligence officers never could.[54] Partners are also critical for interrogating and incarcerating suspected terrorists and determining whether U.S. investigators can have access to them.[55] Beyond providing access to investigators, partner services have considerable influence over how many U.S. intelligence officers are allowed in their country and how much freedom of movement they enjoy. The United States was engaged in counterterrorism intelligence cooperation with over one hundred countries by 2004.[56] The following year, a senior CIA official testified that, outside of Iraq, the capture or kill of almost every suspected terrorist owed at least in part to cooperation from foreign intelligence services.[57]

Reliance on foreign intelligence services is absolutely critical, but it can also be problematic. Although partner services are able to collect raw intelligence, many of them do a poor job analyzing it effectively. As a result, they may not have a clear picture of the jihadist problem or the factors that contribute to it. Some foreign services also struggle with more technical aspects of intelligence, such as tracking terrorist financing. The United States has attempted to build partners' intelligence collection and analytical capacity through training programs and exchanges. In addition to poor capabilities, the potential for human rights violations by foreign intelligence and security services can hamper the U.S. ability to share information. Partners also sometimes fail to protect classified information adequately, thereby exposing U.S. sources and methods of collection, because of poor protocols or corruption.[58] It is worth noting that the United States has also been guilty of disclosing secret cooperation as a result of U.S. government oversight, court proceedings, or media leaks. Foreign intelligence services sometimes withhold information, provide misinformation to serve their own agendas, or deliberately compromise intelligence given to them by the United States. Mistrust has been especially problematic if a partner's intelligence or security service is or previously was penetrated by jihadist sympathizers. Many of the challenges related to intelligence cooperation are amplified in instances where a partner service shares more intelligence than it receives.[59] Compensating for intelligence asymmetries by providing political or military assistance is one solution, but it does not eliminate dependency and can make it harder to use this assistance as leverage to obtain other forms of cooperation.

As the decade after 9/11 wore on, American intelligence officials reduced their reliance on difficult partners. The United States sometimes used reliable partners to help offset unreliable ones. For example, in Yemen, the United States relied more heavily on Saudi intelligence against AQAP to reduce its dependence on Yemeni intelligence. Collecting on partners provides another way of militating against some of the dangers related to asymmetric relationships.[60] U.S. agencies also have retained the services of various contractors and consulting firms—some more legitimate than others—to collect intelligence in different countries or through open-source intelligence.[61] Most notably, the United States has improved its unilateral intelligence collection and operations in several ways.

First, the CIA created a new career track for targeting officers. By 2011, roughly 20 percent of CIA analysts had become "targeters" responsible for piecing together intelligence to locate individuals to recruit as informants, arrest, or eliminate.[62] These manhunters are able to leverage the increasingly powerful U.S. intelligence apparatus, the reams of data it produces, and the information gathered from operations, thereby reducing the need for information from foreign services to track terrorist targets. Second, the CIA began using signature strikes in places like Pakistan and Yemen. Targeting military-aged males based on certain patterns of activity that could be observed via video surveillance from a hovering drone decreased the need for gathering intelligence about specific individuals on the ground. Drone strikes also became a mechanism for generating intelligence because remote operators could monitor where suspected militants went after a strike. Third, American intelligence officers built their own spy networks in countries like Pakistan and Yemen where intelligence cooperation was not forthcoming. Although these unilateral collection efforts made the United States more flexible in certain areas, they did not obviate the need for intelligence cooperation.

DETAINEES

The 9/11 attacks and the U.S. response to them spawned numerous books, including this one. Among the most unique and disconcerting is a coffee-table book about the practice of extraordinary rendition and the network of secret prisons used after 9/11. Titled *Negative Publicity*, with a cover that depicts an entirely redacted document, it contains pictures of former detention sites, detainees' homes, and various government locations. Some of the prisoners were ultimately sent to the Guantanamo Bay detention facility. Others, according to the book, remain unaccounted for.[63]

Extraordinary rendition is the transport of prisoners from one country to another without formal extradition proceedings. The United States began carrying out these renditions during the Reagan administration, although they were not used as a counterterrorism tool at the time.[64] In the mid-1990s, the United States began using them to "take men off the street who were planning or had been involved in [terrorist] attacks on the U.S. or its allies."[65] There were at least seventy cases of extraordinary rendition before 9/11 against suspected terrorists with outstanding foreign arrest warrants.[66] After the September 11 attacks, rendition provided a way to dispense with some detainees and to gather intelligence through interrogation.[67] Individuals captured on the battlefields of Afghanistan and Iraq or seized elsewhere were sent via rendition to other countries. The most common destinations for detainees reportedly were Egypt, Morocco, Syria, Jordan, Uzbekistan, and possibly Saudi Arabia, all of which practiced methods of interrogation prohibited by the United States.[68] Some of these countries, such as Egypt, also assisted in reverse renditions, helping capture individuals in third countries who were then handed over to the United States. It is worth noting that extraordinary rendition sometimes provided the United States with a way to service another country's needs by delivering valuable detainees to it. This was yet another form of barter when it came to intelligence cooperation.[69]

Various countries, including Thailand and some in Eastern Europe, allowed the CIA to establish secret prisons, known as "black sites," on their territory. This covert prison system was established soon after September 11 and also included sites in Afghanistan. These black sites were set up to enable the CIA to hold high-value detainees in complete isolation and to hide their whereabouts from the world. The covert prison system required cooperation from various partners, not all of which shared U.S. concerns about the threat. Some of them, like Poland, appear to have cooperated in an attempt to bolster bilateral relations with the United States. When the existence of CIA black sites became public, it caused domestic political difficulties for partners and in some cases negatively affected counterterrorism cooperation.[70]

The United States began transporting enemy combatants to the Guantanamo Bay detention camp in January 2002. Because the American naval base at Guantánamo, Cuba, was outside the United States, Bush administration lawyers postulated that prisoners there were outside of U.S. legal jurisdiction. This meant that detainees could be held indefinitely without trial and subjected to methods of interrogation that American laws did not permit. By classifying detainees as enemy combatants and not soldiers, the Bush administration also believed it could circumvent the Geneva Conventions. In 2004, the Supreme Court shot down the theory that Guantanamo was beyond the reach of U.S. law, but by then the damage was done.[71] The detention center became an enduring stain on America's image and a potent recruiting symbol for al-Qaeda and other jihadists. Moreover, by creating a new legal status for enemy combatants and then torturing some of them, the Bush administration made it impossible to try these men in U.S. courts. Military commissions, where defendants have fewer rights than in criminal courts, were established to try some detainees. Others were simply held indefinitely.

President Obama signed executive orders on his second day in office ordering the Guantanamo detention camp closed and directing the CIA to shut any remaining secret prisons. The move was a first step in rewriting the rules for detention of suspected terrorists and constituted a reversal of Bush's detention policies. The Bush administration had already returned over five hundred prisoners to their home countries, where they were often incarcerated, or to a third country that agreed to monitor them.[72] The orders Obama signed to close Guantanamo Bay required a review of the 245 detainees still being held to determine if they should be transferred, released, or prosecuted.[73] Congress blocked Obama's efforts to close the prison, which remains open at the time of this writing. Administration attempts to transfer detainees to American prisons and to prosecute them in U.S. courts were also thwarted by Congress.[74] Obama relented and reinstated the use of military tribunals for detainees designated for eventual prosecution.[75] He also pushed to speed the transfer of remaining detainees to their home countries or other states willing to take custody of them.

Asking other countries to accept prisoners marked an important shift in terms of the type of cooperation the United States was seeking from certain partners on detention-related issues. Obama only transferred half as many detainees as Bush (there were fewer prisoners to begin with) but placed greater emphasis on this enterprise because of his desire to close Guantanamo. Because the Obama administration had taken a strong stand on the use of enhanced interrogation techniques, it faced problems in terms of transferring people to states where they might be tortured. This challenge, combined with the fact that the remaining inmates in Guantanamo were often more difficult cases, made transferring them even harder. Furthermore, sending detainees to other countries was intrinsically tied to Obama's efforts to close Guantanamo, which Republicans opposed, and so these transfers became more politically charged than they had been under Bush. Ironically, recidivism in terms of prisoners rejoining the fight against the United States was lower among Obama-era transferees.[76] Nevertheless, the potential for recidivism had become apparent; thus the need to ensure recipient nations were willing and capable of keeping detainees locked up or otherwise limited in their ability to engage in terrorist activities was greater. The cumulative result was that what had been a matter of routine cooperation during the Bush years became a higher and more complicated priority under Obama.

DRAINING THE SWAMP

In the wake of 9/11, the Bush administration made its "freedom agenda" a lynchpin of U.S. counterterrorism strategy.[77] Promoting democracy in the Arab world was intended to address political alienation, which the Bush administration viewed as the main driver of terrorism, and help the United States win the war of ideas against al-Qaeda.[78] This constituted the main effort to combat radicalization and terrorist recruitment during the first half-decade after 9/11. Radicalization connotes the changes in an individual's mindset that leads to the sanctioning and, possibly, involvement in violence in pursuit of a given agenda (in this case, a jihadist one). Recruitment involves the practical steps by which a person joins a violent group or movement. It is possible to radicalize without ever joining an organized group or engaging in violence. Conversely, not all recruits are radicalized. Some of them join for money, power, adventure, to protect family members, or because they are already disposed toward violence for other reasons and are looking for an outlet.

Bush's freedom agenda was intended to address political alienation, which the administration viewed as a main driver of terrorism, and provide an alternative and more appealing ideology than jihadism, namely, democracy. This was an overly simplistic approach. There is no single factor, cause, or pathway that can lead to radicalization or recruitment, though researchers have identified "push" and "pull" factors. "Push" factors create conditions that make individuals or communities more susceptible to recruitment and radicalization. They include political or economic grievances, a sense of injustice or marginalization, social alienation and exclusion, or a personal crisis and tragedy. These factors may be the product of events in an individual's life. They are often connected to structural conditions in society, such as poor governance, corruption, inadequacies in terms of the rule of law, economic underperformance, underinvestment in education and infrastructure, demographic pressures, and religious, ethnic, or tribal schisms. "Pull" factors draw an individual toward an extremist group or cause. These may include the search for meaning in life, a desire for belonging or power, a quest for adventure, a romanticized view of an ideology, or the possibility of heroism or redemption.[79]

The "freedom agenda" focused on getting leaders to hold free elections at the expense of many other issues. Promoting democracy without addressing other societal deficiencies was unlikely to solve the jihadist problem. It could also be dangerous because countries going through democratic transitions are prone to higher levels of instability and civil conflict. Even if democracy had been a silver bullet, it could not be imposed. Many of the Muslim-majority countries aligned with the United States were either monarchies or autocracies that had no interest in reforming their political systems. Bush insisted that "America's vital interests and [its] deepest beliefs are now one," but the contradictions between democratization and the pursuit of other U.S. security interests remained.[80] Moreover, although the freedom agenda and its explicit connection to Iraq gave the impression that the Bush administration intended to impose democracy, local elites were prepared to do more to prevent democratization than Washington was to promote it. The freedom agenda thus produced the worst of both worlds: it failed to ameliorate the political conditions that contributed to jihadism while simultaneously antagonizing allies necessary to combat jihadists.

The freedom agenda fared no better when it came to the war of ideas. Democracy promotion became a rallying cry for the invasion of Iraq after the original assumption that Saddam Hussein possessed weapons of mass destruction turned out to be wrong. This connection with Iraq, which fueled radicalization and recruitment in many countries across several continents, robbed Bush's freedom agenda of legitimacy. The administration's detention policies and public embrace of torture also damaged America's reputation and may have inadvertently sent the message to partner nations that it was acceptable to continue engaging in repressive policies that fueled jihadism.

DEVELOPING AND INTERNALIZING CVE

In 2004, an al-Qaeda-inspired network executed simultaneous bombings against the commuter-train system in Madrid, Spain, killing almost two hundred people. A year later, four young British jihadists blew themselves up on three London underground trains and a bus. As concerns about homegrown terrorism grew, so did the focus on how to prevent people from adopting a mindset that leads to political violence. Some European countries were already moving into this field before the first incidents of homegrown terrorism occurred. The attacks in Europe catalyzed a more serious effort in the United States to understand and counter radicalization.[81] This marked the advent of countering violent extremism (CVE) as a field of focus for U.S. policy makers.[82] The United States was initially focused on preventing homegrown terrorism, and this objective took on greater resonance after the 2009 Fort Hood attack. President Obama also promoted unilateral, bilateral, and multilateral initiatives to counter radicalization and jihadist recruitment in Middle Eastern, Arab, and Asian countries with large Muslim populations.

The Obama administration defined CVE as "the preventative aspects of counterterrorism as well as interventions to undermine the attraction of extremist movements and ideologies that seek to promote violence."[83] Two CVE practitioners offered a more concise definition: "reducing the number of terrorist group supporters through non-coercive means."[84] Lack of consensus about why individuals become radicalized or susceptible to recruitment has made it difficult to reach consensus on how to craft an effective CVE policy. Some officials and experts have argued for staying narrowly scoped on CVE-specific initiatives that directly focus on keeping people at risk of executing or supporting terrorist violence from doing so. Others insist on the need for a more wide-ranging approach that also includes CVE-relevant activities to address myriad societal risk factors.[85] As a result, CVE could theoretically range from individual interventions to society-level ones. Because it is still a relatively new field, the evidence for what works is also weak. Efforts to counter radicalization and recruitment have reflected the abstruse nature of the problem.

Unlike other aspects of counterterrorism, where governments (and their security forces and intelligence services) generally are the sole partners, CVE also includes cooperation with and support for local communities. CVE practitioners argue that civil society organizations and other nongovernmental actors, including religious leaders, teachers, and local businesses, are critical players when it came to countering radicalization and recruitment.[86] As a result, the United States has worked with national governments and other nongovernmental partners. Unilateral efforts augment these activities. For example, the Obama administration established the Center for Strategic Counterterrorism Communication in 2011 at the State Department to develop CVE-related messaging and communication strategies.[87] Simultaneously, Washington has supported partner governments and civil society organizations in their efforts to develop and deliver countermessaging. When Obama expanded the use of CVE-related economic development, these programs ranged from dispensing economic support funds (ESF) to governments to supporting local communities that ran vocational training programs for at-risk youth.[88]

In September 2011, the United States shepherded the creation of the Global Counterterrorism Forum (GCTF), bringing together twenty-nine countries and the European Union. U.S. policy makers saw it as a multilateral mechanism to advance the rule of law and CVE initiatives, which were at the center of GCTF activities.[89] For instance, a CVE working group co-chaired by the United Kingdom and United Arab Emirates led to the creation of an international center for CVE best practices in Abu Dhabi.[90] The instability wrought by the Arab uprising, rise of ISIS, and its ability to attract legions of foreign fighters and inspire terrorism across the globe created an even greater sense of urgency about internationalizing CVE. The White House held a Summit on Countering Violent Extremism in 2015 to draw attention to the issue. A year later, the U.S. Department of State and the U.S. Agency for International Development (USAID) released their first-ever Joint CVE Strategy. It was an incredibly ambitious document that situated programming to improve CVE initiatives by partner nations within a wider effort to "promote good governance and the rule of law, respect for human rights, and sustainable, inclusive development."[91] In other words, the United States aimed to pursue a range of CVE-specific and CVE-relevant initiatives.

It is incredibly hard to demonstrate conclusively why something—in this case an individual becoming radicalized or joining a terrorist group—does not occur. This makes it even more important to develop rigorous methods that enable evaluating specific programs to ensure they are achieving concrete objectives. Identifying these objectives will remain difficult as long as there is disagreement on the main factors that contribute to radicalization or recruitment and on how to counter them. This problem has not been simply a substantive one. As with many major initiatives, multiple offices in the U.S. bureaucracy have also wanted a piece of the pie. When Will McCants, who served as a U.S. State Department senior advisor for countering violent extremism, asked the National Counterterrorism Center for a spreadsheet of every agency that justified a program as CVE, the response he received was a "horse blanket." According to McCants:

> [It] included large chunks of State's budget. DoD also justified FOBs [Forward Operating Bases] in Afghanistan as CVE. It was all over the place. When the NSC [National Security Council] tried to scrap the

> CVE language and use something more specific in its national CT [counterterrorism] strategy, the interagency revolted. As I was candidly told by a colleague at State, the more precise definition would mean cuts to too many programs, which was intolerable.[92]

Unless and until the U.S. government is clear about what it considers CVE, rigorous assessment will be almost impossible. Nevertheless, it is still possible to make several observations about how partner nations perceive and implement CVE. First, the partners in this book were more willing to implement direct or CVE-specific initiatives than they were to embrace indirect or CVE-relevant reforms related to governance, rule of law, or other structural factors. This tracks with other research, which has found that countermessaging work has attracted a disproportionate amount of attention, at the expense of the role that governments play in creating the conditions that can make individuals more susceptible to radicalization and recruitment.[93] Second, governments that implement programs to counter violent extremism often simultaneously undercut these efforts by restricting space for nongovernmental organizations to function. States across the Middle East, South Asia, and Africa, including some of those this book studies, have adopted overly broad definitions of terrorism and violent extremism in order to repress opposition groups and civil society organizations.[94] Thus, one important metric for CVE cooperation is whether governments allow civil society to function. Third, all the partner nations discussed in this book and several surveyed for other projects were more willing to provide aspects of tactical cooperation or launch domestic counterterrorism operations against belligerents than they were to undertake comprehensive CVE efforts. The United States typically made that trade.

BEYOND BORDERS: REGIONAL COOPERATION

Southeast Asia was already on America's radar screen as a potential jihadist front when terrorists there killed over two hundred people in Bali, Indonesia, in 2002. By the time Indonesia and other Southeast Asian countries committed to a comprehensive counterterrorism campaign,

America already had its hands full. It was fighting in Afghanistan and Iraq and pursuing al-Qaeda across much of the globe. Thankfully, the United States had an ace in the hole. Australia, which was a stalwart American ally, played a major role coordinating regional capacity-building and counterterrorism efforts among various Southeast Asian nations.[95] This type of regional coordination became increasingly important as jihadist groups and networks expanded their operations across national borders. However, replicating the Southeast Asian experience proved difficult in the Middle East, Africa, and South Asia, where mistrust among countries often militated against collective counterterrorism arrangements in general and especially against any one country acting as a regional enabler. The United States also lacked an enabler analogous to Australia, which was a staunch and highly capable American ally, knew the region, was able to work with all the key players, and shared U.S. counterterrorism objectives.[96]

The United States did succeed in creating the Trans-Saharan Counterterrorism Partnership in North Africa and the Sahel. It combined military capacity building with diplomacy and development. Ten countries participated. Coordination between them remained relatively limited, but it was nevertheless a step beyond the previous bilateral approach the United States had taken. U.S. assistance and facilitation also played a critical role in supporting the African Union Mission in Somalia, which was a multinational force organized and deployed in 2007 to win back southern and central Somalia from al-Shabaab.[97] More recently, the United States provided similar support for the Multinational Joint Task Force, which is composed of military units from different African countries. Its mandate expanded in 2012 to include counterterrorism operations, and it has since played a major role in combating Boko Haram in West Africa.[98] In supporting these efforts, the United States was essentially playing the part of a coalition enabler.

In addition to promoting regional counterterrorism coordination and enabling other coalitions, the United States built military coalitions for the war efforts in Iraq and Afghanistan and against ISIS.

Partner-nation support was especially important in Afghanistan, where the United States kept a smaller troop presence until the end of the decade after 9/11 and relied heavily on the NATO-led International Security

Assistance Force for stabilization and reconstruction operations. NATO invoked Article 5 for the first time after 9/11. It states that an attack against one ally is considered an attack against all allies. Although some member countries shared or came to share U.S. threat perceptions regarding al-Qaeda and associated groups, many of them contributed to the U.S.-led military coalition in Afghanistan because they were close American allies. Non-NATO treaty allies including Australia, Japan, and the Republic of Korea also contributed for similar reasons. Many Muslim-majority countries were sensitive to supporting a perceived U.S. occupation in Afghanistan. Jordan and the United Arab Emirates were the only ones that sent troops to Afghanistan, and then only in small numbers. Both countries have benefited considerably from U.S. security cooperation, place a substantial premium on maintaining strong military-military relations with the United States, and have been resolute in their attempts to keep jihadists from conducting operations on their soil.[99] In addition to direct military contributions, the United States also looked to other countries to help finance nation-building efforts in Afghanistan. The international community, led by the United States, had appropriated over $100 billion in assistance to support reconstruction efforts in Afghanistan and help rebuild its economy as of 2015.[100] This was on top of financing from multilateral institutions such as the World Bank.

Many states considered Iraq an unjust war that had nothing to do with counterterrorism. Indeed, jihadists were not a major force there until after the invasion. Most Muslim-majority countries opposed the war. None sent troops. However, some, such as Saudi Arabia and Egypt, provided access for basing and overflight. Even some NATO members came out against the invasion. The Bush administration cobbled together a "coalition of the willing" that included stalwart allies such as Britain and Australia and various Eastern European and Latin American countries that were seeking a way to improve relations with the United States.[101] However, this was very much America's war. The total number of non-U.S. troops in Iraq dropped from a high of 25,000 in 2005 to slightly under 5,000 by January 2009, by which time the United Kingdom and Romania were the only other troop-contributing countries. Even at the high-water mark in 2005, non-U.S. forces constituted only 14 percent of the total coalition-force presence.[102] In short, with the exception of a small number of countries whose highly capable forces were on the front lines, a major contribution of many coalition members was to provide the veneer of multilateralism.

More than sixty countries contributed military resources, logistical resources, or both to the anti-ISIS coalition, which as noted earlier, consisted of overlapping coalitions. In addition to the military component, coalition countries also agreed to cooperate to stop the flow of foreign fighters, cut ISIS's access to money, provide humanitarian relief, and undertake steps necessary to reduce radicalization and ISIS recruitment. The military part of the coalition was named Operation Inherent Resolve and had several elements. First, coalition partners aimed to arm and advise the local forces in Iraq needed to retake and hold territory. Second, while the Obama administration sought a diplomatic solution to the Syrian civil war, coalition partners simultaneously attempted to train and equip rebel groups that would take the fight to ISIS. Third, coalition partners provided ground forces in Iraq with air support and also directly targeted ISIS leadership as well as the group's oil convoys and financial stores.[103]

As of January 2016, seventeen countries had joined the United States in deploying military personnel to build the capacity of local forces. Twelve coalition partners had conducted air strikes against ISIS targets, and nineteen provided supporting aircraft to help with transport, surveillance, and aerial refueling.[104] The United States still carried the lion's share of the load in terms of air strikes and put more troops on the ground in Iraq than any other country. Although NATO was not a part of the coalition, many of its member states were among the most active contributors. Muslim-majority countries played a greater role than they had in the other coalitions discussed. Bahrain, Jordan, Saudi Arabia, Turkey, and the United Arab Emirates conducted air strikes in Iraq, Syria, or both countries. All these countries, except for Bahrain, helped train local forces either on the ground in Iraq or by providing training grounds on their own territory for Syrian rebels. Qatar also contributed to the training effort.[105]

The U.S. effort to build an inclusive anti-ISIS coalition is the most clear-cut example since 9/11 of an attempt to recruit Muslim-majority countries based on a common threat from a jihadist organization. Recruiting Muslim-majority countries from the Middle East and North Africa was critical for several reasons. To begin with, the Obama administration was not prepared to execute a large-footprint military intervention. American forces probably would have been able to defeat ISIS on the battlefield, but then they would once again have to occupy Iraq in order to keep the group or another jihadist analogue from reemerging. The participation of Sunni states in air strikes against ISIS was also important because it reduced the perception of U.S. unilateralism or an American war on Islam. However, although regional partners were clearly involved, these metrics don't tell the whole story. The contributions these countries made was often a function of how they ranked the ISIS threat relative to other threats and the utility they ascribed to various warring parties involved in the conflict.

ISIS and its affiliates launched attacks in Egypt, Lebanon, Saudi Arabia, and Turkey, among other places. It made an enemy of everyone and constituted the ultimate shared threat. Yet with the exception of Jordan, America's most important regional coalition partners were more invested in toppling the Syrian regime and pursuing other agendas than they were in battling ISIS. Saudi Arabia and the United Arab Emirates not only placed greater importance on overthrowing the Iranian-supported Assad regime but, as chapters 6 and 7 illustrate, also expended substantially more blood and treasure attacking the Iranian-supported Houthis in Yemen than they did targeting ISIS in Iraq and Syria. Turkey considered both the Syrian government and Kurdish forces fighting in Iraq and Syria to be greater threats than ISIS. (Turkey has faced a decades-long challenge from Kurdish nationalists who were closely linked to Syrian and Iraqi Kurds fighting ISIS on the ground.) It was a necessary ally against ISIS. However, Turkish support came with strings attached, and Istanbul has often hampered coalition efforts as much as it helped advance them.[106]

Despite the contradictory objectives and perception of various countries, the U.S.-led coalition in cooperation with local Iraqi and Kurdish forces on the ground nevertheless made progress rolling back ISIS. However, as ISIS lost territory, the competition among regional and extraregional actors has fueled struggles over liberated areas and complicated attempts to build on military gains. This highlights the need for a political solution to the conflicts in Iraq and Syria and the importance of diplomacy.

Diplomatic cooperation has always been a critical component of modern counterterrorism. This took various forms before 9/11, including international conventions, for example against hijackings; bilateral or multilateral agreements to enforce sanctions against terrorist groups or their state sponsors; and collective efforts to pressure state actors like the Sudanese government or Taliban regime in Afghanistan to hand over or evict terrorists before 9/11. Diplomacy has played an even greater role historically in ending violent conflicts. These two tracks converged after 9/11 and especially in the aftermath of the Arab uprisings because jihadists became consequential participants in civil wars, sometimes seizing territory and attracting local and foreign fighters. As a result, help with reaching political settlements to armed conflicts became increasingly important to the U.S. pursuit of its counterterrorism objectives. In the chapters that follow, we will see how the United States appealed to Pakistan for help getting the Afghan Taliban to the negotiating table, attempted to bring Saudi Arabia along on diplomatic efforts to end the civil wars in Syria and Yemen, and backed Algerian efforts to negotiate a peace deal between Tuareg fighters and the Malian government to end the conflict in northern Mali.

Considering its external nature, it is not surprising that regional cooperation—whether in terms of counterterrorism coordination, contributions to military coalitions or stabilization operations, or diplomatic initiatives—is an area where the factors governing traditional alliance and coalition behavior factor heavily. A country's relationship with the United States is a major determinant of whether and how it cooperates on regional issues. For example, some of the countries that participated in the coalitions formed for Afghanistan and Iraq were influenced more by their desire to build or maintain relations with America than by their threat perceptions regarding terrorism. However, as with traditional alliance and coalition dynamics, some states will "free ride" if they think they can count on the United States or other countries to do the heavy lifting.

A partner's relationships with other countries involved in a given regional activity also matter. For example, rivalries or mistrust between countries can thwart collective regional counterterrorism arrangements and diplomatic initiatives. Alternatively, a state might become more involved in these activities if its leaders believe doing so will help it curry favor with the United States vis-à-vis a regional competitor. In addition to these alliance dynamics, some states may embrace certain types of regional activities and eschew others for historical reasons that have little do with counterterrorism. And as with all elements of counterterrorism, the nature of the partner's threat perceptions, capabilities, and utility it ascribes to the affected terrorists are factors.

* * *

The United States has built a robust counterterrorism architecture for operations overseas, enabling it to target ISIS, al-Qaeda, their affiliates, and associated groups and networks. Many of the instruments and challenges described in earlier sections of this chapter remain useful. Incentives and offers of security assistance can help the United States obtain military access. Intelligence cooperation is still vital to capturing or killing ISIS and al-Qaeda operatives and thwarting planned attacks. But dealing either group a strategic defeat requires robust counterterrorism campaigns, addressing the underling risk factors for jihadism, and regional cooperation to end the complex civil conflicts where jihadists have become key players. Yet across a range of cases over the last fifteen years, many partners have provided different types of tactical cooperation to the United States while simultaneously subverting broader U.S. counterterrorism objectives because these partners were more concerned about other threats or unwilling to undertake painful reforms. It is to these cases that we now turn.

4

PAKISTAN

The Paradox

IT TOOK SOME TIME to arrange the phone call. Finally, on May 2, 2011, at three in the morning, local time, U.S. Chairman of the Joint Chiefs of Staff Admiral Michael Mullen connected with Pakistan's Chief of Army Staff General Ashfaq Parvez Kayani.[1] Mullen was calling with big news. U.S. Navy SEALs had killed Osama bin Laden at a compound in Abbottabad, an upscale city where the Pakistan Military Academy is located. The raid was a national triumph for the United States. According to the Pakistani commission empanelled to investigate how bin Laden had lived undetected—and how the United States had managed to kill him without Pakistan's military and intelligence agencies knowing—the raid was a "great humiliation" and an "act of war."[2] The commission's report said publicly what numerous Pakistani and American officials already acknowledged privately: the two countries were not natural partners, their priorities were not aligned, and their objectives conflicted when it came to certain militant groups in Pakistan.

The Abbottabad raid was the latest bump in a historically rocky relationship characterized by hasty marriages and messy divorces. Pakistan aligned with the United States against the Soviet Union during the Cold War to extract military assistance useful for balancing against India. Periods of engagement were sometimes tumultuous. The disengagements that followed led Pakistanis to argue that Washington always abandoned them. This argument is overly simplistic and exculpatory toward Pakistan.

Ultimately, each side had legitimate grievances regarding the other. After cooperating closely to support the anti-Soviet jihad during the 1980s, the relationship went into a deep freeze. In the 1990s, the United States cut off military aid and imposed sanctions on Pakistan for its pursuit of nuclear weapons. The September 11 attacks forced America to reengage. President Bush told his Pakistani counterpart, Pervez Musharraf, who had taken power in a bloodless military coup in 1999, that he had a choice: Pakistan could be a partner or a target in the War on Terror.[3] With that, the U.S.-Pakistan relationship was reborn.

Some of the Pakistan army's corps commanders argued that cooperating with the United States would imperil Pakistan's national security.[4] Two objectives dominated Pakistan's foreign policy: resisting Indian hegemony in the region (and recovering Indian-administered Kashmir) and promoting a pro-Pakistan government in Afghanistan.

Pakistani leaders have believed that India poses an existential threat to their state since the two countries were created via Partition in 1947. India and Pakistan went to war almost immediately over the disputed region of Kashmir. When the first war ended, Pakistan controlled roughly one-third of Kashmir (Pakistan-administered Kashmir), and India controlled the other two-thirds (Indian-administered Kashmir). This made India the status-quo power. Pakistan's revanchist ambitions are a cornerstone of its foreign policy and led it to start a second war over Kashmir in 1965. This one ended in a stalemate. The two neighbors fought a third war in 1971. Because Pakistan was contoured to include the Muslim-majority regions of the British Raj, it consisted of two separate pieces of territory—West and East Pakistan—divided by one thousand miles of land belonging to India. Civil war ensued after East Pakistan seceded to become Bangladesh. India joined the battle on Bangladesh's side and inflicted a humiliating defeat on Pakistan's military. This reinforced Pakistani beliefs that India wanted to wipe it from the map and heightened fears about dismemberment from within.

In addition to its rivalry with India to the east, Pakistan had antagonistic relations with Afghanistan to its west. The Afghan government in Kabul supported Pashtun separatists living in Pakistan after Partition and, to this day, has refused to recognize the two countries' shared border. Making matters worse, Afghanistan historically had close relations with India.

This fueled Pakistani fears of encirclement by its enemies. Islamabad responded by attempting to promote Islamic unity between Pakistan and Afghanistan. These efforts began in the 1950s and laid the foundation for the Islamist movement that later emerged in Afghanistan.[5] In 1974, Pakistan began providing sanctuary and other support to Afghan Islamists who opposed the communist government.[6] After the Red Army rolled into Afghanistan five years later, Pakistan gave the Afghan mujahedeen sanctuary, money, weapons, equipment, and military training.[7]

Pakistan's support for the anti-Soviet jihad in Afghanistan was accompanied by important developments at home and in Indian-administered Kashmir.

First, General Zia ul-Haq, the chief of army staff, seized power in a military coup two years before the Soviet intervention. He was not the first military leader to take over the country. Pakistan spent more than half of its first sixty years alternating between civilian and military rule. Even when not in power, the military exercised disproportionate influence, especially over the country's foreign and security policy. When the United States and its partners began providing covert support to the Afghan mujahedeen, who were based in Pakistan, Zia received almost complete control over the dispersal of the weapons and supplies.[8] This strengthened the military's overall position and helped its Inter-Services Intelligence Directorate (ISI), which coordinated support for the mujahedeen, to grow into the powerful intelligence organization it is today.

Second, since Partition, civilian and military governments had appealed to Islamic sentiment in order to bolster their domestic legitimacy. Although Islamist and religious parties were sometimes repressed in the early years, they were ultimately integrated into the political system.[9] In the 1980s, Zia, a supporter of Pakistan's most prominent Islamist party, launched a massive effort to Islamize the country.[10]

Third, Pakistan had a long history of tapping into the concept of jihad to support the use of militant proxies. This practice reached new heights beginning in the 1980s, when religious parties played a major role in mobilizing Pakistanis to fight in Afghanistan. Indigenous Pakistani jihadist groups formed to wage jihad against the Soviets. While supporting the anti-Soviet jihad, Pakistani leaders were simultaneously planning to replicate that model in Indian-administered Kashmir.[11] Instead, an indigenous uprising erupted before they had the chance. The ISI reoriented the nascent Kashmir insurgency from one led by nationalists seeking independence to an Islamist-led jihad designed to deliver the disputed territory to Pakistan. It supported numerous Pakistani jihadist groups and other militant organizations that began fighting there in the 1990s.

Pakistani support for Islamist militancy in Afghanistan and Kashmir became closely intertwined during the decade before 9/11. Pakistan continued to support Afghan factions involved in the internecine violence that erupted after the Soviet withdrawal and ultimately threw its weight behind the Taliban. As the Taliban took control over more territory, it inherited Afghan-based training camps that had serviced Pakistani militants fighting in Indian-administered Kashmir. The ISI moved additional camps to Afghanistan after the Taliban came to power.[12] In addition to training in Afghanistan, numerous Pakistani jihadist groups contributed cadres to fight alongside Taliban soldiers against the Northern Alliance.[13]

Although Pakistan experienced sectarian violence between Sunni and Shiite organizations, its active support for indigenous jihadist organizations helped inoculate the country against revolutionary violence before 9/11. Pakistani jihadists believed the country should be an Islamic state, but most of them prioritized fighting against external enemies. The state encouraged these sentiments, redirecting the few revolutionary actors who emerged toward external fights.[14]

Given this state of affairs, the corps commanders were understandably concerned about the consequences of siding with the United States against the Taliban. Regionally, Pakistan finally had a friendly Afghan government that did not maintain relations with India. Domestically, siding against the Taliban could demoralize groups fighting in Kashmir and even lead some of their members to turn against the state. Musharraf acceded to U.S. demands despite the domestic and foreign policy costs because the possibility of American reprisals loomed larger.[15] He pressed for and received an end to sanctions and additional economic assistance to show that Pakistan benefited from cooperating with America.[16]

Negotiations conducted soon after 9/11 ironed out the cooperation Pakistan would provide for the U.S. invasion of Afghanistan. Musharraf agreed to withdraw diplomatic and material support for the Taliban government, provide access to Pakistani facilities and intelligence, pursue al-Qaeda members and other foreign fighters fleeing into Pakistan, and stop Pakistani volunteers from crossing into Afghanistan to fight alongside the Taliban.[17] Islamabad delivered on most of these promises. Pakistan shared intelligence, provided access to airspace and naval and air bases, and deployed over 35,000 troops to protect U.S. forces at these bases. The Pakistan army stationed more than eighty battalions to patrol the border and intercept fleeing militants on land. The navy conducted operations to capture those attempting to flee by sea.[18]

Numerous al-Qaeda members and other foreign fighters were captured and handed over to the United States, but sealing the porous border would have been difficult under the best of circumstances. Several factors further hampered this effort. First, the United States did not deploy enough troops on the Afghan side of the border and thus was overly reliant on Pakistan.[19] Second, the thousands of troops Pakistan initially stationed along the border proved insufficient. More were on their way when the Pakistan-supported Jaish-e-Mohammad attacked the Indian parliament in December 2001. After India went on a war footing and massed soldiers along Pakistan's eastern border, Pakistani forces being used to seal the border with Afghanistan were redeployed to face off against them. Third, the CIA reportedly intercepted communications between Pakistani officers allowing some foreign fighters to escape. It is unclear whether this was official policy or the result of sympathy at the lower ranks in the army or ISI.[20]

The U.S. invasion toppled the Taliban regime in Afghanistan but failed to eradicate al-Qaeda. Because many of its members fled across the border, Pakistan remained a frontline state in the War on Terror. A mix of incentives and coercion had secured support for the invasion of Afghanistan. Continued foreign assistance initially facilitated follow-on operations against al-Qaeda. The security forces hunted down al-Qaeda members, killing or capturing hundreds of them during the first few years after 9/11. Intelligence cooperation, including access for U.S. intelligence officers, supported this effort. U.S. troops remained in Afghanistan, and ongoing access through Pakistan was necessary to supply them. Large amounts of security assistance, combined with Pakistan's desire to maintain its relationship with the United States, helped keep the necessary supply lines open, albeit with some notable interruptions. However, the utility of these instruments of statecraft decreased over time when it came to counterterrorism cooperation against al-Qaeda. They were even less useful in terms of changing Pakistan's behavior regarding supporting for various militant groups.

After reluctantly abetting the U.S. invasion of Afghanistan, Pakistan provided sanctuary to the Taliban and support for its insurgency against U.S. and NATO forces in Afghanistan.[21] As Pakistan's efforts against al-Qaeda declined after the first half-decade after 9/11, its support for the Taliban-led insurgency grew. These developments coincided with increasing jihadist violence in Pakistan. American assumptions that Islamabad would cease using militant groups as an instrument of state policy once faced with its own jihadist insurgency proved incorrect. Instead, the state continued to support some groups while targeting others.

To suggest a clear divide between state-allied and antistate organizations misses the wider range of terrorist-state relationships in Pakistan. The security establishment had collaborative relations with some groups, viewed others as belligerents, tolerated a third cohort, and treated a fourth set as frenemies. Pakistan's approach was predicated on the utility that militants provided and the perceived threats they posed relative to other threats. It is critical to recognize the heterogeneous nature of the state when discussing this segmented approach toward terrorism. The military, which continued to control Pakistan's security policies even after General Pervez Musharraf resigned from the presidency in 2008, was more wedded to a policy of supporting militants than civilian leaders were. Conversely, the civilian governments that led Pakistan after 2008 were more reluctant to confront militants attacking the state. Civilian politicians and the military were also guilty of using various militants to pursue their own parochial political interests.

This chapter focuses primarily on Pakistan's evolving domestic counterterrorism efforts and tactical cooperation with the United States in juxtaposition with its ongoing support for state-allied militants and its unwillingness to attempt to dismantle the militants' infrastructure. CVE was not a top priority for the United States and will be discussed briefly in the penultimate section of this chapter. The final section looks at Pakistan's involvement in attempted political settlements to the conflict in Afghanistan.

A RELATIONSHIP REBORN OF NECESSITY: 2002–2005

Musharraf's primary motivation for supporting the U.S. invasion of Afghanistan was to keep Pakistan from becoming a direct target in the War on Terror. His government also aimed to rekindle the bilateral relationship with the United States, which was at its nadir by 9/11. Pakistan was increasingly isolated internationally because of its nuclear proliferation and support of terrorism. The country was in a "position of extreme vulnerability" economically, according to the World Bank.[22] Building better relations with America offered a way for Pakistan to come in from the cold and secure much-needed economic and military aid. Pakistani leaders also wanted help advancing their position on Kashmir and to maintain the status quo in South Asia, wherein the United States treated India and Pakistan equally.[23] This included limiting the Indian-supported Northern Alliance's influence in a post-Taliban Afghanistan.

Pakistan received over $2 billion in economic aid, approximately $2 billion in security assistance, and over $5.5 billion in Coalition Support Fund (CSF) reimbursements during the first five years after 9/11.[24] Reimbursements were used to pay for Pakistani military efforts against al-Qaeda and other foreign fighters who took refuge in the Federally Administered Tribal Areas (FATA). The United States authorized billions more in arms sales to Pakistan, including plenty of "big-ticket" platforms more suited to conventional war against India than to counterterrorism.[25] Bush named Pakistan a major non-NATO ally in 2004, entitling it to access to additional military platforms not generally available to non-NATO countries.

The political support Pakistan hoped for did not materialize. After promising to limit the influence of the Indian-supported Northern Alliance, the United States backed an Afghan government and military in which former Northern Alliance members played a disproportionately large role.[26] India's economic and diplomatic footprint in Afghanistan grew thereafter and included construction near the Pakistan border, which heightened Pakistani anxieties about Indian encirclement.[27] More generally, Washington sought a strategic relationship with India, which was a more valuable long-term partner than Pakistan. India was a rising Asian power and possibly a future global one, the world's largest democracy, and a potentially vast economic market. And, unlike Pakistan, which had a record of nuclear proliferation and support for terrorism, India obeyed the rules of the road.

The U.S.-Pakistan relationship was largely transactional. America provided large amounts of aid and sought specific counterterrorism cooperation in return. Strategic divergence between the two countries in terms of their visions for the region and approaches to realizing them ultimately made a closer and more mutually beneficial U.S.-Pakistan relationship impossible.

Figure 4.1 provides a notional depiction of U.S. and Pakistani threat perceptions. Figure 4.2 approximates the location of the most notable groups in Pakistan based on their usefulness to the state and the threats they posed relative to other threats. These figures do not include every militant entity operating in Pakistan. Table 4.1 provides a key for the organizations found on these figures.

Three points are worth noting about figure 4.1. First, the United States considered the Indian and Afghan governments to be partners, whereas Pakistan viewed both as significant threats and supported terrorist groups against them. In addition to these two state-based threats, Pakistan also confronted a separatist insurgency in Balochistan that began in 2003.

Second, the United States prioritized the al-Qaeda threat well above any other militant threat in Pakistan. Bush did not enforce his red line on states that sponsor terrorism when it came to Pakistan's ongoing support for various state-allied organizations. For almost a half-decade after 9/11, Washington did not consider the Taliban or Haqqani network to be top-tier threats or seriously pressure the Musharraf regime to end its support for them.[28] The United States ranked myriad other groups even lower and did not always differentiate between them.

Third, al-Qaeda members and other foreign fighters received protection from local tribal militants in the FATA who were also conducting cross-border attacks into Afghanistan. This led to U.S. pressure on Pakistan to conduct military incursions into the FATA. Some of the local tribal militants, such as Nek Mohammad, began attacking Pakistani forces. Al-Qaeda also worked with renegade members of Pakistani jihadist organizations to conduct terrorist operations in Pakistan, including attempting to assassinate

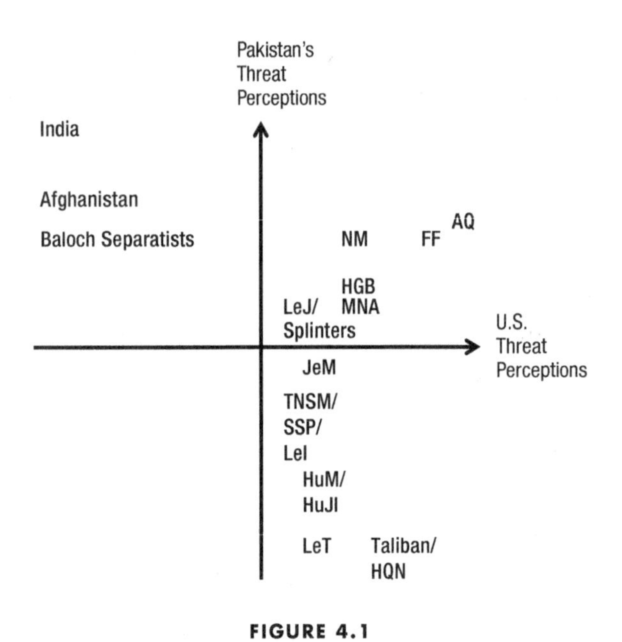

FIGURE 4.1

U.S. and Pakistani Threat Perceptions

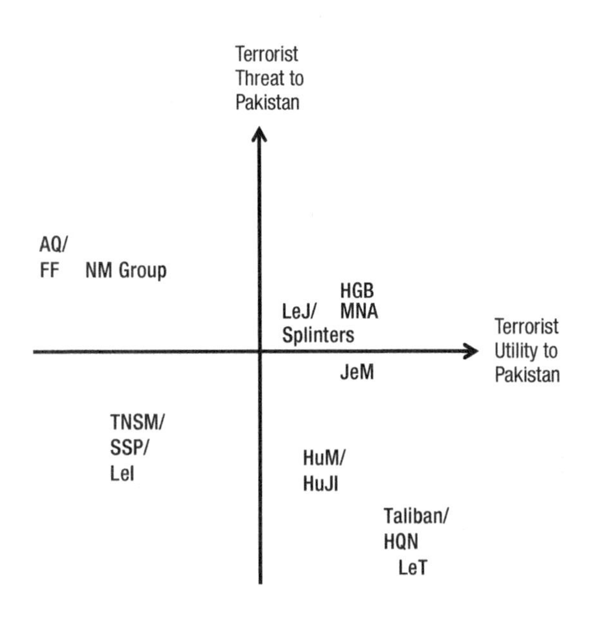

FIGURE 4.2

Terrorist Threat and Utility to Pakistan

TABLE 4.1 KEY FOR SELECTED MILITANT ORGANIZATIONS IN PAKISTAN

ABBREVIATION	FULL NAME OR DESCRIPTION	LOCATION	TARGET OF VIOLENCE
AQ	Al-Qaeda	Cities, FATA	• U.S. homeland and U.S. allies • U.S. and NATO forces in Afghanistan • Pakistani government and military
FF	Foreign Fighters	FATA	• U.S. and NATO forces in Afghanistan • Pakistani military forces in the FATA
HGB	Hafiz Gul Bahadar's militia	FATA	• Vigilante violence to impose interpretation of Islamic law in the FATA • U.S. and NATO forces in Afghanistan. • Pakistani military forces in the FATA
HQN	Haqqani Network	FATA	• U.S. and NATO forces in Afghanistan
HuM	Harkat-ul-Mujahideen	Punjab province	• India • Secondarily, U.S. and NATO forces in Afghanistan
HuJI	Harket-ul-Jihad-al-Islami	Punjab province	• India • Secondarily, U.S. and NATO forces in Afghanistan
JeM	Jaish-e-Mohammad	Punjab province	• India • Secondarily, U.S. and NATO forces in Afghanistan
LeI	Lashkar-e-Islam	FATA	• Sectarian and vigilante violence to impose interpretation of Islamic law in the FATA

(*continued*)

TABLE 4.1 KEY FOR SELECTED MILITANT ORGANIZATIONS IN PAKISTAN (*continued*)

ABBREVIATION	FULL NAME OR DESCRIPTION	LOCATION	TARGET OF VIOLENCE
LeJ	Lashkar-e-Jhangvi	Punjab province	• Sectarian violence • Pakistani government and military
LeT	Lashkar-e-Taiba	Punjab province	• India • Secondarily, U.S. and NATO forces in Afghanistan
MNA	Maulvi Nazir Ahmad's militia	FATA	• Vigilante violence to impose interpretation of Islamic law in the FATA • U.S. and NATO forces in Afghanistan • Pakistani military forces in the FATA
NM	Nek Mohammad's militia	FATA	• Vigilante violence to impose interpretation of Islamic law in the FATA • U.S. and NATO forces in Afghanistan • Pakistani military forces in the FATA
SSP	Sipah-e-Sahaba Pakistan	Punjab province	• Sectarian violence
Taliban	Afghan Taliban	FATA, Balochistan	• U.S. and NATO forces in Afghanistan
TNSM	Tehreek-e-Nafaz-e-Shariat-e-Mohammadi	NWFP	• Sectarian and vigilante violence to impose interpretation of Islamic law in the FATA
Splinters	Factions that split from HuM / HuJI / JeM / SSP / LeJ	Punjab province, FATA	• Pakistani government and military forces, sectarian violence • Secondarily, U.S. and NATO forces in Afghanistan

Musharraf. As a result, the United States and Pakistan confronted a common terrorist threat from these actors. However, they did not prioritize or perceive this threat equally.

Pakistani leaders were at least as concerned about other militants as they were about al-Qaeda and still much more worried about India and Afghanistan. Moreover, although some FATA-based militants were actively targeting Pakistan's security forces, others were focused mainly on conducting attacks in Afghanistan. Islamabad sought to avoid actions that might lead this latter cohort to take up arms against the state. Additionally, FATA was geographically remote from the capital and urban areas where elites were based and materially insignificant in economic terms.[29] All these factors informed the mitigation approach that Pakistan ultimately pursued in the tribal areas.

As figure 4.2 indicates, Pakistan continued to support or enable numerous state-allied organizations that had utility against India or in Afghanistan.[30] Perceptions about an organization's reliability informed how it was treated. For example, the Pakistani military considered Lashkar-e-Taiba (LeT) to be its most loyal, capable, and cohesive state-allied group against India. Other India-centric groups, such as JeM, were closer to the Taliban and splintered after 9/11 over whether to attack the state. As a result, they were less useful and posed a higher threat. The Taliban and the Haqqani network, which was its most lethal arm, were Afghan organizations that were receiving sanctuary and support. Pakistani leaders did not expect U.S. forces to remain in Afghanistan for long and viewed these groups as useful for ensuring that whatever government emerged there would be friendly to Pakistan and not to India.[31]

Musharraf's regime adopted a live-and-let-live approach to various other groups, including the FATA-based militias that were forming but not actively targeting the Pakistan military or security forces. Some of these organizations were sheltering al-Qaeda and conducting cross-border attacks in Afghanistan.[32] The sectarian-oriented Sipah-e-Sahaba Pakistan (SSP) based mainly in Punjab was also tolerated, partly because it had domestic utility for the military and civilian politicians.

Pakistan treated a number of groups as frenemies. The authorities cracked down hard on LeJ, which was a sectarian group, but also used it as a scapegoat for attacks committed by India-centric splinters in Pakistan.[33]

LeJ had some utility against Baloch separatists as well. Militants who split from India-centric groups and began launching attacks after 9/11 were considered useful if they could be brought back into the fold. These actors were co-opted in some cases and targeted in others.[34] Islamabad adopted a similar approach toward certain FATA-based militias that oscillated between attacking Pakistani security forces and fighting in Afghanistan. The government took a belligerent position toward al-Qaeda, other foreign fighters, and the Pashtun tribal militias attacking Pakistani troops. However, it was never fully committed to defeating them. Moreover, belligerents and frenemies benefited from relationships with state-allied and tolerated organizations. This hampered domestic counterterrorism efforts against them.

THE DOUBLE GAME BEGINS

Because al-Qaeda members fled across the border and U.S. troops remained in Afghanistan, the United States required two things from Pakistan: ongoing access into Afghanistan and help hunting down al-Qaeda in Pakistan. The Musharraf government continued to provide access to land routes and air corridors so the United States could supply forces in Afghanistan. Although Musharraf refused to allow U.S. special operations forces to conduct independent operations against al-Qaeda in Pakistan, he gave them access to provide training and intelligence for Pakistani operations.[35] Pakistan also accepted an influx of U.S. intelligence officers to support the hunt for al-Qaeda members. CIA and FBI agents worked with their Pakistani counterparts to track down al-Qaeda members and other foreign militants.[36] To facilitate intelligence cooperation, the United States encouraged and funded the formation of an ISI entity responsible for internal counterterrorism (ISI-CT). It was sometimes at odds with ISI-S, which is responsible for managing the militant portfolio.[37]

Pakistan's domestic counterterrorism campaign could be divided into two aspects. The first, which was the more effective, consisted of well-resourced intelligence-led law enforcement operations outside of the FATA. Some of al-Qaeda's highest-ranking leaders were arrested in Pakistan's cities. These included the 2003 arrest of Khaled Sheikh Mohammad (KSM), who masterminded the 9/11 attacks, and Abu Yasir al-Jaza'iri. The latter was the group's "ambassador in Pakistan," according to bin

Laden's confidential secretary, and knew the locations of various al-Qaeda operational centers in the country.[38] Capturing these men and others like them produced intelligence from interrogations and document exploitation about not only the whereabouts of additional targets but also the al-Qaeda organization.[39]

Second, in response to a combination of U.S. incentives and pressure, the Musharraf government launched a series of military incursions into the FATA to root out al-Qaeda militants and other foreign fighters. These jihadists and the tribesmen hosting them were launching cross-border attacks against American forces in Afghanistan. After these incursions sparked retaliations, operations expanded to include the tribal militias targeting Pakistani forces.[40] However, neither the Musharraf government nor the military were committed to the mission.[41] Pakistan pursued an economy-of-force approach intended to mitigate the militant threat rather than decisively defeat it. Although Islamabad deployed over 70,000 troops to the FATA, many of them were poorly trained and equipped members of the paramilitary Frontier Corps. Most of the time, Pakistani troops stayed at their posts. When they did confront the enemy, engagements were typically short-lived.[42] Pakistani forces normally retreated when they encountered resistance rather than pressing the fight.

After tribal militants led by Nek Mohammad gave them another bloody nose in 2004, the army signed the Shakai Agreement with him. The deal was signed at Nek's madrassa, giving the impression that the army had surrendered.[43] It was the first of many peace deals signed with tribesmen who were harboring and fighting alongside al-Qaeda. Pakistan claimed that this appeasement strategy was intended to secure the handover of al-Qaeda members through negotiated settlements. In reality, peace deals were a mechanism to contain the growing violence.

As the military and ISI hunted al-Qaeda in Pakistan, they simultaneously supported various state-allied organizations fighting in Afghanistan and against India. Most notably, Pakistan backed the Taliban and Haqqani network, which regrouped in the first few years after 9/11 and soon launched an insurgency against U.S. (and NATO) forces in Afghanistan. This backing included hosting training camps and assisting with recruitment.[44] Support for the Taliban-led insurgency not only harmed U.S. interests in Afghanistan; it also further hamstrung counterterrorism efforts in Pakistan. Al-Qaeda and tribal militias taking up arms against the state were co-located in the FATA with Taliban and Haqqani fighters. As a result, they enjoyed a de facto safe haven from incursions by Pakistani security forces, who deliberately avoided targeting state-allied groups.[45] In addition to backing the Taliban-led insurgency, Pakistan also continued to support groups fighting in Kashmir and executing terrorist attacks elsewhere in India. Their training camps remained open, although these were temporarily closed and occasionally moved in an attempt to avoid detection by the United States. Some of these organizations, such as LeT, also benefited from other forms of active support as well.[46]

Along with their support to specific groups, the Pakistani authorities also maintained the infrastructure that supported the militants' jihad against India and in Afghanistan.[47] Terrorist fundraising, recruitment, and the dissemination of propaganda were restricted to different degrees for different groups, but all these activities continued. I point out Pakistani counterterrorism efforts regarding this enabling infrastructure where relevant throughout the remainder of this chapter, but it is important to stress that this infrastructure was still extant when this book went to press in 2017.

Despite Pakistani support for militants fighting in Afghanistan and against India, Washington was relatively satisfied with the cooperation it received during the first few years after 9/11. The peace deal with Nek Mohammad was troubling, but it was quickly followed by permission to fly armed drones over parts of the tribal areas. Musharraf was already allowing the United States to use Pakistani bases for drones operating in Afghanistan. The decision to allow their use in Pakistan came about after Nek Mohammad abrogated his peace agreement with the army. The CIA promised that Nek would be the first person targeted if it was allowed to conduct drone strikes. As part of the arrangement, Pakistani intelligence officials insisted on preapproval of every strike and narrow "flight boxes" in which drones could fly (in order to avoid overflight of nuclear facilities, training camps for India-centric jihadists, or Taliban infrastructure in Balochistan).[48] The United States also pledged not to acknowledge the strikes, which were operated under the CIA's covert-action authority rather than by the U.S. military.[49] On June 18, 2004, a missile fired from a

CIA-operated drone ended Nek in a "goodwill kill."[50] Pakistan claimed credit, saying it had targeted him with an air strike.[51]

THE SEAMS BEGIN TO SHOW: 2005–2008

On July 7, 2005, four young British men blew themselves up on three London Underground trains and a bus. The 7/7 attacks, as they are commonly known, killed fifty-two civilians and injured hundreds more. Two of the men responsible had made multiple trips to Pakistan in the years before. During their last trip, they leveraged connections with LeT and JeM to access al-Qaeda camps.[52] A former commander in JeM who maintained his ties to the group helped coordinate the attack. He also spearheaded al-Qaeda's plot a year later to bring down transatlantic airlines using liquid explosives.[53] These attacks were a clear sign that Pakistan's segmented counterterrorism approach was hindering U.S. objectives. Al-Qaeda was able to leverage ties to state-sponsored terrorist organizations in Pakistan's cities. It had also taken advantage of the growing militant safe havens in the FATA and adjacent North-West Frontier Province (NWFP) to reopen training camps and regenerate its transnational attack capabilities.[54]

Pakistani forces had captured and handed over to the United States at least three hundred al-Qaeda members and other foreign fighters by this time, including several high-value targets.[55] However, these counterterrorism efforts had tapered off as Pakistan pursued peace deals in the FATA.[56] Major deals were signed in 2005, 2006, and early 2008, along with many more informal ones.[57] They allowed militants to consolidate and expand their control over territory. The tribal areas became a jihadist safe haven where the Pakistan security forces struggled to project power. By the middle of the decade, tribal militants were expanding their writ into parts of the NWFP.[58] These nonstate actors exerted such sway in some areas that they determined when military convoys were allowed to use various roads.[59]

Pakistani elites had hoped that agreeing to peace deals with militant factions would keep violence from spreading beyond the FATA and spare the military heavy losses, which its leaders feared could sow discord among the rank and file and harm their institution's reputation.[60] This gambit failed. There is perhaps no better example of the perils of Pakistan's appeasement strategy than Baitullah Mehsud. A former gym instructor, Mehsud harbored foreign militants and raised a powerful militia that fought against Pakistani forces in South Waziristan. He agreed to a ceasefire in February 2005 but soon resumed attacks. Mehsud's militia remained a frenemy until the summer of 2007, when Pakistani forces raided an Islamabad mosque and madrassa, whose pro-Taliban leaders had been challenging the government over a host of issues. The FATA erupted following the raid, and numerous militants, including Mehsud, turned decisively against the state.

In December 2007, militant commanders in each of Pakistan's seven tribal agencies and a number of NWFP districts united to form the Tehrik-e-Taliban Pakistan (TTP, or Pakistani Taliban). Baitullah was appointed the TTP's leader. Under his command, the TTP became the driving force behind a full-blown revolutionary jihad against the Pakistani government and military. Terrorist attacks soon came to Pakistan's heartland province, Punjab; to its capital, Islamabad; and to its economic center, Karachi.

Even as Pakistan faced a growing jihadist threat at home, its support for the Taliban-led insurgency in Afghanistan increased. Attacks against coalition forces jumped threefold from 2005 to over five thousand the following year.[61] The Haqqani network was responsible for many of the more devastating attacks against U.S. and NATO forces. Bush and other senior officials belatedly began to pressure their Pakistani counterparts to curtail support for the Taliban-led insurgency.[62] This pressure only resulted in superficial crackdowns.[63] The infrastructure that supported India-centric groups also remained extant. Musharraf came under U.S. pressure to crack down on them after the 7/7 attacks. He curtailed attacks in Kashmir and temporarily closed down some training camps but stopped short of further action.[64] In November 2008, ten LeT militants rampaged through Mumbai, India, killing 166 people, including six Americans. The attacks were a bloody indication of the group's capabilities, which had actually increased since Pakistan signed up to the War on Terror.

The Bush administration was slow to challenge Pakistan on its declining efforts against al-Qaeda, growing support for the Taliban, policy of appeasement in the FATA, or ongoing support for LeT.[65] Many of the president's top advisors were concerned that pressuring Musharraf to take too hard a line could lead to a popular uprising that might enable Islamists to take power.[66] For all his tough talk about countries having to choose between siding with America or the terrorists, Bush was reluctant to take Musharraf to task. He belatedly began pressing the Pakistan leader on the Taliban in 2006. These calls for action grew more forceful by the time Bush was preparing to leave office.[67] They went unheeded. After rebuilding their relationship on the back of narrow counterterrorism cooperation following 9/11, the two countries were on a collision course as a result of their strategic divergences.

COLLISION COURSE: 2008–2011

Two days after winning the presidency, Barack Obama met with the director of national intelligence (DNI) at a federal building in Chicago. U.S. forces were fighting in Iraq and Afghanistan. Al-Qaeda in the Arabian Peninsula was months away from announcing its formation in Yemen. None of these countries was the top priority, Obama was told. The most immediate threat, according to the DNI, came from Pakistan.[68] The core of al-Qaeda had regenerated. The Taliban-led insurgency in Afghanistan was going from strength to strength, thanks in no small part to support from Pakistan. LeT's attacks in Mumbai raised the specter of a new global threat. And the jihadist insurgency in Pakistan threatened to destabilize a nuclear-armed power.

It was clear that U.S. policy toward Pakistan was not working. Something had to change. Pakistani leaders had complained for years that the United States pursued a transactional relationship with their country while forging a strategic one with India. They also voiced anxieties that the United States would abandon Pakistan once the War on Terror ended and pointed to U.S. actions after the anti-Soviet jihad as evidence. This argument was historically inaccurate and exculpatory toward Pakistan, whose leaders had pursued nuclear weapons in the 1990s with the full knowledge that doing so could result in U.S. sanctions.[69] Nevertheless, American officials thought that if they could make Pakistani leaders, especially in the military, feel more secure, this might reduce the country's reliance on nonstate militants. In late 2009, Obama offered Pakistan a strategic relationship and promised that "America will remain a strong supporter of Pakistan's security and prosperity long after the guns have fallen silent."[70] This offer was backed up by bipartisan congressional legislation. The Enhanced Partnership with Pakistan Act of 2009 (commonly called the Kerry-Lugar-Berman Act, or KLB) authorized up to $1.5 billion annually in nonmilitary assistance for five years and "such sums as may be necessary" for security assistance.[71]

KLB was supposed to serve two additional purposes. First, Musharraf had resigned from office in 2008. However, the military still controlled Pakistan's foreign and security policies despite the election of a civilian government. KLB was designed to demonstrate the U.S. commitment to Pakistan beyond the narrow confines of counterterrorism and show that the U.S. partnership with Pakistan was not just with its military but also its citizenry. Second, authorizing $7.5 billion for civilian aid theoretically created space for the United States to withhold military assistance without risking accusations of abandonment. KLB prohibited certain forms of military assistance and arms transfers unless the secretary of state certified that the Pakistani security forces were not subverting the political or judicial processes, that Pakistan was continuing to cooperate with U.S. efforts to dismantle nuclear weapons–related material-supplier networks, and that Pakistan was demonstrating progress toward combating the Taliban and LeT, among others.[72] However, KLB also included a provision allowing the executive branch to waive certification on national security grounds.

While attempting to reassure Pakistan with offers of a strategic relationship and use military assistance as leverage, U.S. officials simultaneously tried to convince Pakistani leaders that militants, not India, posed the greatest threat to their country. They pointed to the domestic insurgency as evidence that separating good jihadists from bad ones was bad policy.[73] This line of argument was intended to change Pakistan's calculus regarding support for state-allied groups and to get its leaders to take the insurgency more seriously. American officials were genuinely worried about Pakistan's stability and fearful that jihadists might get their hands on Pakistan's nuclear weapons.[74] This fear was overblown, but Pakistani leaders deftly exploited it to deflect U.S. pressure for action against state-allied groups while pushing for more assistance to deal with the insurgency. This gambit worked. Although Congress put conditions on some military assistance, it also established two new programs—the Pakistan Counterinsurgency Fund and the Pakistan Counterinsurgency Capability Fund—to help Pakistan conduct counterinsurgency operations. Pakistan received roughly $2.3 billion from these funds, which were excluded from the limitations imposed by KLB, between FY2009 and 2012.[75]

U.S. efforts to change Pakistan's strategic calculus failed. The two countries had conflicting strategic interests and increasingly divergent understandings of the threat environment (figure 4.3). American officials still considered India and Afghanistan to be important partners and saw Pakistan as a victim of its own insecurity. They believed the jihadist insurgency resulted from decades spent promoting jihadist causes. As the TTP-led insurgency gained steam, Pakistani leaders increasingly recognized the danger antistate jihadists posed to the state. However, they still considered India a greater threat and remained committed to shaping the future government in Afghanistan. Many in Pakistan's security establishment were convinced that cooperating with the United States had triggered the jihadist rebellion. They also believed that India and Afghanistan, which had supported separatist movements against Pakistan in the past, were covertly aiding antistate jihadists and Baloch separatists.[76] Thus, U.S. assumptions that Pakistan's internal security concerns could outweigh its geopolitical compulsions overlooked the fact that Pakistani decision makers did not view the two in isolation. From their perspective, the wisest course of action was to avoid targeting groups that still abjured attacks in Pakistan and, where possible, to reconcile with jihadists at war with the state.[77]

Figure 4.4 offers a notional depiction of terrorist-state relations by the end of the decade. Table 4.2 updates the key provided earlier for contextualizing the various militant organizations in Pakistan. Four points stand out.

First, relations between TTP factions, which included militias represented on figures 4.1 and 4.2, along with many other groups, were characterized by coordination and competition. Clashes sometimes resulted from tribal or personal feuds. Different ideological camps existed under the TTP umbrella. Some factions emphasized revolutionary jihad in Pakistan. Others focused primarily on fighting in Afghanistan.[78] Prioritizing jihad in one country did not preclude operations in the other, but a faction's

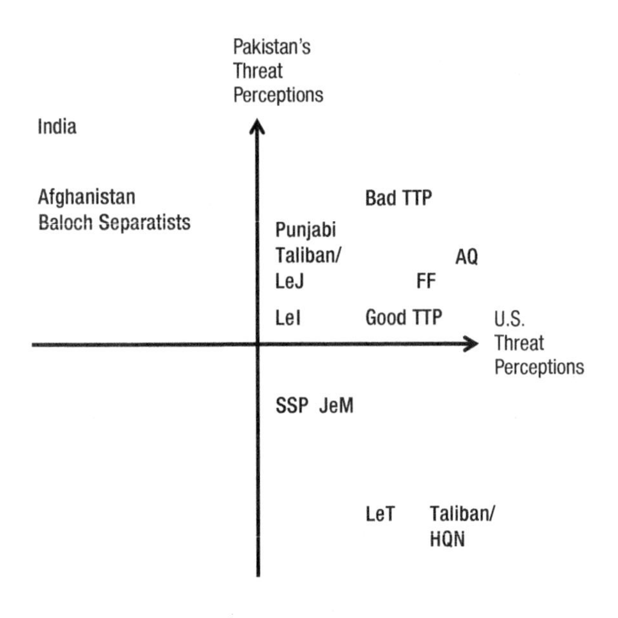

FIGURE 4.3

U.S. and Pakistani Threat Perceptions

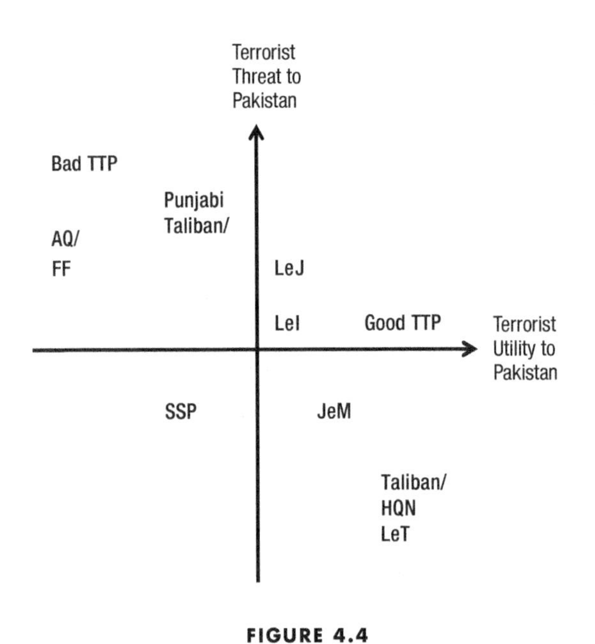

FIGURE 4.4

Terrorist Threat and Utility to Pakistan

TABLE 4.2 KEY FOR SELECTED MILITANT ORGANIZATIONS IN PAKISTAN

ABBREVIATION	FULL NAME OR DESCRIPTION	LOCATION	TARGET OF VIOLENCE
AQ	Al-Qaeda	FATA, NWFP	• U.S. homeland and U.S. allies • U.S., NATO, and Afghan forces in Afghanistan • Pakistani government and military
FF	Foreign Fighters	FATA, NWFP	• U.S., NATO, and Afghan forces in Afghanistan • Pakistani military forces in the FATA
HQN	Haqqani Network	FATA	• U.S., NATO, and Afghan forces in Afghanistan
JeM	Jaish-e-Mohammad	Punjab province	• India • Secondarily, U.S., NATO, and Afghan forces in Afghanistan
LeI	Lashkar-e-Islam	FATA	• Sectarian and vigilante violence to impose interpretation of Islamic law in the FATA • Sporadic attacks on Pakistani military forces in the FATA
LeJ	Lashkar-e-Jhangvi	Balochistan, Punjab province	• Sectarian violence • Pakistani government and military
LeT	Lashkar-e-Taiba	Punjab province	• India • Secondarily, U.S., NATO, and Afghan forces in Afghanistan
Punjabi Taliban	Network of anti-state militants from JeM, LeJ, HuM, HuJI, and SSP.	FATA, NWFP, Punjab province	• Pakistani government and military • Secondarily, U.S., NATO, and Afghan forces in Afghanistan

(*continued*)

TABLE 4.2 KEY FOR SELECTED MILITANT ORGANIZATIONS IN PAKISTAN (*continued*)

ABBREVIATION	FULL NAME OR DESCRIPTION	LOCATION	TARGET OF VIOLENCE
SSP	Sipah-e-Sahaba Pakistan	Punjab province	• Sectarian violence
Taliban	Afghan Taliban	Balochistan, FATA, NWFP	• U.S., NATO, and Afghan forces in Afghanistan
Good TTP	TTP factions that prioritize fighting in Afghanistan and largely abide by peace deals. Includes factions led by Hafiz Gul Bahadar and Maulvi Nazir.	FATA, NWFP	• Vigilante violence to impose interpretation of Islamic law in the FATA and NWFP • U.S., NATO, and Afghan forces in Afghanistan. • Sporadic attacks on Pakistani military forces in the FATA and NWFP
Bad TTP	TTP factions that prioritize fighting in Pakistan and do not abide by peace deals. Led by Baitullah Mehsud and includes TNSM.	FATA, NWFP	• Vigilante violence to impose interpretation of Islamic law • Pakistani government and military forces • Secondarily, U.S., NATO, and Afghan forces in Afghanistan

priorities did impact its treatment by the state. The military viewed factions that prioritized fighting at home as the "bad TTP," treating them as belligerents and targeting them accordingly. Factions that continued to abide by peace deals and prioritized fighting in Afghanistan or against antistate rivals were "good TTP." These latter factions were treated as frenemies and managed through peace deals and ad hoc assistance.

Second, the United States and Pakistan still shared a threat from al-Qaeda and other foreign fighters, but Pakistan considered it a lower priority than both Baloch separatists and TTP factions that prioritized revolutionary jihad. Pakistan also faced a growing threat from militants who split from India-centric and sectarian groups and turned their guns on the state. Analysts used the term "Punjabi Taliban" to describe the network that these militants formed to pool resources and improve coordination.[79] These militants developed strong connections with the TTP, whose revolution-focused factions relied on them to project power from the FATA into Pakistan's capital and major cities.

Third, the Taliban, Haqqani network, and LeT had become much greater threats to the United States but remained critical allies for Pakistan, mainly for the utility they provided against India or in Afghanistan. These groups also became increasingly useful domestically. The Taliban and Haqqani network were used to reorient antistate jihadists toward fighting in Afghanistan. LeT was deployed to degrade some of these jihadists and was also used against Baloch separatists. In addition to their utility, Pakistani decision makers feared that cracking down or reducing support for these groups could lead them or their members to turn on the state. As many Pakistani officials said to me and to other U.S. officials over the years, "if we don't hit them, then they won't hit us."

Fourth, the militant infrastructure spread across territory in Pakistan's control and across contested areas in the FATA. There was growing cross-pollination between state-allied groups, antistate groups, frenemies, and others that fell somewhere in between on the terrorist-state spectrum. These connections meant that antistate militants could leverage the infrastructure—mosques, madrassas, safe houses, and training camps—belonging to state-allied groups. Radicalization and recruitment continued apace. Young men became involved in militancy for different reasons, but many of them were simply inspired to do jihad at a mosque, madrassa, or public school. Whether they joined a group fighting India, fighting in Afghanistan, or fighting against Pakistan often depended more on who inspired them than their own personal predilections.[80] Jihadist propaganda was abundant. Money still flowed in from the Gulf, but funds were also raised in Pakistan through the open solicitation of donations, via criminal enterprises, and even through investments in the legitimate economy. The Financial Action Task Force, a global body that combats money laundering and terrorist financing, put Pakistan on its blacklist because of strategic deficiencies in these areas.[81]

Considering this state of affairs, it is not surprising that U.S. efforts to use assistance to change Pakistani policy failed. Incentives may have helped optimize cooperation against al-Qaeda after 9/11, but they were not the decisive variable. Musharraf secured as much assistance as possible after bowing to coercion. By the time the United States offered Pakistan a strategic relationship and enacted KLB, the dynamics had changed. The United States was making maximalist demands but only threatening to cut some military aid. Decision makers in the Pakistani security establishment were prepared to forgo several hundred million dollars in assistance and additional arms transfers rather than risk breaking with state-allied militant organizations. They also calculated that the U.S. desire for continued cooperation and fears about instability in the region would lead American officials to blink first. This hunch paid off. In 2011, the secretary of state issued the first and only certification that Pakistan was in compliance with KLB conditions, despite considerable evidence to the contrary. Thereafter, the administration repeatedly waived certification.

Why did American officials cave? First, the United States still needed logistical access to Afghanistan to supply U.S., NATO, and Afghan forces there. Second, policy makers recognized that Pakistan's increasing counterinsurgency efforts in the FATA could be helpful even if they did not target al-Qaeda directly. These officials and their military counterparts also feared that the insurgency in Afghanistan could become even deadlier if these efforts reduced or ceased entirely. Third, whether or not they were well-founded, U.S. concerns about the jihadist threat to Pakistan's stability persisted. Fourth, American policy makers recognized that Pakistani support would be critical for any possible negotiated settlement with the Taliban. Given these concerns, how did the United States pursue its counterterrorism objectives in the region? In short, Washington took what it could get. America wanted more cooperation against al-Qaeda and for Pakistan to reduce support to the Taliban, Haqqanis, and LeT. It settled for supporting Pakistani operations against the TTP that had indirect effects against al-Qaeda while simultaneously taking advantage of Pakistan's acquiescence to drone strikes to target the various groups threatening to the United States.

INDIRECT RETURNS

The Pakistan military belatedly committed to a well-resourced campaign against antistate Pakistani jihadists in the FATA and the neighboring province of Khyber Pakhtunkhwa (formerly the NWFP). Operations occasionally hit al-Qaeda and other foreign fighters but mainly targeted the TTP factions focused on overthrowing the state. Nevertheless, the presence of Pakistani forces in the FATA made it difficult for al-Qaeda members to move about freely. Documents recovered from bin Laden's compound confirm the difficult operating environment al-Qaeda faced as a result of the Pakistan military's presence in the FATA.[82] In other words, Pakistan's operations had indirect counterterrorism benefits for the United States. It is important to be clear that the negative impact on al-Qaeda was a secondary consequence of operations that Pakistan was undertaking to secure its own interests. It is also critical to note that Pakistan's approach included co-opting TTP factions and other militants who favored fighting in Afghanistan over waging jihad at home. The military and ISI sometimes exploited competition with factions from competing tribes, forging temporary accords with some in order to weaken others.[83] As a result, various militant factions alternated between attacks against and collaboration with the military.

Pakistani forces scrupulously avoided targeting state-allied groups that had utility abroad but refrained from attacks at home. These organizations also played important roles when it came to internal security. For example, in addition to waging jihad against India and in Afghanistan, LeT carried out propaganda campaigns against antistate TTP factions and al-Qaeda, gathered intelligence on them for the ISI, and sometimes launched attacks against TTP targets. LeT provided similar services against separatists in Balochistan.[84] The Taliban and Haqqani network maintained close relationships with most TTP factions and splinter groups that turned against the state. Both organizations helped reorient some of these antistate jihadists toward Afghanistan and to mediate ceasefires and peace deals in the FATA.[85] JeM was also used to recruit renegade jihadists and redirect them toward Afghanistan or India.[86] In other words, Pakistan was not only supporting state-allied groups in Afghanistan. It was also actively promoting jihad against U.S. and coalition forces there as part of its domestic counterterrorism strategy. And although military operations in the FATA limited al-Qaeda's freedom of movement, the group remained able to leverage its relationships with the Taliban and Haqqani network for sanctuary, training, and access to the Afghan front.[87]

DEATH FROM ABOVE

As U.S. frustrations with Pakistan mounted, its reliance on drone strikes increased. By the end of Bush's second term, it was clear that Pakistani intelligence was delaying planned strikes in order to warn state-allied militants who, often along with al-Qaeda members, would disperse. In June 2008, after being presented with evidence of collusion between the ISI and Haqqani network, Bush ordered an escalation of strikes.[88] After conducting only ten between 2004 and 2007 and four during the first half of 2008, the CIA executed thirty-two more by year's end. These targeted al-Qaeda and the Taliban and Haqqani network equally.[89] Bush also directed that U.S. officials provide the Pakistanis with "concurrent notification" of strikes, meaning that they were told only when an operation was already underway or over.[90] The CIA had few intelligence sources in the FATA when the United States began launching drone strikes there in 2004.[91] Numerous local sources had been recruited by the time Bush left office. Combined with communications intercepts and satellite and drone imagery, these sources made the United States less dependent on Pakistan for intelligence.[92]

Obama inherited both the escalating drone campaign in Pakistan and the intelligence resources to expand it further. While attempting unsuccessfully to change Pakistan's strategic calculus about support for state-allied groups, the Obama administration simultaneously unleashed a withering assault on al-Qaeda, the Taliban, Haqqani network, and various TTP factions. The United States launched fifty-four drone strikes in 2009, one hundred the following year, and another seventy-two in 2011.[93] Many of these were "signature strikes": they did not target distinct individuals but instead were launched based on certain patterns of activity such as "military-aged males" observed carrying weapons and moving in and out of a suspected militant training camp.[94] The use of signature strikes was partially intended to constrict al-Qaeda's operating environment and remove large swaths of the organization's middle management, making it more difficult to regenerate or plan overseas attacks. Signature strikes were also used to protect forces in Afghanistan. These forces could not regularly launch cross-border raids into Pakistan, so death from above was the next best thing.

Drone strikes heavily damaged al-Qaeda in Pakistan between 2008 and 2011.[95] According to a letter written in 2010 by Atiyah abd al-Rahman, who was bin Laden's right-hand man in Pakistan, "The mid-level commands and the staff members are hurt by the killings. Compensating for the loss is going slowly."[96] When considering what made drone strikes so effective in terms of degrading core al-Qaeda, it is important to remember that al-Qaeda was a hierarchical organization with limited human resources. Drone strikes may have contributed to the radicalization of segments of the population, but most new recruits enlisted in local organizations fighting in Afghanistan or Pakistan. They did not join al-Qaeda, which was an Arab organization that regulated the number of South Asians in its ranks.

In addition to damaging al-Qaeda directly, the U.S. drone-strike campaign had the indirect benefit of making it harder for the group to plan attacks. First, these strikes created a hostile environment for surviving members, forcing them to focus on self-protection. As Atiyah wrote to bin Laden, "we need to reduce operations and activities, focus on 'persevering and survival.'" He requested guidance on the acceptability of "stopping many of the operations so we can move around less, and be less exposed to strikes."[97] Bin Laden concurred.[98] Focusing on survival encumbered communication as well as operations, making it difficult for core al-Qaeda to provide direction to its affiliates.[99] Second, incessant strikes hampered the recruitment of Western volunteers needed for attacks in Europe and the United States. New volunteers often arrived without formal vetting because counterterrorism efforts in the West were disrupting the networks responsible for this task. Many would-be jihadists were turned away or rushed through training out of concerns they would bring drone strikes in their wake.[100]

Pakistani officials repeatedly denied that Pakistan was allowing the United States to launch drone strikes, which they criticized as violations of Pakistan's sovereignty. This fueled already high levels of anti-American sentiment.[101] Such public posturing masked the fact that Pakistani decision makers had secretly allowed the CIA to use Shamsi Airbase for Predator drones, acquiesced to their use in Pakistan, and sometimes requested strikes against TTP militants.[102]

ACTS OF WAR

Although drone strikes constituted the primary mechanism for eliminating militants fighting in Afghanistan, U.S. forces conducted a handful of cross-border operations.[103] CIA-backed Afghan militants also carried out missions into the FATA, albeit primarily for intelligence-gathering purposes.[104] These operations angered Pakistani leaders and fueled tensions between the United States and Pakistan. The CIA and ISI, which had collaborated closely to hunt down al-Qaeda targets after 9/11, were increasingly antagonistic toward each other by this time as well. Despite increasing restrictions on their freedom of movement, American intelligence officers had been able to build an independent network to support U.S. drone strikes.[105] The civilian government that came into power after Musharraf left office also authorized an influx of CIA operatives and U.S. special operations personnel.[106]

The CIA's ability to operate in Pakistan without sanction was deeply alarming to the ISI. The situation came to a head in February 2011, when Raymond Davis, a U.S. contractor working in Pakistan, shot dead two men who approached him with guns drawn at a traffic intersection.[107] Davis was providing security for a CIA team that was tracking LeT, the ISI's closest jihadist ally.[108] The two men Davis gunned down were with the ISI either as "full paid-up agents or local informants."[109] It is unclear whether they intended to harm or only scare Davis. Either way, the incident suggested the United States had crossed a red line by focusing more closely on LeT and that the two countries' intelligence agencies had become adversaries. U.S. officials denied Davis's CIA affiliation and claimed he had diplomatic immunity. Pakistani authorities saw through the façade and held Davis in custody for over a month, releasing him after the dead men's families were paid blood money to compensate for their loss.[110]

Approximately six weeks after Davis was spirited out of Pakistan, U.S. Navy SEALs killed Osama bin Laden. The raid was a national triumph for the United States. For Pakistan, it was a great humiliation. Pakistan's military and intelligence agencies had been kept in the dark because U.S. officials did not trust them. Many Pakistani officials, including members of the Abbottabad Commission, which was formed to investigate both how bin Laden had escaped detection and how the United States had pulled off the raid, acknowledged they understood why the United States launched the unilateral raid. But they also considered it an "act of war."[111]

In November, on the heels of the bin Laden raid, U.S.-led NATO forces killed Pakistani security forces during an accidental clash at two Pakistan military checkpoints in Salala, near the border with Afghanistan. The United States refused to apologize for the incident, which many Pakistanis incorrectly believed was deliberate. Pakistan closed the ground-based supply lines into Afghanistan. America froze CSF reimbursements. The relationship cratered.

MUDDLING THROUGH: 2012–2016

Because by 2011 the United States was already concerned about Pakistan's reliability, it had created another supply route, the Northern Distribution Network (NDN), into Afghanistan. When Pakistan closed the supply lines, the NDN enabled the United States to continue supplying forces in Afghanistan, albeit at a much higher cost. Pakistan also suffered financially because it was losing hundreds of millions in CSF reimbursements. Leaving aside the financial hardships, which were not insignificant, the nonmonetary costs of a rupture in the relationship were simply too high for both countries. They walked back from the precipice. After the U.S. government issued a muted apology in the summer of 2012 for the Salala incident, Pakistan reopened the supply lines.[112] The United States released approximately $1.6 billion in military and economic aid to Pakistan and resumed CSF reimbursements.[113]

To make the relationship work, U.S. officials focused on expanding cooperation on issues of mutual concern. In practice, this meant doubling down on supporting Pakistan's military campaign against the TTP-led insurgency. The TTP had trained and funded Faisal Shahzad, a Pakistani-American citizen who attempted a car bombing in Times Square in May 2010. The group therefore constituted a shared threat. However, the TTP was the primary militant threat facing Pakistan and only a secondary concern for the United States. Nevertheless, helping Pakistan counter the TTP at least provided the indirect benefits vis-à-vis al-Qaeda described previously and theoretically created space for increased cooperation in the future.

The divergences between U.S. and Pakistani threat perceptions remained relatively unchanged, as did Pakistan's approach to the militants on its soil, with the exception of several notable developments (figures 4.5 and 4.6). First, as Pakistan made gains against antistate militants and the Taliban-led insurgency in Afghanistan went from strength to strength, the utility of some "good TTP" factions declined. They and LeJ were increasingly treated as belligerents. Second, Pakistani militants displaced by military incursions had regrouped in Afghanistan by this time and began launching cross-border raids into Pakistan. Afghan intelligence officers sometimes enabled these operations to hit back at Pakistan. Although this assistance was nowhere near as robust as Pakistan's support for the Taliban-led insurgency, it nevertheless reinforced the perception among some Pakistanis that Afghanistan (in concert with India) was behind the jihadist threat to their state.[114] Third, al-Qaeda launched a South Asian affiliate (al-Qaeda in the Indian Subcontinent, or AQIS) in 2014.[115] This ensured a long-term presence for al-Qaeda in the region and enabled a division of labor whereby core al-Qaeda (populated mainly by foreigners) could focus on attacking the United States and AQIS (made up mostly of Pakistanis) could take the lead on waging jihad in Pakistan and expanding operations in the region.[116] Fourth, ISIS established a regional branch in January 2015. The Islamic State Khorasan Province (ISKP) was based primarily in eastern Afghanistan but also operated in Pakistan. It was mainly composed of former TTP members.[117]

There were no signs of a strategic shift in Pakistan's policy of supporting state-allied militant groups. After retaking control of territory in much of the FATA, the Pakistan military finally launched a long-awaited military incursion in the summer of 2014 into the North Waziristan tribal agency where the Haqqani network was headquartered. Pakistani leaders promised the operation would target it along with antistate militants, but Haqqani militants were tipped off before the operation began and conveniently relocated.[118] Efforts to disrupt and degrade militant networks in Pakistan's urban areas similarly avoided state-allied groups like LeT.

Despite its segmented approach toward militancy, Pakistan made counterterrorism gains. Terrorist attacks declined by 48 percent in 2015 over the

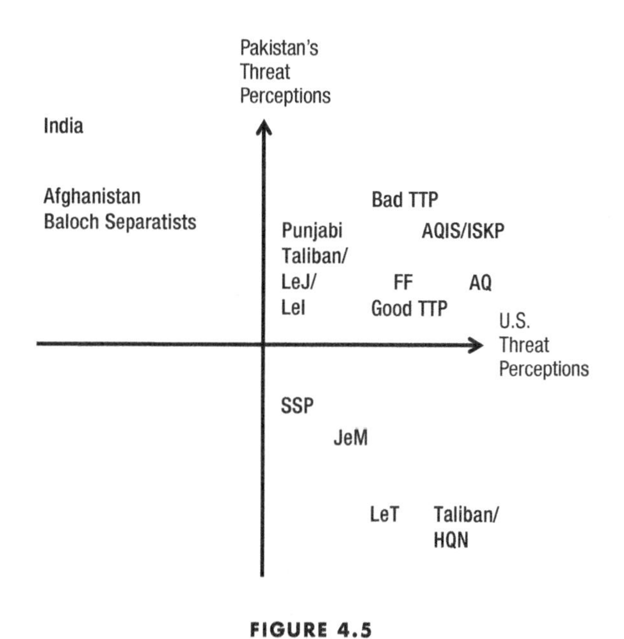

FIGURE 4.5

U.S. and Pakistani Threat Perceptions

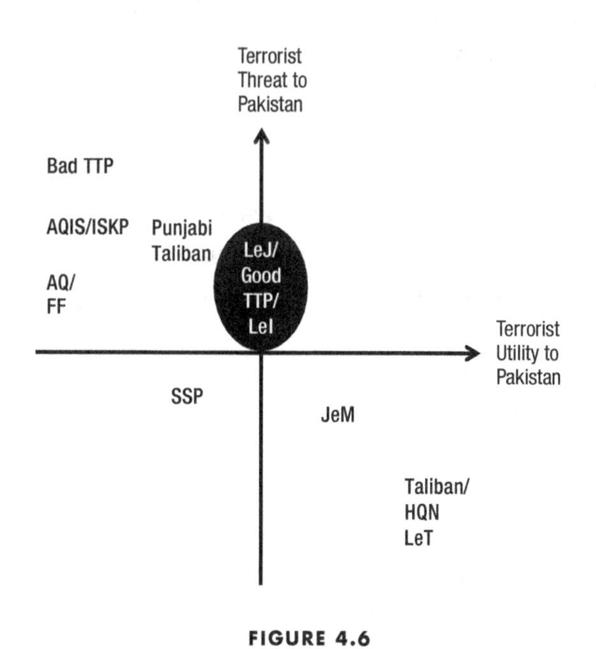

FIGURE 4.6

Terrorist Threat and Utility to Pakistan

previous year.[119] Pakistan was still ranked fourth among countries most affected from terrorism, but it was trending in the right direction.[120] The situation improved further in 2016, with a reported decline of 28 percent in acts of terrorism from the previous year.[121] This still amounted to approximately 450 terrorist attacks across Pakistan that killed roughly 900 people.[122] But the country was stabilizing. As the security services made progress against antistate militants, they also expanded their efforts to target some frenemies, including various TTP factions that prioritized fighting in Afghanistan.[123] In an acknowledgment of Pakistan's improved efforts to combat terrorist financing, FATF removed it from its blacklist in 2015. However, these actions did not indicate a strategic shift in Pakistan's policy toward militants. There was no indication of expanding counterterrorism operations to target state-allied groups.

Congress imposed additional conditions on CSF and PCF that made the disbursement of funds contingent on Pakistan keeping the supply lines into Afghanistan open, making demonstrable efforts against al-Qaeda, and not supporting terrorism against coalition forces in Afghanistan, among other things.[124] The secretary of defense, in coordination with the secretary of state, was allowed to waive most of these restrictions if it was in the U.S. national security interest. Multiple secretaries exercised this right. None ever certified.

Congress added a new condition on CSF after the Pakistan military launched its 2014 operation in North Waziristan. It made $300 million of the $1 billion authorized for CSF contingent on certification that Pakistan was significantly disrupting the Haqqani network's sanctuary and freedom of movement.[125] Congress stipulated certification could not be waived. Subsequent legislation retained this model and raised the amount withheld to $350 million in 2016.[126] No secretary of defense has ever certified. This cost Pakistan $650 million in reimbursements as of 2017—a price it was prepared to pay.

Although America and Pakistan patched up their relationship and Pakistan made progress in its own war on terror, the space for cooperation had shrunk considerably. As the number of U.S. and NATO forces in Afghanistan declined, so did the need for access to supply them. Some ground access remained necessary. Access to airspace was a bigger issue when it came to moving supplies into and out of Afghanistan and to conducting sorties in support of Afghan forces fighting the Taliban. In addition to preserving this access, the United States also sought to maintain modest intelligence cooperation. There was not much happening beyond that when it came to counterterrorism cooperation.

The core al-Qaeda organization had been seriously degraded by U.S. drone strikes. Parts of its remaining infrastructure shifted to Afghanistan once U.S. forces there drew down, and some leaders migrated to countries in the Middle East.[127] The Pakistan military's operations in the FATA and activities of the intelligence services throughout the rest of the country made it more difficult for al-Qaeda to return or for AQIS and ISKP to operate. U.S. assistance might have helped enable these operations, but Pakistan would have conducted them anyway. And it was clear that no amount of assistance or threats to withhold it would lead the Pakistani security establishment to turn on the Taliban, Haqqani network, or other state-allied organizations. The infrastructure and climate of support for these groups hindered Pakistan's already limited efforts to counter violent extremism.

A HANDICAPPED EFFORT: CVE IN PAKISTAN

President Bush made spreading democracy a key component of America's war of ideas against al-Qaeda, but he did not embrace democratization in Pakistan until the end of his second term. General Pervez Musharraf, who took power in a military coup before 9/11 and held onto it by winning rigged elections thereafter, was considered too vital a partner to be replaced. Washington only stepped up to promote a transition to civilian governance once Musharraf was already losing his grip on power. The Obama administration took up this mantle and attempted to support the primacy of civilian institutions in Pakistan. KLB was partially intended to begin righting the civil-military imbalance in Pakistan and in U.S.-Pakistan relations, which for decades were characterized by Washington's overreliance on the military.

U.S. interests in promoting democracy were driven primarily, although not exclusively, by the ambition to reduce the military's grip on Pakistani security policy. Pakistan's two major civilian parties favored normalizing relations with India and Afghanistan and were not tied to supporting state-allied militants. American officials assessed that if civilians could exercise real control, they might bring about shifts on Pakistani policies in these areas. Unfortunately, the civilian government that came into power after Musharraf resigned essentially abdicated governing on security matters, ceding those responsibilities to the military. The next government, led by a rival party, tried and failed to establish parity with the military.

Broader efforts to counter violent extremism in Pakistan expanded under Obama but were never a top U.S. priority.[128] Moreover, these initiatives were sometimes misguided as a result of faulty understandings of the problem. Two examples are telling.

First, U.S. policy prescriptions included a healthy focus on addressing perceived socioeconomic drivers for radicalization and recruitment, whereas subsequent research indicated the connections between poverty and support for militancy in Pakistan were tenuous at best.[129] Even if economic factors did play a more critical role, U.S. programs would have been insufficient palliatives given Islamabad's failure to address wider socioeconomic deficiencies and lack of political integration in the country.

Second, much of the discourse on extremism in Pakistan focused on the role that radical madrassas play. Musharraf-era efforts to bring madrassas under state oversight and ensure that problematic ones did not teach a curriculum that promoted jihad or sectarianism failed.[130] Madrassa reform, even if successful, would not have been a silver bullet. Indeed, research suggested that the number of problematic madrassas was exaggerated.[131] For example, madrassa reform did not address the public-school curriculum, which interpreted jihadist causes as positive responses to Indian aggression and as religiously valid enterprises.[132] To his credit, Musharraf ordered curriculum reform in 2004, and a new national curriculum was developed two years later. The United States and United Kingdom supported these efforts.[133] They also flopped. The failure to reform the curriculum is unsurprising considering that it was "a direct product of state policy and a narrative that justifies the existence of Pakistan with respect to India."[134]

As U.S. officials developed a more sophisticated understanding of CVE, the United States refined its approach in Pakistan. The State Department began conducting CVE programming at Pakistani universities and in prisons. USAID explored different theories of change and tested them through trial-based, small-scale projects that were followed by the production of lessons learned. The United States Institute of Peace (USIP) led and funded research mapping youth trends related to militancy.[135] In 2011, the U.S. embassy in Islamabad opened a new office to support CVE initiatives. It took a trial-based, grassroots approach that sought proposals from Pakistani civil society centered on expanding media and community engagement.[136] Embassy programs also endeavored to foster a counter-narrative through a dialogue series involving religious leaders.[137] USIP awarded grants that would facilitate efforts by the Pakistan Broadcasting Corporation and private FM stations to promote diversity and tolerance.[138] Although Pakistan allowed these initiatives, its intelligence services sometimes hampered the civil society organizations implementing them and intimidated their staffs.[139]

Rigorous metrics and more time are needed to assess U.S. efforts, but at best they chipped away at the problem. It would be tough to expect anything more, considering that Pakistani leaders had spent decades pursuing policies that created a political-ideological environment that fostered extremism and promoted militancy. They marketed the activities of militants fighting in Afghanistan and against India as legitimate jihads, promulgated a vehemently anti-Hindu discourse, and passed various laws discriminating against religious minorities.[140] Clerics were encouraged to reinforce extremist narratives, which have remained prominent in the educational system and media. The state also allowed some jihadist groups to engage in the provision of social services, which has contributed to the perception among portions of the population that they can be positive, or at least benign, actors.[141] Homegrown terrorism was presented as something external—the result of Indian meddling, spillover from the conflict in Afghanistan, or the consequences of Pakistani cooperation in the U.S.-led War on Terror.

Pakistan belatedly began implementing some CVE initiatives after years of domestic terrorist attacks, but these efforts remained ad hoc.[142] In 2014, Pakistan developed a National Internal Security Policy (NISP) that theoretically made constructing a national narrative against extremism, sectarianism, and terrorism a cornerstone of the government's efforts.[143] The NISP also envisioned incorporating madrassas into the mainstream educational framework. A National Action Plan, which was passed the same year and delineated steps for dismantling the militant infrastructure, promised a crackdown on hate speech and media outlets trafficking in it or giving space to terrorist messaging.[144] Enforcement was inconsistent. The authorities arrested some clerics who extolled sectarian violence.[145] Dozens of madrassas that were unregistered or associated with fomenting sectarian violence were raided or shut down.[146] However, militants—especially ones belonging to state-allied groups—still enjoyed access to the airwaves, newspapers, and social media. And many problematic mosques and madrassas, especially those associated with state-allied organizations, remained open for business.

Pakistani deradicalization efforts were also characterized by half-measures. Pakistan established deradicalization centers in the Swat Valley after its forces completed a major offensive to retake jihadist-occupied territory in 2009. Militants went through psychological screening, religious counseling, and vocational training.[147] Most of the participants were young, local men captured on the battlefield. Another program was established in Punjab Province in 2011 to rehabilitate former members of sectarian and state-allied India-centric groups. It was closed a year later.[148] Neither of these programs focused on disarming, demobilizing, and reintegrating members of jihadist organizations. The Swat program did not attempt to dissuade participants from fighting in Afghanistan or counter the common Pakistani narrative that the United States was an infidel occupying force. According to the administrator of one of the Swat centers, if participants wanted to go to Afghanistan, that was a separate issue, as long as they did not wage jihad at home.[149] And therein lay the rub. Any effort, regardless of how well funded or correctly targeted, cannot succeed unless Pakistan stops promoting jihad as an instrument of state policy. The impact of this policy on the U.S. war effort in Afghanistan was impossible to ignore.

NO EASY WAY OUT

In August 2017, President Donald Trump unveiled his long-awaited plan for Afghanistan. Fears that international terrorist groups might once again use Afghanistan as a safe haven to strike America led him to commit additional U.S. forces who would stay as long as necessary to prevent the Taliban from taking over.[150] Although his speech focused mainly on how America would kill its way to victory, Trump held open the prospect of reconciliation with the Taliban. The fact that the war in Afghanistan will end with a political settlement is one of the few points everyone familiar with the conflict agrees on. However, the modalities of negotiation have bedeviled U.S. policy makers since the Obama administration began making overtures to the Taliban in 2010.

Afghanistan, the United States, and the Taliban each have been internally divided about when to pursue negotiations, how to sequence them, who should lead them, and what concessions to make, among other things. Some U.S. officials have favored moving more quickly to the negotiating table, whereas others have argued it is necessary to make sufficient gains against the Taliban first in order to negotiate from a position of greater strength.[151] In either case, attempts at reconciliation are unlikely to succeed without at least some buy-in from Pakistan.

The Pakistan military has set its sights on a settlement that enables Taliban leaders to participate in Afghan politics without actually running the country like they did in the 1990s. The aim is to counterbalance Indian influence in Afghanistan, while simultaneously avoiding an outright Taliban victory that could strengthen its militant brethren in Pakistan. These strategic interests have militated against pushing the Taliban too hard to cut a deal or allowing the movement to negotiate on its own. The military and ISI have detained or killed Taliban members who pursued talks without Pakistan's blessing and subverted negotiations that did not sufficiently account for Pakistan's equities in Afghanistan. Speaking about the arrests of Taliban leaders who attempted to negotiate directly with the Afghan government toward the end of the decade after 9/11, one Pakistani intelligence officer admitted they were intended to "punish people who want to betray Pakistan."[152]

One of the most infamous episodes occurred in 2010, after three years of painstaking work by Norwegian diplomats to bring the Taliban and Afghan officials together. This process overlapped with efforts by other countries, including Saudi Arabia, to bring the Taliban to the table. It appeared to be making the most progress despite setbacks, including the

2008 bombing of a Taliban representative's house in Quetta right before he and others were to meet members of the Afghan government. In February 2010, just when the highest-level engagement ever between the Afghan government and six Taliban members was about to occur, Mullah Abdul Ghani Baradar was arrested in Pakistan. Baradar was the Taliban's deputy leader and one of the six representatives scheduled to engage with the Afghan government. According to a Norwegian government report, "The ISI's position was made clear by the arrest of Mullah Baradar," which effectively spoiled the peace process.[153]

People involved in the Saudi-facilitated process also interpreted Baradar's arrest as a sign of Pakistan's opposition to their efforts.[154] Saudi Arabia began facilitating secret negotiations between the Afghan government and Taliban in 2006. Agha Jan Motasim, the Taliban's former finance minister who traveled to Saudi Arabia several times a year to raise money, was a key interlocutor. A power struggle in the Taliban and the movement's refusal to meet a major Saudi demand to cut ties to al-Qaeda may have helped doom the peace process. But it effectively ended several months after Baradar's arrest, when a gunman shot Motasim twelve times outside his home in Karachi, Pakistan.[155]

It is important to note that the United States was not directly tied to either of these initiatives and for years was unwilling to negotiate with the Taliban. Once this position changed in 2010 and the United States began making overtures to the Taliban, Pakistan's history of meddling informed how U.S. officials approached the process. The Obama administration supported the opening of a Taliban office in Qatar in 2013 partly to enable its representatives to negotiate more independently of Pakistan and represent the movement's real positions.[156] Yet U.S. officials also recognized that progress on negotiations would be impossible without Pakistan's support or at least acquiescence.

If the United States could not convince Pakistan to stop providing the Taliban with sanctuary, then it at least needed Pakistan to use its influence to facilitate a political settlement. In practice, this could mean empowering Taliban factions that favored negotiations and pressuring recalcitrant ones, curtailing financing and weapons, denying factions sanctuary, and arresting or helping the United States assassinate especially problematic actors. U.S. attempts to secure this cooperation have not panned out. This is partly because Pakistan's objectives in Afghanistan are existential and have trumped anything the United States has promised or threatened. Pakistan also has finite leverage over the Taliban and does not wish to exhaust that leverage on America's behalf. Indeed, Pakistani decision makers are undoubtedly aware that pressing too hard could promote further fissures in the insurgency, drive factions to turn to Iran or even Russia for support, and possibly prompt a violent backlash at home.

After he was inaugurated as Afghanistan's president in September 2014, Ashraf Ghani launched an effort to improve ties with Pakistan. Ghani assessed that the Taliban had fragmented since Mullah Omar's death was announced and that therefore the representatives in Doha could not be effective interlocutors. He also believed that Pakistani support was a critical, albeit not exclusive driver of the Taliban-led insurgency. Thus, bringing Pakistan to the table was essential to ending the conflict. This led him to expend considerable political capital in a failed quest for better relations with Pakistan, which did not respond favorably by reducing its support for the insurgency. The Afghan government held a round of talks in Pakistan in 2015, but they went nowhere. The legitimacy of the Taliban representatives, whose attendance Pakistan facilitated, was a major issue. One of them was perceived to be working more or less directly for the ISI.[157] In January 2016, diplomats from Pakistan, Afghanistan, China, and the United States met for the first time. The Quadrilateral Coordination Group (QCG) was intended to jumpstart negotiations between Kabul and the Taliban.[158] This effort has yet to bear fruit.

Five months after the QCG first met, a car carrying Mullah Akhtar Mohammad Mansour was headed toward Quetta, the capital of Balochistan, when a missile from a U.S. drone blew it to smithereens. Mansour had officially led the Taliban since word had leaked out in 2015 that Mullah Omar had died two years earlier in a Karachi hospital.[159] Obama reportedly authorized the strike after efforts to pressure Mansour to join negotiations failed.[160] The drone strike that killed him was the first one ever conducted in Balochistan Province. This may have been intended to send a message to the Taliban leaders that Pakistan could not protect them and to Pakistan that the United States was losing patience with it. According to several Afghan officials, Taliban outreach regarding talks increased temporarily.[161]

According to a *New York Times* investigation, however, Agha Jan Motasim, the former Taliban finance minister and peace mediator, and others believe Mansour was ready to negotiate when he was killed. Evidence has reportedly emerged that led some Afghan officials, Taliban commanders, and Western analysts to believe that Pakistan might have engineered Mansour's death. The Taliban leader still relied on Pakistan for financial and other support at the time of his death but was seeking similar assistance from Iran and Russia.[162] Diversifying support was partially intended to enable Mansour to conduct negotiations on his terms, rather than Pakistan's, according to a one-time Taliban commander who is close to Mansour's former inner circle. The commander compared the drone strike with Pakistan's detention of senior Taliban commanders like Mullah Baradar who dared to negotiate directly with Kabul.[163] Ultimately, the machinations behind Mansour's death may remain shrouded in mystery. Yet one thing is clear: no discernable progress on negotiations had been made. Sixteen years after using a mix of incentives and coercion to secure Pakistan support for its invasion of Afghanistan, U.S. officials were still searching for the right instruments to compel their Pakistani counterparts to deliver the Taliban and end the conflict there.

* * *

There are no magic bullets for solving the vexing problems related to working with Pakistan. Coercion combined with incentives worked when it came to getting Pakistan to support the U.S. invasion of Afghanistan after 9/11. Additional assistance helped secure cooperation against al-Qaeda in the early years thereafter. Yet this cooperation was not indicative of a change in Pakistan's strategic calculus. During the Cold War, a string of Pakistani leaders aligned with the United States to build their country's military capacity and balance against India. Committing to the War on Terror may not have appeared entirely different from aligning with America against the Soviet Union. However, U.S. expectations turned out to be considerably greater than during the Cold War and grew more intrusive over time. Early counterterrorism cooperation obscured strategic disagreements over the future of Afghanistan, America's relationship with India, and Pakistan's ongoing support for terrorism. These divergences deepened until they stretched the fabric of the relationship to its seams.

Even after Pakistan's support for insurgents and terrorists with American blood on their hands was blindingly obvious, the United States was reluctant to get too tough. U.S. officials feared destabilizing the nuclear-armed nation, especially once it faced its own jihadist insurgency, and were wary of squandering the limited but vital cooperation Pakistan still provided. Pakistani operations in FATA were narrower than U.S. policy makers wanted, but they nevertheless constrained the freedom of movement for al-Qaeda and other groups that might threaten the United States. As long as American troops were in Afghanistan, the United States required access to move materiel into and out of the country. Ground-based supply lines became less important, but access to Pakistani airspace was still critical. Intelligence cooperation might theoretically be useful to thwart terrorist plots against the United States, even if the days of close CIA-ISI coordination were long past. Although Pakistan might not be able to deliver the Taliban to the negotiating table, its buy-in was still seen as an important component of any peace process.

Sixteen years after 9/11, it was clear that no realistic incentives were likely to change Pakistani behavior with regards to supporting terrorism. Space for cooperation had shrunk, and frustration was high throughout the U.S. government. There was an emerging consensus in Washington that the United States needed to take a tougher line but no agreement on what this line should look like or how far to go if Pakistan retaliated to coercion rather than capitulate. One thing was clear. Pakistan had always been a deeply problematic partner, but it was increasingly at risk of being treated like a hostile state.

5

SAUDI ARABIA

Arsonist and Firefighter

IN EARLY 2002, President Bush took Crown Prince Abdullah bin Abdul-Aziz Al Saud, who was next in line for the throne, on a forty-five-minute drive around his Texas ranch. It was a last-ditch effort to build rapport and salvage a visit that was going poorly. The crown prince arrived hoping to talk about resolving the Israeli-Palestinian conflict. Bush wanted to discuss counterterrorism.[1] Fifteen of the nineteen 9/11 hijackers were Saudis. Al-Qaeda's ability to recruit them owed heavily to the enabling infrastructure in the kingdom, which was also the biggest source of jihadist financing in the world. The driving tour helped break the ice, but the two countries remained out of sync in terms of their priorities and perceptions of the terrorist threat.

Security cooperation and American interests in maintaining the global availability of Saudi oil have anchored one of the oddest yet most durable geopolitical relationships in modern history. The separation of religion and governance and the promotion of liberty and equality are core American values. Saudi Arabia is an Islamic theocratic monarchy where political pluralism is largely absent, civil liberties are severely limited, and religious intolerance is actively promoted.[2]

King Abdulaziz ibn Saud formed the modern Saudi state in 1932 by making common cause with the descendants and followers of the eighteenth-century zealot Sheikh Mohammed ibn Abdul-Wahhab. To establish the primacy of political power in the new state, Ibn Saud drew upon the

Wahhabi doctrine of the duty of obedience to the ruler and instituted a grand bargain between religious and political leaders.[3] The ulema (religious scholars) recognized the predominance of the royal palace in matters of economic, foreign, and security policy and provided it with religious legitimacy. In return, the ulema received the authority to dictate and enforce societal norms based on the rigid Wahhabi interpretation of Islam. This included promoting enmity against non-Muslims and "deviant" Muslims, especially the Shi'a.[4] The Saudi kingdom expended enormous sums of money to support the ulema domestically and export Wahhabism internationally through mosques, religious schools, and charities. Salafi movements throughout the world are heavily influenced by Wahhabi doctrine. Salafism refers to a universalistic and puritanical approach to Islam whose adherents seek to practice the faith in strict accordance with how they believe the Prophet Mohammad and his Companions did. Most jihadists situate themselves within the Salafi movement and have been heavily influenced by Wahhabi teachings.[5]

Efforts to export Wahhabism went hand in hand with Riyadh's promotion of pan-Islamic causes. These policies served geopolitical and domestic interests and reached new heights after the Soviets intervened in Afghanistan in 1979. Saudi Arabia was a staunch U.S. partner in the battle against godless communism, and the anti-Soviet jihad quickly became a major front in the Cold War. Supporting it also provided an opportunity to back a popular pan-Islamic cause at a time when the kingdom faced new regional and domestic challenges. The Iranian revolution brought a Shiite theocracy to power in early 1979. Later the same year, an apocalyptic Sunni sect laid siege to the Grand Mosque in Mecca, fueling fears of a possible revolutionary challenge to the regime.[6] Saudi Arabia's marginalized Shiite minority was growing increasingly restive around this time, too.[7] And Saudi Islamists began pressuring the government to undertake political reforms during the 1980s.[8] Supporting the anti-Soviet jihad helped boost the regime's legitimacy and deflect attention from these domestic challenges while simultaneously enabling it to counter Iranian influence.[9]

Saudi leaders agreed to match U.S. contributions to the Afghan mujahedeen and allowed the United States to use their territory as a transit point for weapons shipments. While Riyadh matched U.S. financial contributions, the ulema steered millions more dollars to the mujahedeen and other foreign fighters. The government encouraged its citizens to support the war effort, famously subsidizing airline flights to Pakistan, and allowed foreign semi-state and nonstate actors to recruit, propagandize, and raise money.[10] This led to the creation of an enabling environment for jihadist causes, which remained extant after the Red Army withdrew from Afghanistan and the Soviet Union collapsed. Riyadh continued to support pan-Islamic jihads during the 1990s for many of the same reasons it had backed the war effort against the Soviets. Numerous Saudis flocked to fight in the civil war in Bosnia-Herzegovina. A smaller number fought in Tajikistan, Ethiopia, and elsewhere during the 1990s.[11] Riyadh also backed various nongovernmental organizations (NGOs) involved in these conflicts. Some of these were legitimate aid organizations; others financed and armed foreign jihadists.[12]

Even as they promoted pan-Islamic jihads abroad, Saudi leaders were aware of the potential for blowback.[13] In 1995, a four-person cell composed of veterans of the anti-Soviet and Bosnian jihads exploded a car bomb in Riyadh outside a U.S.-administered National Guard training center.[14] Riyadh responded with mass arrests and harsh interrogations, transforming some Saudis who had participated in state-supported pan-Islamic jihads into revolutionaries.[15] The state briefly reduced space for jihadist mobilization, then reversed course. Al-Qaeda and other jihadist organizations remained able to fundraise and recruit inside the kingdom and to tap into the Saudi-sponsored global network of charities, mosques, and educational institutions that spread Wahhabi Islam.[16] Saudi men in search of jihadist training flocked to Taliban-controlled Afghanistan during the late 1990s. Many of them gravitated toward al-Qaeda camps.[17]

During the Cold War, divergences in the bilateral relationship were subordinated to the common struggle against the Soviet Union and U.S. need for oil. Washington encouraged Saudi support for Islamic militants in Afghanistan and endorsed the kingdom's promotion of Wahhabism to advance geostrategic objectives.[18] The Cold War's end and growing U.S. concerns about terrorism caused a rethink of these policies. As the al-Qaeda threat increased, so did U.S. requests for cooperation, especially on intelligence sharing about terrorist financing and access to detainees.[19] The regime was reluctant to provide detailed information to the United States in several key cases, including the 1995 bombing and a thwarted al-Qaeda attack on the U.S. consulate in Jeddah in 1998.[20] American officials were also refused access to a top al-Qaeda financial official after he turned himself in to the Saudi authorities.[21] Some U.S. officials believed information sharing in this case might have implicated important members of Saudi society, perhaps including royal family members, in supporting jihadist causes.[22] However, this was not simply an issue of a few bad apples.

The enabling infrastructure provided genuine geopolitical and domestic utility to the regime, whereas attempting to dismantle it could cause general instability. Moreover, Saudi authorities appear to have believed that the jihadist threat to the kingdom was manageable and that cracking down on support for jihadist causes would make the problem worse. In short, the United States and Saudi Arabia viewed the terrorist threat differently. This disconnect must be understood within the context of a relationship on the decline by the end of the 1990s. The two countries were at odds over various regional issues, including how best to manage shared threats from Iraq and Iran and what to do about the Israeli-Palestinian conflict.[23] It is also important to note that although the Saudi government resisted cooperating, Washington did not make terrorism a priority before 9/11.

The September 11 attacks radically reordered U.S. priorities, but they did not have the same impact on Saudi Arabia. Counterterrorism cooperation was initially limited and might have remained so if al-Qaeda had not launched a terrorism campaign inside the kingdom in 2003. Saudi threat perceptions changed dramatically, and the government has been unyielding in its commitment to enemy-centric counterterrorism operations ever since. The bilateral intelligence relationship also became vital for U.S. counterterrorism, especially after the rise of al-Qaeda in the Arabian Peninsula in neighboring Yemen. Despite these advances, the Saudi government's approach to the enabling infrastructure on its soil has been muddled. Changes in Saudi threat perceptions led to increased efforts to combat terrorist financing and some introspection about the dangers of promoting the country's rigid Wahhabi doctrine. Yet promoting pan-Islamic causes and exporting Wahhabism continued to provide Saudi leaders with a way to exert influence abroad. These policies were also intertwined with the kingdom's identity as Islam's holiest land and partly a function of the grand bargain that existed between religious and political leaders. As a result, the United States and Saudi Arabia converged in some areas of counterterrorism but diverged in others.

The rich history of the bilateral relationship enhanced cooperation in areas where the two countries converged and sometimes helped mitigate divergences, but it was not enough to overcome them. When investigating U.S.-Saudi cooperation, it is important to keep in mind that the relationship was not reducible to counterterrorism. Saudi Arabia was a longstanding partner and major oil producer whose stability was considered critical to U.S. interests in the Middle East and to the global economy. Although the kingdom was not a treaty ally, the United States was committed to helping protect it against external threats and supporting government efforts to counter internal challenges. Security assistance was not a critical feature of the U.S.-Saudi relationship, but arms sales were. The kingdom was a major buyer of American military hardware.[24] Because these purchases benefited American defense manufacturing and enhanced Saudi military capacity, leverage related to arms sales went both ways. It is also important to recognize that divisions existed in the kingdom between the royal family and the religious establishment and that hardliners and reformers exist in both. This sometimes created situations where American officials received conflicting signals about Saudi policies or where the policies themselves were inconsistent.

This chapter explores U.S.-Saudi cooperation over the course of three periods from 2001 to 2016: the first period lasted from 2001 to 2003, when cooperation was most limited; the second stretched from 2003 to 2011, when cooperation expanded considerably, thanks to changing Saudi threat perceptions; and the third began after the Arab uprisings in 2011. Tactical cooperation and efforts to counter terrorist financing remained extant during this third phase, but divergences in the increasingly important area of regional cooperation reduced the overall efficacy of the U.S.-Saudi counterterrorism relationship. Discussion of Saudi policies regarding jihadist ideology is interwoven throughout this chapter to illustrate how even at the height of counterterrorism cooperation, the kingdom continued to produce the mood music to which many jihadists danced.

A RELUCTANT PARTNER

The 9/11 Commission "found no evidence that the Saudi government as an institution or senior officials within the Saudi government funded al Qaeda."[25] But the kingdom was clearly a major source of money for bin Laden's organizations and other jihadist groups. U.S. officials and policy makers paraded through the kingdom after 9/11, calling on their Saudi counterparts to shut down the domestic infrastructure and global networks that funded al-Qaeda and other jihadists.[26] The newly appointed U.S. ambassador also increased pressure on the government to rein in the religious establishment. "What you teach in your schools and preach in your mosques now is not an internal matter," the ambassador told his Saudi counterparts, adding, "it affects our national security."[27] Saudi Arabia's response to U.S. entreaties was disjointed and generally underwhelming. On balance, the authorities did not view combating al-Qaeda as a priority. In some instances, this position stemmed from an ideological affinity for bin Laden's organization. In others, Saudi leaders feared blowback because the United States was unpopular with most Saudis, whereas support for al-Qaeda was strong.[28] The internal security forces also mistakenly believed that they had eliminated al-Qaeda networks in the 1990s.[29] This assessment began to change in late 2002 after the police uncovered al-Qaeda plots, but even then the authorities did not appreciate the extent of the threat.

Conspiratorial thinking about the 9/11 attacks hampered cooperation. The king was incapacitated by a stroke, and many of the senior princes suspected the attacks were part of a Zionist conspiracy. Crown Prince Abdullah initially bought into this trope. When presented with evidence by U.S. officials, however, he became the first senior prince to accept that most of the hijackers were sons of Saudi soil.[30] Abdullah was a would-be reformer who favored close ties to the United States, but he was still out of step with the Bush administration. Prince Saud Al-Faisal, the Saudi foreign minister, was more gung-ho. He began pushing for a joint U.S.-Saudi counterterrorism taskforce soon after 9/11. The White House was eager for more cooperation but slow to create this type of coordinating body.[31] Prince Nayef bin Abdul-Aziz Al Saud, who was aligned with hard-line anti-American elements of the religious establishment, was on the other side of the spectrum.[32] He repeatedly and publicly questioned whether fifteen of the hijackers were really Saudis, hinting instead at a Jewish plot.[33] Prince Nayef's position was critical; he headed the Interior Ministry. His son, Mohammed bin Nayef, was given the responsibility for counterterrorism.

The Bush administration's decision to invade Iraq further strained bilateral relations, making it harder for U.S. and Saudi leaders to get on the same page about counterterrorism.[34] The Saudi ambassador to the United States, Prince Bandar bin Sultan, was a notable exception. He encouraged Bush to invade, falsely claimed his country was secretly supportive of the war, and backed the invasion among his fellow princes.[35] This may have fueled the misperception in some quarters of the administration that the United States and Saudi Arabia were in agreement about Iraq. But Prince Bandar was an outlier. Abdullah deeply opposed the invasion, as did most senior princes.[36] They had no love for Saddam Hussein, but he was still a Sunni leader who kept Iraq's Shiite majority down. Saudi Arabia had a restive Shiite minority, which was based mainly in the areas where oil reserves were located. This made the regime even warier of growing Shiite influence in the region. In addition to its concerns about the potential for Shiite rule and attendant Iranian influence in Iraq, the Saudi royal family was displeased with the democratization objectives that provided part of the rationale for the invasion. Saudis were generally skeptical of U.S. motives and resolve when it came to promoting democracy, but members of the royal family still worried that if America succeeded in facilitating the emergence of a genuine democracy in Iraq, this might inspire their citizenry to demand a similar political system.[37]

The United States and Saudi Arabia shared threats from Iran and al-Qaeda, but they prioritized the latter differently (figure 5.1). Riyadh did not consider al-Qaeda a major threat and viewed the constituent parts of the enabling infrastructure on its soil as a net positive because they provided legitimacy at home and influence abroad (figure 5.2). A comprehensive effort to degrade or dismantle this infrastructure could have negative ramifications for internal security. Addressing the underlying factors that permitted the construction of an enabling infrastructure in the first place could put the regime and religious establishment at odds, leaving the former vulnerable to accusations it had betrayed Islam to satisfy America. As

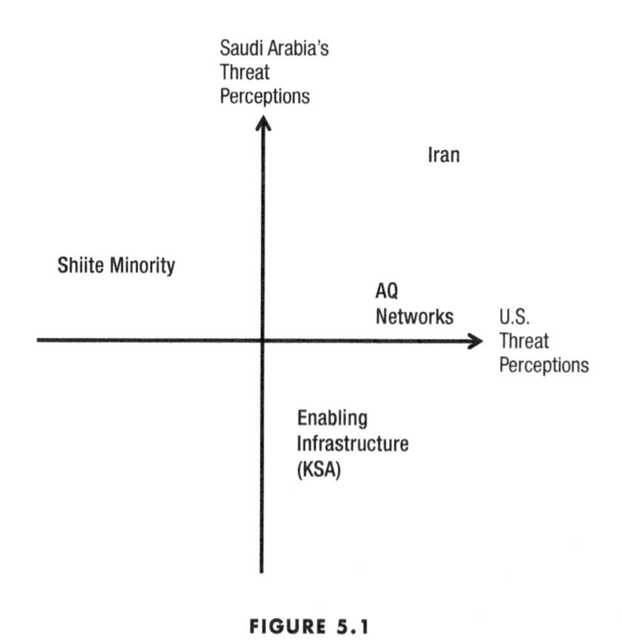

FIGURE 5.1

U.S. and Saudi Threat Perceptions

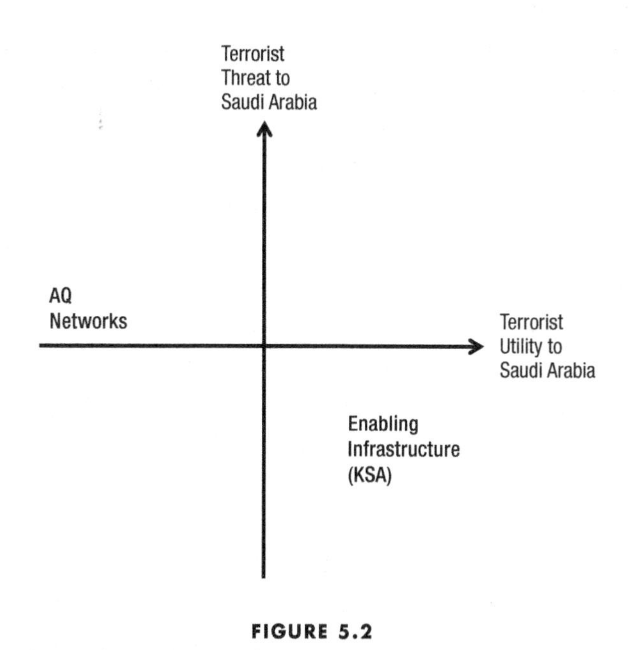

FIGURE 5.2

Terrorist Threat and Utility to Saudi Arabia

a result, U.S.-Saudi counterterrorism cooperation was limited in the first two years after 9/11.

PRO FORMA COOPERATION

Saudi Arabia provided the United States access to basing and airspace for the invasion of Afghanistan.[38] Despite its opposition to the Iraq war, the regime allowed the United States to use Saudi territory as a launching point for airstrikes, special operations forces missions, refueling tankers, and intelligence-gathering flights.[39] The provision of access was largely a function of preexisting security cooperation, especially U.S. efforts to build up Prince Sultan Air Base for American military operations in the region. The United States used the base for the invasions of Afghanistan and Iraq. This access was not heavily publicized, largely because both wars were unpopular in the kingdom.[40] Following the Iraq invasion, the U.S. Air Force moved its assets to Qatar. No U.S. planes were based in Saudi Arabia after September 2003. Most American forces also departed, leaving only a small number of military trainers.[41]

In spring 2002, a U.S. delegation led by then treasury secretary Paul O'Neill traveled to Saudi Arabia for "an uncomfortable discussion about terrorist financing," to quote one of the officials involved.[42] The Treasury delegation focused on closing down branches of the Saudi-based al-Haramain Foundation, which had offices around the world to raise money for Muslim causes. The organization disbursed between $40 million to $50 million annually.[43] It supported legitimate charitable causes but also served as a platform for al-Qaeda and other jihadist groups to raise and move money. If the United States could get Saudi agreement on shuttering some of the most problematic branches, then over time it might be possible to close down the entire al-Haramain network.[44] In March 2002, the United States and Saudi Arabia made a joint submission to the United Nations designating the Bosnian and Somalia branches. This was a first step, but it was still unclear at this point whether the Saudis would take additional actions that could have real strategic effects on al-Qaeda's ability to raise money.

September 11 catalyzed debates over the religious establishment's proper place in Saudi Arabia. However, the attacks had less of an effect on the kingdom's export of the Wahhabi doctrine that contributed to the theological foundation for jihadist ideology. Several senior princes challenged the idea that affairs of state should be decided jointly by rulers and religious scholars, arguing that the latter should act only in an advisory capacity.[45] The debate was less about whether there was a role for the ulema in politics than what that role should be and which clerics should represent the religious establishment.[46] These were existential questions about the nature of governance in the kingdom and were intimately tied to the debate about the essence of the Saudi polity. Reformers argued that the best way to counter the spread of jihadist ideology was to transform the kingdom into a constitutional monarchy.[47] Some of them also questioned the use of pan-Islamic jihad as an instrument of foreign policy.[48] The regime showed little indication of changing its policies, but Crown Prince Abdullah did embrace reformist calls for national dialogues to discuss these and other issues. The first dialogue was scheduled for June 2003. It occurred amid a new sense of urgency, coming on the heels of al-Qaeda's first major terrorist attack in the kingdom.

GETTING INTO THE FIGHT

The Saudi authorities maintained a nonconfrontational approach toward the broader jihadist community until mid-2002, by which time it was too late. Yusuf al-Uyayri took advantage of this operational space. An illegal street-racing enthusiast in his younger days, Uyayri used to joyride around his hometown at breakneck speeds in stolen cars. He dropped out of school in 1991 and flew to Afghanistan. Uyayri later became a bodyguard for bin Laden before being dispatched back to Saudi Arabia to begin building an al-Qaeda network in the late 1990s to lay the groundwork for a future jihad.[49] Abdul Aziz al-Muqrin, another al-Qaeda leader and also a high-school dropout, took a more circuitous route back home. He traveled to Afghanistan in the late 1980s to fight the Soviets, joined the jihad caravan that went to Bosnia-Herzegovina, and may have run guns to jihadists in Algeria during its civil war in the 1990s. Muqrin was captured in Ethiopia in the late 1990s while fighting alongside Somali separatists and extradited to Saudi Arabia. His four-year prison sentence was halved as a reward for memorizing the Qur'an.[50] After his release, Muqrin built a separate al-Qaeda network in Saudi Arabia.

Bin Laden sent hundreds of Saudi militants home in early 2002 to augment these twin networks.[51] The police treated most returnees with kid gloves, detaining them for no more than a few weeks, if at all.[52] Saudi Arabia's longstanding support for pan-Islamic jihad made it difficult to justify imprisoning men coming back from Afghanistan. The country's history of supporting jihad abroad also meant that returnees were not considered a major threat. As the police uncovered more al-Qaeda plots in mid-to-late 2002, they started taking a more confrontational approach toward the jihadist community. The authorities' efforts were neither comprehensive nor consistent and managed to fuel jihadist mobilization without actually hampering jihadist capabilities.[53]

Before 9/11, al-Qaeda leaders had believed that it was necessary to weaken the U.S. willingness and ability to intervene abroad before launching revolutionary jihads in Muslim countries, lest America come to their aid. They saw launching a jihad in the kingdom as counterproductive, given Saudi Arabia's importance as a source of recruits and money. However, with the loss of Afghanistan, al-Qaeda no longer had a place to train Saudi recruits or safely plan major terrorist operations. The group also needed to capitalize on the momentum of the 9/11 attacks, and jihadists still enjoyed reasonable freedom of maneuver in Saudi Arabia. Against this backdrop, al-Qaeda leaders directed Uyayri to initiate terrorist operations.[54] In May 2003, his network attacked three compounds used by American and other expats. The Saudi state responded swiftly, killing Uyayri and severely degrading his network.[55] Members of Muqrin's network escaped the dragnet. They formally declared themselves to be "al-Qaeda in the Arabian Peninsula" (commonly called QAP, in contrast to AQAP, established in Yemen in 2009). In November 2003, QAP struck a residential compound for Westerners. The attack killed mostly Arabs and Muslim expats. This sparked a public backlash against the group.[56] It also hardened the regime's resolve to crush QAP. One U.S. diplomat quipped that it was after the November attack that the government really "got religion" when it came to counterterrorism.[57] The Saudis launched a robust campaign that eliminated QAP networks over the next three years.

Saudi Arabia was not a poor or failing state. Its counterterrorism budget was substantial, totaling approximately $8.5 billion in 2004 and growing to $10 and then $12 billion over the next two years.[58] As a result, the kingdom did not require or receive robust U.S. security assistance to enable its campaign against QAP. However, Saudi capabilities were lacking in certain areas where foreign assistance was helpful. The United Kingdom trained the Saudi special forces. Washington and Riyadh established a joint intelligence taskforce enabling analysts and technical experts from the CIA and FBI to work side by side with their Saudi counterparts.[59] This helped the security forces prosecute operations more effectively and set the stage for broader counterterrorism cooperation.[60] Changes at the top helped as well. Bush appointed a single point person to handle the U.S.-Saudi counterterrorism portfolio, which focused mainly on helping the Saudis combat QAP and coordinating enhanced efforts to counter terrorist financing.[61] In 2008, the two countries agreed to establish a U.S. interagency "critical infrastructure protection advisory mission" to the kingdom. This Saudi-funded initiative embedded U.S. advisors in key offices within the Saudi government.[62]

U.S. objectives vis-à-vis cooperation with the kingdom expanded after Yemeni and Saudi al-Qaeda members officially united to form AQAP in Yemen in January 2009. Saudi officials considered the potential for AQAP attacks in places like Riyadh, Jeddah, or Abqaiq (where processing facilities for the Saudi Arabian Oil Company, or Aramco, are located) to be a major security threat.[63] These fears were heightened after AQAP attempted to kill Assistant Interior Minister Prince Mohammed bin Nayef, the director of the kingdom's counterterrorism campaign, in 2009.

U.S. and Saudi threat perceptions about al-Qaeda's Gulf branches clearly converged after 2003, as figure 5.3 illustrates. Four points are notable. First, the al-Qaeda threat to the kingdom was not uniform—Riyadh understandably worried more about QAP from 2003 through 2006 than it did about AQAP once the latter activated in 2009. Second, America's main counterterrorism focus inside Saudi Arabia, especially once QAP was dealt with, was on stemming the flow of money to al-Qaeda Central, its affiliates, and associated groups. The Saudis increasingly shared this concern, especially because of al-Qaeda's potential for inspiring and directing jihadist attacks in the kingdom. As a result, Saudi authorities began to view the enabling infrastructure on their soil as a greater threat. Third, securing intelligence cooperation against AQAP in Yemen became a major regional counterterrorism objective for the United States. Fourth, Iran constituted another shared threat, although not as immediate a threat for Saudi Arabia as QAP was during the time when that group was active. After a brief period when Riyadh tried to accommodate Iran, which included calls for Washington to engage in talks with Tehran, the Saudi government reverted to a policy of balancing against it and rolling back Iranian influence wherever possible.[64] Saudi leaders were especially sensitive about perceived Iranian support for Shiite Houthi rebels in Yemen, even though the rebels were motivated by local grievances, not sectarian identity. Houthi rebels launched attacks along and across the Yemeni border against Saudi forces at various times, prompting the kingdom to respond with air and artillery barrages in 2009.[65]

The ongoing competition with Iran is one of the main reasons why the enabling infrastructure in the kingdom still had utility for Riyadh. Saudi authorities cracked down reasonably hard on money flowing into al-Qaeda's coffers after 2003 but still allowed other regional militant groups to raise money. The government also continued to export Wahhabi Islam. As was the case in the past, these practices were intended to avoid domestic instability in addition to achieving geopolitical objectives. At the same time, Saudi officials recognized the dangers this infrastructure posed and took steps to begin degrading elements of it. Figure 5.4 captures this conflicted approach by situating the enabling infrastructure in the upper-right quadrant to indicate both its ongoing utility and the Saudis' growing appreciation for the threats it posed.

A MORE COMPREHENSIVE EFFORT

As the security services hunted down QAP militants, the group continued to strike U.S. and other Western targets. These attacks mainly consisted of fatal shootings but also included one beheading of an American contractor. An assault against the U.S. consulate in Jeddah killed four Saudi security guards and five local staff.[66] QAP never attacked Saudi government officials or infrastructure, but a strongly antiregime subcurrent was present

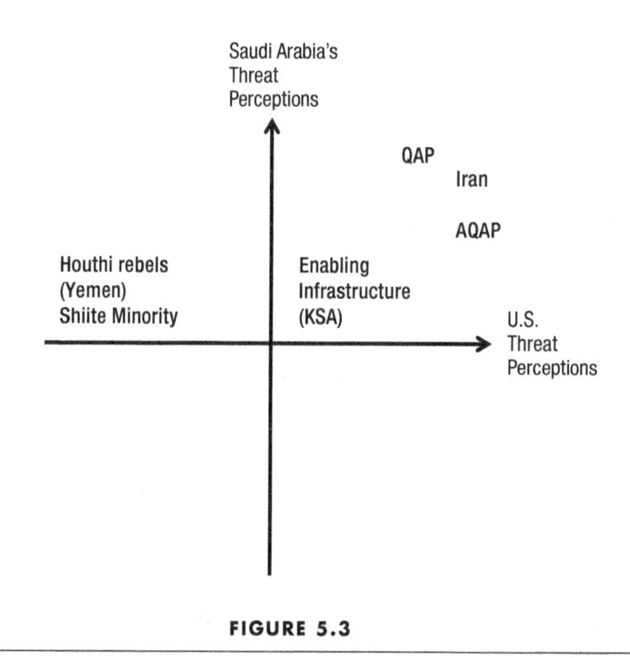

FIGURE 5.3

U.S. and Saudi Threat Perceptions

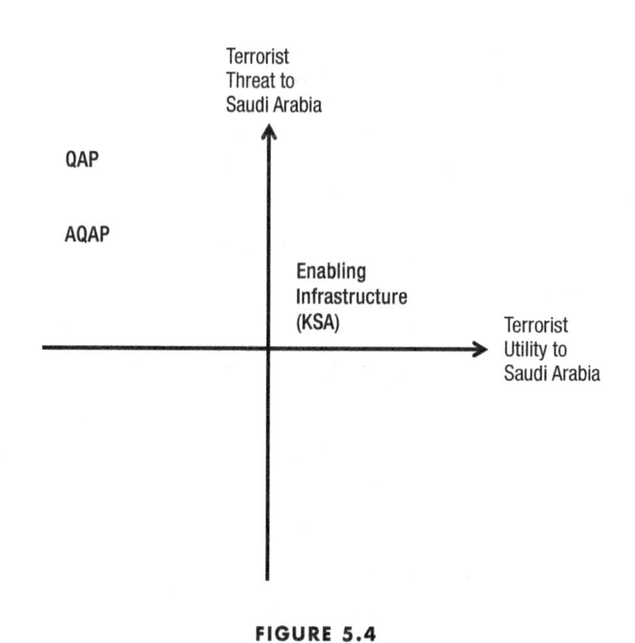

FIGURE 5.4

Terrorist Threat and Utility to Saudi Arabia

in its ideology and its discourse.[67] The state's counterterrorism campaign hastened QAP's expansion to include revolutionary jihad. When faced with a brutal crackdown by the state and a dearth of support from the population, QAP began attacking the Saudi security forces.[68] These forces foiled numerous attacks, arrested hundreds of suspected militants, and killed twenty-three on their most-wanted list of twenty-six militants, including Muqrin.[69] The group was flagging by the summer of 2004. Two years later, QAP's campaign sputtered to an end. How did the kingdom achieve this domestic counterterrorism success?

To begin with, Saudi Arabia pursued a comprehensive counterterrorism campaign characterized by a high level of effort and resources. Riyadh raised the salaries of the security forces and provided them with more counterterrorism training.[70] These forces benefited from improvements in technical surveillance and forensics, which the United States helped foster.[71] At the same time, steps were taken to root out potential jihadist sympathizers within the security forces' ranks.[72] The cumulative result was to increase the security forces' determination and effectiveness. These forces avoided indiscriminate violence in their counterterrorism operations, largely refrained from torturing captured militants, and endeavored to be transparent about how prisoners were treated. This helped prevent detainees from becoming even more radicalized and robbed QAP of a potent recruitment tool.[73] The authorities also used amnesties to peel off reconcilable members of QAP and publicized defections to reduce the group's morale.[74]

The government took steps to damage QAP's reputation and make it hard for the group to recruit outside of limited and easily monitored circles of jihadist veterans with preexisting connections to its members.[75] Saudi authorities arrested a cohort of clerics who provided ideological support to QAP, robbing it of "a crucial legitimizing resource."[76] Riyadh also took advantage of the taboo against revolutionary violence in the country, whose citizens were more accustomed to supporting pan-Islamic jihads against non-Muslims. Using various information channels, including the media and education system, Saudi leaders demonized QAP militants for killing fellow Muslims. The religious establishment, which was always supportive of pan-Islamic jihads in other countries, likewise condemned the group for launching attacks in the kingdom.

Efforts to stem jihadist recruitment were robust, but they were narrowly targeted against QAP and sometimes ran counter to U.S. interests. While leading clerics rebuked QAP for its revolutionary activities, they simultaneously called on Saudis to wage jihad against U.S. forces in Iraq and endorsed fighting in Afghanistan.[77] The government permitted these pronouncements, just as it had allowed previous appeals for Saudi youth to join pan-Islamic campaigns. The authorities interdicted and imprisoned some Saudis attempting to access the Iraq front. Yet there are reports that others were allowed or even encouraged to go, including one that suggests elements in the Saudi government offered to facilitate the participation of Muqrin (the QAP leader) and other QAP fighters in the Iraq jihad.[78] Saudi officials also did not treat returnees from Iraq as harshly as captured QAP militants.[79] After decades of supporting pan-Islamic jihad, and considering the widespread anger over the U.S. invasion, stifling calls for Saudis to fight in Iraq or cracking down too harshly on those who did could have helped fuel QAP's jihad. Conversely, encouraging participation in the Iraq jihad provided would-be recruits with a more attractive and "legitimate" alternative to revolutionary violence. As one scholar observed, the Iraq war divided pan-Islamic and global jihadists in Saudi Arabia to the latter's disadvantage.[80] QAP struggled to recruit new members, whereas approximately 1,500 Saudis mobilized for Iraq.[81]

As part of its counterterrorism campaign, Saudi Arabia began to address the terrorist-enabling infrastructure that had existed in the kingdom for decades. The state improved its border controls and clamped down on the sizeable illegal arms market, thereby making weapons and explosive materials more difficult to acquire.[82] In subsequent years, the authorities also worked hard to stamp out the production of forged passports in order to circumscribe Saudi militants' ability to travel abroad.[83] The most consequential reforms came in the area of countering terrorist financing. The kingdom was the "epicenter" for al-Qaeda financing, according to David Aufhauser, the Treasury Department's general counsel at the time of the May 2003 attacks.[84] Riyadh lacked a financial regulatory system, practiced almost no oversight of domestic charities, and often did not collect even basic financial data from its citizens.[85] The authorities had made little effort to address these deficiencies since the first delegation from the U.S. Treasury Department visited in the spring of 2002.[86]

QAP's campaign compelled Riyadh to devote more attention to combating terrorist financing, which became a critical pillar of the U.S.-Saudi counterterrorism partnership. The Saudi government launched a spate of new initiatives. These included establishing a Saudi Anti-Financial Crime Unit, creating the Permanent Committee on Combating the Financing of Terrorism, enacting an anti–money laundering law, taking additional steps to increase the regulation of informal money transfers, expanding prohibitions on charitable donations outside the kingdom, and augmenting the monitoring of various charitable organizations.[87] Little more than a year after the May attacks, the Financial Action Task Force, the part of the Organization for Economic Cooperation and Development that combats money laundering and terrorist financing, determined that the kingdom was compliant or largely compliant with international standards in most areas.[88] In another sign of their increased commitment, Saudi officials ultimately shut down the entire al-Haramain organization and prosecuted its director for financial irregularities.[89]

The United States helped enhance the Saudis' capabilities to close financial loopholes and track terrorist financing. Recall that after the May attacks, the two countries set up a taskforce focused on capturing the perpetrators. They subsequently established another joint taskforce to counter terrorist financing and share intelligence about threats to the United States.[90] Additionally, agents from the FBI and Internal Revenue Service worked with their Saudi counterparts to set up a center focused on bank accounts, computer records, and other financial data. The U.S. government also trained Saudi officials and investigators on how to counter terrorist financing.[91] In 2008, the United States created a Treasury attaché office in the embassy in Riyadh to enable daily interaction and information sharing with Saudi officials.[92] By end of the decade, the Saudi government was increasingly willing to take actions it had previously resisted, especially holding individual financiers legally accountable and freezing suspect accounts.[93] The regulations Saudi Arabia put in place initially focused on charities but did not apply to direct donations from private donors.[94] Thus, Riyadh's willingness to begin arresting and prosecuting suspected jihadist financiers was a notable step forward. Documents recovered after the bin Laden raid in May 2011 detailed chronic cash shortages.[95] Saudi efforts were not solely responsible for this, but they did hamper al-Qaeda's ability to raise money.[96]

Despite this progress, donors in the kingdom still constituted the greatest source of funding for Sunni militant groups.[97] For example, the Taliban, Haqqani network, and other Pakistan-supported groups fighting against U.S. and coalition forces in Afghanistan raised millions annually from Saudi sources.[98] Al-Qaeda, which was allied with some of these organizations, benefited indirectly because it could rely on them for funding. As a result, terrorist financing remained a "constant irritant" between the United States and Saudi Arabia.[99] Limited capabilities remained part of the problem. The Saudi Interior Ministry continued to depend heavily on the CIA for direction on terrorist financing. Thus, success was contingent on the United States' ability to provide analytical support and actionable intelligence. Even as the authorities became more adept at regulating activities inside the kingdom, they were slow to tackle the international aspects of terrorist financing.[100] The regime was also slow to close certain loopholes. Because Saudi Arabia was a wealthy, cash-based society where carrying large sums of money was common, would-be donors could circumvent restrictions by using couriers to transfer cash to jihadist organizations.[101] Financiers connected to al-Qaeda and other jihadist groups leveraged the hajj (the annual Muslim pilgrimage to Mecca) to collect cash and smuggle it out of the kingdom.[102] U.S. officials pressed their Saudi counterparts to deny access to pilgrims who were also potential fundraisers. Riyadh refused, opting for monitoring instead. These efforts met with limited success, which is understandable when one considers the vast numbers of people coming into and out of the country for the hajj.[103]

The problem was not simply a matter of boosting Saudi capabilities or closing loopholes. Saudi leaders were reluctant to address fully either the demand side or supply side of terrorist financing. In terms of demand, the authorities still tacitly allowed members of foreign jihadist organizations that did not threaten the kingdom directly to travel to Saudi Arabia and raise money. Much of the money raised went to groups that Saudi Arabia saw as constituting a Sunni firewall to contain Shiite Iran across South and Central Asia.[104] On the supply side, Saudi leaders and clerics had spent decades encouraging the citizenry to support various jihadist causes. The government took tactical steps after 2003 to discourage financing jihadist causes but remained reluctant to arrest Saudi donors, provided they did not threaten the kingdom. More importantly, the ideological apparatus that promoted certain jihadist causes remained in place, and a portion of the population remained committed to supporting them. As Prince Mohammed bin Nayef, who led the Saudis' antiterrorism activities told one U.S. official, "if money wants to go" to jihadist causes, "it will go."[105] Addressing this issue required wrestling with broader issues related to Saudi Arabia's religious character.

TARGETED CVE

Efforts to counter radicalization and recruitment can be defined narrowly to include only CVE-specific initiatives focused on potential terrorists or supporters of terrorism or more broadly to encompass CVE-relevant activities that are meant to address myriad societal risk factors. Saudi Arabia took a relatively narrow approach composed of three interconnected programs aimed at prevention, rehabilitation, and aftercare (PRAC). Wahhabism, which stresses obedience and loyalty to the ruler, was central to this approach because it reaffirmed the state's legitimacy and its authority as the arbiter of true Islam. Extremists were depicted as lacking the proper understanding of religious doctrine and the authority to call for violence in the name of Islam. These actors were said to be illegitimate precisely because they pervert the true faith. While taking an ideological approach, the government simultaneously employed longstanding Saudi policies of co-optation, patronage, and coercion where necessary.[106]

Prevention took various forms but focused heavily on informing the public about the proper interpretation of Islam and delegitimizing extremists who promoted violence against other Sunni Muslims.[107] Special attention was given to the education sector. The government took steps to combat radicalization and recruitment in schools by warning students about the dangers of becoming involved in terrorism. Teachers who propagated extremist ideas were sent for retraining or fired, but instruction regarding the dangers of extremism remained inconsistent.[108] Afterschool programs and other activities to keep students occupied when not in class were created to keep them from getting into trouble with jihadist recruiters or on the internet.[109]

A larger effort to reform the education curriculum accompanied these initiatives. Saudi officials acknowledged that elements of the official school curricula, which maligned non-Muslims and the Shi'a, argued that Islam was under attack, and exalted participation in pan-Islamic jihad, were problematic and sometimes downright "abhorrent."[110] Abdullah made a concerted effort to revamp the country's education system.[111] A considerable amount of bigoted material that maligned other religions was excised from school textbooks.[112] Other books deemed to include extremist content were removed from school libraries.[113] Although the government made progress, studies conducted over a decade after 9/11 found that some texts still taught enmity toward other religions, labeled Jews and Christians "enemies of the believers," lauded jihad against the infidels, called for apostates to be put to death, and promoted other extremist ideas.[114]

Saudi Arabia established a program to deradicalize captured militants and reintegrate them into society. Inmates were assessed upon arrival to identify social or psychological factors that may have led to their involvement in jihadist activities. Psychologists and psychiatrists along with other researchers tracked participants' progress in the program. Religious clerics and scholars played a major role, challenging jihadist ideology on theological grounds. There was a special emphasis on the dangers of takfir, which is the accusation that another Muslim is an apostate. Religious experts drove home the messages that the use of violence within the kingdom was un-Islamic and that only legitimate scholars and the government were authorized to call for jihad.[115] Inmates judged to have been rehabilitated were released but monitored and encouraged to continue meeting with clerics. The authorities helped create educational opportunities for graduates of the program and find them employment. Many received cars so they could commute to and from work. To encourage released inmates to settle down into a stable life, the state gave many of them money for a dowry.[116] Social support was also provided to prisoners' families, who were expected to help keep them out of trouble.[117]

The kingdom's deradicalization program made it easier for the United States to repatriate Saudi detainees from Guantanamo Bay. Riyadh was also willing to take custody of non-Saudis in some cases, including Yemenis the Obama administration was reluctant to send back to Yemen, where prisons were notoriously porous. Approximately three thousand detainees went through the program by the end of the decade, and roughly half of them were released.[118] Saudi officials claimed an 80 percent success rate. The 20 percent who failed included both detainees who refused to participate and ones who were released and then rearrested.[119] According to Saudi authorities, the latter group was less than 5 percent of all released detainees.[120] Not all of the men who relapsed were rearrested. Some of them, including detainees repatriated from Guantanamo, fled to Yemen, where they later helped lead AQAP.[121]

What recidivism rates do not reveal is whether released detainees have really been deradicalized or have simply disengaged from jihadist activity. Disengagement by itself is a worthy objective but does not preclude the possibility that released prisoners may relapse or help radicalize other Saudis.[122] Many of the participants who graduated also never engaged in terrorism domestically. They were veterans of jihad campaigns abroad who were rounded up after QAP launched its terrorist campaign in the kingdom. Detainees involved in terrorism inside Saudi Arabia were not released, and most of them either refused to participate in the program or were deemed ineligible. Rehabilitating low-level operatives can keep them from participating in future jihad campaigns, which is a worthy objective, and can help prevent them from moving up the chain to become operational leaders. However, this is still not the same as deradicalizing hardliners.[123]

It is impossible to assess deradicalization efforts without placing them in the context of wider debates about Wahhabi Islam. According to program officials, many detainees knew relatively little about Islam, and this made them susceptible to extremist messaging from jihadist ideologues. Thus, replacing misunderstandings about Islam with what the Saudi authorities considered the correct interpretation was a lynchpin of the program.[124] Yet the "correct" interpretation of Islam in Saudi Arabia delegitimized terrorism in the kingdom but often encouraged pan-Islamic jihad and justified violence against non-Muslims and the Shi'a.

The limited and largely superficial revision of Wahhabi Islam that did occur took place via a series of National Dialogue conferences. The crown prince initiated these in response to calls for reform after 9/11. The initial gathering in June 2003 consisted exclusively of clerics. Not all of them were Wahhabis. Leaders of other Muslim communities, including Shiite clerics, were also present.[125] This was a notable step forward. Participants who were not religious scholars attended subsequent meetings; a total of eight were held between 2003 and 2010. After the first session, intended to promote intellectual dialogue, subsequent meetings focused on fighting extremism, women's rights, young people's expectations, dealing with world cultures, education, employment, and health services. Although dialogues enabled discussion, not many concrete actions emerged.[126]

After imprisoning clerics who legitimized QAP's jihad, Saudi authorities fired another 3,500 imams for refusing to renounce extremist views. Approximately twenty thousand more were sent for retraining, according to the Saudi government. Yet virulently anti-Semitic, anti-Christian, and anti-Shiite sentiments still appeared in sermons delivered by clerics as well as in the official media. The government still banned most forms of public religious expression other than that of Wahhabi Islam, arrested or detained Shiite dissidents, and otherwise cracked down on non-Wahhabi Muslims. Individuals continued to be imprisoned for apostasy and blasphemy.[127]

On balance, the Saudi approach focused more on pull factors, which draw an individual toward an extremist group or cause, than on the push factors that create conditions for recruitment and radicalization. Saudi efforts were undercut not only by their reluctance to confront fully the consequences of promoting Wahhabi Islam but also by their ongoing repression of civil society. The security forces continued to monitor and tightly limit political and social activism. Several prominent reformers who questioned the idea of Wahhabi Islam as the basis for the Saudi state were fired from their jobs. One was sentenced to seventy-five lashes for speaking out.[128] Critics calling for a reexamination of the more exclusivist and violent parts of Wahhabism were given only a short leash.[129] As a result, the role Wahhabi Islam would play in the kingdom and what form it would take remained unanswered. And the government continued to spend substantial sums of money to export Wahhabism across the Middle East, Asia, Africa, and Europe through a sophisticated network of mosques, charities, NGOs, and Saudi-trained clerics.[130]

FIGHTING FIRES

Intelligence cooperation expanded considerably once the Saudi authorities began taking the al-Qaeda threat seriously. Saudi ownership of the jihadist problem on its soil was the primary cause for improvement, but the United States also made adjustments. Streamlining counterterrorism engagements through a single point person helped, as did U.S. efforts to build Saudi capabilities. U.S. officials had previously demanded cooperation without providing actionable intelligence. Once they committed to share more sensitive information, Riyadh responded positively.[131] Saudi intelligence collection and information sharing was valuable for the United States and other countries that were trying to track established and would-be jihadists operating throughout the Gulf region.[132] This was especially true in Yemen, where the kingdom's intelligence service stepped up its collection efforts after al-Qaeda regenerated there during the latter years of the decade.[133]

U.S.-Saudi intelligence cooperation on AQAP was robust.[134] Saudi intelligence established a station in Sanaa, the Yemeni capital, and its networks stretched deep into Yemen's tribal areas.[135] These networks helped with hunting down Yemen-based AQAP operatives. Saudi Arabia also played a pivotal role in disrupting two of the group's three major attempted terrorist attacks against the United States. In 2010, AQAP hid bombs in FedEx and UPS packages aboard two cargo planes. Saudi intelligence provided the key tip about the plot, enabling the United States to coordinate with the United Arab Emirates and the United Kingdom to halt the flights in time.[136] In 2012, an agent run by Saudi intelligence who had infiltrated AQAP thwarted the group's second attempt to bring down a commercial airline using a nonmetallic "underwear bomb." The agent was one of several operatives sent into Yemen with a Western passport, enabling them to pose as "clean skins" capable of traveling into Europe or the United States. He allowed himself to be fitted with the bomb, then turned it over to his Saudi handlers inside Yemen.[137]

The Saudi government also allowed the CIA to begin operating a secret airbase for unmanned drones used to target AQAP militants across the border. The base was constructed after a December 2009 cruise-missile strike in Yemen unintentionally killed dozens of civilians, including women and children. In September 2011, a drone flown from the Saudi base killed Anwar al-Awlaki, the U.S.-born cleric who inspired numerous Western jihadists and had a hand in planning several of the aforementioned AQAP attacks. Thereafter, Saudi-based drones were used to hunt other high-value targets in Yemen.[138] Although the longstanding partnership between the United States and Saudi Arabia probably helped smooth the way for drone basing, Riyadh's anxieties about the AQAP threat almost certainly factored as well. The shared threat from AQAP and the U.S. need for tactical cooperation remained important features of the counterterrorism partnership, even as tensions mounted in the wider bilateral relationship after the Arab uprisings and Iran nuclear deal.

COUNTERTERRORISM AT A CROSSROADS

Close U.S.-Saudi cooperation on terrorist financing and intelligence, especially against AQAP, existed in parallel with growing divergences over regional security threats and responses to them. The Arab uprisings exposed these divergences, which were exacerbated by developments in Egypt, the conflicts in Syria and Yemen, and the U.S. pursuit of a nuclear deal with Iran.

Although Saudi Arabia remained remarkably stable as revolutions roiled other countries, the Arab uprisings reinvigorated debates among Saudis about the nature of their society and polity. Issues including political reform, human rights, corruption, and religious freedom in the kingdom also became more prominent in U.S.-Saudi relations.[139] Saudi leaders were deeply unsettled by the Obama administration's response to the uprisings in other Arab countries because of what it possibly portended for them. Riyadh had viewed the Bush administration's democracy agenda cynically, questioning "both American motives and resolve," according to one close observer of the U.S.-Saudi relationship.[140] President Obama took America's foot off the democracy pedal after coming into office, but that changed when the Arab uprisings began.

Where the Obama team saw the opportunity to promote democracy, good governance, and rule of law, the Saudi regime perceived potential threats to its regional position and possibly to its existence.[141] U.S. policy toward Egypt was especially troubling in this regard. Egypt under the military-backed regime of Hosni Mubarak had been a critical Arab ally for the kingdom. Among other things, both the Saudi and Egyptian governments had shared an antipathy toward the Islamist Muslim Brotherhood. Thus, Obama's decision to call for President Mubarak's ouster and then to support the Brotherhood-led government that replaced him was a blow to the kingdom's regional fortunes. The fact that the United States had sided against a longstanding partner also set a dangerous precedent for the Saudi regime and its willingness to work with a government led by the Muslim Brotherhood was salt in the wound.

Although Washington and Riyadh coordinated to support certain rebel forces in the Syrian civil war, their priorities and approaches diverged. Toppling the Iran-supported Assad regime and replacing it with a friendlier government was Saudi Arabia's main objective. Obama was prepared to use force to combat ISIS but not the Syrian regime. Saudi leaders were especially incensed after the president backed away from his pledge to use military force after Assad crossed a "red line" and used chemical weapons. Moreover, they complained that Washington had strengthened Assad's hand by preventing America's Sunni partners from giving Syrian rebels powerful weapons, like antiaircraft missiles, out of fear they would fall into the hands of terrorists.[142] From Obama's vantage point, the Saudis were too consumed by their competition with Iran and therefore too willing to fuel a proxy war in Syria that ultimately benefited ISIS and al-Qaeda's Syrian affiliate.[143]

A growing U.S.-Saudi rift over Iran underlay much of the tension between the two countries. Recall that in 2012 the five permanent members of the UN Security Council plus Germany (P5+1) and the European Union began secretly negotiating an international agreement with Tehran to curb the Iranian nuclear program in exchange for sanctions relief. The Obama administration believed the deal, which was being openly negotiated by 2013 and was signed in 2015, offered the best bet for avoiding a nuclear escalation in the Middle East. Saudi leaders were not only skeptical that Iran would abide by the terms of any arrangement but also recognized that the relaxation of sanctions could enable Tehran to wield greater regional influence. From Riyadh's perspective, the nuclear deal was at best another sign of U.S. naivety or, worse, an indicator that Washington might tilt toward Tehran.

One Middle East analyst summed up the Saudi state of mind about the nuclear deal when he said, "It's a frightening period for the Saudis," who needed to be "reassured—psychologically, politically—that, in fact, Saudi Arabia remains a staunch American ally and is protected from that encroachment by Iran."[144] The administration attempted to assuage Saudi anxiety about Iran or U.S. abandonment by agreeing to sell the kingdom billions of dollars of expensive, high-tech weaponry, including F-15s that were "messaged as a means of pushing back against Iran," according to one U.S. defense official.[145] The U.S. arms deal failed to mollify Saudi Arabia. Saudi concerns about Iran were magnified when Shiite Houthi rebels took control of the capital in Yemen in 2015. Although the Houthis were motivated mainly by local grievances, Saudi leaders believed Iran was "winning" in Yemen. Saudi Arabia and its Gulf allies argued that because the United States was embracing Iran instead of deterring it, they had no choice but to intervene.[146]

The Arab uprisings and their aftermath, combined with the Iran nuclear deal, clearly impacted Saudi threat perceptions. Figure 5.5 highlights the fact that although the United States and Saudi Arabia still shared common threats, regionally the two countries increasingly perceived and prioritized them differently. The biggest jihadist challenge to Saudi Arabia came from ISIS affiliates in the kingdom, which successfully recruited numerous Saudis, often via the internet, and launched a series of strikes intended to trigger an uprising.[147] Regionally, ISIS in Iraq and Syria (ISIS core) and AQAP in Yemen also threatened Saudi Arabia, although not to the same degree.[148] However, Riyadh perceived Iran and the Houthis to be a bigger regional threat and prioritized rolling back their advances. The United States viewed Iran as a threat and was wary of the Houthis, especially once they overthrew the government in Yemen in early 2015. But U.S. perceptions and prescriptions for dealing with these challenges diverged from Riyadh's. This hampered regional cooperation, which became increasingly important to the United States after the Arab uprisings. U.S. attempts to mollify Saudi Arabia by supporting its ill-fated intervention against the Houthis has also drawn America further into the Yemeni civil war. As this occurred and as Iranian support for the Houthis increased, the Houthis began to pose a greater threat to U.S. interests. (This shift is reflected in figure 5.5 and discussed in greater detail at the end of the next chapter.) Meanwhile, the Saudi government's policies toward the enabling infrastructure on its soil remained conflicted (figure 5.6). Also, as the figure indicates, AQAP remained a belligerent, but its usefulness increased, albeit only marginally, because it sometimes fought with the Saudi-led coalition against the Houthis in Yemen.

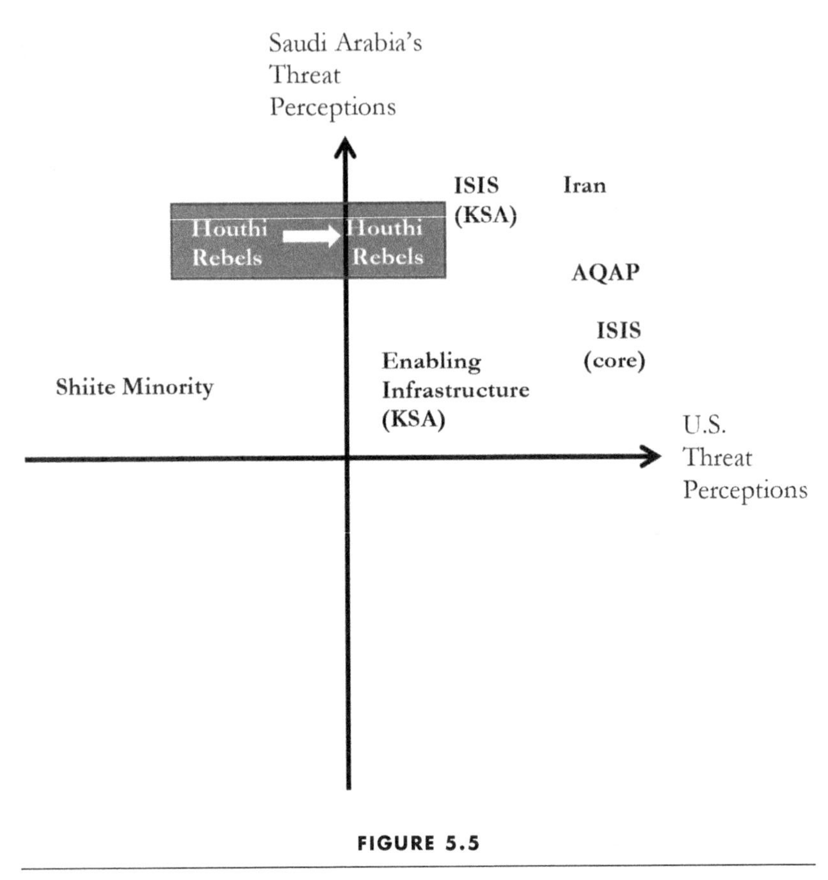

FIGURE 5.5

U.S. and Saudi Threat Perceptions

ARSONIST AND FIREFIGHTER

U.S.-Saudi intelligence cooperation remained close and critical to American counterterrorism efforts. Saudi intelligence continued to recruit spies, develop plans to eliminate AQAP operatives, and track others for targeting by U.S. air and drone strikes.[149] U.S. support for Saudi Arabia's domestic counterterrorism efforts also remained extant. Despite a series of deadly attacks against the security forces and members of the kingdom's Shiite minority, the Saudi state's robust domestic counterterrorism apparatus kept local ISIS affiliates from gaining too much momentum inside the kingdom. Persistent pressure disrupted the group's networks. Many hundreds of ISIS supporters, financiers, and recruits were arrested.[150]

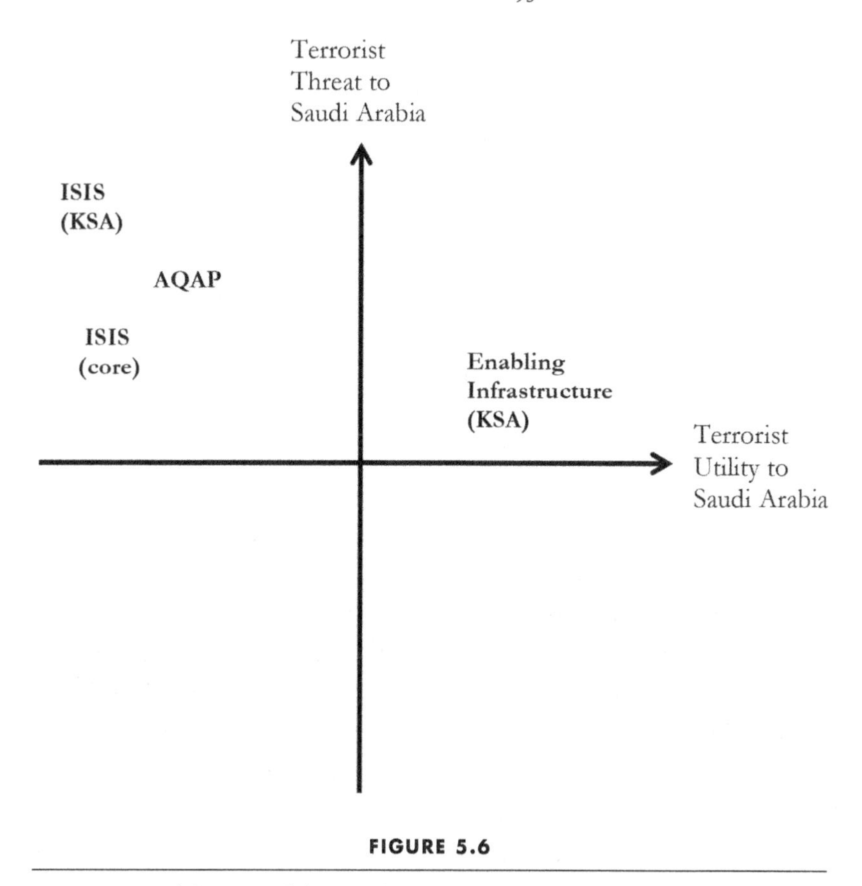

FIGURE 5.6

Terrorist Threat and Utility to Saudi Arabia

Saudi authorities forbade citizens from traveling to Syria to participate in the conflict there and established prison sentences for Saudis found to have traveled abroad to fight with extremist groups.[151] Approximately two thousand would-be foreign fighters were arrested and imprisoned before they could make the trip.[152] However, an equivalent number managed to leave the kingdom to join jihadist groups in Syria and Iraq by the spring of 2015, according to the Saudi Interior Ministry.[153] These numbers suggest that the pull of pan-Islamic jihad remained strong inside the kingdom.

Efforts to cut off financing, although still not as comprehensive as U.S. officials would have liked, nevertheless stemmed the flow of funding directly to ISIS and al-Qaeda.[154] According to the U.S. government, "Despite serious and effective efforts to counter the funding of terrorism originating within the kingdom, Saudi Arabia [was] still home to individuals and entities that continue to serve as sources of financial support for Sunni-based extremist groups."[155] Ongoing support for regional al-Qaeda affiliates, such as the Nusrah Front in Syria, remained especially problematic, according to the U.S. State Department's 2015 Country Report on Terrorism.[156] The report found that although the Saudi government had tightened banking and charity regulations and stiffened penalties for financing terrorism, the challenges posed by hawala networks and by fundraising conducted during the hajj were still extant. The conflicts in Iraq and Syria and growth of social media, which enabled entities outside Saudi Arabia to solicit donations from Saudi donors, contributed to these challenges. Decades spent encouraging support for jihadist causes also hampered Saudi efforts to stem the tide of private money. And the ulema continued reinforcing the theological foundation on which jihadist ideology was based.

It is impossible to ignore the fact that various jihadists, of whom ISIS was the most extreme manifestation, adopted an exclusionary, expansionary, and sectarian worldview on the basis of their reading of Wahhabi Islam.[157] ISIS tapped into widespread fears among Sunnis of Shiite domination in the region, presenting itself as the only actor able and willing to halt this advance. Its leaders and supporters also justified sectarian violence by drawing on the inherently anti-Shiite aspects of Wahhabism and pointing to official teachings of the Saudi religious establishment.[158] Indeed, at the apex of its power ISIS behaved like a Wahhabi protostate. It engaged in the same type of expansionist jihad against fellow Sunnis and sectarian violence against the Shi'a as had the first Saudi-Wahhabi state that formed in the eighteenth century.[159] In a major embarrassment for Riyadh, until ISIS was able to produce its own study materials, it republished numerous works by Sheikh Mohammed ibn Abdul-Wahhab and used official Saudi textbooks in the schools under its control.[160]

Most Saudi clerics were slow to condemn ISIS after it seized territory and declared a caliphate. Only after a public rebuke from then king Abdullah did the Saudi grand mufti finally declare that "the ideas of extremism, radicalism and terrorism do not belong to Islam in any way, but are the first enemy of Islam, and Muslims are their first victims, as seen in the crimes of the so-called Islamic State and Al Qaeda."[161] Saudi clerics subsequently began issuing routine condemnations, but these were sometimes most notable for their attempts to shift blame and forestall any real introspection. Many of them indulged in conspiratorial thinking that described ISIS as a product of various foreign bogeymen, including the Baath party, Muslim Brotherhood, international intelligence agencies, and, of course, Israel.[162] Nevertheless, the government's use of state-backed clerics to denounce ISIS signaled its belligerent attitude toward the group. The authorities also cracked down on clerics who deviated too far from the state's antiterrorism messaging.[163]

The government allowed more public criticism of Wahhabism than in the past, clamped down on clerics who openly supported ISIS, and prodded others to condemn the group.[164] Yet scholars who preached intolerance of the Shi'a were not muzzled. On the contrary, some Saudis, smarting from growing Iranian influence in the region, saw ISIS as "a comeback for 'Team Sunni.'"[165] Riyadh made a conscious decision to widen and leverage the Sunni-Shi'a divide to increase support for its agenda and isolate Iran.[166] As the civil war in Syria stretched on and spilled over into Iraq, anti-Shiite sermons, rhetoric, and opinions, many of which circulated via social media, became both more common and more virulent.[167] This contributed to sectarian polarization in which both Sunnis and Shi'a increasingly dehumanized the other.[168]

Regional cooperation became more important to the United States after the Arab uprisings, but Washington often found itself at variance with Riyadh on key issues. The kingdom was one of many members of the anti-ISIS coalition created in 2014 to retake territory in Iraq and Syria and ultimately defeat the group. However, Saudi forces made only meager contributions because they were preoccupied fighting against the Houthis in Yemen. Saudi fighter pilots flew only a handful of initial strike missions in Syria and none in Iraq. Within a year of the coalition's formation, the U.S. Department of Defense was referring to Saudi involvement in the past tense.[169]

The kingdom contributed weapons and money to a secret CIA-led program that began training select Syrian rebel groups in 2013.[170] It also provided bases for training.[171] However, Washington and Riyadh diverged over Saudi support for Salafi rebel groups that were unacceptable to the United States because of their ties to al-Qaeda's Syrian affiliate Jabhat al-Nusra.[172] The two countries were also often at odds over a political solution to the conflict. There was plenty of blame to go around for the failure to end the civil war. Eliciting a greater commitment from Saudi Arabia or other Sunni partners and bringing Iran and Russia, both of which supported the Assad regime, to the negotiating table required America to bring its considerable political and military strength to bear. The Obama administration was not prepared to shoulder the costs this would entail.

In Iraq, Saudi Arabia finally reopened diplomatic offices in December 2015, following a twenty-five-year absence. This was an important step toward normalizing Saudi-Iraqi relations and occurred after Hayder al-Abadi replaced Nouri al-Maliki as the Iraqi prime minister in 2014. However, Saudi Arabia remained suspicious of the Shiite-led government, despite Abadi's relative closeness with United States and his attempts to formulate more inclusive and ecumenical policies than his predecessor.[173] Riyadh's refusal to lend more support to Abadi's government threatened to make it more difficult to institute the types of steps necessary to keep ISIS from regenerating once its caliphate began to crumble.

In Egypt, the Saudis embraced the military's 2013 coup d'état that ousted the elected government led by Mohammed Morsi. They also provided billions of dollars in financial assistance to the military-backed government that replaced him at a time when the United States was attempting to exert leverage over it by threatening to withhold aid. The kingdom obtained Egyptian support for its military intervention in Yemen.

Saudi Arabia had played a positive role in Yemen during the years immediately before the Arab uprisings. It co-chaired the Friends of Yemen program along with the United Kingdom and the Republic of Yemen.[174] This program was established in January 2010 to bolster international support for Yemen and to assist Yemeni-led efforts to address some of the underlying causes of instability in the country. After the Arab uprisings spread to Yemen, Riyadh took the lead in crafting and implementing the Gulf Cooperation Council plan that eased Yemeni President Saleh out of power in February 2012. The Saudis helped manage the transition process and pledged over $3 billion to support the new government.[175] When Saleh's desperate bid to keep power created a security vacuum that AQAP exploited, Saudi Arabia cooperated with the United States to airdrop supplies for Yemeni military units and flew bombing raids to relieve pressure on them.[176] In short, Saudi Arabia was helping stabilize Yemen and degrade AQAP. However, as we will see in chapter 7, Riyadh also influenced post-transition politics in ways that seriously disadvantaged Houthi rebels.

After the Houthis drove interim Yemeni President Abd-Rabbu Mansour Hadi into exile in Saudi Arabia, the kingdom began launching airstrikes against them. Saudi Arabia also constructed its own coalition of Sunni countries, some of which contributed to the air campaign and put boots on the ground.[177] The Saudi-led intervention was indicative of a more assertive foreign policy, one shaped by events both inside and outside the kingdom. King Abdullah died two months before the intervention occurred. Salman bin Abdul-Aziz ascended to the throne. His son, Prince Mohammed bin Salman, who was young and relatively unknown, became the defense minister and architect of the military campaign in Yemen.[178] Some observers assessed that the prince was seeking to move beyond the kingdom's historical reliance on U.S. military power and perhaps to cultivate a heroic image domestically by stoking Sunni-based Saudi nationalism in advance of future succession battles.[179]

The influence of internal dynamics does not cancel out the importance of real geopolitical concerns. Saudi Arabia was clearly attempting to roll back Iranian encroachment in the Gulf. Its intervention in Yemen was part of the same regional power struggle that fueled the Syrian civil war. In some respects, the stakes for Saudi Arabia were even higher because its geography meant that it faced the threat of an Iranian proxy right next door. Thus, the kingdom perceived both a wider threat of Iranian encirclement on the Arabian Peninsula and a direct one on its southern border.

The Saudi government pressed for assistance from the United States for its intervention in Yemen. The Obama administration struggled to develop a coherent response. On the one hand, Riyadh and the United Arab Emirates, which was a major contributor to the campaign in Yemen, were already skeptical of U.S. resolve to protect their core interests. Failing to back them would have damaged relations even more. On the other hand, U.S. officials believed the Saudi-led campaign was unlikely to succeed and could further destabilize Yemen and hinder counterterrorism efforts against AQAP.[180] In the end, the Obama White House reluctantly supported the intervention with weapons, intelligence, and logistical support in order to placate Saudi (and Emirati) leaders and in the hopes of limiting civilian casualties.[181] As the United States was drawn further into the civil war as a result and Iranian support for the Houthis increased, the Houthis began to pose a greater threat to U.S. interests. (This is reflected in figure 5.5 and discussed in greater detail in the next chapter.)

The State Department approved the sale of over one billion dollars of smart bombs to help Saudi forces replenish their munitions for use in Yemen and (theoretically) against ISIS.[182] In addition to supplying weapons and midair refueling for Saudi coalition fighter jets, the United States has also provided logistical and intelligence support to help the Saudi-led coalition conduct air strikes, control Yemeni airspace, and blockade Yemen's seaports to keep Iranian vessels from resupplying the Houthis.[183] In addition to mollifying Riyadh, targeting assistance and smart bombs were also intended to help reduce civilian casualties resulting from airstrikes.[184] Despite this assistance, Saudi airstrikes routinely hit nonmilitary targets in Yemen, killing thousands of innocent civilians.[185] As casualties mounted, the Obama administration blocked the sale of additional smart bombs to Saudi Arabia and cut back on intelligence sharing.[186] U.S. officials also pressed their Saudi counterparts to reach a political settlement that would bring an end to the conflict. Despite a series of truncated ceasefires, the conflict continued as of late 2017.

The Saudi-led intervention helped turn a local power struggle into a regional and sectarian conflict that claimed the lives of over ten thousand civilians by 2017. In addition to the staggering toll of human suffering, this had negative ramifications for U.S. counterterrorism efforts. ISIS and AQAP both took advantage of the conflict to expand their operations in Yemen.[187] AQAP remained more robust and capable than ISIS's Yemeni affiliate and benefited to an even greater extent from the conflict. The kingdom refrained from airstrikes against AQAP strongholds, and Saudi-backed forces sometimes fought alongside AQAP militants against the Houthis.[188] As a result, AQAP faced "no pressure except from the occasional U.S. drone shot" for approximately a year after the intervention began.[189] In March 2016, Saudi interior minister Mohammed bin Nayef finally convinced his counterparts in Riyadh to adjust their strategy and target AQAP, albeit still not with the same vigor as the Houthis.[190] As of late 2017, the Saudi-led campaign continued to distract from the fight against AQAP. This has enabled the group to continue expanding its zones of support, which U.S. intelligence officials assess could enable it to execute external attacks.[191]

* * *

Saudi Arabia was the first country Donald Trump visited as president. It was a major break from tradition—most of his predecessors went to Canada or Mexico. While there, Trump delivered a speech to leaders of more than fifty countries, in which he called on Muslim states to do more to combat terrorism, announced an agreement to sell his hosts at least $110 billion worth of weapons, and expressed an eagerness to ally with Sunni autocrats against Shiite Iran. In his speech, Trump identified areas where he sought greater efforts from Saudi Arabia and other countries in the region: "starving terrorists of their territory, their funding and the false allure of their craven ideology."[192] These demands were not new. They fit squarely within the framework of U.S. counterterrorism objectives since the September 11 attacks.

Whether a country actually comes through depends on the threats that terrorists pose to it and the utility those terrorists offer. Saudi Arabia is a perfect example. It did not take al-Qaeda seriously after 9/11 because it did not view the group as a major threat. This changed only after al-Qaeda began launching attacks inside the kingdom in 2003. Since then, Saudi authorities have been ruthlessly committed to keeping their house in order. The Saudis are likely to continue to do so because it is in their interests, not because America sells them arms or takes their side against Iran.

The same calculus that dictates whether a state takes the fight to terrorist groups also informs whether it commits to dismantling a supportive infrastructure. Again, Saudi Arabia is a good example of the possibilities and limits of cooperation. For decades, Saudi Arabia championed charitable giving for extremist causes. After Saudi leaders committed to combating al-Qaeda's affiliate in the kingdom, they also began working harder to stanch the flow of money to the group internationally. The Saudis have made similar efforts vis-à-vis the ISIS. Yet the government has also allowed conditions favorable for jihadist fundraising to persist, and the kingdom's citizens remain one of the greatest sources for jihadist financing.[193] Moreover, even as Saudi Arabia made progress on domestic counterterrorism efforts and became a critical partner in terms of intelligence cooperation, its export of Wahhabism has remained incredibly problematic.

The kingdom's uncompromising version of Islam has formed the theological foundation that inspires ISIS, al-Qaeda, and other Sunni extremists.

The government's promotion of Wahhabism is a function of its longstanding arrangement with the Saudi ulema but also a useful way to promote its own domestic legitimacy and project influence regionally. In late 2017, Mohammed bin Salman, who earlier that year became the crown prince, announced plans to curb the power of Saudi clerics and push for a more tolerant brand of Islam. This is widely viewed as part of the crown prince's bid to consolidate power in the kingdom; an effort that has also included detaining his rivals in the royal family.[194] It is too soon to tell how genuine these promised reforms are, what they portend in terms of counterterrorism, or whether they will succeed, considering the deeply conservative nature of Saudi society and the entrenched religious bureaucracy. It is clear that Saudi Arabia, which has been a remarkably stable albeit difficult partner, appears to be poised to enter a period of tumult.

While the crown prince has consolidated power at home, the Saudi-led intervention in Yemen that he championed continued. During his visit, Trump cited the intervention as an example of the kingdom's contributions to regional security despite the fact that it has distracted from the fight against ISIS and created space for AQAP to expand, recruit, and bring in money. And although he used his Saudi speech to blame Muslim leaders for not doing enough to combat terrorism, Trump embraced the Saudi agenda in the Middle East and singled out Shiite Iran as the main culprit responsible for fueling the fires of sectarian conflict and terrorism in the region. In doing so, Trump not only signaled that he views Iran as a greater threat than Obama did. He also brought U.S. threat perceptions more in line with Saudi Arabia's.[195]

Taking a tougher line on Iran could help improve the tone and tenor of U.S. relations with Saudi Arabia and other Sunni states, but it is not clear that this will necessarily produce any positive and sustainable outcomes on counterterrorism efforts against AQAP, ISIS, or other jihadist groups. However, Trump's rhetoric and actions may have signaled to Saudi Arabia and its Sunni allies that they are free to expand their rivalry with Iran heedlessly. The further escalation of sectarian tension likely to result from such an expansion would threaten U.S. security objectives across the Middle East and make combating jihadist terrorism more difficult than it already is.

6

YEMEN

An Unstable Partner

IN AN AL-QAEDA VIDEO released several months before the October 2000 attack on the USS *Cole*, Osama bin Laden wears a *jambiya*. The short curved dagger is popular in Yemen, which was bin Laden's ancestral home and a place where al-Qaeda's networks had operated relatively unmolested before September 11. However, Yemen was not an ideological state like Pakistan and Saudi Arabia, where there was a consistent logic, which continued across multiple governments, underlying policies toward jihadists. Yemen's security paradigm, to the degree one existed, boiled down to Ali Abdullah Saleh, his family, and his allies doing whatever was necessary to keep power. This objective heavily influenced Yemen's dealings with al-Qaeda before and after 9/11 as well as with the United States.

Saleh became president of the Republic of Yemen (hereafter Yemen) when North Yemen and South Yemen united in 1990. He had already ruled North Yemen for twelve years, taking power after a series of assassinations claimed the lives of several previous leaders. Before unification, the two countries were bitter rivals. They fought a brief war in 1979, after which forces supported by the Marxist-led government in South Yemen continued to wage a low-level insurgency. Saleh organized Saudi-financed religious and tribal groups into an Islamic Front to assist his counterinsurgency campaign. He later integrated many Islamic Front members into the army and police.[1]

Although Saleh's personalized style of rule had a disproportionately large effect on his government's policies before and after unification, state capacity was too low for him to exercise authoritarian rule. Instead, he used a combination of patronage and skillful manipulation to keep power. Saleh famously referred to his style of governance as dancing on the heads of snakes. He granted autonomy to Yemen's well-armed tribes, which were the most long-lasting and consequential social institution. Saleh also integrated Islamists from the Muslim Brotherhood into the political system and provided space for a Salafi movement to develop.[2] These policies were intended to keep the peace but also to undercut Marxist influences from South Yemen.[3]

The enabling environment that al-Qaeda took advantage of during the 1990s had its roots in Saleh's support for the anti-Soviet jihad the previous decade. Unification was looming, and Saleh recognized the utility that battle-hardened fighters would have if conflict ensued. North Yemen's tribes were also committed to sending volunteers to the Afghan front. It is questionable whether the government could have stopped them had it wanted to, and supporting these efforts brought Saleh legitimacy.[4] North Yemen's intelligence and internal security service, the Political Security Organization (PSO), and elements of the army took an active role in channeling fighters to the Afghan front.[5] Some returning Yemeni fighters were integrated into the security services. The anti-Soviet jihad in Afghanistan ended not long before North and South Yemen unified. Saleh's government allowed foreign jihadists leaving the Afghan battlefield to operate in the newly unified country.[6]

Despite a power-sharing agreement, competing northern and southern power centers struggled to reconcile with one another. Tensions escalated until civil war finally erupted in 1994. Once civil war broke out, a Northern Army Brigade composed mainly of Yemeni and Egyptian veterans of the anti-Soviet jihad fought against southern forces. The war lasted only three months and ended with the southern leadership fleeing the country. Saleh had won. He placated Yemeni jihadists who fought in the civil war with land, salaried positions in the government, or other forms of patronage.[7] Many remained in the PSO. Some retained the connections they had forged with al-Qaeda in Afghanistan.[8] In 1996, the authorities began deporting foreign jihadists, who no longer had much utility and might pose a problem.[9] However, Saleh's government turned a blind eye to the network of Yemeni al-Qaeda members that had developed on its territory.

The newly unified Yemen remained poor and regionally fragmented. The government exercised only nominal control in remote areas of the country, where strong tribes still held sway. Allowing al-Qaeda to operate unmolested fit with Saleh's practice of avoiding confrontation wherever possible. He reportedly used al-Qaeda members to eliminate political opponents as well.[10] Some of the group's operatives also benefited from their ties to the country's security services. As a result, al-Qaeda was able to use Yemen for recruitment and logistical support.[11] It ran multiple guesthouses in the country and leveraged connections with Yemeni intelligence to obtain fake passports and travel visas.[12] Al-Qaeda operatives involved in multiple terrorist plots before 9/11 had direct links to Yemen.[13] In October 2000, the group transitioned from using Yemen as a support base to treating it as a theater of operations.

The U.S.-Yemen bilateral relationship was still in its infancy when al-Qaeda bombed the USS *Cole* during a port call in Aden, killing seventeen American sailors. Washington had ostracized Saleh for most of the 1990s after he sided with Iraq during the Gulf War, costing Yemen mightily. The *Cole* attack threatened to derail the rapprochement and usher in another period of international isolation. Yet the authorities were not cooperative when FBI agents arrived to investigate. Yemeni stonewalling enabled the *Cole* attack's mastermind and other al-Qaeda operatives to flee the country. Some suspects identified for Yemeni intelligence by the CIA also managed to slip through the net, raising questions about whether sympathetic PSO members had tipped them off.[14] Yemeni authorities belatedly arrested dozens of suspected al-Qaeda operatives and shut down bank accounts and businesses that U.S. officials believed were connected to the group. U.S. investigators were allowed to interrogate some, though not all, of the al-Qaeda members the Yemeni authorities had in custody.[15] This cooperation helped put a small dent in the group's local infrastructure, but its Yemeni networks remained operational. As a result, U.S. officials were predisposed to view Saleh's regime in a negative light after September 11.

In the wake of the attacks, Saleh worried that his country might become a target of America's War on Terror.[16] His fears were not misplaced. Senior

U.S. officials included Yemen on a list of possible targets for military operations.[17] However, Saleh also spied an opportunity to improve his standing with a potential superpower patron and extract economic and military aid that could be used to strengthen his hold on power. When he visited Washington in late November, then CIA director George Tenet confirmed that Yemen could either be a target or a beneficiary of the War on Terror.[18] President Bush reinforced this message and bluntly told his Yemeni counterpart that cooperation against al-Qaeda would define relations between their two countries.[19]

Incentives and coercion can facilitate limited domestic counterterrorism efforts. Fear of U.S. military action combined with offers of assistance convinced Saleh's government to conduct a counterterrorism campaign against al-Qaeda in Yemen (AQY) and to provide U.S. forces with access to assist with these efforts. Critically, AQY provided limited utility to Saleh's regime, which did not face any other threats at the time. The campaign Yemen conducted was an economy-of-force approach that mixed periodic raids with outreach to local tribal leaders. This proved sufficient because al-Qaeda's networks were fragile and overly reliant on a few strong leaders at the top. They collapsed within two years, which meant there was no need for a sustained campaign. However, the conditions that allowed these networks to form in the first place remained extant.

U.S. instruments of statecraft proved less useful once al-Qaeda reemerged in Yemen in 2006, for several reasons. First, Saleh's threat perceptions had changed. Houthi rebels launched an insurgency against the state in 2004 that continued on and off for the remainder of the decade. Not long after AQY regenerated, a southern separatist movement also mobilized. The Houthis and southern separatists each posed a considerably greater threat to Saleh's rule than did al-Qaeda's revitalized organization. This remained the case after AQY merged with Saudi al-Qaeda members to form al-Qaeda in the Arabian Peninsula (AQAP) in 2009. Thus, although the United States and Yemen shared a common terrorist threat, their threat perceptions were not aligned. The United States viewed AQY after it regenerated and then AQAP following the merger as the top threat in Yemen; Saleh was more worried about the other indigenous challenges he faced.

Second, American interest in Yemen waned considerably after al-Qaeda appeared defeated in 2004. Washington reengaged once the group reemerged, but this led Saleh to believe that the United States was a fickle partner that would abandon him again if the jihadist threat were eradicated entirely. Thus, AQY and then AQAP, despite posing a threat to the regime, also had potential utility as a mechanism for keeping U.S. assistance flowing.

Third, Saleh no longer feared being targeted by the United States. American forces were bogged down in Iraq and Afghanistan. It had also become clear that large-footprint deployments of U.S. military forces to unstable and failing states was unsustainable. And Washington was fearful of losing the limited cooperation it was receiving.

U.S. assistance helped incentivize limited actions against AQY after it reemerged and then against AQAP, but the government's threat perceptions and the group's potential utility militated against robust counterterrorism operations. It often seemed to American officials that the security forces were doing just enough to keep aid flowing. Assistance was more helpful in terms of securing access for small numbers of U.S. forces and for air and missile strikes. Unilateral action was necessary because Yemeni forces were not getting it done—a result of their severely limited capacity and the government's questionable commitment. The United States spent large sums of money to build up the security forces, but the outcomes were mixed at best. U.S. efforts to promote development and counter violent extremism were more limited and less successful. The Arab uprisings offered a chance for a fresh start and better cooperation after Saleh belatedly resigned from office. However, Yemen's competing power centers could not unify to overcome the country's fragmentary politics. Egged on by outside actors with their own agendas, they pitched Yemen into civil war.

This chapter explores the U.S.-Yemeni counterterrorism partnership over the course of three periods from 2001 to 2016. The partnership focused mainly on U.S.-supported domestic counterterrorism operations by Yemeni forces, the provision of access to the United States, and limited intelligence cooperation. There were no major government initiatives when it came to countering violent extremism; U.S. efforts during the Obama administration are discussed briefly. The first period of cooperation lasted from 2001 to 2004, when incentives and coercion led Yemen to destroy al-Qaeda's networks. This was followed by an interregnum from 2004 to 2006. The second period stretched from 2006 to 2011. Counterterrorism cooperation during this time helped keep the U.S. homeland safe but failed to degrade the al-Qaeda threat. This period ended with the Arab uprisings in 2011. The third period was poised to be more fruitful but stopped abruptly when Yemen descended into civil war in 2015. Cooperation thereafter was severely limited, although the United States remained able to conduct some operations and reluctantly supported the Saudi-led coalition fighting to restore the Yemeni government to power.

GETTING ON BOARD

Following Saleh's pledges of cooperation in the wake of the 9/11 attacks, the United States deployed military trainers to build Yemeni forces' capabilities. Yemen's security apparatus was composed of a series of power centers, most of which Saleh controlled through family members or other allies. The army was hopelessly corrupt and largely inept. Moreover, some of its top leaders were considered too closely connected to Yemen's jihadist community.[20] Saleh pressed the United States to focus on the Special Operations Forces (YSOF) and on the Republican Guard, commanded by his son. U.S. trainers invested heavily in building YSOF's capabilities, which had already received training from the Jordanian military and benefited from more funding and kit relative to the rest of the army.[21] Saleh came to consider these forces too valuable for counterterrorism and rarely used them for this purpose. They became his U.S.-trained and equipped praetorian guard. U.S. (and British) efforts to train and equip the Interior Ministry's Central Security Forces (CSF), led by the president's nephew, built up the CSF counterterrorism force that took the lead in the fight against al-Qaeda.[22]

The Political Security Organization (PSO), Yemen's primary intelligence entity, was infested with veterans of the anti-Soviet jihad. Shortly before Saleh left for the United States, the CIA provided the PSO with information about a list of suspected terrorists. The men fled the country, stoking U.S. suspicions that they had been tipped off.[23] In another instance, U.S. analysts conducting a post-9/11 review of intelligence collected before the attacks uncovered tapes of Abdul Salam Ali al-Hilah, a PSO officer, talking about "airplanes" and an upcoming attack. The U.S. government subsequently alleged Hilah had supported al-Qaeda.[24] Just as it had built a CT division within the Pakistani ISI after 9/11, the United States helped stand up the National Security Bureau (NSB) in Yemen in an attempt to work around the PSO.[25] Another one of Saleh's nephews became the deputy director of the new intelligence service.

U.S. security assistance, which had been paltry before 9/11, increased thereafter and totaled almost $60 million from 2002 to 2004. Most of the aid came in the form of foreign military financing and antiterrorism assistance. Yemen also received excess defense articles from the United States.[26] Some U.S. assistance supported weapons systems the United States had already sold Yemen.[27] CIA Director Tenet arranged for Saleh's government to receive helicopters, eavesdropping equipment, and weapons.[28] The United States provided approximately $15 million worth of computers and scanners to help the Yemenis control their borders, airports, and seaports.[29] This investment was intended to reduce al-Qaeda's ability to use Yemen as a transit and staging point for international operations. Because the *Cole* attack had laid bare Yemen's inability to police its ports or coastal areas, the United States helped stand up a modern coast guard that could patrol the Bab al Mandab Strait, where the Red Sea meets the Gulf of Aden.[30]

Economic aid also increased after 9/11, but not nearly as much as security assistance. It came to approximately $30 million between 2002 and 2004.[31] The U.S. Agency for International Development (USAID), which had closed after Saleh backed Saddam Hussein in the Gulf War, reopened its mission in Yemen in 2003. This was critical because it helped ensure that money was not only appropriated by Congress but also spent by the U.S. embassy. It is also important to note that these small sums of economic aid were augmented by nontraditional assistance. For example, the United States agreed to a debt-forgiveness package in 2002 that reduced Yemen's debt by $75 million.[32] Even so, U.S. economic aid was not sufficient, consistent, or targeted enough to insulate Yemen's deprived areas from becoming future safe havens for al-Qaeda. However, it is also important to note that the challenges in Yemen were substantial. It was a poor country, greatly in need of development, and governed by a corrupt leader who enriched himself at the expense of his citizenry.[33]

In terms of U.S. objectives, the Bush administration was focused on capturing or killing high-value targets, including al-Qaeda's commander in Yemen Abu Ali al-Harithi. U.S. officials mainly wanted Saleh's government to go after these individuals and then to eliminate any residual al-Qaeda infrastructure. The United States also aimed to ramp up its intelligence and military presence in the country.[34] These elements would assist the Yemenis in their counterterrorism efforts while simultaneously giving America the option of scaling up to conduct unilateral operations if the Yemeni security forces were deemed unable or unwilling to do the job.[35] To this end, the United States secured access to fly armed drones over Yemeni territory. In addition to these goals, the FBI also pressed for continued cooperation on the USS *Cole* investigations.[36] After the Iraq war began, U.S. officials urged Saleh's government to interdict would-be foreign fighters as well.

Yemen did not face any specific threats at the time of 9/11 and had no major geopolitical competitors. Tensions with Saudi Arabia historically ran high, but Saudi attempts to stoke instability in Yemen declined after the two countries reached an agreement defining their shared border in 2000.[37] Saleh's primary concern was keeping Yemen's major tribes content enough to maintain stability in the country. His government was not unconcerned about jihadists, having dealt with attacks by the Aden-Abyan Islamic Army (AAIA) in the late 1990s, but al-Qaeda was tolerated, and its members sometimes provided helpful political muscle. As noted earlier, Saleh was seriously concerned about the danger of U.S. military action immediately after 9/11. This, combined with the lure of inducements, led him to cooperate with the United States.

A growing sense of a shared threat from al-Qaeda may have reinforced the regime's commitment once Yemen began cooperating. Al-Qaeda's commander in the country, Abu Ali al-Harithi, spearheaded a series of bombings targeting the Yemeni intelligence and security forces. The bombs don't appear to have been intended to kill but rather to intimidate the regime into ceasing its cooperation with the United States and releasing many of the men it had arrested.[38] Al-Qaeda then attempted a rocket attack against the U.S. embassy in August 2002. The plot failed so miserably that the intended target was not even immediately clear. Saleh may have believed the attackers were gunning for him. He requested and received U.S. assistance in investigating the attack.[39] Two months later, Abd al-Rahim al-Nashiri, al-Qaeda's chief of operations for the Persian Gulf and the mastermind behind the *Cole* bombing, successfully executed a seaborne suicide strike against the MV *Limburg*, a French oil tanker.[40] The attack threatened Yemen's already weak economy and likely reinforced the government's commitment to counterterrorism.[41]

As figure 6.1 suggests, the United States still considered al-Qaeda in Yemen (AQY) to be a greater threat than Saleh did. Nevertheless, had this snapshot been taken before 9/11, AQY likely would have fallen in the lower-right quadrant. More importantly, a pre-9/11 depiction of figure 6.2 would have put AQY in the upper-right quadrant to indicate its utility to Saleh. Once his government began targeting AQY leaders after 9/11, the group's utility declined. Yet the Yemeni president still worried about internal stability. These concerns led him to pursue a policy of catch and release with many lower-level militants.

WILLING AND ABLE ENOUGH

Yemen's campaign against al-Qaeda relied on limited force, combined with assistance from tribal leaders, in its pursuit of high-value targets. The security forces tracked down Harithi, the al-Qaeda commander in Yemen, in December 2001. This was not difficult. He was living openly at his compound. Mohamed Hamdi al-Ahdal (aka Abu Assem al-Mekki), an al-Qaeda financier who was considered another high-value target, was located close by. After attempts to negotiate their surrenders failed, Yemeni forces were deployed to capture them. Security forces traveling in armored personnel carriers were easily detected, and Harithi was long gone when they arrived. The effort to capture Ahdal went even worse. It erupted into a firefight between the security forces and local tribesmen. Nineteen soldiers died.[42] Although the failed efforts to capture the two high-value targets demonstrated some level of commitment, it raised questions about Yemeni capabilities. Moreover, legitimate concerns remained about sympathies for al-Qaeda within the regime and security forces. In the summer of 2002, U.S. intelligence finally located Harithi, who had vanished soon after the failed operation to capture him. While the U.S. and Yemeni governments mustered to respond, U.S. intelligence intercepted a call to the al-Qaeda commander's phone from the Yemeni defense ministry, warning him about the impending operation.[43] Harithi disappeared once again.

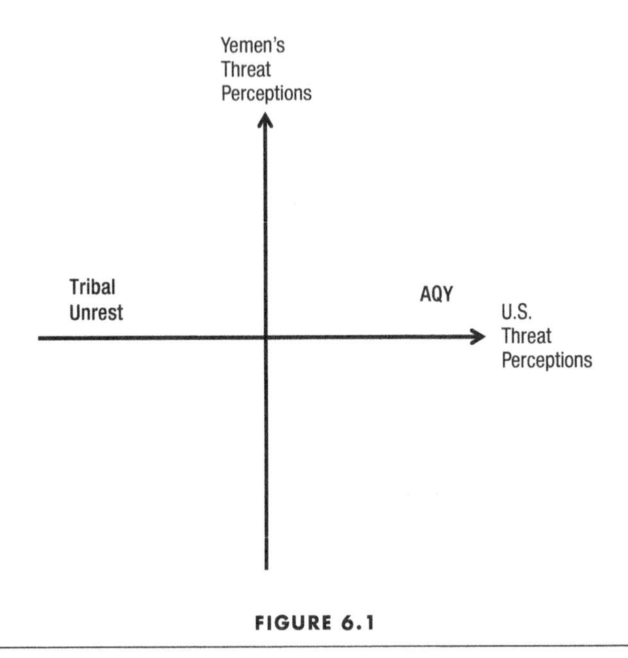

FIGURE 6.1

U.S. and Yemeni Threat Perceptions

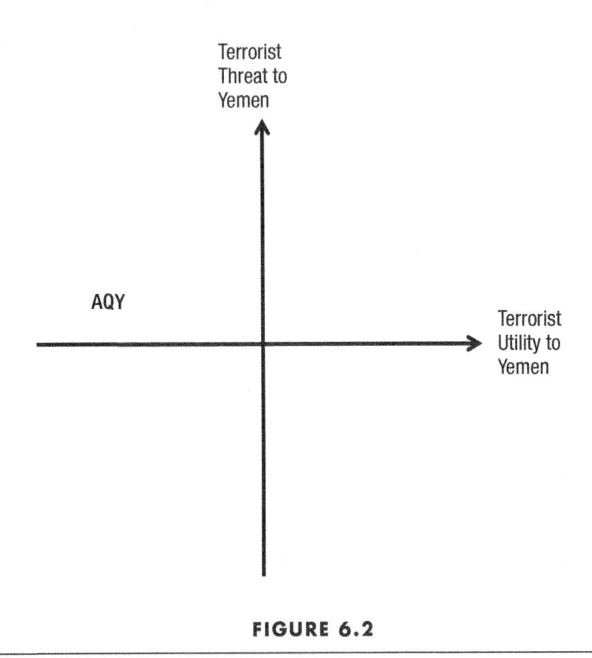

FIGURE 6.2

Terrorist Threat and Utility to Yemen

Efforts to apprehend high-value targets were augmented by sweeps that arrested scores of potential al-Qaeda suspects. These sweeps were intended as much to demonstrate action as to actually weaken al-Qaeda.[44] As the months dragged on with few results, some in the Bush administration began agitating for unilateral combat missions there.[45] The United States built up its military and intelligence presence there, including trainers for the security forces, CIA officers, a cryptologic support group from the National Security Agency, and a small clandestine force from the Joint Special Operations Command (JSOC), whose members entered the country under official cover.[46] JSOC could conduct surgical strikes, but planning always included options for heavy air power in the event U.S. forces were trapped.[47] Unfamiliar terrain and inability to access discretely the remote locations where potential targets might be hiding increased the chances this would occur. As a result, Edmund Hull, the U.S. ambassador, pushed back hard against unilateral action, which he believed could result in heavy civilian casualties.[48]

The first major victory in Yemen resulted from access the United States received. On November 3, 2002, the NSA's cryptologic support group team tracked Harithi via his mobile phone. A JSOC Predator drone launched from Djibouti locked onto Harithi's vehicle and delivered a missile strike, killing him and five others.[49] U.S. involvement was supposed to remain secret.[50] After the car carrying Harithi and his colleagues was obliterated, Yemeni officials contained the site and claimed the men were killed when a bomb they were transporting exploded.[51] Then deputy defense secretary Paul Wolfowitz shot holes through this cover story two days later when he confirmed rumors the United States killed Harithi. Saleh belatedly owned up to the drone strike, claiming it was executed at his request.[52]

Al-Qaeda's chief of operations for the Arabian Gulf was arrested in the United Arab Emirates not long after Harithi was killed, but progress against remaining high-value targets in Yemen was halting.[53] As one Bush administration official said at the time, "We have to hold their [the Yemenis'] feet to the fire to carry through on anything."[54] The army remained inept, and the U.S.-trained Yemeni special forces were kept in the stable because Saleh deemed them too valuable to risk against al-Qaeda. Instead, the CSF's counterterrorism unit took the lead. The government reportedly allowed small groups of U.S. special operations forces and CIA agents to help in "identifying and rooting out al-Qaeda cadres."[55] By the summer of 2003, the security forces had captured Ahdal (mentioned earlier) and Harithi's top two lieutenants. Decapitation strategies are typically more successful when a terrorist entity is highly dependent on one or two leaders. This was the case in Yemen. Al-Qaeda had not built up a resilient network of sophisticated cadres there, and Harithi's death was a major blow. Once the remaining top players were removed, al-Qaeda's networks collapsed.

After the United States invaded Iraq, Yemeni jihadists who escaped the dragnet refocused their efforts abroad. With the al-Qaeda leadership in Yemen destroyed and the United States occupying a country in the heart of the Muslim world, this shift made sense.[56] Plenty of Yemenis who were not part of the jihadist community also went to Iraq. As smuggling networks sprang up to help volunteers reach the Iraqi front, the United States pressed Yemen to crack down. The government outlawed travel to Jordan and Syria (two main entry points into Iraq) without government approval for males under age thirty-five. Many Yemenis still reached Iraq, thanks to poor policing that often bordered on indifference.[57] Others were arrested and incarcerated.[58] In August 2003, as counterterrorism cooperation appeared to be improving, ten suspects in the *Cole* attack escaped from a PSO prison in Aden by digging through a wall. U.S. officials suspected the escapees had help from the inside.[59] It took almost a year, but the top operatives who escaped were finally tracked down, along with several minor players. They were rearrested, prosecuted, and convicted.[60] With that task complete, Yemen ceased to be a priority for the United States.[61]

CATCH AND RELEASE

After 9/11, Saleh's regime ordered hundreds of suspected al-Qaeda sympathizers arrested in order to show it was serious about counterterrorism.[62] Although some suspects stood trial, the lack of either effective counterterrorism laws or evidence in many cases made prosecution challenging.[63] Many detainees came from tribes whose loyalty was needed to maintain stability.[64] Saleh turned to a junior cleric, Hamud al-Hitar, to develop a religious reeducation program that would enable the government to release prisoners and reintegrate them back into society. Yemen's program was a far cry from the sophisticated and expensive one developed by Saudi

Arabia. Hitar was essentially a one-man band. Other clerics wanted little to do with the effort. No research or evaluations were conducted. Scores of men were released beginning in late 2002. Many were given money or jobs.[65] Follow-up was minimal, at best.

Prison radicalization and recruitment is not unique to Yemen. Yet it was especially acute because of the government's revolving-door prison policy and refusal to allow outside monitoring.[66] Some Yemenis arrested trying to go to Iraq were held in the same PSO prison as hardcore al-Qaeda members who were not released through Hitar's program. Al-Qaeda enjoyed such control over their section of the prison that guards were excluded from it.[67] Al-Qaeda leaders preached to their fellow inmates that Saleh claimed to be a Muslim but actually worked for the American government, which was responsible for their collective incarceration.[68] The Iraq war made this argument easier. Prisoners saw the U.S. invasion of Iraq as no different from the Soviet intervention in Afghanistan two decades earlier, except for the fact that Saleh had supported jihad in one case but not the other. This complicated Hitar's deradicalization efforts. Participants argued that if the president did not endorse the Iraq jihad then he must not be a genuine Islamic leader. Hitar failed to convince many of them otherwise. Instead, prisoners were released provided they promised not to stage attacks in Yemen or use Yemen to plot attacks elsewhere.[69] In other words, the religious reeducation and reintegration program became a tacit peace accord between Yemen's jihadist community and the state. Moreover, some men released left prison more committed to the jihadist cause than when they entered because of their exposure to al-Qaeda leaders. Hitar's program ended in 2005 after reports that at least three of its graduates had carried out suicide attacks against U.S. forces in Iraq.[70] U.S.-Yemeni cooperation and relations had deteriorated by this time, and a new threat to Saleh's government had emerged.

DRIFT: THE 2004–2006 INTERREGNUM

In 2002, Sheikh Hussein Badreddin al-Houthi, a dissident cleric based in the northern governorate of Saada near the Saudi border, began organizing protests against Saleh's regime. The protestors were Zaydi Shiite Muslims.

Their grievances stretched back to the 1962 revolution that had brought an end to the millennium-long rule of the Zaydi imamate and to the creation of the Yemeni Arab Republic (North Yemen before unification).[71] The Zaydis were economically and politically marginalized thereafter. Successive regimes supported the import of Sunni Salafism into the north to subvert their influence, contributing to a concomitant fear of religious marginalization. Sheikh Hussein formed the Organization for Youthful Believers to protect Zaydi interests.[72] It focused on reducing sectarian marginalization and securing economic development for Saada, one of the poorest regions in the country.

State fragility was ultimately a political challenge rather than merely a development one. Saleh and his family alone were not to blame for Yemen's political and economic failures, but years of misrule by his regime certainly contributed to them. The government failed to forge an inclusive and legitimate compact with marginalized segments of the society. Disunity extended beyond the north-south divide, and, as was apparent from the aforementioned protests, the government faced challenges to its authority and legitimacy in the north as well as the south. Saleh's regime used patronage to maintain power but did not distribute goods equally. Resources were extracted from various parts of the country but used mainly to benefit the capital Sanaa and the surrounding northwestern highland region. The higher the perceived imbalance in the distribution of resources, the more likely it was that regional identities would strengthened in opposition to a shared national identity.[73] For years, the Zaydis in Saada had been on the short end of the stick.

By 2004, weekly clashes were occurring between the police and Zaydi demonstrators.[74] Saleh dispatched the First Armored Division to deal with Sheikh Hussein's well-armed tribal supporters. The military deployed helicopter gunships, used fighter aircraft to carry out bombing runs, and engaged in collective punishment against the local population. These actions led numerous previously neutral tribesmen to join the rebels, who became known as Houthis, after their leader. Hundreds of Yemeni troops were dead by summer's end. The military lost millions in equipment, including helicopters and planes brought down by rebels armed with shoulder-launched surface-to-air missiles. Houthi losses were probably even higher and included Sheikh Hussein, who was gunned down in September.[75] A tentative ceasefire brought the fighting to an end. It held until March 2005, when fighting erupted once again. This conflict lasted only a month, but it was clear there would be more battles to come.

When Saleh visited Washington in late 2005, he came with a shopping list of weapons he would need for anticipated future conflicts with the Houthis.[76] The Yemeni president thought he would be rewarded for cooperating against al-Qaeda. All of America's high-value targets were dead or in prison. Lower-level suspects were being released, but the security forces continued to target jihadist cells when they popped up.[77] For all his wiliness, Saleh failed to read the Bush administration. Yemen did not matter much to the United States before 9/11. Afterward, the United States viewed it mainly as a battlefield against al-Qaeda. Once that battle was seemingly won, the Bush administration turned its attention elsewhere.

Saleh did not receive the major boost in military assistance he had hoped for. And U.S. officials made clear that the moderate amounts of assistance Yemen did continue receiving was not for use against the Houthis, which Washington considered a domestic problem.[78] After being chastised by then secretary of state Condoleezza Rice about corruption and the need for political reforms, Saleh also learned that Yemen had not qualified for economic assistance from the newly established Millennium Challenge Corporation (MCC).[79] The MCC was established in 2004 to provide assistance to countries deemed eligible based on their performance across a range of political and socioeconomic indicators. Thus, all Saleh appears to have received on his trip was the unintended message that playing the counterterrorism card was the only way to get America's attention.

In February 2006, not long after Saleh returned from the United States and Hitar's deradicalization program ended, twenty-three prisoners, including bin Laden's former personal secretary Nasir al-Wuhayshi and other senior al-Qaeda leaders, escaped from prison. A dozen PSO officers were later convicted for abetting the jailbreak.[80] The escapees reorganized in Yemen's remote tribal areas. Wuhayshi and Fawaz al-Rabi'i, the most senior member of the original al-Qaeda organization in Yemen, began building a more durable successor. Al-Qaeda did not have strong alliances with Yemeni tribes before 9/11 despite U.S. concerns to the contrary. AQY leaders sought to rectify this. They appointed local commanders from major tribes to direct operations in their home districts and encouraged AQY members to marry into local tribes.[81] Building these alliances and blood relations helped ensure that any conflict with the state would not be a two-sided affair because tribes would take revenge if their kin were killed or the security forces launched operations in areas under their control.[82]

The regenerated al-Qaeda entity was more revolutionary than the one destroyed after 9/11. Its leaders recognized that a narrowly global focus was not possible as long as Yemen was cooperating with the United States. Some members of al-Qaeda's old guard in Yemen still favored a tacit non-aggression pact with the regime. In a June 2007 statement, AQY leaders declared that their organization was ready to wage jihad against Saleh's regime and asserted that it was time for the old guard to choose sides.[83] The group released a second statement not long after, demanding that the government release al-Qaeda members still in prison, remove restrictions on travel to Iraq, cease counterterrorism cooperation with the United States and other enemies of Islam, and implement sharia (Islamic law). If Saleh's government did not comply, then al-Qaeda would destroy it.[84]

While AQY was regrouping, the Bush administration remained preoccupied with Iraq. To the degree senior officials focused on Yemen, it was with regard to staunching the flow of foreign fighters to Iraq, addressing the pitfalls of the government's house-arrest system, and securing the extradition of Jamal al-Badawi and Jabir al-Banna.[85] Badawi was involved in the USS *Cole* attack, escaped in the 2003 PSO prison break, and was sentenced to death after being recaptured. Banna was an American citizen wanted by the FBI in connection with the Lackawanna Six, a group of Yemeni-Americans convicted of providing material support to al-Qaeda. Both men were among the twenty-three escapees in the 2006 prison break. Badawi surrendered to Yemeni authorities. Rather than return him to prison, Saleh's government placed Badawi under house arrest on the provision that he promise to give up terrorism. Banna briefly disappeared before turning up in a Yemeni courtroom and claiming that he was a free man thanks to a private deal with Saleh. Bush administration officials were livid. They demanded that Yemeni authorities rearrest and extradite both men.[86] Saleh refused and cited a constitutional ban on extradition.[87]

The MCC had finally approved a $20 million threshold program for Yemen to help it meet standards necessary for a substantially larger economic-development package. Angry about Saleh's treatment of Badawi and Banna, the Bush administration cancelled the threshold program. When Yemen had failed to qualify several years earlier, U.S. officials refrained from giving it a pass on governance because of its counterterrorism cooperation. Now the administration was tacitly linking the two in order to punish Saleh for his intransigence. Hull, the former ambassador, opined, "The linkage was understandable on an emotional level but betrayed shaky logic. In undermining Yemeni reform, the United States was acting against its own best interests."[88] Canceling the MCC undercut Yemeni advocates of political reform and might have made it even more difficult to address some of the underlying risk factors enabling AQY recruitment. It also contributed to growing estrangement between Washington and Saleh's regime, making counterterrorism cooperation with an already difficult partner even harder.

REENGAGING

AQY announced its reemergence in September 2006 with operations against oil facilities that could have crippled Yemen's oil industry had they succeeded.[89] In the summer of 2007, AQY began killing tourists in bombings and gun attacks.[90] The group bombed the U.S. embassy in March 2008, killing two people outside. An attack against a housing compound for American diplomats followed a month later.[91] As the pace of operations quickened, the group's focus expanded to include the government and security forces. AQY attacked army checkpoints, the Central Security Forces, and the presidential palace.[92] In September 2008, AQY militants, including three graduates of Yemen's deradicalization program, launched a second, more sophisticated strike against the U.S. embassy.[93] By this time, the group was not only emerging as a major threat to U.S. citizens and infrastructure in Yemen. It was also on its way to turning the country into a pivotal base linking various jihadist theaters, including Afghanistan, Iraq, and Somalia. Yemen became a place for the rest and refit of foreign fighters and a training ground for militants from other groups.[94] Most notably, the Somali jihadist group al-Shabaab sent members there to learn bomb making and other techniques.[95]

The September 2008 attack on the U.S. embassy was a wake-up call for the United States, which, for the second time in a year, authorized the departure of all nonessential personnel from the embassy.[96] Security assistance jumped to $75 million in 2009.[97] Most of the money came from the Section 1206 authority that Congress created to help build the capacity of foreign partners' national military forces for counterterrorism operations. The increase reflected the renewed AQY threat and the maturation of the 1206 program. However, the repeated departures of U.S. personnel and challenging security climate for those who remained made disbursement more difficult. Moreover, when President Obama took office in January 2009, Admiral Mike Mullen, then chairman of the Joint Chiefs, told him that "adequate plans" still did not exist for dealing with al-Qaeda in Yemen.[98]

Less than a week after Obama's inauguration, AQY announced its merger with remnants of Saudi Arabia's al-Qaeda organization to form al-Qaeda in the Arabian Peninsula (AQAP). Nasir al-Wuhayshi, the Yemeni who had spent years at bin Laden's knee in Afghanistan, led the new organization. Said Ali al-Shihri, a Saudi who had also been in Afghanistan before 9/11 and spent time in Guantanamo Bay before being repatriated to Saudi Arabia, was his deputy.[99] Within a year of its formation, AQAP surpassed core al-Qaeda in terms of the capability to organize centrally directed attacks against U.S. and Western targets. AQAP was not only able to attract foreign recruits to Yemen, where the operating environment was more favorable by this time than in Pakistan.[100] The group also had a master bomb maker named Ibrahim al-Asiri in its ranks. On Christmas Day 2009, the group deployed Umar Farouk Abdulmutallab to bring down a transatlantic airline. Asiri constructed a nonmetallic bomb that Abdulmutallab concealed in his underwear. The explosive passed through airport security undetected and would have brought down the airplane had Abdulmutallab detonated it correctly.[101] A year later, AQAP placed printer cartridges containing explosives on U.S.-bound cargo flights. The attack probably would have succeeded if not for a tip from Saudi intelligence.[102]

AQAP also inspired lone-wolf attacks in the United States. Anwar al-Awlaki, the Yemeni-American cleric who fled the United States in 2002, played a disproportionately large role in the group's inspirational capabilities. Awlaki arrived in Yemen in 2004. The authorities detained him in mid-2006 on a kidnapping charge and released him in December

2007. Awlaki believed the arrest was executed at America's request.[103] Although he ultimately contributed to AQAP's international operations, Awlaki was chiefly a propagandist. Speaking in colloquial, American-accented English in videos posted to YouTube and through writings on his website, Awlaki endorsed terrorism as a religious duty. His calls for individual jihad had influenced almost ninety known extremists in the United States and Europe by 2016.[104] Working with Samir Khan, a Pakistani-American member of AQAP, Awlaki also developed the online English-language magazine *Inspire*. It combined incitement to jihad with operational guidance for how individuals could execute terrorist attacks. The first issue of *Inspire* included an article titled "Make a Bomb in the Kitchen of Your Mom."[105] The Tsarnaev brothers who executed the 2013 Boston marathon bombing used it to build their pressure-cooker bombs.[106]

Befitting a group formed through a merger of members from Yemen and Saudi Arabia, AQAP also targeted both countries in addition to the United States. It managed only a small number of operations against Saudi targets. The group was much more active in Yemen, where it was based and where the operating environment was more conducive to militant activities. In 2009, AQAP leaders created Ansar al-Sharia to facilitate a division of labor between their global terrorist operations and local activities in Yemen. It was essentially a front group, albeit one with a degree of autonomy. A senior AQAP official admitted that "the name Ansar al-Sharia is what we use to introduce ourselves in areas where we work, to tell people about our work and goals, and that we are on the path of Allah."[107] This enabled AQAP to build support among the population, especially local tribes, and thus reduce the chances of an indigenous challenge along the lines of the Sunni Awakening in Iraq.[108] While it aimed to avoid a backlash among the local population, the group did not shrink from clashes with the army, police, and other security forces. AQAP increased the pace and intensity of local attacks in 2010, including a sustained assassination campaign of Yemeni military and intelligence officers who had tortured al-Qaeda members in prison or worked closely with the United States.[109]

The al-Qaeda threat in Yemen festered during the latter half of Bush's second term, but the U.S. government was becoming increasingly concerned about AQY by the time Obama took office. He commissioned a review of U.S. policy toward Yemen and prioritized strengthening counterterrorism cooperation with Saleh's regime.[110] A CIA assessment in 2010 determined that AQAP posed the most urgent terrorist threat to the United States, outpacing the core al-Qaeda organization.[111] President Saleh did not rank the jihadist threat as highly as the United States (figure 6.3). He was more worried about the Houthi rebellion in the north and a burgeoning secessionist movement in southern Yemen. In 2007, Saleh declared "all-out war" on the Houthis, which he viewed as a potential existential danger to his regime.[112] Al-Hirak began as a southern protest movement that sought redress for grievances dating back to unification in 1990. It launched a campaign for secession after the state responded to southerners' demands for better treatment with intimidation and violent repression.[113]

Just as U.S. officials struggled to get Saleh to take the jihadist threat more seriously, he grappled with how to convince America to view the Houthis as a shared enemy. The Yemeni president played up Iranian support for the Houthis and boldly claimed he was fighting them on behalf of the United States.[114] Neither the Bush nor Obama administrations showed any inclination to support Yemen's war against the Houthis, who were motivated by local grievances, not supportive of an Iranian agenda, and had not shown any inclination to attack U.S. targets. Thus, although the United States would arm Yemeni forces to fight against al-Qaeda, it would not support the war against the Houthis. Saleh claimed the U.S. refusal undermined the bilateral relationship.[115] This asymmetry of threat perceptions complicated an already difficult partnership.

Pinning down the Saleh regime's approach to AQY when it reemerged and then to AQAP after the merger is difficult (figure 6.4). AQY members claimed that before they joined forces with Saudi jihadists, his government "asked us to fight against the followers of Imam al-Houthi of Saada. In return, Yemeni security forces will ease the persecution of our members."[116] This accusation is difficult to confirm, although U.S. intelligence and military officials reportedly corroborated it.[117] The Yemeni president also allegedly offered AQAP a truce soon after it formed, promising to refrain from targeting the group if it ceased attacking Yemeni forces. AQAP leaders reportedly rejected the offer, most likely because their organization already enjoyed a permissive security environment and thus had little need to strike a peace accord with the government.[118]

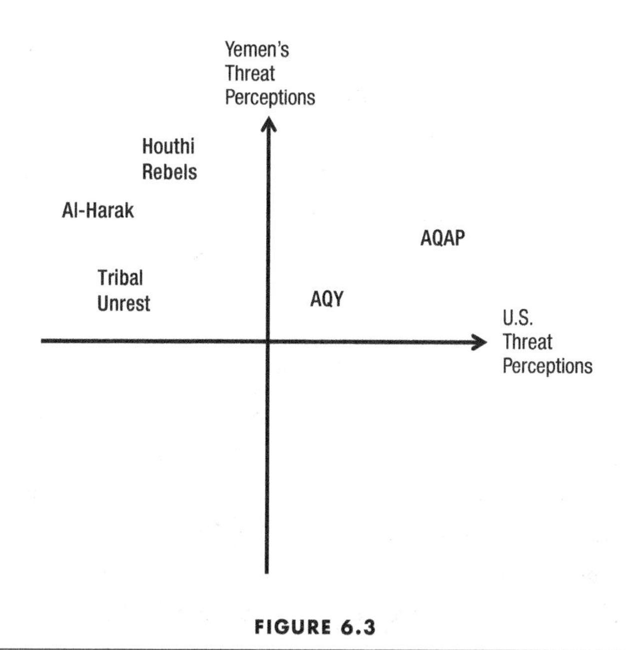

FIGURE 6.3

U.S. and Yemeni Threat Perceptions

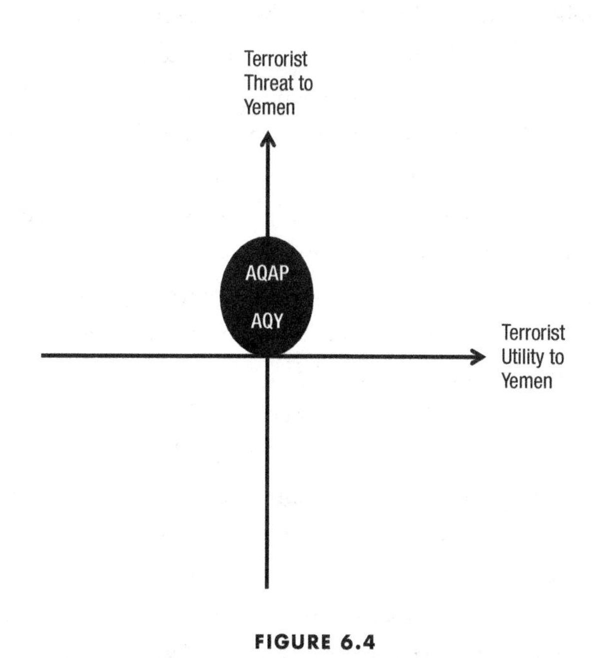

FIGURE 6.4

Terrorist Threat and Utility to Yemen

One could argue that having failed to secure a tacit peace accord (if the evidence is accurate), Saleh's regime had a belligerent relationship with the group but lacked the will or capability to execute an effective counterterrorism campaign. It is also reasonable to suggest that even without a tacit accord, Saleh and some of those closest to him in the government considered AQY/AQAP to have some utility as a vehicle for extracting assistance. Past experience likely led the Yemeni president to conclude the United States was a fickle partner that would only provide assistance were there an active jihadist threat. The fact that U.S. messaging to Yemen focused overwhelmingly on counterterrorism reinforced his assessment, according to current and former U.S. officials.[119] Thus Saleh's regime had a stake in making sure the al-Qaeda threat was never totally resolved. Various elements of the security services, including the PSO, Republican Guard, and the Central Security Forces, are alleged to have provided jihadists with supplies, safe houses, and intelligence.[120] It is unclear whether they were doing so unilaterally or on behalf of the government in order to elevate Washington's threat perceptions and keep aid flowing. The fact that Yemeni jihadists were close to tribal elements Saleh needed to maintain power further complicated dynamics between the government and AQY/AQAP and, in turn, between Washington and Sanaa.[121] At the very least, it is fair to say that Yemen under Saleh combined an economy-of-force counterterrorism effort with willful neglect because the jihadists were useful for extracting assistance, close with tribes that could hurt him, or both. Notably, Saleh's regime was also always ready to exploit jihadist attacks after they occurred. One U.S. official summed it up by saying, "Saleh played both sides and obstructed a lot. He wanted to keep jihadist elements or at least sympathizers placated and remain in our good graces, and he did a pretty good job balancing those two."[122]

The United States had limited leverage. A mix of incentives and coercion led Saleh to cooperate after 9/11. Almost a decade later, his government was committed to doing just enough to keep aid flowing. Meanwhile, the United States was war-weary from the conflicts in Iraq and Afghanistan. It was also clear that major military operations in Muslim-majority countries were a boon for jihadists. As a result, the coercive instruments available to the United States were more limited. Washington could threaten to withhold or cut off aid, but this might further erode stability in

Yemen and lead it to curtail its already limited counterterrorism operations. Punitive actions might also jeopardize access for special operations forces and missile, air, and drone strikes, all of which became more important as Yemeni forces proved unable or unwilling to contain the growing jihadist threat.

DIY COUNTERTERRORISM

The security forces sometimes took the fight to AQY/AQAP, but not with the frequency or skills necessary to keep it on the defensive. They sometimes employed overwhelming firepower during specific engagements, including the use of tanks and helicopters to provide force protection for soldiers conducting raids. On the whole, however, Saleh's government assumed a reactive posture and pursued an economy-of-force mission. The regime sometimes leaned on various tribal leaders to stop providing refuge to jihadists but never developed a coherent strategy or dedicated sufficient resources to isolate them from the local population. For example, after a 2008 suicide car bombing at a military compound in Hadramawt killed and wounded mostly civilians, Yemenis around the country condemned al-Qaeda. Rather than seize the initiative, as the Saudi government had done in 2003, Saleh's regime merely released a lukewarm statement. The cell that planned the attack was only brought to justice because police stumbled onto the safe house where its members were hiding.[123] Far too often, counterterrorism operations were executed only after terrorist attacks occurred or in response to U.S. requests. Yemeni forces did launch several major offensives. The first, in August 2010, followed a spate of assassinations of military and intelligence officials. Another conveniently coincided with a visit by Obama's senior counterterrorism adviser, John Brennan, a month later.[124]

The Obama administration pursued a tripartite approach to Yemen: build the security forces' capacity, employ direct action when necessary, and use targeted economic assistance to chip away at some of the underlying factors that enabled jihadist recruitment. Economic aid, which had never crossed the $15 million threshold before 2008, jumped to over $36 million in 2009 and almost doubled the following year.[125] The United States supported the Friends of Yemen program established in January 2010 to bolster international support for Yemen and assist Yemeni-led efforts to address the underlying causes of instability.[126] However, even tens of millions in economic and development assistance could only do so much in a country rife with corruption and ranked near the bottom of the human-development index.[127] U.S. officials also struggled to implement assistance programs because of the difficult security climate.[128]

President Obama made Yemen a testing ground for his approach of working with and through indigenous security forces while augmenting their efforts with direct action. Despite years of security assistance and training, Yemeni security forces remained largely inadequate. According to one Department of Defense report, Yemeni forces' "inability to conduct precision counterterrorism operations allows Al Qaeda in the Arabian Peninsula to destabilize the region and both indirectly and directly harm U.S. interests."[129] Part of the problem was that train-and-equip efforts had been inconsistently funded and executed for most of the decade. The Obama administration attempted to rectify this with an infusion of security assistance, which skyrocketed from $75 million in 2009 to over $175 million in 2010.[130] Yet challenges to effective capacity building remained. For instance, the fact that the security forces were engaged in multiple internal conflicts complicated training efforts. U.S. officials especially needed to remain on guard for attempts by Saleh's government to redirect training and equipment to support his Republican Guard or operations against the Houthis.[131] Building partner capacity can take years to bear fruit even under the best of circumstances, which clearly did not exist in Yemen. It could be even longer before the United States saw benefits from economic and development assistance—if these materialized at all. This did not mean such efforts were not necessarily worthwhile. But the threat was immediate, and the United States did not have a capable or trustworthy partner.

As the United States ramped up its training of Yemeni forces, it simultaneously sought approval from Saleh to expand joint operations and unilateral strikes against AQAP.[132] General David Petraeus, head of the U.S. military's Central Command, which is responsible for U.S. security interests in twenty states stretching through the Arabian Gulf into Central Asia, visited Yemen in June 2009. He confirmed to Saleh that U.S. military aid would increase, which it did, as noted above, and more vociferously pressed the Yemeni president to go after AQAP. Simultaneously, he and other U.S. officials moved forward with a joint CIA-military effort to target AQAP directly.[133] Several months later, Saleh met with Obama's senior counterterrorism advisor, John Brennan, and approved U.S. operations in Yemen. In return, the Yemeni leader appealed for increased military assistance, which U.S. officials surmised he planned to use against the Houthis. Allowing the United States to conduct its own operations against AQAP was also a way for Saleh to free up his security forces to devote themselves and their limited resources to fighting Houthi rebels. The Yemeni president even boldly proclaimed that because he had granted access for the United States to conduct its own counterterrorism operations he was no longer responsible for future attacks against America or American targets in Yemen.[134] Saleh was essentially attempting to outsource much of the effort against AQAP while also requesting more security assistance in exchange for granting the United States the right to be part of this effort.

The Obama administration increased the number of Joint Special Operations Command (JSOC) forces in Yemen. Their official mission was to train, advise, and assist Yemen forces to conduct counterterrorism operations. In this capacity, U.S. military personnel not only trained their Yemeni counterparts. They also participated in joint ground assaults against AQAP targets, provided helicopter transport for Yemen forces, and deployed personnel undercover to perform reconnaissance.[135] According to one former aide to a senior JSOC leader, "we were training and building the indigenous security forces in Yemen. Simultaneously we were targeting and then killing people who were suspected or had been confirmed to be al-Qaeda extremists in and around the Peninsula, and within Yemen itself."[136]

JSOC and CIA personnel also helped coordinate U.S. air and missile strikes. The United States launched a volley of cruise missiles from ships based off Yemen's coast on two separate occasions in December 2009. These operations marked a significant escalation in the U.S. war against AQAP. Saleh's government claimed the strikes were executed by his air force in an attempt to keep the U.S. role secret. The Yemeni press quickly identified the use of munitions that Yemen's air force did not possess.[137] U.S. officials soon confirmed America's role.[138] The first cruise-missile strike targeted an AQAP training camp but mainly killed Bedouin families living nearby.[139] Cruise missiles are less precise and more lethal than drone strikes, and they take longer to hit their targets from the time they are launched. In early January, President Saleh granted access to Yemeni airspace for U.S. manned and unmanned aircraft to strike when actionable intelligence was available.[140] According to the *Long War Journal*, which tracked data for U.S. air and drone strikes in Yemen, the United States conducted four in 2010.[141]

The United States required more than access to Yemeni territory and airspace. It also needed intelligence. Yemen provided this but could not be trusted to do so on a consistent basis. There were three areas of concern. First, it was unclear whether the Yemeni government, PSO, NSB, and security forces possessed the capacity to collect and willingness to share timely and accurate information. Second, U.S. officials were reluctant to share intelligence because they feared that sympathizers in any of these institutions might tip off the intended targets. Third, an incident in May 2010 led Washington to worry about Yemeni officials using U.S. direct action to settle political conflicts. Acting on Yemeni intelligence, the United States launched a drone strike that killed the deputy governor of Maarib when he was meeting with members of AQAP. It later turned out the deputy was attempting to convince them to surrender, and that he was involved in a feud with members of Saleh's family. U.S. officials believed they got played.[142] While the intelligence relationship still had value, especially with the NSB, the United States also had others ways of collecting intelligence that did not entail relying on the Yemenis.[143]

In addition to access and intelligence cooperation, the administration also sought help on detainees. There were approximately one hundred Yemenis being held at Guantanamo when Obama took office.[144] Closing the detention facility required finding some place to send them. Considering the prison breaks that occurred on Saleh's watch and the faulty rehabilitation program he initiated, U.S. officials did not trust the Yemeni government to take custody of these prisoners. Instead, the United States wanted permission to transfer Yemeni detainees to Saudi Arabia. Saleh rebuffed these requests and demanded not only that the prisoners be repatriated to Yemen but also that the United States and Saudi Arabia fund a rehabilitation center for them.[145] Although he later relented, the Obama administration canceled the scheduled repatriation of over thirty Yemenis because of the "unsettled situation" in Yemen.[146] The situation grew even more unsettled a year later, after the Arab uprisings spread to the country.

A FRESH START GOES ROTTEN

Protests against Saleh's regime began in January 2011. The Yemeni president offered dialogue and promised concessions but hung on to power and directed his security forces to crack down on demonstrators.[147] These efforts failed to suppress the challenge. Instead, the regime's violence contributed to schisms within the ruling party, the military, and security forces along the lines of different powerbrokers.[148] The United States suspended military training in February and withheld most other security assistance to ensure it would not be used against peaceful protesters.[149] Yet U.S. officials refrained from publicly pressuring Saleh to moderate his behavior or step down from power because he was considered a critical counterterrorism partner.

Saleh's position and U.S. support for him became untenable by April, at which time Washington stepped up efforts to help arrange a transfer of power that would not impair ongoing counterterrorism cooperation.[150] The Gulf Cooperation Council brokered a deal in November that paved the way for a political transition and included amnesty for Saleh and close members of his circle. He stepped down in February 2012, after which U.S. military assistance and training resumed. Vice President Abd-Rabbu Mansour Hadi was elected president for a two-year period. The UN-sanctioned National Dialogue Conference (NDC) was established to address the nation's manifold political challenges and longstanding regional divisions.[151] Once the NDC process was complete, the transitional government would oversee the drafting of a new constitution.

AQAP took advantage of the security vacuum created by Saleh's response to the Arab uprisings and launched an offensive in southern Yemen in early 2011. A belated Yemeni counteroffensive backed up by U.S. drone strikes and intelligence support helped halt AQAP's advance, but the group still retained control over parts of two governorates in the south.[152] It began the slow process of building credibility among the population by providing security, social services, and the administration of justice.[153] AQAP also recruited new members, many lured by the promise of a decent salary.[154] These efforts were conducted under the Ansar al-Sharia banner to avoid the baggage that came with the al-Qaeda brand. Governing territory provided the group with an opportunity to experiment with how far it could go in terms of imposing its interpretation of sharia. The AQAP leadership was divided between maximalists, who argued for rigid enforcement of the group's concept of Islam, and gradualists, who favored a step-by-step approach.[155] Although the group theoretically took what its leader considered a tolerant approach to sharia enforcement, in reality, summary executions, amputations, and violence against locals who challenged strict religious mores were not uncommon.[156]

The Yemeni government's threat perceptions shifted dramatically once Saleh was ousted. President Hadi made it a top priority to combat AQAP and increased counterterrorism cooperation with the United States (figures 6.5 and 6.6).[157] His government also took seriously the threat from an ISIS affiliate (ISIS Yemen Province, or ISIS-YP) that emerged in 2014. Hadi's posture was heavily influenced by the fact that AQAP had seized control of Yemeni territory, whereas the Houthi and Hirak threats appeared to have dissipated once Saleh left power and political reforms got underway. The interim president's enthusiasm for counterterrorism cooperation was also a function of the fact that he lacked a natural constituency and thus was reliant on U.S. and international support to maintain his position.

Hadi deployed the security forces to retake the territory under AQAP control. They benefited from U.S. air support and from cooperation with locals who were displeased with the jihadists' harsh form of governance and created popular committees to fight them.[158] He also granted the United States broad permission to conduct drone strikes.[159] After launching nine strikes in 2011, including one that killed Anwar al-Awlaki, the United States executed fifty-six in 2012.[160] This withering assault, combined with the security forces' ground operations, forced AQAP to abandon the territory under its control after losing approximately five hundred men.[161] But the drone strikes also helped fuel jihadist recruitment. In Pakistan, al-Qaeda was a foreign organization, and young men seeking revenge for drone strikes predominantly joined local organizations. In Yemen, angry tribesmen

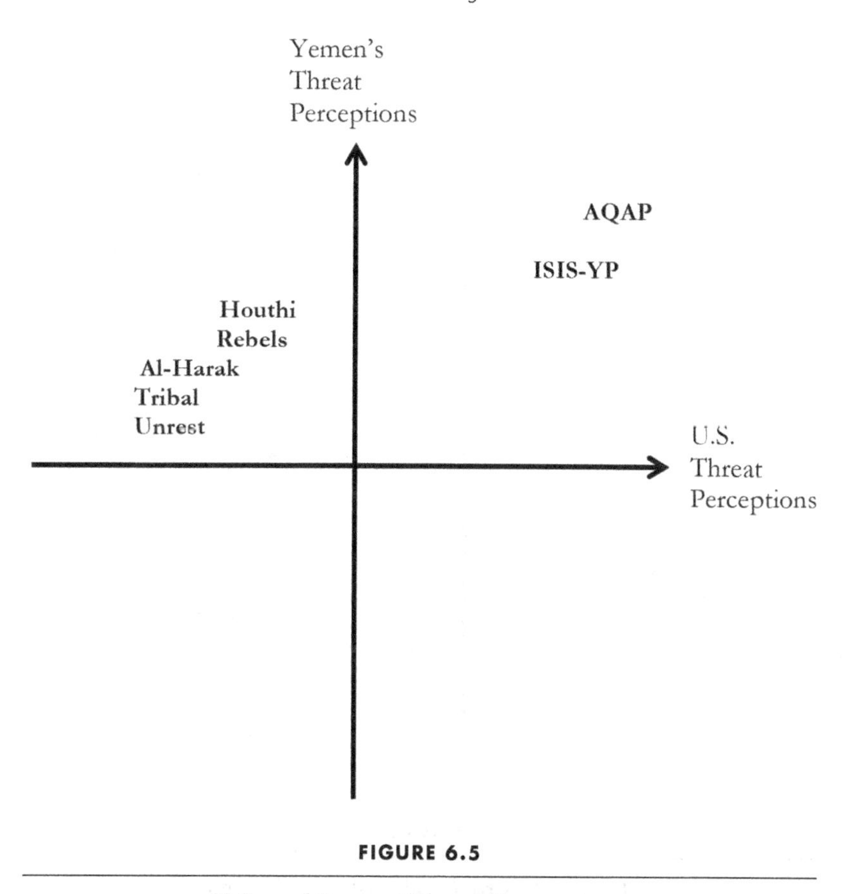

FIGURE 6.5

U.S. and Yemeni Threat Perceptions

signed up with AQAP or its parochial analogue Ansar al-Sharia.[162] Of course, not all militants are created equal, and some U.S. officials probably would have traded an influx of locals for eliminating experienced members who helped make the group a transnational terrorism threat.[163]

In addition to launching a domestic campaign against AQAP and increasing access, Hadi also followed through on U.S. requests to pursue security-sector reform.[164] While Saleh was in power, the United States worked with him and family members and loyalists in the security establishment when it had to and worked around them where it could. Hadi took steps to reorganize the military, sacked Saleh's family members and other loyalists, and pursued various other reforms once in office.[165] He also pledged to U.S. officials that he would do more in the way of military and

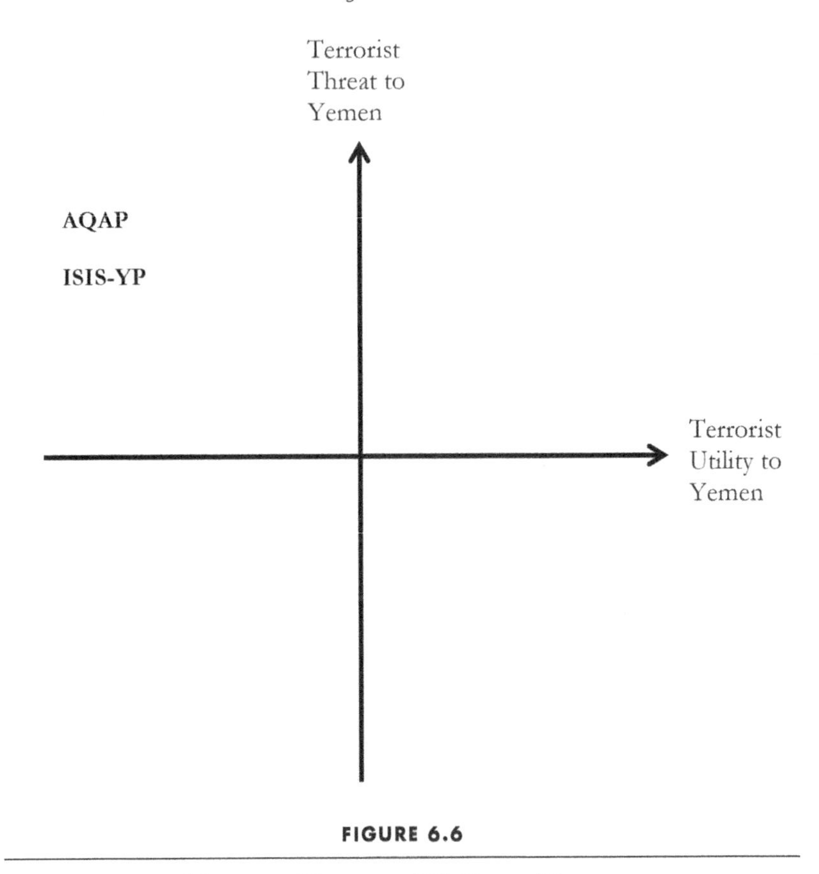

FIGURE 6.6

Terrorist Threat and Utility to Yemen

intelligence oversight. These were essential steps for improving the efficacy of U.S. capacity-building efforts and putting Yemen on a path toward becoming a more functional country. As a result, years of U.S. security assistance finally began to pay off once Hadi made these changes.[166] The United States was at long last getting from Hadi the type of counterterrorism cooperation it had long been denied while Saleh was in power. Then it all fell apart.

The NDC process was beset by political and structural problems from the outset, including the exclusion of the Houthis and Hirak movement, who were unhappy with the resultant contours of the new federal system.[167] Saudis Arabia, which was heavily involved and influential in the GCC-led transition process, encouraged Hadi's hard line against the Houthis.[168] The United States did not push back vigorously against their exclusion. One former U.S. official acknowledged the United States could have done more to urge accommodation of the Houthis before the Arab uprisings and certainly during the NDC process.[169] While the rest of the government and security forces were preoccupied with Saleh's fate and then with rolling back AQAP's advances, the Houthis consolidated power among the northern tribes.[170] In 2014, unhappy with the outcome of the dialogue process, the Houthis started making their way southward. They bested the military in a series of clashes and entered the capital in September.[171]

Houthi leaders were not initially seeking to topple the Hadi government. Instead, they negotiated a National Partnership Plan with it. This plan established a more technocratic government and created mechanisms to address unresolved political and economic issues.[172] The situation appeared resolved, but it deteriorated after some Houthi leaders began agitating for more power. They put Hadi under house arrest in January 2015, catalyzing a confrontation. Some forces in the military backed the president. Others remained loyal to Saleh, whose family members had been allowed to keep their positions in the military and security services as part of the deal brokered by the Gulf Cooperation Council. Saleh leveraged these connections and forged an alliance with his onetime nemesis, the Houthis.[173] His support enabled them to control elements of the Yemeni military and provided a decisive advantage over forces loyal to Hadi, who fled the capital and then the country for Saudi Arabia.[174]

Riyadh had already clashed with the Shiite Houthis on its southern border and viewed them as a cat's paw for Iran, which was providing the rebels with material support.[175] Acceptance of arms and training did not indicate political compliance with Iranian aims, and the Houthis rarely defined their struggle in sectarian terms. Rather than confessional identity, the Houthi movement was motivated by local grievances.[176] This did not keep Tehran from claiming credit for the Houthis' success in driving Hadi from power or stop Riyadh from overreacting.[177] Saudi Arabia, which had previously launched airstrikes against the Houthis in response to cross-border raids into the kingdom, led a military intervention to roll back the Houthis and restore Hadi to power. The Saudi-led intervention helped turn a local power struggle into a regional and sectarian conflict. Yemen slid into civil war and ceased functioning as a unitary state.

Washington closed the U.S. embassy, which was the primary base for U.S. intelligence operations in Yemen, in February 2015. CIA and military personnel, including senior officers who worked closely with Yemen's intelligence and security services to target al-Qaeda operatives, were among the many Americans evacuated.[178] The last 125 U.S. special operations advisors left the following month.[179] Because the United States was not solely reliant on the Yemenis for intelligence, drone strikes did not abate entirely. In June 2015, as civil war raged on the ground, a drone strike killed AQAP's leader Nasir al-Wuhayshi.[180] But U.S. direct action was not enough to keep the group from expanding amid the chaos of the conflict.

Counterterrorism cooperation ground to a halt after the Houthis toppled Hadi because there was no host-nation government with which to partner. Houthi forces in concert with forces loyal to former president Saleh and backed by Iran controlled northwestern Yemen, including the capital.[181] Forces loyal to Hadi backed by the Saudi-led coalition retreated to the south and east. America still considered AQAP the biggest threat in Yemen, followed by ISIS-YP, but other parties to the conflict did not share this perception. Hadi's forces and his coalition backers prioritized defeating the Houthis. AQAP, which operated in the same areas as Hadi's forces, exploited the sectarian tensions and security vacuum that resulted during the civil war to retake territory: it seized control of Mukalla, which is the capital city of the Hadhramaut coastal region, and governed through local proxies from April 2015 to April 2016.[182]

AQAP had never been motivated by an anti-Shiite agenda, but it adopted one after the Houthi takeover. It did not jettison its revolutionary or global objectives; instead, it conflated them with sectarianism.[183] This served two important purposes. First, ISIS had burst onto the scene by this time, fueling and feeding off the sectarian current flowing in the region. It was seeking to build up its presence in Yemen. Promoting a sectarian agenda helped AQAP head off an ISIS challenge. Second, appealing for Sunni unity against the Houthis enabled AQAP to make inroads among the population. Sunni communities that previously had resisted the group started to see AQAP as a useful counterweight to the Houthis.[184] The exiled government and its backers in the Saudi-led coalition sometimes did, as well. AQAP fighters have fought alongside coalition and Hadi government forces against the Houthis and were sometimes integrated into their ground units.[185]

Once Yemeni forces loyal to the government backed by the Saudis shored up control of southern Yemen, Hadi's government attempted to reconstitute. The United States established a small special operations presence along the coast, where they worked with Emirati troops to keep tabs on AQAP.[186] The United Arab Emirates, which had initially focused mainly on fighting the Houthis, transitioned to put more emphasis on the battle against the jihadists. In late 2016, U.S. forces worked with Emirati troops to evict AQAP from Mukalla.[187] Yet by this time the group had accumulated a war chest of approximately $100 million in money taken from banks and revenue raised from administering the Mukalla port and selling oil on the black market. AQAP fighters had also looted abandoned army bases and loaded up on advanced weaponry, including shoulder-fired missiles and armored vehicles.[188] And although AQAP had been evicted from Mukalla, it still had robust zones of support in southern Yemen.

After countless attempts at UN-led negotiations failed, the Obama administration pressed the key parties—the Saudis, the Houthis, and the Yemeni government—to accept a roadmap for ending the conflict. However, the fighting continued, and the country remains riven at the time of writing. Hadi was not the only spoiler, but he was one of them. The man who once had been such a promising partner repeatedly scuttled deals because they would have required him to leave office. Hadi's Saudi patrons, who kept him under house arrest in Riyadh, were unwilling to compel him to agree and were themselves quick to make unreasonable demands that prolonged the conflict.[189] Meanwhile, with none of the main players prioritizing counterterrorism operations against AQAP or ISIS-YP, both groups had plenty of space to operate.

* * *

At a dinner in the White House residence five days after taking the oath of office, President Trump gave his conditional go-ahead for a risky raid on an AQAP compound. He officially signed off the next day.[190] U.S. Navy SEALs and special forces from the United Arab Emirates were detected as they advanced on the AQAP compound. An intense firefight broke out, leaving one SEAL dead and another three injured. A U.S. airstrike called in during the fighting killed numerous civilians. Hadi's government in exile suspended permission to the United States to mount ground operations but quickly backtracked.[191] The botched raid and its aftermath focused immediate attention on the risks related to conducting aggressive military operations. It also highlighted the degree to which AQAP had used the civil war in Yemen to entrench itself further in the country, the difficulty of conducting operations where intelligence is lacking, and the need to continue targeting the group directly despite these challenges. Also lost in the background was the rising civilian death toll from the conflict, a surging cholera outbreak, and widespread famine that, combined, made Yemen the largest single-nation humanitarian crisis in the world.[192]

Yemen had once appeared to be a success story, at least when it came to counterterrorism. The Bush administration successfully employed incentives and coercion to secure cooperation that led to the destruction of al-Qaeda's networks in the country. However, it quickly turned its attention elsewhere and invested little to ameliorate the conditions that could enable al-Qaeda to regenerate. In the meantime, the Saleh regime confronted new threats from Houthi rebels. His appeals for assistance were denied, a move that may have led him to conclude that the presence of an active jihadist threat was the key to maintaining U.S. support. The Bush administration reengaged once al-Qaeda reemerged, but Saleh's government faced greater threats from Houthi rebels and a southern secessionist movement.

Al-Qaeda in the Arabian Peninsula announced its merger days after Obama took office. He made combating the group a priority but inherited an incredibly problematic partner who had an incentive in making sure the jihadist threat was never extinguished.

Counterterrorism cooperation improved considerably once Saleh was ousted. The U.S. partnership with the Hadi government became a model of what President Obama aspired to: local forces, supported with security assistance and backed up by direct action, taking the fight to the enemy. Yet the fundamental structural problems in Yemen, many of which stretched back before unification, could not be overcome. The United States kept AQAP from striking the American homeland without putting American troops on the ground in considerable numbers, but it was unable to prevent

Yemen's descent into chaos. AQAP seized on the conflict to prove it could "govern" and provide basic services, deepen its ties with local tribes, and integrate its fighters with some of the forces fighting against the Houthis.

With forces loyal to the Hadi government and the Saudi-led coalition backing him focused primarily on the Houthis, this has left the United States to rely on airstrikes and commando raids like the one Trump approved soon after taking office. U.S. operations against AQAP began to ramp up again during Obama's last year in office and have gained steam under Trump. The United States conducted over 100 strikes against AQAP between January and October 2017, in addition to raids carried out by U.S. special operations forces against high-value targets.[193] The U.S. military has also begun targeting ISIS-YP fighters in Yemen.[194]

This escalation has been accompanied by intensifying U.S. efforts against the Houthis. There appear to be at least three reasons for this. First, Iran's campaign in Yemen has led it to supply the Houthis with antiship cruise missiles that endanger freedom of maritime navigation in and around the Arabian Peninsula.[195] Ensuring the flow of commercial vessels, especially ones carrying oil and gas, is a critical U.S. interest, which the Houthis had become able to threaten.[196] Second, supporting the Saudi-led intervention led the United States to become drawn it into the civil war. The Houthis launched missile attacks against the USS *Mason* near the Bab al Mandab Strait in October 2016, leading the U.S. military to destroy three radar sites in Yemen in response.[197] A year later, a U.S. drone was shot down in territory under the Houthis' control where jihadists are not known to operate.[198] Third, the United States appears to be increasingly prioritizing the Iranian threat, as discussed at the end of the last chapter.

It is unclear how far Trump is willing to go in terms of escalating U.S. involvement in the civil war. It is clear that despite U.S. military operations, AQAP and ISIS-YP are still exploiting the conflict to strengthen their position. They are likely to continue doing so until a political settlement is reached that allows the United States, Saudi-led coalition, and Yemeni forces to focus on combating them.

7

MALI

The Weakest Link

IN 2002, A YEMENI LINKED to the USS *Cole* attack arrived in Mali. His name was Emad Abdelwahid Ahmed Alwan, and he was an emissary dispatched by al-Qaeda to assess the Sahel as a potential new base for operations. With its weak states, porous borders, and expanses of sparsely populated territory, the Sahel had all the makings of a potential jihadist sanctuary. The security capacity of states there was substantially lower than in Algeria or other North African countries, corruption was endemic, and conflicts between central governments and minority ethnic groups were common.[1]

Alwan met with two commanders from the Salafist Group for Preaching and Combat (GSPC): a one-eyed militant named Mokhtar Belmokhtar and Amari Saifi, who was known as al-Para because he had been an Algerian paratrooper.[2] Both were Algerians, part of a large cohort of jihadists who grew disillusioned with the Armed Islamic Group (Groupe Islamique Armé, or GIA), which had been the main jihadist organization and most militarily powerful nonstate actor in the Algerian civil war that had raged during the 1990s. After the GIA engaged in numerous civilian massacres from 1996 to 1998, this cohort broke away to form the GSPC. The GIA had since fizzled, but the GSPC was still active in Algeria as of late 2017. Belmokhtar and Amari Saifi were part of a GSPC contingent that came to northern Mali before 9/11 in search of new supply lines to support the war effort and to carve out a sanctuary.

Al-Qaeda's emissary, Alwan, was killed en route to meet with the GSPC leadership in Algeria. There are indications that he might have been helping to plan an attack on the U.S. embassy in Mali's capital, Bamako, at the time of his death.[3] His appearance in the region rattled U.S. officials already worried that the Sahel might become a new al-Qaeda safe haven. According to one former U.S. intelligence official, "after 9/11 the U.S. thought we'd squeezed the toothpaste in Afghanistan and these guys were just going to squirt into all these different ungoverned spaces."[4] The presence of a GSPC battalion, which operated in the undergoverned territory that stretched across southern Algeria, northern Mali, and into Mauritania, reinforced these fears. Although Mali had no indigenous jihadist movement, the number of Salafi missionaries from the Gulf was also growing in northern Mali, and money coming in from Saudi Arabia was increasing.[5]

The U.S. European Command, which was responsible for Africa at the time, pressed for action in the Sahel.[6] U.S. special operators began conducting reconnaissance there in 2002.[7] A year later, Amari Saifi kidnapped thirty-two European tourists in southern Algeria and held them for ransom in northern Mali. He released his hostages in exchange for roughly €5 million and invested much of the money to enhance GSPC smuggling networks and reinforce relationships with local power brokers.[8] The U.S. military tracked Saifi and considered targeting him with a drone strike. Instead, the United States helped facilitate his capture.[9] Around the same time, the military also started tracking Belmokhtar and proposed launching either an operation to capture him at a training camp in northern Mali or airstrikes against him.[10] Belmokhtar had established an elaborate smuggling network in the region and used the money he made to acquire weapons for the GSPC in Algeria.[11] He was clearly a bad guy. But he had never threatened the United States. And U.S. officials in Bamako feared that an operation could catalyze a backlash against America. For these reasons, the U.S. ambassador to Mali vetoed the operation and the U.S. government refrained from pursuing direct action.[12]

The Bush administration wanted to roll back the GSPC, prevent al-Qaeda from relocating to the Sahel, and keep the region from becoming a launching pad for international terrorist attacks. Other than that, America did not have any real national security interests there. Countries in the region were not requesting American forces, and the threat to the United

States was not sufficient to warrant pressuring the region's leaders to accept them. Instead of a taking military action, the Bush administration opted to assist local forces in doing the fighting themselves.

All of the countries in the Sahel lacked the capacity to execute counterterrorism operations against the GSPC. Mali also lacked the political will. The United States wanted Bamako to police its own territory. As with Yemen, Washington was not looking for it to take action beyond its borders or change its foreign policy. However, even keeping jihadists off its soil was too much for the Malian government. It viewed the Tuareg tribes in the north as a much bigger threat than the GSPC and was wary of taking any action against the group that could destabilize the area. This contributed to Bamako's decision to pursue a tacit peace accord with the jihadists.

Like the other cases in this book, Mali illustrates the importance of a partner nation's security paradigm. This is most apparent in terms of the government's prioritization of the local ethnic threat at the expense of the jihadist one. Mali also provides a useful contrast to the other case studies discussed so far, which involve countries considered essential for achieving U.S. counterterrorism objectives. Although the U.S. government described Mali as a key counterterrorism partner in West Africa, it was not treated as a frontline state. The United States did not consider the GSCP a top-tier threat, and Mali had no strategic significance. This remained the case even after the GSCP joined al-Qaeda in September 2006 and became al-Qaeda in the Islamic Maghreb (AQIM) the following year. (For the purpose of clarity, I use GSPC when referring to the group before 2007, AQIM when discussing it thereafter, and either GSPC/AQIM or "the jihadists" in instances where overlaps between the two time periods occur.) It was also the case that Mali was the democratic darling of the region and often viewed through a development lens rather than a counterterrorism one. America and other Western countries held up Mali as an island of political freedom on a coup-ridden continent.[13]

After a coup in 1991 ended twenty-three years of military rule, Mali's new leaders created a multiparty system, put in place a constitution that guaranteed a separation of powers, and held elections the following year. Presidential elections were held every five years thereafter, the press was relatively free, and Malians enjoyed freedom of speech and assembly. Despite these positive steps, good governance and rule of law were seriously deficient. Corruption was rampant, and the country ranked incredibly low on the Human Development Index.[14] The socioeconomic situation was especially dire in northern Mali, where the Tuaregs, who were a minority population, were located. As in Yemen, state fragility was ultimately a political challenge as well as a development one. The Malian government failed to forge an inclusive and legitimate compact with its entire citizenry, leaving some segments of society marginalized. These deficiencies contributed to the indigenous security challenges Mali faced and created opportunities that GSCP/AQIM exploited.

Because jihadist groups in Mali were not a top-tier threat for the United States, officials believed that they had time and space to build Mali's counterterrorism capacity through train-and-equip efforts. The United States also attempted to counter violent extremism—the Malian government facilitated these efforts as well as ones by civil society organizations, but it did little on its own. Studying these initiatives affords an opportunity to explore the pitfalls of inconsistent security cooperation and the dangers of corruption and weak rule of law when it comes to creating conditions that make it more difficult to combat jihadists. This discussion is broken into two time periods after 9/11, based on evolving U.S. and Malian threat perceptions. The third time period begins with the 2012 conflict that erupted in northern Mali and paved the way for jihadists to seize and govern large swaths of territory.

A BLIND EYE

The biggest security threat to the Malian government came from the Tuaregs, not jihadists. Tuareg tribes dwell in numerous Sahelian countries and are traditionally nomadic, although many became sedentary over time. The Tuaregs' largest concentration is in northern Mali, where they have long sought regional autonomy. Some Tuareg tribes resented their incorporation into Mali after its independence from France in 1960 in part because they were separated from kin in other countries.[15] Ethnic divisions in Mali exacerbated animosity between the Tuareg and the government in Bamako. The Tuareg were one of four main ethnic groups in northern Mali. The Mandé was the dominant ethnic group in the south, typically the best educated in the country, and the main contributor to the country's ruling elite.[16] Well before Mali's independence, Tuaregs had helped enslave black Africans. This contributed to the view held by many in the Mandé-dominated government that formed after independence that the Tuareg were racist and reactionary. Many Tuareg are light-skinned and viewed themselves as being Arab rather than African. Segments of the Tuareg population chafed at being ruled by black southerners.[17] Successive governments in Bamako pursued policies that further alienated the Tuaregs. Malian leaders failed to invest in the north, where the poverty rate was substantially higher than in the south.[18]

Economic and political grievances, combined with ethnic and cultural divisions, led Tuareg tribes to rebel twice before 9/11: first in 1963–1964 and again on and off in 1990–1996. In addition to these grievances and divisions, the ambitions of individuals, groups, clans, and tribes in northern Mali pursuing their own parochial agendas also helped catalyze the rebellions. The armed forces brutally suppressed the 1963–1964 rebellion, and the government placed the Tuareg-populated northern regions of Gao, Kidal, and Timbuktu under a repressive military administration. The second rebellion died down after Algeria mediated the Tamanrasset Accords in January 1991. The government and rebels signed the National Pact of Reconciliation the following year. Bamako failed to deliver on funds promised to the north as part of the peace process, and the army continued its repressive behavior.[19] Violence flared again in 1994 and continued until 1996. Hostilities ceased that year, but tensions remained high.[20] The National Pact of Reconciliation promised integration of the Tuareg into the armed forces and economic development for northern Mali, among other things.[21] Promised economic programs and new infrastructure never materialized. Despite its democratic bona fides, Mali was poorly governed and corrupt.[22] A considerable portion of the millions of dollars that America and other international donors poured into Mali never made its way to the people.[23] This was especially true in the north, where major Tuareg towns remained virtually inaccessible.

The government's failure to follow through on agreed-upon reforms, combined with internecine competition among some Tuareg leaders, contributed to the outbreak of a third Tuareg rebellion on May 23, 2006. The conflict began when Tuaregs who had previously been integrated into the Malian army as officers led attacks against army outposts. Other Tuareg rebel commanders soon joined the fight. They formed the May 23 Democratic Alliance for Change (ADC) and demanded that Bamako honor the provisions of the National Pact, which ended the rebellion in the 1990s. The Algiers Accord signed by the government and ADC in July 2006 renewed some of these provisions and was intended to end the fighting.[24] When Bamako's implementation of the accord stalled, some ADC commanders broke away and renewed their rebellion. Fighting spread beyond northern Mali into other parts of the country. A combination of battlefield victories by the Malian army and the fragmentation of the Tuareg alliance led to the rebellion's end in 2009.[25]

Bamako's appeasement policy regarding GSPC/AQIM must be understood within the context of the repeated Tuareg rebellions and the group's own history. Bamako perceived the Tuareg to be a much greater threat than the one posed by the jihadists and feared that sending military units into northern Mali to combat them would upset the fragile détente with Tuareg tribes.[26] Once another rebellion erupted in 2006, this further militated against confronting the jihadists because the armed forces were preoccupied with a greater threat. Because the GSPC had expanded into the Sahel to support its jihad back home against the Algerian regime, Mali's leaders did not view it as a real threat to their country and were reluctant to take actions that could turn it into one. Moreover, the government of Amadou Toumani Touré, who became Mali's president in 2002, considered the jihadists to be an Algerian export and therefore Algeria's problem.[27] Touré actually gave Algeria the right to launch operations against the group up to one thousand kilometers into Malian territory.[28] The Algerians never took advantage of this offer, for a variety of reasons discussed in the next chapter. However, the fact that Touré was prepared to allow Algerian forces to operate in his country suggests he either adamantly believed that it was not Mali's responsibility to deny the jihadists safe haven or was firmly opposed to fulfilling this responsibility.

Despite the fact that Bamako was clearly guilty of turning a blind eye to jihadist activities, neither the Bush nor Obama administrations attempted to coerce it into executing counterterrorism operations or turned to unilateral direct action. This fact highlights the importance of U.S. threat perceptions, which informed American objectives and the tools used to achieve them. As figure 7.1 illustrates, the United States was more concerned about GSPC/AQIM than Bamako was, especially after the merger with al-Qaeda, but even then did not consider the group to be a top-tier threat. The United States also did not seek to use Malian territory as a transit point or base for regional action. Nor did Washington seek robust intelligence cooperation.[29] Mali rarely had intelligence to share, according to current and former U.S. officials. Indeed, much of the threat information the United States collected reportedly came from open-source reporting produced by the American-sponsored Native Prospector program, which relied on Malian nationals who aggregated information from local sources.[30]

It is unclear whether the Touré government's nonaggression pact with the jihadists was actually, if informally, negotiated or if the peace accord was implicit. In either case, while Bamako did not view the GSPC/AQIM as a threat, it also did not see the group as having utility to the state (figure 7.2). There are rumblings that Touré or other state actors sometimes colluded with the GSPC/AQIM to subvert Tuareg militants.[31] However, even if true, this does not appear to have been a consistent policy, and the government did not actively support the group or deliberately create or sustain an infrastructure to enable it. This does not mean that GSPC/AQIM was not useful to individuals in positions of power. It became a useful vehicle for personal enrichment for them. Political elites, military and intelligence officers, and allied power brokers and militias in northern Mali benefited financially from criminal activities that the GSPC/AQIM was also involved in. Although the financial benefits of collusion were not an initial determinant of the government's policy toward the jihadists, they ultimately reinforced the tendency toward appeasement rather than confrontation. Moreover, this collusion was linked to broader patterns of corruption in northern Mali, which further militated against doing anything about the jihadist problem.

A BAND-AID ON A BULLET WOUND

The United States launched the Pan-Sahel Initiative (PSI) in late 2002 to build the capacity of the armed forces in Mali, Mauritania, Niger, and Chad. A total of $7.75 million was allocated to train and equip six

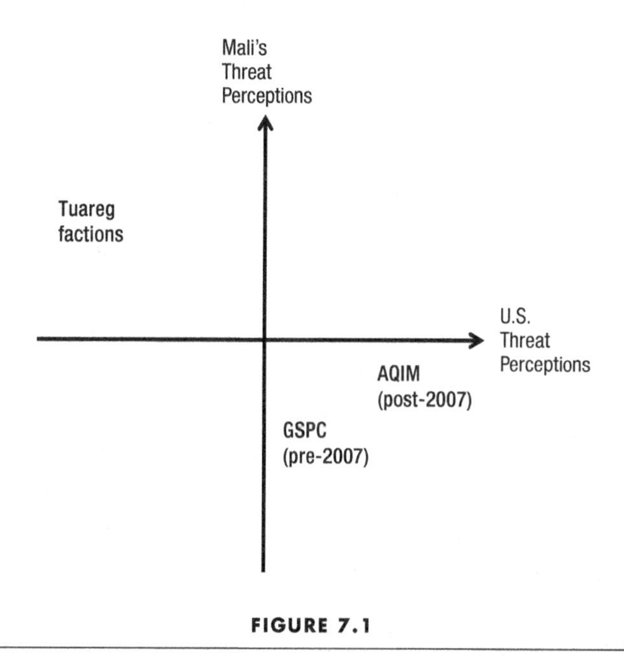

FIGURE 7.1

U.S. and Malian Threat Perceptions

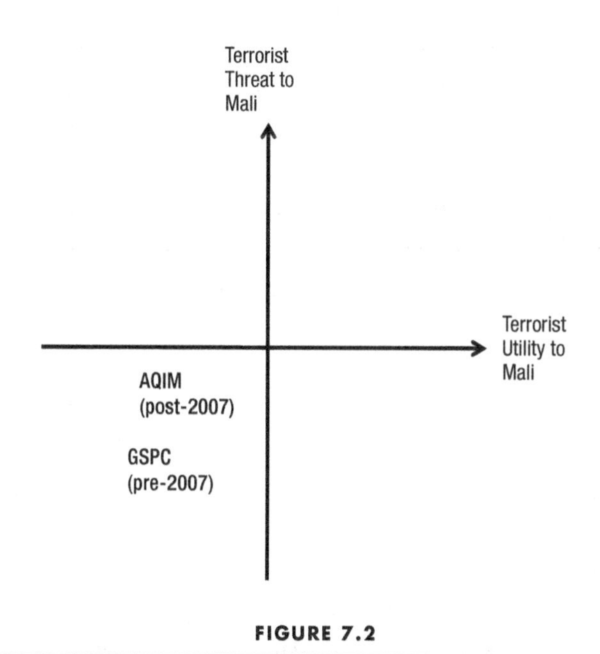

FIGURE 7.2

Terrorist Threat and Utility to Mali

company-sized (about 150 soldiers each) rapid-reaction counterterrorism forces in the four countries.[32] The money did not begin flowing until 2004.[33] A year later, the United States replaced the PSI with the Trans-Saharan Counterterrorism Partnership (TSCTP), which was better funded and more comprehensive. The TSCTP grew geographically to include Algeria, Burkina Faso, Morocco, Nigeria, Senegal, and Tunisia along with the original PSI countries. It also expanded functionally to include development and diplomacy programs in addition to security cooperation. These new efforts were intended to address the perceived socioeconomic risk factors that enabled terrorists to thrive and promote coordination among participant countries. According to the U.S. Government Accountability Office, TSCTP participant countries collectively received almost $340 million between fiscal years 2005 and 2013. Mali was the second largest recipient between 2005 and 2008 and the largest from 2009 to 2013.[34]

The security aperture enlarged beyond the narrow PSI focus to include work with the recipients' gendarmerie, police, and customs and border patrol. However, military capacity building remained the predominant security-centric feature of the TSCTP. U.S. special operations forces worked in participating countries to strengthen their individual military capabilities to capture or kill terrorists and enhance regional military-to-military cooperation. Bilateral security cooperation and assistance focused on tactical skills such as marksmanship, operational planning, communications, and land navigation.[35] The U.S. Department of Defense also initiated a regional counterterrorism interoperability exercise called Flintlock.

The TSCTP's construct—combining defense, development, and diplomacy—appeared sound in theory, and some programs achieved their individual objectives. For instance, a 2011 evaluation found that USAID efforts focused on good governance, youth empowerment, and media and outreach support had positive outcomes, especially in the area of civic engagement.[36]

Yet on the whole, there were numerous barriers when it came to implementation. In addition to the normal hurdles found in other capacity-building efforts, the TSCTP required interagency coordination across multiple countries.[37] Moreover, even successful programs like the USAID one were limited interventions. On balance, although the resources allotted for the TSCTP were not insubstantial, they were still insufficient to accomplish the program's objectives. Perhaps more important than dollar figures or interagency hurdles, the program's efforts, although noble, overlooked a host of issues related to poor governance and rampant corruption, dysfunctional security sectors, and a lack of societal integration, to name just a few. Failure to address these issues devalued security and economic assistance in recipient countries. As one former American official observed, the drivers of instability in the region were so immense that the TSCTP programming was akin to "throwing a Band-Aid on a chest wound."[38] This was certainly the case in Mali, where the array of governance-related challenges and Bamako's security paradigm combined to impede domestic counterterrorism operations, U.S. capacity-building efforts, and the reforms necessary to create a less hospitable environment for GSCP/AQIM.

Mali was a major recipient of development assistance from the United States, Europe, and the international community.[39] Indeed, Mali received approximately twenty times as much in U.S. economic development aid as it did in security assistance during the decade after 9/11.[40] Between the mid-1990s and 2010, the various sources of foreign assistance helped Mali reduce poverty by over 30 percent and achieve gross domestic product growth of approximately 5.5 percent annually.[41] Despite this progress, the country still ranked near the bottom of the 2010 Human Development Index.[42] Moreover, progress was not uniform. The north remained severely disadvantaged relative to other parts of the country. As part of the TSCTP, the United States funded counterterrorism-related development initiatives to improve infrastructure, social service delivery, and educational and vocational opportunities in northern Mali. The United States also financed civil society–led youth programs and peace-building initiatives there. These initiatives were intended to reduce support for the jihadists, increase northern Mali's integration with the rest of the country, and enable government forces to operate there more effectively.[43] In addition to increasing spending for these programs, the Obama administration supported FM radio stations to counter extremist messaging and other CVE-related initiatives.[44]

It is difficult to measure the efficacy of development and CVE initiatives, but three major shortcomings are apparent. First, the United States was arguably more committed to improving socioeconomic conditions in northern Mali and integrating it with the rest of the country than Bamako was. This type of asymmetric commitment to development is not unique to Mali, as we saw in the last chapter. Second, American officials were often unable to travel to northern Mali because of the security situation and lack of infrastructure. This made implementing programs difficult and sometimes led U.S. officials to focus on areas where the need was less acute but that were more accessible.[45] Third, democratization had not led to good governance. Successive leaders, all democratically elected, had plundered the state's coffers for personal gain and transformed the civil service into a mechanism for dispensing patronage, diverting resources to the political party in power, and coercing rivals.[46] The influx of international assistance since the 1990s may have helped Bamako redress some of its socioeconomic deficiencies, but reliance on foreign aid also reduced the government's accountability to its citizenry.[47] A culture of impunity developed in which officials abused their positions with little risk of reprisal.[48] Washington did little to promote better governance and rule of law, especially as they pertained to criminality and corruption. Although technical assistance was provided to strengthen the security sector and judicial system, there was little effort to press Malian leaders to undertake the political reforms necessary to combat corruption and organized criminality. These illicit activities not only hampered socioeconomic development nationwide, and especially in the north. They also facilitated the growth of GSPC/AQIM and increased the barriers to action against it.[49]

Touré claimed his government would be able to do more to dislodge the jihadists from their bases in northern Mali if it had greater military capacity.[50] Current and former U.S. officials were skeptical. They questioned whether Bamako really wanted to build sufficient capacity, which would rob it of an excuse for inaction.[51] A researcher who interviewed numerous Malian officers and enlisted soldiers for a project exploring the army's strategic culture offered a different interpretation. The army had more training (from the Soviet Union during the Cold War), and the government had shown it greater support before 1991, when the military dictatorship of Moussa Traoré was overthrown. Since then, the government's approach to internal security challenges from the Tuareg was to solve them through negotiations. The army's role, to the degree it had one, was to "fight the Tuaregs to the negotiating table," not to defeat them on the battlefield.

This informed how the state approached GSPC/AQIM, which it sought to manage politically rather than defeat militarily or drive out of the country through force of arms. Thus, government leaders did not need the army to be capable of eliminating the group or evicting it from the country because they had no intention of using it for this purpose.[52] Moreover, fear of another military coup or other form of political interference led successive civilian governments, including Touré's, to withhold resources from the military.[53]

The United States was not terribly committed to building Mali's military capacity, either. The State Department referred to Mali as "one of the key U.S. Global War on Terrorism (GWOT) partners in West Africa and a major participant in regional efforts to identify and stop the transit of weapons and terrorist movement throughout the Sahel region."[54] Yet in reality, engagement was limited. The PSI stood up three 150-person rapid-reaction counterterrorism units in Mali and trained them in basic infantry skills, marksmanship, first aid, and navigation.[55] Capacity building for elite units continued after the TSCTP was created.[56] However, training for these units was episodic. Overall, Mali received less than $6 million in security assistance between 2002 and 2006. The United States appropriated over $7 million to train and equip two Malian counterterrorism units in 2007, perhaps reflecting the creation of new security-assistance authorities, growing concerns about the jihadist threat, or both.[57] Malian forces also participated in the annual Flintlock training exercise. The two main ongoing training initiatives were the Counterterrorism Fellowship Program and International Military Education Training. The former trains mid- and senior-level defense and security officials on counterterrorism issues. The latter is the primary instrument for professionalizing military partners.

Two broad observations result from putting these activities in context. First, Mali's military was weak, riddled with corruption, and beset by other institutional problems. Senior military officers engaged in graft and nepotism. Political leaders meddled with recruitment and promotion.[58] The confluence of low defense spending and high levels of corruption left most Malian units mismanaged and poorly equipped. Morale was understandably low as a result.[59] The military also struggled with planning and lacked even a basic doctrine. Moreover, the Ministry of Defense was poorly run. Yet there was no planning or defense institution-building component to the U.S. effort. IMET and CTFP typically occurred in the United States or at other regional centers, making them appealing boondoggles. Participation could also help with promotions. Some Malian officers reportedly bribed their superiors in order to ensure selection. Thus, the people attending these courses were not always capable or committed to professionalizing the force.[60] Even the best trainees were unlikely to have much success actualizing what they learned as long as the military as an institution remained corrupt and mismanaged.

After the Malian army folded in the face of the joint Tuareg and jihadist onslaught that began in 2012, critics decried the failure of years of training by U.S. special operations forces to build a more durable force. What many of these postmortems missed was the fact that the armed forces overall had not actually received much training. Because the capacity-building efforts had prioritized training for specific counterterrorism units, they failed to address the myriad deficiencies in the Malian armed forces or adequately account for them in a way that would enable a mitigation strategy.

Second, even narrowly focused efforts to build capable counterterrorism units were poorly implemented. Far from an ongoing, robust train-and-equip initiative, engagements were limited and episodic. Moreover, training engagements for these units only began occurring with any regularity after 2008. Even then, training remained sporadic, as we will see in the next section. This training also focused almost exclusively on basics like marksmanship or technical matters, such as how to operate the limited equipment that units received.[61] Engagements never progressed to the point where participants became proficient in mounting the types of coordinated operations necessary to dislodge the jihadists from their fortified bases.

While U.S. capacity-building efforts floundered, GSPC/AQIM worked to ingratiate itself with local actors. The group dispensed cash collected from smuggling operations and ransom money from kidnappings, beginning with the estimated €5 million from the 2003 abduction of European hostages. It provided gifts, including four-wheel-drive vehicles, and opened up opportunities in its kidnap-for-ransom enterprise to locals.[62] To win over members of the wider population, jihadists overpaid for local goods, provided cellular-phone service, and even sometimes dispensed medical care.[63] Some GSPC/AQIM members, including Belmokhtar, married into prominent tribes.[64] By the end of the decade, AQIM was established enough to tax local tribes and render justice in certain areas.[65]

Bamako relied on local power brokers and armed militias to maintain a modicum of control in northern Mali. Many of these actors were engaged in transnational criminal activity.[66] A range of criminal networks smuggled people, weapons, and drugs. West Africa also became a major transshipment area for cocaine coming from South America to Europe.[67] The government and army allowed local elites to engage in all manner of criminal activity in return for their assistance in keeping the north from sliding back into conflict.[68] Army and security personnel offered protection to traffickers and armed groups, including GSPC/AQIM, in exchange for monetary compensation.[69] Ruling elites in Bamako also benefited financially from these criminal activities. This reinforced the government's policy of neglect, which remained largely intact even after the government's threat perceptions and the U.S. approach to capacity building began to change.

A LIMITED ENGAGEMENT

Mokhtar Belmokhtar staged the GSPC's first attack outside Algeria in 2005 when his brigade raided a Mauritanian military outpost, killing a dozen soldiers.[70] AQIM officially declared a jihad against the "apostate" government of the Islamic Republic of Mauritania in 2009.[71] AQIM militants also began focusing more on Western targets in Mauritania, murdering an American teacher-cum-missionary and attacking the French embassy that year. These attacks followed a similar expansion in Algeria, where the group also began striking Western targets after merging with al-Qaeda. As it was ramping up these operations, AQIM initiated a separate kidnap-and-ransom campaign targeting Westerners in the region.

The kidnappings started with two Austrian tourists, who were taken hostage in southern Tunisia in 2008 and subsequently transported to northern Mali. AQIM finally released both hostages to the Malian army.[72] The Austrian government reportedly paid a $3.2 million ransom.[73] Additional kidnappings of Europeans followed and brought the group millions in ransom money. In some cases, Tuareg tribesmen are believed to have carried out the abductions and then sold the hostages to AQIM.[74] The influx of funds enabled the group to reinforce its position with segments of the population in northern Mali and to become a funding engine for other inchoate jihadist organizations, such as the Nigerian Boko Haram.[75] Mali had signed up to various international conventions against terrorist financing, but AQIM's practice of raising money through ransoms and smuggling operations rendered traditional counter threat finance practices moot.[76] More importantly, government and military elites personally reaped financial benefits by helping facilitate ransom exchanges and from the jihadists' smuggling operations.

U.S. officials saw the group as a bigger threat after it became an al-Qaeda affiliate. The affiliation, combined with AQIM's decision to begin attacking Western targets in Algeria and Mauritania, reinforced growing U.S. concerns. However, the level and nature of the AQIM threat was hotly debated. Some analysts and officials worried AQIM could become a global threat. Others argued the group remained regionally focused and that if it were to begin launching international attacks, then European countries were the most likely targets.[77] Intelligence services in these states had shown themselves capable of suppressing GSPC/AQIM networks.[78] Yet even if the group remained regionally focused, the threat it posed in the Sahel had clearly grown. AQIM's kidnapping campaign not only posed a direct danger to Western citizens but also had yielded the group millions of dollars in ransom payments that it could use to purchase more sophisticated weapons and support other local jihadist movements.[79]

The Touré government still did not view AQIM as a major security threat, but by 2009 it was indicating a greater readiness to move against it for several reasons.[80] First, AQIM's kidnap-and-ransom campaign imperiled the tourism trade.[81] Second, Touré was feeling the heat from Mali's neighbors, which were increasingly frustrated with his appeasement of the jihadists.[82] His sense of isolation increased as the group became more active in attacking Mauritania and kidnapping Westerners. Yet Touré still insisted that the main barrier to action was the lack of support from Mali's neighbors. He continued to castigate them for leaving it up to his country, with its weak military, to deal with AQIM. If the United States and regional partners provided the necessary support, then Touré maintained that Mali would confront the group.[83] Third, as the president grappled with these issues, the latest round of fighting between the state and Tuareg rebels was winding down. Between January and June 2009, the factions that rejected the 2006 Algiers Accord were routed, fragmented, or agreed to stop fighting and disarm.[84] With the latest Tuareg crisis over, the military began planning for an operation against AQIM. There was no timetable for when the offensive might occur and little indication it would take place in the near term.[85]

It was unclear whether the government had really adopted a belligerent position toward the jihadists on its soil or if, despite the aforementioned developments, it still viewed them with indifference and was playing for time. AQIM's actions added a sense of urgency and swung the needle away from neglect and toward confrontation.

The group sometimes demanded prisoner releases in addition to ransom payments but almost always settled for the latter. The one notable exception occurred after a group of four European tourists were abducted in 2009. AQIM demanded money and that the United Kingdom release Abu Qatada from Long Lartin jail.[86] Qatada was a jihadist ideologue and staunch supporter of the revolutionary jihad in Algeria during the 1990s. His release was specifically tied to the fate of Edwin Dyer, the only British citizen among the four hostages. On May 31, after it was clear the British government would not release Abu Qatada or pay ransom, AQIM executed Dyer at one of its bases in northern Mali.[87] The order to kill him reportedly came from al-Qaeda senior leaders in Pakistan and was communicated directly to an AQIM commander in northern Mali.[88] Abdelhamid (Hamidu) Abu Zeid, the commander in question, was a rival of Belmokhtar's. Dyer's execution led to factional infighting between the two. Belmokhtar had gone out of his way to preserve northern Mali as a safe haven. He feared that killing a British citizen would make maintaining this sanctuary more difficult. He was right. The Malian authorities responded to Dyer's execution by arresting some AQIM members.[89] That might have been the end of it for the time being, except for what happened next.

On the night of June 10, AQIM militants assassinated Lieutenant Colonel Lamana Ould Bou, a senior Malian intelligence officer, in his home in Timbuktu. Intrigue surrounds his death. The timing makes it appear that his murder was retaliation for the arrests. That might be the case, although there were also allegations that Bou was murdered over an arms or drug deal or some other criminal engagement with AQIM that went awry.[90] Whatever the motive, the assassination outraged Touré and others in his government. Bou had been an important go-between for Mali's Directorate General of State Security (Direction Générale de la Sécurité d'État, or DGSE) with local militias, smugglers, and AQIM.[91] In this capacity, he served as an intermediary with AQIM on hostage negotiations and other criminal-related matters.[92] Perhaps more importantly, Bou was also a key interlocutor with the Arab militia in Timbuktu that Touré relied on to help manage the Tuareg problem.[93]

Hours before Bou was gunned down, the president had requested U.S. military planners to travel to Mali to help the military refine its plan to confront AQIM and to determine the training, equipment, and support necessary to implement it.[94] However, although Bamako was beginning to consider military operations, there was little indication up to this point that it was prepared to execute them. The assassination spurred Touré to action, and he launched a hasty military operation.

Mali's offensive was short-lived. Planning existed on paper, but the military had not properly positioned forces or logistical stocks. Malian forces killed a number of militants, seized one of the group's bases, and gave chase to fleeing AQIM fighters. The soldiers soon ran low on fuel and supplies but continued their pursuit. With minimal intelligence and air support, they were unable to engage AQIM. Unlike the military, the jihadists were prepared for a protracted engagement. They accessed weapons caches and took up defensive positions that enabled them to keep Malian forces at bay with heavy weapons. On July 4, AQIM militants ambushed Malian forces at a makeshift camp, inflicting the largest number of casualties on the military in a single day since 1991. This stunning assault effectively brought the operation to a halt.[95] Three days after the ambush, AQIM issued a statement blaming Bamako for breaking the tacit peace agreement between them: "You know very well that we do not have to fight you. . . . We only came your way in the past after you captured our brothers and you committed acts of aggression against us."[96]

States respond to losses like this one in different ways. Some go on the offensive in order to send a message to the enemy, avenge fallen troops, or because they wake up to the existence of a looming threat. Other states recoil because they fear further losses. Mali recoiled. It saw the jihadists as a bigger

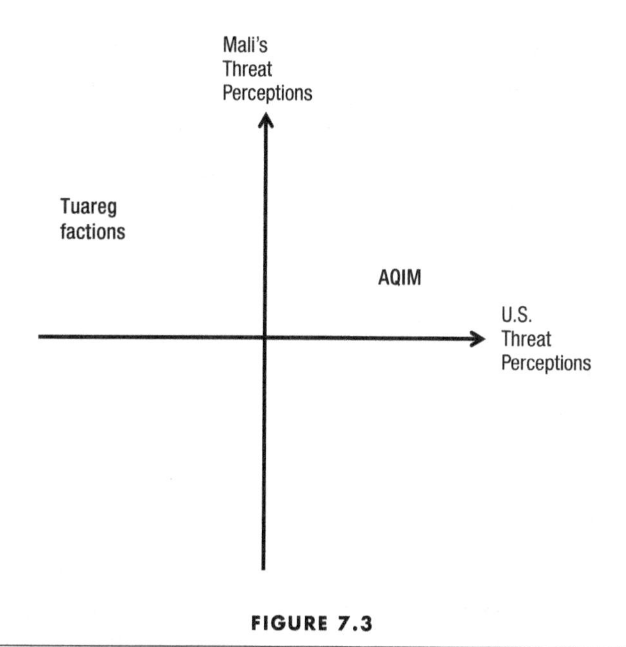

FIGURE 7.3

U.S. and Malian Threat Perceptions

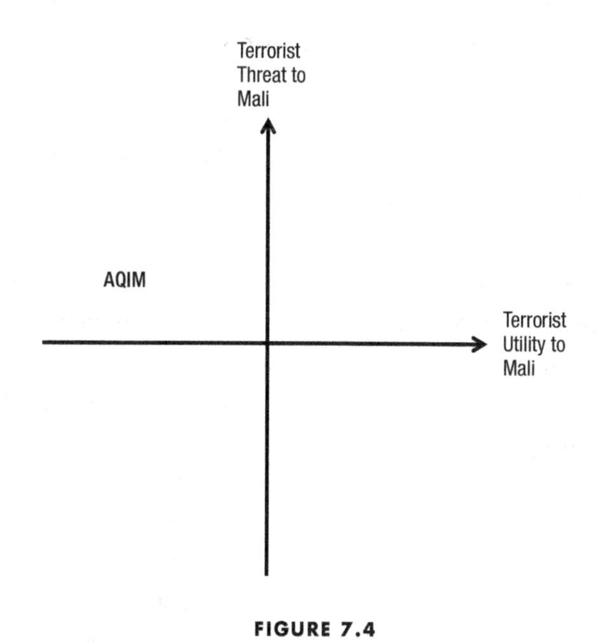

FIGURE 7.4

Terrorist Threat and Utility to Mali

threat than in the past (figure 7.3). Yet although Mali's relationship with AQIM, based on its threat perceptions, was now defined by belligerence (figure 7.4), its approach to dealing with the group did not change all that much. U.S. officials rightly predicted that Bamako would seek additional assistance from its partners before launching another offensive.[97] This assessment, combined with the failure of Mali's military effort and growing U.S. concerns about AQIM, led U.S. special operations forces to begin revamping their approach to train-and-equip programs in Mali. Between mid-2009 and 2012, Malian military units were training harder in anticipation of confronting AQIM, but the government never launched a sustained campaign.

TOO LITTLE, TOO LATE

In a belated attempt to extend Bamako's writ into the north, Touré initiated the Special Program for Peace, Security, and Development in northern Mali in 2010. The program was intended to establish eleven secure zones in northern Mali that would be manned by three thousand military and development officials.[98] Bamako officially launched the program a year later. Bilateral and multilateral partners, including France, Canada, and the European Union, contributed to its approximately €50 million budget. The effort had various flaws. One of the most damaging was Bamako failure's to address concerns among populations in northern Mali about the reintroduction of a "southern" military presence.[99] As a result, an effort intended to dislodge AQIM and other criminal networks in the north instead further alienated the local populations.

Reliance on local power brokers in northern Mali who were involved in criminal activities and the complicity of senior officials in these same activities made it even more difficult to address the socioeconomic problems there and further damaged the government's legitimacy.[100] Many of the same local power brokers and militias the government relied on to keep the peace also acted as mediators for AQIM hostage negotiations. Backing certain mediators provided Bamako with another way to reward its allies. Until the most recent Tuareg conflict ended in 2009, money gleaned through ransoms was also used to fund northern militias fighting against rebels.[101] Individuals in the army, intelligence services, and government continued to benefit financially from AQIM's kidnap-and-ransom campaign too.[102] In one of the most egregious examples, Touré's wife was reportedly detained while shopping in Paris with marked euros from one of the hostage exchanges.[103]

While fumbling its efforts in the north, Bamako also failed to ameliorate its neighbors' concerns about terrorism. Algeria and Mauritania both recalled their ambassadors to Mali in 2010 to protest Bamako's decision to free four suspected jihadists in exchange for a single hostage.[104] Mauritania began taking matters into its own hands that year. Its forces conducted several raids against AQIM camps in northern Mali. The first raid was launched in concert with French forces in July 2010. Mauritanian forces conducted another one in June 2011 and launched airstrikes in October. It is notable that Mauritania officially described the June raid as a coordinated operation with the Malian army, whereas Bamako issued a separate statement claiming it had only secured the area to prevent AQIM militants from fleeing. In other words, the Touré government took pains to publicly deny sending its military back to face off against the group.[105] There are also reports that Mali's neighbors and international partners actually limited the information they shared with the Malian army and intelligence service about these operations for fear that some individual officers might alert AQIM.[106]

Bamako viewed the group as a threat and was not pursuing policies deliberately intended to enable it. But corruption in the government, military, and intelligence service nevertheless produced a similar effect. And there was no telling if or when Touré's government might turn the corner and decided to commit to confronting the jihadists dwelling on its soil. However, it was clear by the end of the decade that Mali's military was not up to the task. The July 2009 ambush was a warning sign for the United States that its capacity-building efforts were failing. A consistent effort to train and equip Malian units to take on AQIM finally began that year. At Mali's request, U.S. special operations forces zeroed in on training exchanges with the Echelon Tactique Inter-Armées (ETIAs). These were motorized infantry units with approximately 160 men each. The ETIAs had been formed by pulling troops from other army regiments. They were ethnically mixed, with a considerable number of Tuaregs in their ranks.[107] The first training event with an ETIA was held in August 2009 and lasted thirty days. A month proved to be too little time given how woefully inadequate the ETIAs were. Trainings expanded to forty-five days and by the summer of 2011 were averaging approximately three months. Engagements occurred concurrently, which meant that U.S. forces were in Mali for the majority of the year training with the ETIAs.

This seemed like enduring engagement, but it was not. Special operations forces were training four ETIA units, so each one typically went six to nine months between engagements. Because ETIA personnel were on a six-month rotation policy, they typically rotated out after one round of training. As a result, U.S. trainers repeatedly had to start at square one with a fresh crop of ETIA personnel and thus could never move beyond imparting basic skills.[108] Put another way, the input of special operations forces' activity was enduring and consistent, but the output in terms of personnel trained continued to be haphazard.

U.S. officials appealed to the Malian Ministry of Defense to change the six-month personnel rotation policy but were rebuffed.[109] Defense institution building or even a greater emphasis on personnel management might have helped remedy this issue, but U.S. engagement with the Ministry of Defense was mainly focused on operational planning. Unable to remedy the ETIA rotation problem, U.S. and Malian officials instead struck an agreement to identify a force whose members would stay in the unit and be available for training annually for a number of years. This effort complimented a French capacity-building initiative to create a similar counterterrorism regiment further north.[110] Canadian Special Forces were also conducting training in Mali.[111] According to one close observer of the Malian military, these disparate programs were not well coordinated.[112] The 33rd Régiment des Commandos Parachutistes, based in Bamako, was chosen as the organization from which to draw personnel for a rapid-reaction battalion based in the center of the country.

In 2010, almost a decade after launching the Pan-Sahel Initiative, the United States was starting from scratch to build yet another elite counterterrorism force. This one would be called the Compagnie des Forces Spéciales (CFS). An SOF assessment of the troops who would form its nucleus found them lacking. This was dispiriting, considering that they came from a unit that had participated in U.S. and French training events since 2001 and was considered among the best trained in the Malian army. U.S. experts determined it would take approximately five years to transform the CFS into an entity with the capabilities necessary to take on AQIM effectively.[113] It was forced into battle sooner than expected.

IT ALL FALLS APART

The buildup to a rebellion that tipped Mali into chaos and led to the creation of a short-lived jihadist protostate began with the formation of the National Movement of the Azawad (MNA) in November 2010. Less than six months later, NATO led the intervention in Libya that ultimately toppled Gaddafi's regime. The Libyan dictator had recruited thousands of Tuaregs from Mali to fight as mercenaries in his military. They appropriated weapons abandoned or left unguarded during the conflict and brought them back to Mali.[114] In October 2011, the MNA merged with another Tuareg organization to form the National Movement for the Liberation of Azawad (Mouvement National pour la Libération de l'Azawad, or MNLA). The MNLA pursued an explicitly separatist agenda and sought to form a new state, Azawad, in northern Mali. Many Tuareg fighters returning from Libya joined the MNLA, infusing the new organization with a cadre of well-armed and battle-tested men.[115]

Other Tuareg fighters flocked to Ansar Dine, an organization formed in December 2011 as an Islamist alternative to the secular MNLA.[116] Ansar Dine's founder, Iyad Ag Ghali, was one of northern Mali's most influential power brokers and a man known for having his fingers in many pies. Ag Ghali was a key commander in both the 1990 and 2006 Tuareg rebellions. In between, he helped facilitate the GSPC's release of European hostages in 2003. After taking up arms in 2006, Ag Ghali subsequently helped broker a political solution with Bamako that led many fighters to lay down their weapons. For his assistance managing these crises, the government rewarded Ag Ghali by appointing him consul general in Jeddah, Saudi Arabia, from 2007 to 2009.[117] After returning, he founded Ansar Dine to do battle against the government he had just finished serving. It reportedly drew some of its manpower from Tuareg fighters serving under Ag Ghali's cousin, an AQIM commander.[118]

Days before Ansar Dine's formation was announced, AQIM members trumpeted their creation of a splinter group called Movement for Unity and Jihad in West Africa (MUJWA). Since expanding beyond Algeria more than a decade earlier, GSPC/AQIM had recruited Mauritanians, Malians, and citizens from other West African countries. MUJWA appears to have broken away as a result of frustration with the continued dominance of Algerian nationals in AQIM.[119] The new organization's leaders were predominantly Mauritanians and members of Arab tribes from northern Mali.[120]

As 2012 approached, all these organizations—the MNLA, Ansar Dine, AQIM, and MUJWA—prepared for war. President Touré remained "apathetic" about dealing with the impending crisis, according to one U.S. intelligence assessment.[121] Hostilities commenced in mid-January. The MNLA led an offensive that handed the Malian army a series of defeats, precipitating protests by military families in southern Mali who condemned the government for failing to provide its soldiers with adequate equipment and protection. Unrest in Bamako led a collection of soldiers to mutiny in late March, culminating in Touré's overthrow six weeks before his term ended.[122] The mutineers defended the coup on the grounds that Touré failed "to provide adequate equipment to the defense and security forces fulfilling their mission to defend the country's territorial integrity."[123] Although the rout of Malian forces catalyzed the coup, discontent had been simmering among junior officers for years as a result of rampant corruption in the government and military's senior ranks.

The coup created a political vacuum in Bamako and added to the chaos in northern Mali, where the rebel coalition took control of the three largest cities: Kidal, Gao, and Timbuktu. In early April, the MNLA declared the new state of Azawad. Not long after, the Islamist-cum-jihadist coalition that had collaborated with the MNLA turned against it. Ansar Dine and MUJWA, with assistance from AQIM militants, seized the major northern cities by late 2012 and began attempting to build an Islamic state. Ansar Dine took control of Timbuktu and Kidal; MUJWA administered Gao. AQIM leaders provided guidance and leadership behind the scenes.[124] Committed jihadists and young men lured by the promise of steady salaries journeyed to Mali to join the state-building enterprise or take advantage of the growing safe haven. They came from neighboring countries such as

Tunisia, Burkina Faso, Algeria, Niger, and Togo and from faraway lands including Pakistan, Afghanistan, Nigeria, and France.[125] Militants from the Nigerian jihadist group Boko Haram reportedly also traveled to Timbuktu for training.[126]

Because the jihadists lacked the military, financial, and structural capabilities to resist international pressure, AQIM's Algeria-based amir Abdelmalek Droukdel warned, "We must not go too far or take risks in our decisions or imagine that this project is a stable Islamic state." He advocated using the captured territory as an opportunity to interact with the local population, peacefully propagate the jihadists' interpretation of Islam, and prove that AQIM and its allies were capable of meeting peoples' daily needs, not simply waging war. Thus, even if the protostate failed, these groups would have increased their integration with the society and solidified important connections with key power brokers.[127] This advice aligned with core al-Qaeda's strategy of slowly building popular support for an Islamic state and was the subject of two letters to the AQIM amir from his counterpart in AQAP. In them, the AQAP leader shared lessons learned from his group's experience attempting to govern territory in Yemen.[128] Despite this advice, the jihadists in Mali were impatient for change. They began implementing their harsh interpretation of Islamic law soon after seizing territory, earning a subsequent rebuke from al-Qaeda leaders.[129]

Droukdel's attempts to work with and through Ansar Dine also failed. Because it was an indigenous organization, he encouraged the group to take the lead in administering territory. This was intended to facilitate engagement with the local population and ensure that the al-Qaeda "brand" did not put the Islamic protostate at risk.[130] However, competing agendas and ethnonational tensions undermined the coalition between Ansar Dine and its jihadist allies. In January 2013, the jihadists made an aggressive southward push and appeared poised to take Bamako.

U.S. security cooperation shrank dramatically after the rebellion erupted because of concerns about counterterrorism assistance being used in an internal conflict. The United States ended security cooperation after the coup, although a small SOF team remained at the American embassy.[131] Washington terminated almost all aid to Mali several weeks later, in accordance with U.S. law prohibiting assistance to the government of any country whose duly elected head of government is deposed by a military coup.[132] The Obama administration chose not to intervene militarily or to begin conducting direct action strikes. Instead, the United States sought to help Mali, its neighbors, and French forces repel the jihadist threat.[133]

Because of its colonial and postcolonial history in Francophone Africa, France had greater and longer-standing interests in the Sahel than the United States did. France was also the main Western target for AQIM in the region. The jihadists' seizure of territory heightened fears among senior French officials. There were more than six thousand French citizens living in Mali. AQIM could kidnap an untold number of them and demand the release of thousands of Islamist prisoners or enormous ransoms.[134] When Mali's interim president requested help after the jihadists made their southward push, French president Francois Hollande answered the call. France led a military intervention—Operation Serval—to retake control of northern Mali. Chad deployed its U.S.-trained and equipped Special Anti-Terrorism Group to support the French operation. Troops from other countries in the African Union and regional Economic Community of West African States also joined the fight.[135] The French-led military intervention drove out Ansar Dine and the jihadists, who melted away into the expansive territory stretching across the Sahel.

There were debates in the United States over how robustly to support the French-led intervention. In addition to disagreements about the AQIM threat, U.S. officials were at odds over whether supporting the intervention could be a slippery slope that would lead to greater American involvement in the conflict.[136] After years in which European powers had failed to meet their financial commitments to NATO, some members of the Obama administration were also reluctant to provide refueling aircraft without the promise of reimbursement.[137] The United States ultimately supported the intervention with in-flight refueling for French aircraft, heavy airlift of French and Chadian soldiers and vehicles, and intelligence.[138] An ongoing shortage of French logistical assets forced the United States to keep American airmen in Mali through the end of the year.[139] A small number of U.S. special operations forces was deployed to provide liaison support to French and African troops.[140] The United States used unarmed drones based out of Niger to conduct reconnaissance for French forces.[141]

The UN Multidimensional Integrated Stabilization Mission in Mali (MINUSMA) was established in April 2013 to carry out security-related stabilization tasks.[142] It took control of the six thousand West African troops already in Mali; the French forces hunted for high-value targets.[143] MINUSMA troop shortages, combined with a deterioration of the security situation in northern Mali in late 2013, led France to maintain a larger force presence for longer than planned.[144] The French government announced plans the following spring to keep one thousand troops in Mali and three thousand in the Sahel region for "as long as necessary."[145] Operation Barkhane replaced Serval in July 2014, and its mandate subsequently expanded to include involvement in the counterinsurgency against the Nigerian-based Boko Haram. French forces have been stretched thin as a result while MINUSMA has continued to struggle.[146]

AQIM and its allies increased the tempo of operations after 2015, including attacks against MINUSMA forces. Mali became had become the site of the United Nations' deadliest ongoing peace operation by 2016.[147] Jihadists also began launching attacks in central and southern Mali.[148] ISIS-affiliated groups in Algeria and Libya posed an added challenge, although AQIM remained the most powerful jihadist group in the Sahel. In November 2015, AQIM, Ansar Dine, and al-Mourabitoun (a splinter group formed by Mokhtar Belmokhtar) all claimed responsibility for an attack against the Radisson Blu in Bamako. Twenty people from six countries were killed.[149] Local and French forces led the hostage rescue operation; a small team of American special operations forces assisted.[150] The three groups that claimed responsibility for the attack later joined forces to form a united jihadist front.[151] Numerous attacks followed, including one in October 2017 when militants ambushed U.S. special operations forces in Niger close to the Malian border, killing four of them.[152]

Mali's weak military capacity meant that UN peacekeepers were forced to shoulder the burden in terms of carrying out stability operations and bore the brunt of attacks as a result.[153] France's military presence provided a degree of protection against major attacks, but there is only so much French forces can do in so great a geographic area against such a diffuse enemy. They have focused on conducting counterterrorism operations in lieu of building the Malian army's capacity. The European Union has attempted to help fill the void. One EU training mission is focused on the Malian army while a parallel EU effort is working on developing the capabilities of Mali's internal security services. Not long before this book went to press, five African nations, Mali, Mauritania, Burkina Faso, Niger, and Chad, officially established the G5 Sahel Force to combat Islamist militants in the region.[154]

U.S. security cooperation resumed in 2014 but has not included a training component for Malian troops. Instead, a small contingent of American forces has focused on training troops from neighboring countries who were deploying to Mali.[155] The United States has continued providing limited support to French and Malian troops. This has mainly entailed sharing video feeds from unmanned drones and other intelligence, but U.S. special operations forces have also reportedly participated in counterterrorism missions alongside French forces.[156]

Democratic rule was restored with the election of President Ibrahim Boubacar Keita in August 2013. Mali's new government and its armed forces grasped that their country faced a serious threat from the jihadists and adopted a belligerent position toward them. As of 2017, this had not translated into effective counterterrorism efforts. Capacity shortfalls were a major hindrance but not the only one. Political will remained the paramount problem. The 2015 Accord for Peace and Reconciliation, agreed to by Bamako, progovernment militias, and a coalition of rebel factions that included the MNLA, theoretically created space for Malian forces to focus on the jihadists.[157] However, many within military and security circles still refused to accept that the rebel factions that signed the accord could ever be integrated into the political process. They either viewed these factions as a greater threat than the jihadists or conflated them with the jihadists because of their history of cooperation. Sometimes, Malian officials and military officers have done both simultaneously.[158] It is therefore highly questionable whether the capacity that international partners are attempting to build in Mali will be used against the terrorist groups for which it is intended.

* * *

The Malian military's poor performance on the battlefield and the coup in Bamako led to soul searching by U.S. civilian and military officials about the type of training provided after 9/11.[159] Narrowly focused counterterrorism training clearly did not address systemic deficiencies in the military. Yet it is questionable whether even a more robust effort would have succeeded. As one U.S. embassy official observed, "How can you have a military that succeeds if you don't have a government that succeeds?"[160] This highlights the broader issue of Bamako's behavior. Despite diagnosing Mali's concerns about Tuareg factions as a major impediment to action against GSPC/AQIM, the United States does not appear to have seriously considered ways to address the issue or work around it.

American investment in Malian democracy boiled down to making sure that multiparty elections were held. Washington invested less in promoting governance and rule of law, especially as they pertained to criminality and corruption. According to one study, which compiled data from multiple assistance programs before the 2012 coup, 97 percent of aid was spent on social or economic development. Although vitally important, this meant that less than 1 percent of the U.S. aid budget for Mali was spent on governance and only about 2 percent was spent on security.[161] Moreover, the limited technical assistance provided to strengthen the security sector did not address corruption and organized criminality, which had both facilitated the growth of GSPC/AQIM and increased the barriers to action against it.[162] The United States never held Touré accountable for the corruption and poor governance that occurred on his watch.

Despite setting out to build Mali's military capacity as early as 2002, these efforts did not really commence in a consistent manner until the end of the decade. This was an instance in which more resources might have helped. A bigger problem was the haphazard nature of the effort. Numerous experts and observers questioned the efficacy of the train-and-equip program after the Malian military collapsed.[163] What these critiques missed was that the military actually had not benefited from years of training. Most of the training engagements were episodic. The CSF, which is the one Malian unit that benefited from enduring engagement, did not collapse during the conflict and indeed performed admirably.[164] Failure to focus on institution building was another squandered opportunity. Professionalizing individuals is very difficult if the institutions they return to are corrupt and poorly managed.

U.S. policy shortcomings on governance and capacity building were partly a result of resources and attention, which were limited. Some of these deficiencies might have been identified and rectified earlier if the departments of State and Defense had rigorous programs in place to assess, monitor, and evaluate security assistance and cooperation. It is difficult to ignore the fact that consecutive U.S. administrations repeatedly privileged partner engagement over any deeper governance reforms. They also did not view GSPC/AQIM as a major threat. In theory, this provided an opportunity to take a patient and comprehensive approach toward Mali. In reality, a lack of urgency may have led the United States to squander the time and space it actually had.

8

EGYPT AND ALGERIA

The Revolutionary Heartland

THE CITY OF LUXOR SITS on the site of ancient Thebes. From the sixteenth to the eleventh century BCE, it was the pharaohs' capital when they were at the height of their power. Today, Luxor is a must-see destination for foreign visitors to Egypt. Tourists flock to the temples and royal tombs that dot the landscape. In November 1997, fifty-eight tourists, along with four Egyptians, were slaughtered while they scampered through the Mortuary Temple of Hatshepsut, a funerary shrine also known as the Holy of Holies. The Luxor massacre, perpetrated by terrorists from the Egyptian Islamic Group (EIG), was the last gasp of a jihadist insurgency that ended not long after. The government of President Hosni Mubarak had been locked in combat with EIG for almost a decade and contending with jihadist violence for far longer. Egypt had successfully defeated the jihadists on its soil by September 11, 2001, and was resolute about not letting them regain a foothold.

For most of the 1990s, Mubarak was frustrated by a perceived lack of support from the United States, which he criticized for failing to do more against international terrorism and for maintaining contacts with "terrorists" from the Islamist Muslim Brotherhood.[1] The organization had eschewed violence for years, but Egyptian authorities still considered it a threat to their hold on power. In the wake of the Luxor attack, Mubarak also lashed out at the United Kingdom and other European countries for granting asylum to Islamist militants.[2] He had already cautioned them—correctly, it turned out—that they would one day become targets of similar groups.[3] When the United States launched its War on Terror after 9/11, Mubarak's Egypt was an eager participant.

Counterterrorism cooperation between the United States and Egypt had already increased during the late 1990s, as Washington grew more concerned about the threat from al-Qaeda. This cooperation was just one element of the bilateral relationship. For decades, the United States had viewed Egypt as a stabilizing force in the Middle East and invested heavily in its armed forces. Egypt is one of the largest recipients of security assistance; historically most of it has come in the form of military financing for major weapons systems. The United States has provided foreign assistance to both Egypt and Israel since the 1979 peace treaty to smooth security cooperation and maintain a balance of power between the two countries. Egypt has received $1.3 billion in military assistance per year since 1987. However, U.S. imperatives for the relationship were not limited to keeping the Egypt-Israel peace treaty intact. They also included eliciting support from Cairo for U.S. policies in the region and maintaining preferential treatment for U.S. military and commercial traffic through the Suez Canal.[4]

U.S. relations with Algeria were far less developed when the 9/11 attacks occurred. Algeria was a leader in the nonaligned movement during the Cold War but tilted toward the Soviet Union, while the United States backed Algeria's regional rival, Morocco. Relations did not improve after the Cold War. U.S. officials strongly criticized the Algerian military's cancellation of elections in 1992, which catalyzed a civil war that claimed almost one hundred thousand lives by the end of the decade. Jihadist groups were the most powerful nonstate actors in the conflict, but they were not the only ones. Although Washington worried about the threats these groups might pose, it also condemned the military-backed regime's brutal suppression of political opposition movements and security-centric approach to countering the insurgency. For their part, Algerian officials blamed the United States for contributing to their country's international isolation in the 1990s.[5] The two countries took initial steps to build a relationship on the basis of shared interests in the energy sector toward the end of the decade.[6] The emphasis quickly turned to counterterrorism after 9/11.

Bush administration officials believed their Algerian counterparts could offer valuable lessons about combating terrorism. They also believed—incorrectly, it turned out—that the remaining jihadist forces in Algeria were allied with al-Qaeda. A "Civil Concord" referendum approved almost unanimously by Algerian voters in 1999 officially ended the civil war, but the Salafist Group for Preaching and Combat (GSPC) was still waging a low-level insurgency on September 11, 2001.[7] (As in the last chapter, I use GSPC when referring to the group before 2007, AQIM when discussing it thereafter, and GSPC/AQIM where overlaps between these time periods occur. Because Algeria viewed both the northern and southern branches as threats but not as equivalent ones, I also distinguish between the two.) Algerian leaders viewed the United States as belatedly waking up to a threat they had faced for years. The 9/11 attacks presented an opportunity for the Algerian regime to make its enemies America's enemies and to forge stronger ties with a superpower in order to end its international isolation, restore its reputation, and attract investment.

Algeria and Egypt had faced robust revolutionary jihadist insurgencies before 9/11. As one would expect, both countries took an extremely belligerent position toward jihadists and prioritized the terrorist threat relative to other threats. In theory, this made them natural partners. In reality, they both helped and hindered America's efforts to achieve its counterterrorism objectives. Thus, exploring cooperation with both countries highlights the complexity of cooperation. The dissimilar nature of their relationships to the United States also makes comparing Egypt and Algeria useful for teasing out how threat perceptions and terrorist-state relations, on the one hand, and bilateral relations, on the other hand, inform different types of cooperation.

Each country's relationship with the United States had no bearing on its commitment to domestic counterterrorism operations. Both countries maintained powerful armies and security services and kept emergency laws in place that helped neutralize or suppress jihadist networks. There was no need to incentivize or coerce either government into taking the jihadist threat seriously. Obtaining regional cooperation, which was a function of threat perceptions and strategic culture, was more difficult. Some countries may be willing to share the burden on regional counterterrorism in order to service their relationship or curry favor with the United States. Egypt and Algeria were not.

The nature of the bilateral relationship and provision of assistance had no discernable impact on U.S. efforts to promote political reforms intended to reduce the risk factors for radicalization. Both countries were led by military-backed authoritarian regimes that used their highly capable security forces not only to combat terrorism but also to repress political opposition movements, suppress dissent, and curb the mobilizing potential of the population. Thus, while their relatively strong capabilities, experience dealing with jihadist violence, and commitment to countering the threat made them helpful partners, Egypt and Algeria simultaneously pursued policies that created the conditions for jihadist recruitment and radicalization. This made it more difficult for Algeria to stamp out the GSPC entirely, and it enabled jihadist groups to reemerge in Egypt despite the state's commitment to suppressing them.

The United States had stronger relations with Egypt and made a stronger push there for political reform, but it came up short. Cairo did not make any efforts to counter violent extremism through targeted initiatives, although it also did not face a substantial, active jihadist threat before the Arab uprisings. U.S. efforts helped bring Algeria into multilateral forums focused on countering violent extremism. The Algerian regime also launched its own initiatives to delegitimize jihadist ideology, allowed some Islamist parties to contest elections, and instituted other incremental reforms. It is difficult to determine how much of an effect Washington's policies had on these developments. Moreover, the regime continued to suppress political opposition and civil society organizations.

Closer relations and a history of cooperation mattered most when it came to access, intelligence cooperation, and coordination on detainees. All three were more fruitful with Egypt. Many U.S. defense policy makers tied the tangible access that the Egyptian government and armed forces offered the United States to the United States' thirty-plus years of investment in Egyptian military aid. Intelligence cooperation was a function of an intelligence-intelligence relationship that preceded 9/11. The two countries also had been cooperating on rendition since the mid-1990s. In contrast, the U.S. and Algerian intelligence services had no real relationship to speak of when 9/11 occurred. Algeria was also not forthcoming on access, largely because of its aversion to military intervention and its anticolonial ethos, and it never exhibited an inclination to cooperate in exchange for assistance. Algerian cooperation on intelligence and regional counterterrorism improved after instability in its near abroad resulting from the Arab uprisings altered Algeria's threat perceptions. This chapter explores Egyptian and then Algerian cooperation with the United States.

EGYPT: KEEPING THE LID

Washington and Cairo shared similar threat perceptions when it came to jihadists. The two main Egyptian jihadist groups active during the 1980s and 1990s were almost entirely eradicated by 9/11. Ayman al-Zawahiri's Egyptian Islamic Jihad existed in exile, had merged with al-Qaeda, and had no presence in Egypt. The leadership of the Egyptian Islamic Group (EIG), which waged the insurgency in Egypt in the 1990s, had renounced armed operations by the end of the decade. The few EIG militants still active were operating in exile. Washington and Cairo were committed to ensuring that Egypt remained an unattractive environment for these or other jihadists. However, the two diverged over the Muslim Brotherhood (figure 8.1). American officials were wary of the world's oldest Islamist organization, but they also did not consider it a threat on par with jihadist groups like al-Qaeda. Cairo did. The Brotherhood had renounced violence in the 1970s but remained the most organized political opposition movement in the country and thus a potential threat to the Mubarak regime's hold on power.

A CANARY IN THE SINAI

Cairo was a signatory to most major counterterrorism-related conventions and made an effort to comply with them when it came to squashing terrorist activities.[8] The Egyptian intelligence and security services were vigilant, unforgiving, and generally effective at rooting out emergent jihadist threats. And Egypt's Emergency Law, in force since the aftermath of Anwar Sadat's assassination in 1981, gave the regime far-reaching powers in the counterterrorism realm. Suspected terrorists were detained and harshly interrogated. Plea bargains were not on offer, and prosecutions sometimes took place in military tribunals or emergency courts, a practice

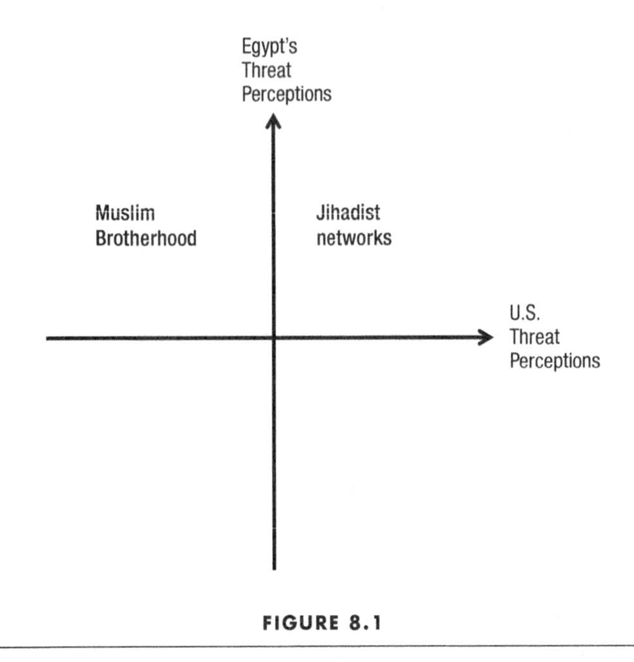

FIGURE 8.1

U.S. and Egyptian Threat Perceptions

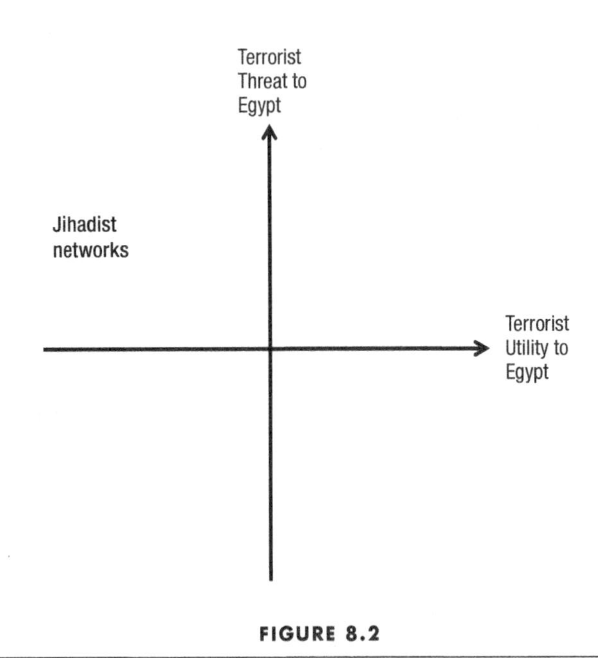

FIGURE 8.2

Terrorist Threat and Utility to Egypt

some analysts suggest increased after the Bush administration began using military tribunals for enemy combatants.[9] Egypt tightened its terrorist finance regulations, in keeping with relevant UN resolutions, and maintained open lines of communication with the United States on the financing issue.[10]

In spite of the security services' vigilance, militants networks in the Sinai Peninsula executed a series of terrorist actions between 2004 and 2006. Israel occupied the Sinai Peninsula from 1967 to 1982, after which it was returned to Egypt as part of the peace accord. Three separate car-bomb attacks targeted seaside resorts in the south of the peninsula: Taba on October 7, 2004; Sharm al-Sheikh on July 23, 2005; and Dahab on April 24, 2006.[11] Separately, two roadside bombs in northern Sinai hit a bus belonging to the Multinational Force and Observers.[12] Ten countries, including the United States, contributed soldiers to the MFO, which maintained a permanent presence in the Sinai after 1982. The attacks in Sinai between 2004 and 2006 cumulatively hit a mix of targets—international peacekeepers, Israeli tourists, and Egyptians—and spurred debates about whether al-Qaeda may have provided assistance or inspiration.[13] The authorities claimed the perpetrators of the bombings had links with the Palestinian movements Hamas and Islamic Jihad. Evidence suggests at least some of the individuals involved in the attacks trained in Gaza.[14] Without ignoring the potential for external assistance or inspiration and the impact of the Israeli-Palestinian conflict, it is important to situate the Sinai militants in the context of the relationship of the peninsula's population to the Egyptian state.

A substantial minority of Sinai residents are of Palestinian origin, even if many were Egyptian-born, and thus they are especially sensitive to events in Gaza and the West Bank. Bedouin tribes with historic origins in Arabia and branches in Israel, Gaza, the West Bank, and Jordan comprise the remainder of the Sinai's population.[15] The Bedouins had an adversarial relationship with the Egyptian state, which believed them to have collaborated with Israel when it ruled the peninsula.[16] Because of their ongoing involvement in smuggling and ties to armed actors across the border, the Sinai's inhabitants were also stereotyped as criminals and sometimes terrorists.[17] Rather than integrate the Sinai's inhabitants into the state, Cairo promoted the resettlement of Nile Valley migrants, whom it favored with jobs and housing at the expense of the local population. The development of tourist enclaves in the south further disadvantaged locals, who rarely benefited from employment opportunities and instead saw their land rights taken away. One local inhabitant referred to the regime as colonialists and lamented that the Sinai had passed through multiple periods of occupation: British, Egyptian, Israeli, and, since 1982, Egyptian again.[18]

The bombings made an already bad situation worse. Egyptian security adopted an "attrition and repression" approach that deployed resources considered sufficient to annihilate the enemy. Thousands of Sinai inhabitants were arrested. An untold number were tortured.[19] The security forces' heavy-handed response seemingly solved the problem. With no terrorist threat that could not be crushed by force, the regime had little incentive to change its approach to either counterterrorism or the Sinai. Yet the smuggling networks that helped enable the attacks and the risk factors that led Sinai-based individuals to launch them still existed.

These developments reinforced U.S. assessments that Egypt needed to improve its counterterrorism and border-security capabilities. This required equipment geared toward activities such as intelligence, surveillance, and reconnaissance. Washington also wanted Egypt to make these improvements so it could play a more active role in promoting regional security and backstopping U.S. military requirements in the Middle East.[20] Egyptian military officials chafed at U.S. efforts to reorient assistance toward arms and equipment more useful for regional counterterrorism and away from fighter jets, battle tanks, and other "prestige" weapons systems that were more suited to conventional combat. The $1.3 billion Egypt received annually was worth less every year owing to inflation. Egyptian leaders had little interest diverting additional money toward the type of kit American officials were pushing, especially considering that American assistance to Israel continued to rise.[21] U.S. efforts to promote political reform also foundered.

TAKING A BACKSEAT ON REFORM

Bush made democratization a key component of his counterterrorism strategy. He proclaimed it was necessary to "shake off decades of failed policy in the Middle East" and to cease tolerating "oppression for the sake of stability." The president promised to pursue a different course, consistently challenge the enemies of reform, and expect a higher standard from America's Arab partners.[22] Bush singled out Egypt as the place where a peaceful democratic transformation of the Middle East should begin. While encouraging other countries to take the first steps toward democracy, he asserted in a 2003 speech that "the great and proud nation of Egypt has shown the way toward peace in the Middle East, and now should show the way toward democracy in the Middle East."[23]

Calls for democracy ran headlong into the core interests of Mubarak's military-backed authoritarian regime. The Muslim Brotherhood was officially banned but generally tolerated and widely considered the most organized opposition vehicle in the country. Egyptian officials raised the specter of an Islamist takeover in response to calls for democratization and pointed to the chaos in Iraq as a reason why they were reluctant to reform.[24] Nevertheless, for a brief moment in 2005, when Egypt held multiparty presidential elections for the first time, it appeared that U.S. entreaties had found traction. However, any hopes for real progress had been dashed by the time the ballots were counted. The regime ensured the nominating process was so onerous that the outcome of the election was guaranteed well in advance. Just to be safe, the security services (sometimes with the help of proregime thugs) attacked opposition supporters, engaged in vote rigging, and arrested hundreds of Islamists and the opposing presidential candidate.[25] In spite of similar attempts at repression during the multiphase parliamentary elections held later that year, Muslim Brotherhood members who ran as independents won eighty-eight out of the 112 opposition seats. Mubarak's party maintained a majority with 311 seats, but the Brotherhood's gains were a fivefold increase over the 2000 election and occurred in spite of mass arrests and intimidation.[26]

Mubarak's regime immediately sought to reassert dominance. It retreated from promises of political reform, tightened its grip on power, and increased its repression of domestic opponents.[27] The state constitutionalized aspects of the Emergency Law, a step that Amnesty International called the "greatest erosion of human rights" in Egypt since the law was introduced.[28] Some analysts believe that in addition to his domestic political compulsions, Mubarak's harsh response may have been intended to send a message to the United States that his regime would not be pressured into political reform.[29] He viewed American efforts to promote democracy as a direct threat to him. Moreover, the regime and military supporting it both considered the prospect of a politically empowered Muslim Brotherhood to be a real threat to their privileged position in the country.

Some U.S. policy makers began looking for ways to use the annual assistance package provided to Egypt as leverage to change Cairo's behavior. Congress started debating whether to condition assistance to Egypt on, among other things, human rights, democratization, efforts to control the Egypt-Gaza border, and religious freedoms.[30] In 2008, after multiple attempts to condition military aid failed, U.S. lawmakers finally passed legislation withholding $100 million in military or economic assistance until the secretary of state certified that Egypt had taken concrete steps to "adopt and implement judicial reforms that protect the independence of the judiciary; to review criminal procedures and train police leadership in modern policing to curb police abuses; and to detect and destroy the smuggling network and tunnels that lead from Egypt to Gaza."[31] The legislation also allowed the secretary of state to waive the conditions. Then secretary of state Condoleezza Rice, who had challenged Egypt to "lead and define" a democratic future in the Middle East in a powerful 2005 address, exercised the waiver option, allowing total funding to Egypt to continue.[32]

These were existential issues for Egypt's leaders, on which they were united and resolute. The stakes were lower for the United States, where officials struggled to formulate a coherent position. This was partly a result of fears that groups like the Muslim Brotherhood would pursue policies counter to U.S. interests if they ever took power. American officials were also reluctant to exercise too much pressure on Egypt because they were afraid of jeopardizing relations with a seemingly stable government that supported U.S. foreign policy goals in the Middle East, granted ongoing access to the Suez, and provided various other forms of tactical counterterrorism cooperation.

BUILDING ON PATTERNS OF COOPERATION

One of the purposes of security cooperation is to develop and sustain relationships with other nations that will allow U.S. forces on their territory and in their airspace. After 9/11, Egypt granted the United States overflight rights for the invasion of Afghanistan. U.S. officials again sought access in March 2003 for Operation Iraqi Freedom. This was a more substantial request, since Mubarak opposed the invasion. As an autocrat, the Egyptian president had little interest in any venture designed to help spread democracy in the region. He also correctly assessed that the war would become a recruiting bonanza for the jihadist movement.[33] Despite his and the Egyptian public's strong opposition to the Iraq war, Mubarak provided U.S. forces access to Egyptian airspace and expedited passage for U.S. warships through the Suez Canal.[34]

Intelligence cooperation with Egypt already existed before September 11. In addition to keeping tabs on their own territory, the Egyptian intelligence services monitored the activities of Egyptian militants in multiple countries and had an abundant amount of information on al-Qaeda and other jihadist groups.[35] The United States and Egypt worked closely on finding individuals of mutual concern. In those instances where that individual was out of reach of the Egyptian authorities, the United States sometimes brought its capabilities to bear. This "hunting dimension" of the counterterrorism relationship worked reasonably well, especially once the United States began executing direct-action strikes.[36] Egyptian intelligence and security services also cooperated on the detention and interrogation of subjects. The government often acted unilaterally to take suspected terrorists off the streets. Many of these individuals were not wanted in the United States, and an untold number of them were probably not involved in jihadist activity. In cases where detainees were involved in terrorist activities, their interrogation sometimes served U.S. intelligence interests.[37] Egyptian authorities also shared evidence with their counterparts in the United States via the Mutual Legal Assistance Treaty, thus enabling the use of this evidence in U.S. courts.[38]

Recall that Cairo was a key partner in the U.S. rendition program that transported prisoners to another country without formal extradition proceedings. Rendition of individuals suspected of involvement in terrorism began in the 1990s. Its use expanded after 9/11, and Egypt took custody of between half and three-quarters of the individuals rendered, depending on the total number of people caught up in the program.[39] The Egyptians also assisted in reverse renditions, helping capture individuals in third countries who were then handed over to the United States. For example, recall from chapter 7 that after 9/11 U.S. analysts uncovered information that Abdul Salam Ali al-Hilah, a member of the Yemeni Political Security Organization, was closely connected to al-Qaeda. In addition to his job with the PSO, Hilah was a representative for Egypt's largest construction company. Egyptian intelligence arranged for the company to request he visit Cairo. When he did, Egyptian agents snatched Hilah, held him briefly in a secret prison, and then turned him over to the CIA.[40]

Collaborative activities like intelligence sharing and rendition are typically smoother when intelligence services from the two countries involved have a history of working together. That was certainly the case with Egypt and the United States. There is not enough evidence in the open source to chart the precise trajectory of intelligence cooperation or rendition, but these activities were relatively insulated from the vagaries of the relationship after 9/11, according to former Bush and Obama administration officials familiar with them.[41] This probably owes to both the longstanding nature of the intelligence-intelligence relationship and mutual concerns about the jihadist threat. The latter changed after the Arab uprisings.

THE LID COMES OFF IN EGYPT

President Obama shifted his administration's focus away from Bush's Freedom Agenda, which had alienated partners like Egypt without bearing fruit. This was part of a wider effort to reset U.S. relations with the Muslim world. In a landmark address delivered in Cairo six months after he took office, Obama reiterated his commitment to "governments that reflect the will of the people" but asserted that "each nation gives life to this principle in its own way."[42] Instead of democracy, Obama and his team emphasized solving the Israeli-Palestinian conflict. Success on this front was viewed as critical to U.S. interests. The issue was also more appealing to Cairo than political reform and thus a way to repair the relationship, which had cooled during the Bush years. Political reform remained a common subject during public and private diplomatic exchanges, but the Obama administration avoided overtly pressuring the Mubarak regime.[43] Then came the Arab uprisings. After almost three weeks of protests, during which support for Mubarak from both the United States and Egyptian military drained away, he left office in February 2011. Power transferred to the Supreme Council of the Armed Forces (SCAF), which dissolved parliament, suspended the constitution, and belatedly appointed an interim prime minister.

The eruption of protests in Cairo's Tahrir Square that led to Mubarak's downfall was accompanied by the disappearance of police and security forces nationwide.[44] The vacuum was especially acute in Sinai, which was already a hotbed of smuggling and other criminal and militant activities. Militancy in the Sinai surged as the security situation deteriorated further during the transition period. Emboldened Bedouin and Palestinian militants increased border smuggling and sacked abandoned checkpoints, police stations, and intelligence offices.[45] An influx of weapons from Libya exacerbated the lawlessness in Sinai. Bedouin smugglers sold these arms to locals and militants from Gaza.[46] After a July 2011 attack against a police station in Sinai's capital, militants calling themselves al-Qaeda in the Sinai Peninsula circulated pamphlets. They called for creating an Islamic emirate in the peninsula and halting discrimination against the Sinai's Bedouin tribes, among other things.[47] The SCAF responded with heavy forces backed up with tanks and Apache helicopters; the military evicted jihadist networks from population centers but did not target militant hideouts or attempt to degrade militant links between Gaza and Sinai.[48] As a result, the burgeoning jihadist groups in the Sinai remained. Ansar Bayt al Maqdis (Supporters of Jerusalem, or ABM) was the most organized among them.[49]

The tumultuous transition period that followed Mubarak's resignation finally ended with the June 2012 election of Mohammed Morsi, a leading Muslim Brotherhood activist, as president. Although the Muslim Brotherhood's victory at the polls complicated U.S.-Egyptian relations, the Obama administration was committed to honoring the outcome of democratic elections and sought to develop a good working relationship with Morsi's regime.[50] However, the new Muslim Brotherhood government had no history of cooperation with the United States. Moreover, Morsi and his advisors did not view jihadists as a long-term threat, because they believed that by establishing a genuinely Islamic government they could remove the rationale for jihadist violence. The United States tried in vain to convince the new government that al-Qaeda and others would not wither away and would target Egypt. U.S. counterterrorism cooperation, especially on the intelligence side, took a big hit as a result.[51]

Morsi ordered the military to reduce its operations in the Sinai. A substantial number of Egyptian forces that deployed to the peninsula were withdrawn. In lieu of a counterterrorism campaign, Morsi emphasized development, which had long been lacking. He also pursued political dialogue with Sinai-based jihadist groups in an effort to reach an accord that would end their incipient revolt.[52] After years of a heavy-handed approach by the military, Morsi was attempting to address the underlying risk factors for militancy. Although these initiatives were long overdue, the withdrawal of troops created space for Sinai-based jihadist networks to grow.[53] Mubarak's approach had been far too focused on hard power at the expense of socio-economic or other reforms in the Sinai. Morsi over-corrected, failing to recognize the need for security when attempting to implement such reforms in an area where militants operate. The Morsi government was also slow to protect the U.S. embassy when thousands of Egyptians protested outside of it on September 11, 2012.[54] The demonstrations coincided with protests in other Muslim-majority countries and the murders of the U.S. ambassador to Libya Christopher Stevens and three other Americans in Benghazi, Libya. Some demonstrators in Egypt scaled the embassy's walls, and this significant security breach reportedly led President Obama to question whether Egypt could still be considered a reliable partner.[55] The tide finally began to turn after ABM targeted Morsi directly. This event helped the United States and Egypt reconstitute collaboration on the intelligence side.[56] Morsi began reengaging on domestic counterterrorism operations as well. Then he was overthrown.

A JIHADIST INCUBATOR

Numerous missteps by Morsi and efforts to undermine him by Egypt's military-led deep state culminated in his ouster.[57] Protest movements, some of which were reportedly backed by the military, returned to the streets in the spring of 2013.[58] On July 3, after deadly clashes between the president's supporters and opponents amid another round of mass demonstrations, the military toppled the government and detained Mohammed Morsi. Although an interim president was appointed, General Abdel Fatah al-Sisi, Egypt's defense minister, held power. Brotherhood members and supporters staged mass demonstrations around the country. The security forces responded with lethal force, killing hundreds in the weeks and months that followed. The Muslim Brotherhood was not blameless for the violence. Encouraging supporters at Cairo encampments to martyr themselves, as protest leaders reportedly did, was hardly a means of deescalating the situation. Muslim Brotherhood members and supporters also traded fire with the security services and targeted Coptic Christians across the country.[59] But it was military leaders who balked at any reconciliation and instead escalated the situation. The military renewed the conflict in the streets, labeled Morsi supporters as "terrorists," banned the Brotherhood, and arrested most of its top leaders, along with hundreds of others, and sent more into hiding. In August, eight hundred Morsi supporters were reportedly killed in a single day.[60] The severity of the crackdown suggests that Egypt's generals believed they could finally rid the country of their bête noire or at least that they preferred to deal with the Brotherhood as a security problem and not as a political actor.

Jihadist attacks in the Sinai skyrocketed after the military removed Morsi from power.[61] Before long, Sinai-based jihadists brought the war to Cairo, assassinating government officials and executing mass car bombings.[62] Various jihadist groups and cells were responsible for this violence. ABM was the most prolific and effective organization.[63] In late 2014, the group's leadership swore allegiance to ISIS and became the Islamic State–Sinai Province (IS-IP hereafter).[64] It still primarily staged attacks against Egyptian targets but also took on a more global dimension. Most notably, IS-IP is believed to be responsible for the bombing that brought down a Russian airline in November 2015.[65] The following year, IS-IP expanded its target set to include the Coptic Christian cathedral in Cairo and other Coptic churches. This sectarian-provocation strategy, which was similar to the one ISIS has deployed in Iraq to pit Sunni against Shia, threatened to rend the fragile ties between Egypt's Muslim and Christian communities. Despite a consistent military onslaught, in 2017 IS-IP still enjoyed the same freedom of movement in the Sinai as it had several years earlier.[66]

The escalation of attacks in Egypt makes it appear as though jihadists were taking up the Brotherhood's cause. In reality, IS-IP and other jihadists had little love for the Brotherhood, which they had not supported when it was in power and believed had sold out long ago.[67] How, then, do we explain the uptick in violence after Morsi's ouster? First, the security vacuum that existed in the Sinai when the Morsi government was in power gave militants based there time to organize. When the armed forces redeployed a massive number of troops in September 2013 following Morsi's ouster, this provided plenty of targets for attack.[68] Second, Egyptian jihadists were opportunistic. The military's coup and attendant crackdown bolstered the case that the only path to power was via the gun and the bomb, not the ballot box. Jihadists used this opening to recruit more disaffected youth and try to peel away erstwhile Muslim Brothers frustrated with their organization's commitment to nonviolence.[69] Third, approximately five thousand Egyptians were fighting abroad with ISIS by this time.[70] A substantial number of them returned home to lead the revolution against Sisi's regime.[71] These men probably helped escalate the scale, tempo, and lethality of attacks.

The security forces' indiscriminate and heavy-handed approach, combined with longstanding, unaddressed socioeconomic grievances, fueled recruitment and contributed to an escalating cycle of violence. The regime pursued a scorched-earth policy in the Sinai, where the military sometimes burned down entire villages in response to jihadist activity.[72] The new military regime also designated the Brotherhood as a terrorist organization and insisted it was responsible for much of the violence, despite substantial evidence to the contrary.[73] Many of the people arrested were affiliated with the Brotherhood and not IS-IP or other jihadist groups.[74] This fixation on the Brotherhood risked diverting necessary manpower, resources, and attention away from the groups actually at war with the state. More importantly, mass arrests swelled Egypt's prisons, where torture was rife. Harsh policies toward the Muslim Brotherhood in the decades before 9/11 contributed to a split in the organization between those opposing and advocating violence and helped foster the development of jihadist groups in the first place. The regime's heavy-handed approach in Sinai and its harsh treatment of the Brotherhood threatened to push another generation of alienated Egyptians toward a new crop of jihadist organizations.[75]

Washington and Cairo agreed on the dangers that IS-IP and other jihadists posed but still disagreed in their perceptions of the Muslim Brotherhood (figure 8.3). Egypt designated it a terrorist organization. The Obama administration recognized it as an Islamist movement that had foresworn violence years earlier.

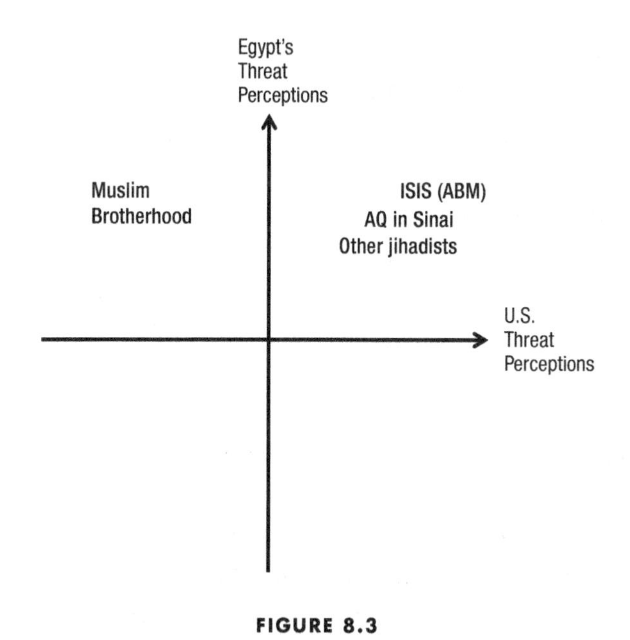

FIGURE 8.3

U.S. and Egyptian Threat Perceptions

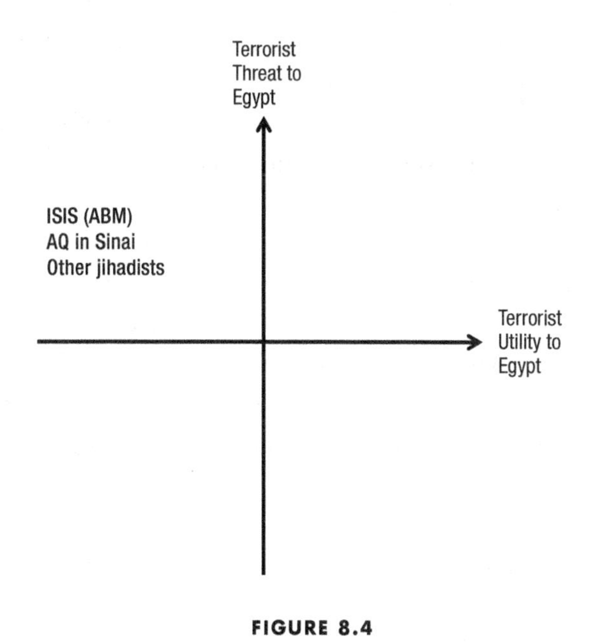

FIGURE 8.4

Terrorist Threat and Utility to Egypt

Differing perceptions of the Brotherhood and how to deal with it was just one of several strategic divergences plaguing the relationship. First, the Egyptian military's ouster of the Morsi-led government strained relations with the United States, forcing American officials to navigate between their avowed commitment to democracy and desire to maintain a critical partnership. Further complicating matters, U.S. law prohibits nearly all assistance to a country whose elected head of government is deposed by a military coup d'état or decree until a democratically elected government is restored.[76] Thus, Egypt's aid package was at risk.

Second, civil society organizations had operated in an environment of limited freedom and selective repression during the Mubarak era.[77] After a brief opening following the 2011 uprising, these organizations were now facing the most repressive environment they had experienced in decades. In December 2011, security forces raided the offices of seventeen American, German, and Egyptian organizations, including the National Democratic Institute and Freedom House.[78] The organizations were shut down, and forty-three of their employees were arrested.[79] The Muslim Brotherhood's Freedom and Justice Party maintained restrictions on these entities.[80] Once the military returned to power, it expanded the repression of journalists, activists, and other members of Egyptian and international civil society.[81] These activities were not only a clear affront to the rule of law. They also undercut organizations best positioned to counter radicalization and jihadist recruitment.

In June 2014, after taking off his military uniform, Abdel Fatah al-Sisi, the de facto leader of Egypt since the coup, was elected president. He garnered 96.91 percent of the vote amid a political environment that the United States diplomatically dubbed "restrictive."[82] A military-backed authoritarian regime was once again ruling Egypt. A new constitution ratified earlier that year codified the military's autonomy from civilian oversight and banned political activity based on religion.[83] Sisi's government accelerated the campaign to repress Egyptian civil society and all political opposition, including the Muslim Brotherhood; muzzle the press; and silence international organizations that received U.S. and European funding to promote democracy, governance, and rule of law. Approximately forty thousand people, mainly members of the Muslim Brotherhood but also journalists, lawyers, and others working in civil society, have been imprisoned. Another 1,700 have been "disappeared" as of 2017.[84] While prosecuting an overly military-centric campaign against IS-IP and other jihadist groups, the Egyptian regime has also used the threats they pose as justification for its repressive policies.

After years spent eschewing a greater role in regional counterterrorism, Egypt's threat perceptions led it to become more active outside its borders. However, it has done so in ways that do not neatly align with U.S. interests. Cairo perceived the Libyan civil war to be a threat to internal security because ISIS and other jihadists can use the safe havens in Libya to execute or support operations in Egypt. The flow of jihadists and arms across its western border led the Egyptian government to intervene in Libya. It launched strikes against terrorists based there; actions that the United States had also taken. However, Egypt also backed Khalifa Haftar, a rogue Libyan general and would-be strongman. This backing included providing intelligence and weapons, in contravention of the UN arms embargo, to Haftar's forces for their campaign against the UN-backed and U.S.-recognized government. Egypt was not the only foreign power backing a faction in Libya. Other countries, including close partners like the United Arab Emirates, were as well. This support prolonged the civil war and ran counter to the Obama administration's policy of promoting reconciliation.[85]

There were vigorous debates inside and outside the U.S. government over whether to prioritize immediate security needs in terms of counterterrorism or longer-term objectives related to governance and the pursuit of the liberal ideals that undergirded the U.S.-backed international system.[86] The fact that Egypt's violations of human rights and the rule of law were creating a breeding ground for jihadism further complicated matters. Washington also needed to preserve its relationship with Cairo if it hoped to retain a degree of influence. The fact that all of Egypt's military assistance was spent on American-made weapons compounded the problem because it meant cutting this aid could harm the U.S. economy.

The U.S. government attempted to walk a fine line, aiming to hold Egypt accountable without damaging the relationship or jeopardizing immediate security concerns. In 2012, Congress began adding new conditions to Egypt's military assistance that required the secretary of state to certify that Cairo was upholding the 1979 treaty with Israel, carrying out the transition to a civilian government, and protecting minority rights. This practiced continued thereafter, but with the exception of 2014, legislators added a national security waiver every year. That year, Congress also passed a law that included language exempting Egypt (and only Egypt) from the coup clause and allowed some military assistance for counterterrorism to be provided regardless of whether a democratically elected government was in place.[87]

The Obama administration never referred to the military overthrow of the Morsi government as a coup d'état, even though it clearly was. It halted the delivery of four F-16 fighter jets after the military began massacring members of the Muslim Brotherhood in July 2013 but also emphasized that the move was not indicative of wider plans to end military-to-military cooperation.[88] As violence escalated over the summer, the Obama administration considered withholding aid until a democratically elected government returned to power.[89] In October, the United States cancelled planned cash transfers of economic aid and placed executive holds on the delivery of Apache helicopters, F-16 aircraft, Harpoon missiles, and M1A1 tank kits to Egypt "pending credible progress toward an inclusive, democratically elected civilian government through free and fair elections."[90] However, U.S.-Egyptian counterterrorism cooperation continued, as did a considerable amount of military assistance.[91]

The administration was attempting to pursue a policy that "maintain[ed] strategic cooperation with Egypt to enable it to respond to shared security threats, while . . . encouraging progress toward restoration of democratic institutions."[92] The Egyptian government proved immovable on issues related to governance and rule of law. Egyptian leaders portrayed the U.S. response as either naïve or malign and lobbied the United States, along with some shared regional allies, for a resumption of full assistance.[93] To have had any hope of changing Egypt's behavior, the United States would have needed to suspend all assistance and coordinate similar cutoffs with other donors. Taking the middle road reduced whatever leverage the United States had.

Concerns about jihadist violence in Egypt and the need for Egyptian support for the anti-ISIS coalition (including access for U.S. military personnel) convinced policy makers that a return to the status quo was a priority.[94] The Obama administration released the Apaches to Egypt in 2014, enabling their use against the jihadist insurgency in the Sinai.

Following Sisi's victory in the presidential election that year, the U.S. government also released $575 million in aid.[95] In 2015, the White House decided to release all of the withheld assistance and announced that it would resume joint military exercises with Egypt.[96] However, U.S. officials also announced that beginning in FY2018, security assistance to Egypt would be reformulated to focus on counterterrorism, border security, Sinai security, and maritime security in addition to the maintenance of weapons systems already in Egypt's arsenal.[97] In addition to its concerns about the growing jihadist insurgency and state of bilateral relations with Egypt, the administration's decision to lift the holds may also have been an acknowledgment that they were not changing the Egyptian government's behavior. While promising to continue to assert principles in keeping with U.S. ideals, Obama explained his administration's reversal: "Our approach to Egypt reflects a larger point: The United States will at times work with governments that do not meet, at least in our view, the highest international expectations, but who work with us on our core interests."[98]

ALGERIA: A STUBBORNLY EFFECTIVE PARTNER

The September 11 attacks helped Algeria rehabilitate its reputation and emerge more quickly from international isolation following the bloody civil war of the 1990s. As part of its effort to build a partnership with the Algerian government after 9/11, the Bush administration lifted the arms embargo imposed on Algeria after it cancelled elections a decade earlier.[99] U.S. security assistance increased after 2002 but only climbed above $2 million a year twice in the decade after 9/11.[100] Much of the funding was used to sustain counterterrorism training for Algerian forces or for regional training programs in which the Algerians participated. Arms sales and security assistance appear to have had almost no bearing on whether Algeria cooperated on various initiatives. According to current and former U.S. officials, Algerian leaders made their decisions based solely on whether they thought the initiative in question was a good idea.[101] These officials also pointed out that almost immediately after 9/11 the United States gave the regime what it craved most: legitimacy.

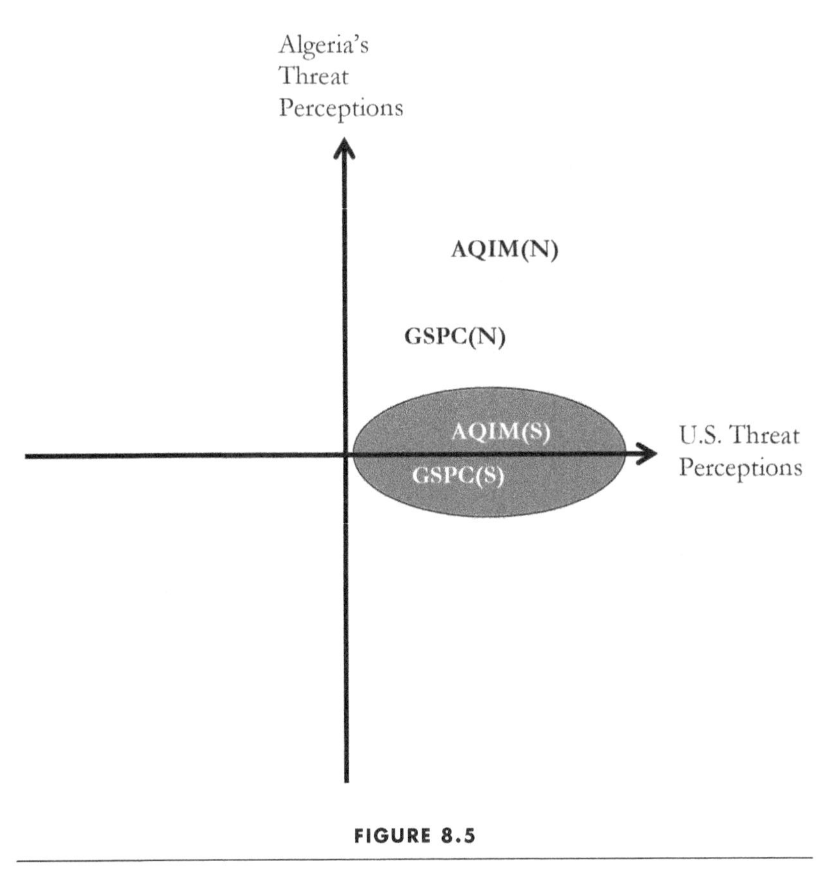

FIGURE 8.5

U.S. and Algerian Threat Perceptions

Assistance was not necessary to incentivize action against the GSPC/AQIM inside Algeria, where Washington and Algiers both considered the group a threat (figures 8.5 and 8.6). Three points are worth noting. First, although Algeria took a belligerent approach toward the GSPC/AQIM's northern branch, it had a more nebulous position toward the southern branch based in Mali. This was partly a function of Algeria's threat perceptions. The government did not consider the southern branch to be as big a threat as its northern analogue and was wary of inciting cross-border blowback. Algeria's traditional aversion to foreign intervention factored as well. As a result, Algeria did not take direct action or engage in robust regional cooperation against the southern branch. Second, it is important to recall that U.S. threat perceptions are presented in

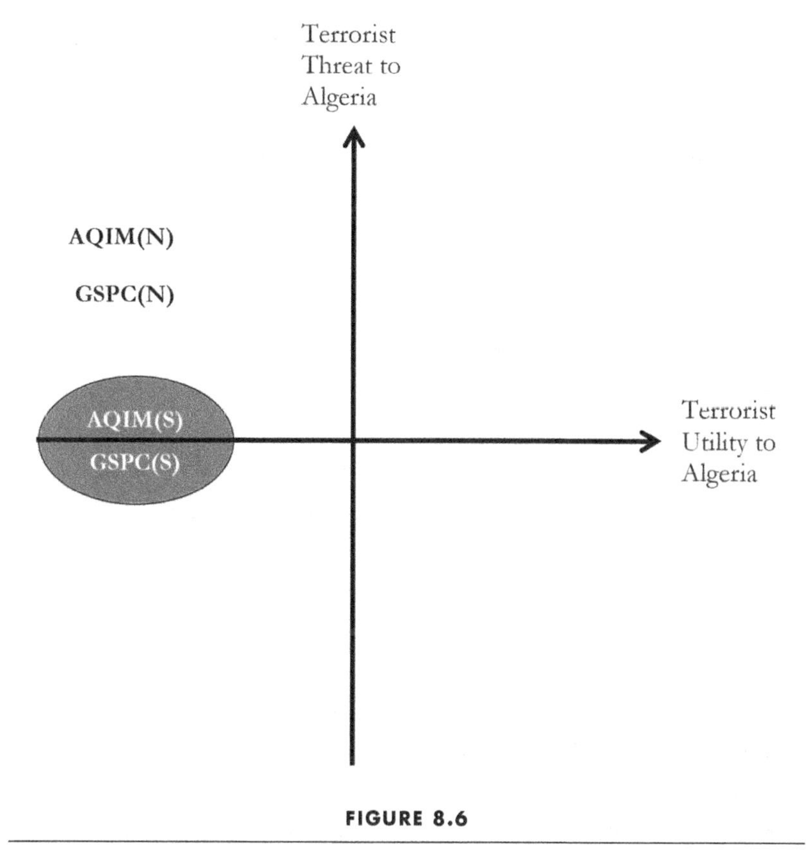

FIGURE 8.6

Terrorist Threat and Utility to Algeria

the context of the relationship with its partner. Regionally, America considered the GSPC/AQIM a major threat. Globally, the group ranked lower than other jihadist organizations. Third, the United States began taking the group more seriously after it became an al-Qaeda affiliate in 2007. It is arguable that this was also a wake-up call for Algeria, whose leaders thought the group's northern branch was essentially defeated at the time.

CONTAINMENT IN KABYLIA

The GSPC was on the defensive by 9/11. After waging a merciless counterinsurgency campaign for most of the 1990s, the Algerian authorities offered an amnesty in 1999 to militants who had not committed rape or murder.[102] Thousands of GSPC members took advantage of the opportunity. The regime continued to pursue an attrition campaign intended to eradicate the remaining hard core while simultaneously leaving the door open for eligible militants who wished to come in from the cold. Most GSPC members still in Algeria were confined to the mountainous Kabylia region east and southeast of the capital.[103] Search-and-destroy missions kept the group bottled up, deprived it of economic resources and personnel, and eliminated remaining insurgents.[104] Local self-defense forces worked with the military, gendarmerie, and police to protect rural and isolated populations and contributed to intelligence gathering. After 9/11, the group's regional and international support networks also came under increased pressure.[105] One GSPC member summed up the group's situation, saying, "We didn't have enough weapons. The people didn't want to join. And money, we didn't have enough money."[106] In 2005, Algeria's president Abdelaziz Bouteflika introduced the National Peace and Reconciliation Charter, which exonerated the military and security forces for the "disappearance" of thousands of Algerians and extended another amnesty offer to militants who had not yet surrendered and were not guilty of mass murder, rape, or bombings against public installations.[107]

Amid these trying times, Iraq became a lifeline for the GSPC. The day after Baghdad fell, the Iraqi embassy in Algiers was "besieged by Algerians who were volunteering to take part in the war against the United States."[108] Bouteflika condemned the U.S. invasion and called for the early withdrawal of foreign troops.[109] The regime and security services initially viewed fighting in Iraq as legitimate resistance and did not clamp down on the flow of fighters there.[110] Numerous networks cropped up to help would-be fighters reach the Iraqi front.[111] GSPC leaders seized the opportunity and called on Algerians to go fight in Iraq. The group tapped into independent networks to help volunteers reach Iraq and set up its own.[112] These moves enabled the GSPC to access a recruiting pool of men too disillusioned by the civil war to join the revolutionary jihad in Algeria. The group quickly became al-Qaeda in Iraq's regional beacon.[113] This position brought the GSPC credibility, money, additional recruits, and access to new networks in Europe.[114] It also led to its merger with al-Qaeda in 2006.[115] According to the former head of the group's media committee, joining al-Qaeda provided badly needed breathing space: "Faced with the national reconciliation process in Algeria, we'd no choice but to stop fighting. But with the merger we gained new authority in people's eyes: it allowed us to project an image of ourselves as a new group."[116]

Algerian officials were assuring the United States that the jihadist insurgency was essentially defeated and urging U.S. officials to downgrade their threat posture in Algeria. According to one former U.S. intelligence official, the message was "we got this, focus on the GSPC in the Sahel."[117] Instead, a renewed jihadist offensive rocked Algeria. The group still focused mainly on local targets but also began attacking foreign ones after the merger with al-Qaeda. AQIM celebrated its rebrand in 2007 by launching a spate of mass-casualty suicide bombings. It was the most prolific and lethal jihadist organization operating outside of the active war zones in Iraq and Afghanistan that year.[118] Although AQIM did attempt to strike various foreign targets, almost all of its suicide bombings were against local ones.[119] A vehicle-borne suicide bombing against the UN Refugee Agency was the most notable exception.

After being caught off guard, the Algerian government and security forces recovered to put AQIM on the defensive less than two years after its first suicide bombing. Algeria's military, intelligence service, gendarmerie, and local police forces collectively had a solid mix of capabilities and experience. Intelligence-led operations ensured that even during the height of the suicide-bombing campaign, AQIM's northern branch remained largely confined to Kabylia.[120] Restrictions were put in place on where and when trucks could circulate (to reduce vehicular bombings), and checkpoints were erected at access points around Algiers and other key cities. The United States and European partners provided technical equipment to help the security services track vehicles. Algerian authorities regulated sales of fertilizer, large amounts of which were required for the rudimentary bombs that AQIM used in its attacks.[121]

The state's counterterrorism offensive benefited from a population still recovering from the trauma of civil war. Suicide bombings were not a common feature of that conflict, but they reminded Algerians of the indiscriminate attacks that were. This translated into a greater number of tips phoned in to the police, who were able to translate intelligence into action directly or cooperate with other security forces that could.[122] Some AQIM officials, including several religious scholars and members of the group's leadership, rejected the use of suicide bombing and surrendered to the authorities.[123] Their surrenders provided the state with additional intelligence and propaganda value and robbed AQIM of well-trained and experienced members.[124]

Although attacks escalated again in 2009, their lethality declined dramatically. Bomb and gun attacks dropped a year later, as did the number of victims killed.[125] The security forces were unable to eliminate AQIM's presence in Kabylia entirely, but the terrorist threat was greatly reduced and largely contained. Algeria continued to refine its own counterterrorism architecture, including the development of specialized counterterrorism judicial procedures to deal with terrorism cases.[126] The regime also developed special legislation to enable the authorities to counter terrorist financing more effectively.[127] These steps were in keeping with international norms but had limited utility because AQIM raised much of its money through criminality. The group brought in millions in ransom money from Western governments as part of its kidnapping campaign in the Sahel. It also kidnapped and ransomed local businessmen in Kabylia.[128] Robberies of restaurants, bars, other businesses, and motorists at fake roadblocks, all of which were practices that dated back to the 1990s, remained common. These activities helped AQIM survive, but it was largely a spent force inside Algeria by the end of the decade.

CVE SANS GOVERNANCE

The Bush administration did not make nearly as strong a push for democracy in Algeria as it had in Egypt, but Algeria took limited steps on its own. After winning the presidential election with military backing in 1999 (after all other candidates withdrew amid allegations of fraud), Bouteflika prevailed in a multiparty contest in 2005 in which the military officially remained neutral. The bureaucracy and judiciary manipulated the process before the election to favor Bouteflika, but he probably would have won regardless, thanks to reductions in terrorist violence, many Algerians' desire for continued stability, and the divided nature of the political opposition.[129] International observers lauded Algeria for making progress toward democratization despite the manipulation that occurred.[130]

It would be a mistake to overestimate progress on political reform. "Le Pouvoir" (the power), a term Algerians use to refer to the political and military elite structures that rule their country, remained firmly entrenched.[131] In the ongoing tussle for influence between these structures, Bouteflika increased the authority of the presidency at the expense of senior military commanders and intelligence officers. But these actors collectively retained political and economic control in the country. Elected representatives still had little real power, and the bicameral legislature remained weak.[132] In short, Algeria was still governed by an authoritarian regime.

Moreover, the Islamic Salvation Front (FIS), whose victory at the polls in 1991 catalyzed the military's coup, remained outlawed. Other Islamist parties participated in the political system, as they had since the 1990s, but they were divided and often co-opted by the regime.[133] The state of emergency declared in 1992 remained in effect and was still used to justify heavy-handed security measures. Reports of security-force abuses and incidents of torture declined, but the practices continued. Arbitrary arrests and prolonged detention still occurred.[134] Although Algeria's economic position improved, largely thanks to income from oil and gas, the regime did little to address the chronically high levels of unemployment and underemployment, income inequality, inadequate education, or any of the other socioeconomic problems that had helped fuel recruitment for the insurgency during the 1990s.[135] Government corruption remained commonplace.[136] Conditions for radicalization and terrorist recruitment were still extant after 9/11 as a result, but the security services' vigilance and lingering trauma from the civil war acted as a check against GSPC/AQIM's growth.[137] Algerian leaders exploited this trauma but also took steps to develop targeted CVE programming.

After being caught flat-footed by the 2007–2008 AQIM offensive, the regime launched a series of initiatives to counter radicalization and recruitment. The government already monitored the sermons that imams gave at their mosques for extremist content. In 2007, the Ministry of Religious Endowments and Islamic Affairs went a step further and established an "anti–suicide bomber" program at local mosques and other religious institutions.[138] The authorities also worked to counter prison recruitment by putting qualified imams in charge of the religious discourse, using infiltrators to sow doubts about jihadist doctrine among prisoners, and isolating militants from the general population.[139] Historically, militants who received amnesty were kept on a tight leash and not allowed to speak publicly about their experiences. As part of its CVE efforts, the government arranged for some of the men who had surrendered after AQIM started executing suicide bombings to explain why they gave up their arms, call on other militants to follow suit, and declare that what AQIM was doing was not jihad.[140] The regime hosted Salafist clerics from other countries to make similar arguments through the media.[141] To reach militants in hiding, the authorities created a television and radio station and produced CD recordings that were airdropped into the mountains. Some AQIM commanders forbade their men from listening to the radio to insulate them from these messages.[142]

AQIM was again on the defensive by the time Obama took office. Because Algeria was not "blowing up," there was time and space to try to foster progress on CVE and rule of law, according to Ambassador Daniel Benjamin, the Obama administration's first coordinator for counterterrorism. He had numerous meetings with his Algerian counterparts on security-sector reform. The United States sent experts to Algeria and delivered a forensic lab, among other things, to advance the rule of law. The two developed and signed a mutual legal-assistance treaty in 2010 and a bilateral contact group on counterterrorism the following year.[143] The U.S. and Algerian governments also collaborated through the Global Counterterrorism Forum, the international body established in 2011 to promote information sharing and collaboration among counterterrorism officials from numerous countries on issues including rule of law and CVE. These efforts resulted in incremental progress, although as Benjamin noted, "Algeria, more than most countries, still did its own thing."[144] This was glaringly apparent when it came to the issues of access and intelligence cooperation.

ACCESS DENIED

American special operations forces were allowed to operate temporarily in southern Algeria to train and equip Algerian forces, but this was the extent of the military access provided.[145] Washington did not seek permission for a permanent military presence. The regime almost certainly would not have granted such access, which it would have viewed as a violation of national sovereignty. Algeria sometimes reacted negatively to proposals for U.S. military bases in other African countries as well.[146] U.S. and Algerian intelligence services had almost no relationship before 9/11, and the two did not develop a close partnership in the years that followed. Algeria sometimes shared intelligence, especially regarding suspected terrorists of Algerian origin, and other times withheld it.[147] According to current and former U.S. intelligence officials, they had to be very specific about the information they wanted. This was difficult because American officials often did not know what information the Algerians had to share in the first place. Even then Algeria was not always responsive to specific requests. For example, despite the United States helping orchestrate the capture of Amari Saifi, the GSPC commander who had kidnapped European tourists in 2003, Algeria denied American officials access to him. It took a long time before they were even able to debrief their Algerian counterparts on Saifi's interrogation. Overall, Algeria was reluctant to share intelligence about GSPC/AQIM activities inside the country and mainly provided information about the group's operations in the Sahel.[148] By focusing on the Sahel, Algerian officials likely hoped to convey a sense of normalcy in their country and leverage the United States to put pressure on Mali to do more about GSPC/AQIM elements based there.

A RELUCTANT REGIONAL PARTNER

After the United States replaced the Pan-Sahel Initiative with the more expansive Trans-Saharan Counterterrorism Partnership in 2005, American officials began asking the Bouteflika regime to become more involved in counterterrorism efforts in the Sahel. The two countries also launched a joint military dialogue that year to foster bilateral exchanges, training, and joint exercises. These activities were not only intended to improve the Algerian forces' effectiveness at home but also to encourage and empower them to contribute to regional counterterrorism efforts.[149] This was around the time when U.S. officials were seeking regional enablers in different parts of the world. Algeria's financial resources, counterterrorism experience, large military, and regional knowledge made it seem like the natural choice in the Sahel. Yet despite Algeria's claims to regional leadership and reputation as a robust counterterrorism actor, its leaders were reluctant to take action outside their country's borders. Algerian leaders agreed to participate in the TSCTP, but that was the extent of their regional cooperation for most of the decade.

Algeria's reticence stemmed from several factors. First, operating across the border might risk inviting more attacks at home. Algerian officials argued they were taking care of the terrorist problem inside their borders, so the GSPM/AQIM's presence in Mali was Bamako's responsibility.[150] Second, Algerian leaders preferred bilateral activities with the United States because they believed these reflected their country's importance.[151] Third, Algeria's reluctance to take on a larger regional role must be understood within the context of its historical experience and political identity. French colonization had scarred the country. Algeria's foreign policy since independence was defined by the principles of respect for national sovereignty and opposition to military intervention.[152] These principles were explicitly elucidated in the country's constitution.[153] Finally, Algeria's commitment to noninterventionism was theoretically intended to legitimize its desired role as an impartial actor that pursued peace and stability through diplomatic means.[154] In reality, this position sometimes constrained Algeria's policy options. Its leaders also had a tendency to undermine regional initiatives when they feared that neighbors were operating independently or to the detriment of Algerian interests.[155] Indeed, critics contended that Algeria sometimes sidelined regional competitors at the expense of coordinating an effective regional response to the terrorist threat.[156]

Fears that AQIM's kidnap-and-ransom campaign could trigger a U.S. or French intervention or that the group's Sahel-based militants might grow strong enough to launch cross-border attacks finally prompted the Algerian regime to get more engaged.[157] In 2008, Algeria deployed thousands of troops to its provinces abutting Mali, Niger, and Mauritania to combat AQIM. The state also began providing arms, ammunition, vehicles, fuel, and training to Mali as well as to Mauritania and Niger.[158] These four countries established a joint command center in the southern city of Tamanrasset in 2010 to coordinate efforts and mount joint operations against AQIM. Yet three years after it was established, the command center still "play[ed] no significant role in regional counterterrorism activity and [was] unlikely to carry out counterterrorism military operations for the foreseeable future."[159] By that time, the Arab uprisings and consequent instability in Algeria's neighborhood had forced it to expand regional counterterrorism efforts in other ways.

WEATHERING THE STORM

Algeria weathered the Arab uprisings without making any major structural changes to its government or polity. When demonstrations erupted, the government adopted elements of the approach taken by other authoritarian regimes in the region: offering limited political and economic concessions while simultaneously deploying the security forces to break up protests. At the same time, security forces in Algeria showed greater restraint than in other Arab countries. Instead of violently crushing the opposition, the Algerian regime played on popular anxiety that political change could undermine stability.[160] Memories of the civil war likely left many Algerians reluctant to rock the boat and thus susceptible to the government's appeals for continuity.[161] Because the regime had co-opted Islamist parties and worked hard to ensure that civil society was atomized, the protests that did occur were not as organized as in other countries. Government spending was increased in response to the uprisings, but most promises relating to political reform remain largely unfulfilled at the time of writing. After repealing the state of emergency in place since the 1990s, the regime replaced it with a new law that imposed harsher penalties for protesting.[162] The government subsequently enacted laws that carried severe penalties for journalists and others who disturbed "the morale of the nation."[163]

While political reforms related to governance and rule of law languished, the civilian government implemented a series of moves that strengthened the office of the presidency and regular army at the expense of Algeria's famously powerful and secretive intelligence service, the Department of Intelligence and Security.[164] It is difficult to discern the full extent or consequences of these moves, especially given the longstanding opacity of the Algerian regime. Some analysts speculated that these shifts could create new opportunities for Western states to engage Algeria and possibly encourage it to take on a greater role in regional security cooperation.[165] Ultimately, it was developments in Libya, Mali, and Tunisia that changed Algerian leaders' threat perceptions and forced them to reassess their country's regional role while remaining on guard at home.

The capture of northern Mali's major cities by Ansar Dine, AQIM, and MUJWA (discussed in the last chapter) heightened the regional dangers Algeria faced. For example, MUJWA, which was the AQIM offshoot that took part in the Malian conflict, conducted suicide attacks against gendarmerie and police bases in southern Algeria in 2012.[166] In Tunisia, the Islamist Ennahda party granted a general amnesty and prisoner release after taking power in 2011. Many prisoners had been unjustly incarcerated, but hardened jihadists were among those set free.[167] Having abandoned violence for activism themselves, Ennahda leaders believed it was possible to bring these jihadists into the political system and thus tolerated increased outreach activities.[168] Jihadists formed Ansar al-Sharia Tunisia (AST) and seized on their newfound operational freedom to engage in nonviolent outreach at home. While encouraging AST to maintain its above-ground activities as long as possible, AQIM simultaneously established its own operational presence in Tunisia. A belated crackdown by the Tunisian authorities on AST triggered escalating attacks against the security forces and high-profile targets frequented by Western tourists.[169] By then AQIM had a new base from which to target northern Algeria and to launch attacks against the Tunisian security forces unilaterally or in coordination with AST.[170]

AQIM also exploited the security vacuum that developed in Libya following Gaddafi's downfall and the easy availability of weapons there to launch attacks against Algeria.[171] Access to weapons and explosives from Libya augmented the flow of arms to AQIM's northern branch from its southern one. Gun and bomb attacks in northern Algeria spread in geographic scope and surged in number and lethality in 2011.[172] Mokhtar Belmokhtar, the one-eyed jihadist commander who helped spearhead the push into Mali before 9/11, rang in the new year in 2013 with a major terrorist attack against the Tigantourine Gas Facility in Ain Amenas, Algeria. His men penetrated Algeria's border and took over eight hundred hostages at the gas plant. The Algerian military stormed the facility, killing twenty-nine militants and capturing others. Thirty-nine foreign hostages were killed during the two-day crisis and subsequent rescue operation.[173] The attack was staged from Libya and executed by thirty-two militants from eight different countries: Algeria, Egypt, Mali, Mauritania, Libya, Nigeria, Tunisia, and Canada.[174]

Algeria's perceptions about regional threats were already shifting by end of the decade after 9/11. This shift intensified after the Ain Amenas attack. Algeria clearly viewed AQIM's southern branch and the congeries of groups connected to it as greater threats than in the past. All of these groups—AQIM's southern branch, Ansar Dine, and al-Mourabitoun (Belmokhtar's group)—had merged by the time of writing. Ansar Dine is separated from the rest of the pack in acknowledgment of allegations that Algerian intelligence has in the past attempted to use it as a mechanism for influencing other actors in Mali.[175] The threat from AQIM's northern branch had also grown. In 2014, a splinter of the group calling itself Jund al-Khilafa (Soldiers of the Caliphate) pledged allegiance to the ISIS emir Abu Bakr al-Baghdadi.[176] Figures 8.7 and 8.8 illustrate these developments.

Algeria's tilt toward greater regional involvement was primarily a function of its security perceptions. However, geopolitical compulsions reinforced the shift. Algerian leaders worried about losing ground to its regional rival Morocco, which had less military capacity but was more willing to partner with the United States on military operations.[177] Despite sharing short-term security interests with the United States and France, Algeria also feared the consequences of a U.S. intervention in the region and considered France a rival for influence in the Sahel. Taking on a greater regional role was a way for Algeria at least to maintain parity with Morocco, balance against French influence, convince the United States and European countries to take its interests into account, and create leverage with these external powers for use when future decisive moments arose. Additionally, Algiers likely hoped that invigorated engagement would encourage Sahelian countries to look to one another and Algeria for regional solutions rather than to outside powers like France or the United States.[178]

PULLING ITS WEIGHT

Algeria responded to rising AQIM attacks in the north with many of the same practices it had employed in the past: aggressive search-and-destroy

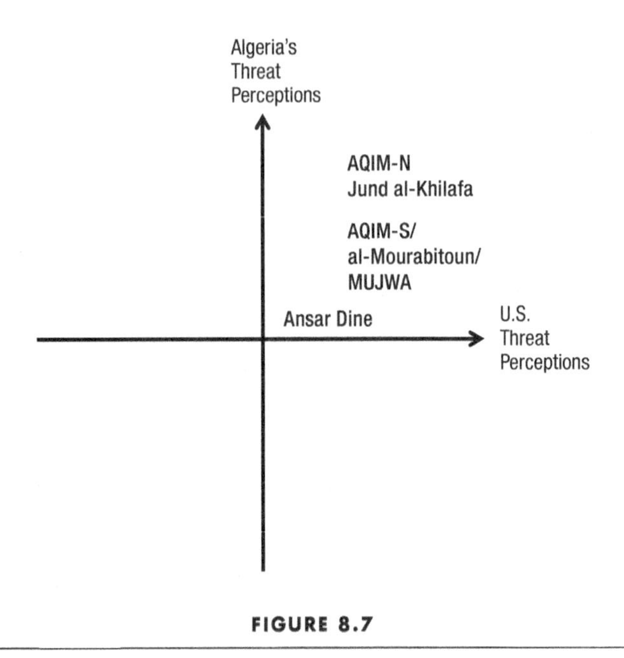

FIGURE 8.7

U.S. and Algerian Threat Perceptions

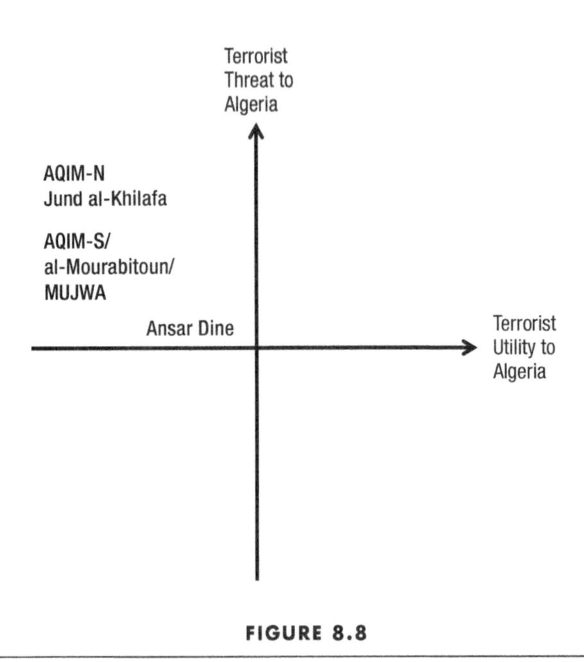

FIGURE 8.8

Terrorist Threat and Utility to Algeria

operations, restrictions on vehicular travel, and increased coverage of possible targets.[179] Operations targeted AQIM's northern units and ISIS's main affiliate, Jund al-Khilafa, whose leader the security forces killed in December 2014.[180] The government also adapted its approach to countering radicalization in part to combat foreign fighter flows to the Syrian conflict. The Ministry of Religious Affairs focused heavily on revitalizing Islamic education to promote tolerance while simultaneously encouraging more supervision of Salafi mosques and imams that operated independently of government control.[181]

As part of its domestic counterterrorism effort to combat cross-border attacks, the Algerian government imposed strict border controls, closed the crossings to Libya and Mali, made access to border zones conditional on military permission, and deployed ground and air forces to enforce these rules.[182] The army created a new military zone along the border with Libya and gave its commander substantial resources to combat the jihadist threat as well as cross-border smuggling.[183] At least 75,000 armed forces were deployed to monitor Algeria's southern and eastern borders. Approximately 50,000 of them were based along the Libyan border.[184]

Algeria had been an active diplomatic player since independence, helping resolve regional conflicts, including multiple Tuareg rebellions in northern Mali. Now it took the lead on facilitating a peace deal in Mali by initiating the Inclusive Inter-Malian Dialogue in January 2014. The dialogue brought together regional governments, multilateral organizations, and various substate Malian groups.[185] Algeria became the chief mediator of the dialogue, which produced a peace and reconciliation agreement in the spring of 2015.[186] Progress on the agreement was sub-par as of 2017, but this does not erase Algeria's help facilitating it. While taking the lead on diplomatic efforts in Mali, Algeria also sought to facilitate a political solution to the crisis in Libya, where the government had split into two competing authorities. The Algeria government launched the Inter-Libyan Dialogue to bring together all Libyan parties to the conflict, including Islamists and Gaddafi-era officials, and coordinated the involvement of ten other governments as well. Finding a political solution was intended to enable the reemergence of state institutions, which were a necessary condition for reducing the external terrorist threat to Algeria.[187]

The biggest adaptation in terms of Algeria's counterterrorism policies came in the areas of intelligence, access, and regional security. Intelligence cooperation with the United States and EU member states improved substantially after the Arab uprisings and accelerated following the Ain Amenas attack.[188] Despite opposing France's military intervention in Mali, Algeria allowed French overflight of its territory. Algerian support for another country's foreign intervention suggested a softening of its own noninterventionist stance.[189] Algeria also increased bilateral cooperation with some of its neighbors, which was another sign that the government in Algiers was prepared to be more flexible when it came to noninterventionism.

After eight Tunisian soldiers were killed in an ambush in the Chaambi Mountains near the Algerian border in the summer of 2013, Algeria boosted its military presence in the area and expanded counterterrorism cooperation with Tunisia.[190] The two countries increased intelligence sharing and coordination of military activities, including training for the Tunisian special forces and joint patrols along their shared border to root out AQIM and ISIS militants.[191] Although the Algerian government denied it, some reports suggested that Tunisia allowed Algerian special forces to cross the border in pursuit of militants.[192] After temporarily withdrawing its military advisers from Mali and stopping delivery of military equipment during the civil unrest there in March 2012, the Algerian government subsequently improved intelligence cooperation with Mali and agreed to plans for joint personnel training and mixed patrols with Malian forces.[193] Algeria still lagged behind in terms of governance and rule of law, but several years after the Arab uprisings it had emerged as an increasingly consequential counterterrorism partner in an unstable region.

* * *

In April 2017, Donald Trump granted Egypt's president Abdel Fattah al-Sisi an audience at the White House. Describing Sisi as a "fantastic guy," Trump lauded Egypt's counterterrorism campaign and made no mention of its human rights abuses.[194] The Bush and Obama administrations recognized the need to work with partners that do not share U.S. values. However, both attempted to promote political reforms, even if competing interests circumscribed their efforts. Trump, on the other hand, has consciously eschewed calls for addressing the political and economic injustices that create conditions for jihadist groups flourish. He appears to have no interest in promoting good governance and rule of law and instead has opted for cheerleading the domestic counterterrorism efforts that countries like Egypt and Algeria would make regardless of their relations with United States.[195]

Comparing the two Arab countries illustrates that both were thoroughly committed to conducting counterterrorism campaigns on their own soil because of their threat perceptions. Similar calculations informed regional cooperation. Although Egyptian and American interests in the region were largely congruent, the Mubarak regime exhibited no interest in taking on the type of regional counterterrorism role the United States would have liked. When Egypt did become more involved regionally after the Arab uprisings, it was mainly in coordination with local Arab partners and not the United States. As of 2017, Cairo, along with the United Arab Emirates, remained a critical backer of Khalifa Haftar's forces in Libya. Washington also struggled to get Algeria to take the lead on regional counterterrorism initiatives. Algeria belatedly took on a larger regional role after new threats in its near abroad emerged following the Arab uprisings. Notably, Algerian leaders were partly motivated by a desire to reduce the potential for other regional countries to look to the United States or France for assistance.

Egypt was much more forthcoming on tactical cooperation, where a partner's relationship with the United States and its interest in the assistance that comes with that relationship have more weight. Algeria was not cooperative on either intelligence or access until after the Arab uprisings, when its regional threat perceptions changed. U.S. efforts to build patterns of cooperation with Algeria may have helped it take advantage of this development. Because Algeria was not in crisis, U.S. officials were able to devote sufficient time to pursuing longer-term objectives related to security-sector reform and CVE. The Arab uprisings highlighted the importance of such endeavors and reinforced the challenges related to working with partner nations that do not share U.S. values, even if they do have overlapping threat perceptions. Optimizing these and other types of partnerships is the topic of this book's conclusion.

CONCLUSION

Making the Most of Cooperation

In the final year of Obama's second term, Lisa Monaco, the assistant to the president for homeland security and counterterrorism, outlined the administration's counterterrorism framework. She focused mainly on ISIS but also voiced concerns about a resurgence of al-Qaeda and its affiliates. The framework Monaco put forward consisted of five pillars: protecting the homeland, engaging U.S. partners, taking direct action on the battlefield, disrupting enabling factors like financing and foreign fighters, and countering violent extremism.[1] Monaco listed engaging partner nations as a specific element of the U.S. strategy, but a close reading of her remarks and of American policy reveals that cooperation with other countries is critical in one way or another to all of these elements.[2] This focus on partners echoed a key theme found in numerous strategy documents produced by the Bush and Obama administrations: almost all aspects of international counterterrorism rely in some way on cooperation with other countries.

Since taking office in January 2017, Donald Trump has embraced the burden-sharing aspect of Obama's "indirect" strategy to combating terrorism. Counterterrorism cooperation with key partners, at least in Europe, has remained reasonably solid, according to current and former officials with whom I spoke in the spring and summer of 2017. This is more of a testament to the professionals who manage these relationships than to the president, who has failed to adopt Obama's focus on building sustainable partnerships. The Obama administration's reliance on local and international partners to fight terrorist groups on the ground was not only intended to share the costs and risks. It was also supposed to make gains more sustainable by giving partners ownership of the fight, building patterns of cooperation with them, and thus avoiding the perception of U.S. overreach by giving counterterrorism a local face.

In contrast, Trump has taken a more transactional approach. Pursuing counterterrorism cooperation in this manner fails to account for the myriad ways that partners can directly and indirectly help or hinder U.S. efforts. It also risks alienating some partners and reinforcing the worst impulses of others.

Trump's overall counterterrorism strategy was still taking shape when this book went to press, but there were already other warning signs of dangers ahead. Although defeating ISIS was a pronounced priority, Trump has evinced a maximalist objective that all Islamist terrorist groups—Sunni and Shiite—are enemies that must be defeated. He also has promoted an overly military-centric approach toward counterterrorism premised on the view that military force is sufficient to accomplish U.S. objectives even if divorced from other tools of national power. Both are reminiscent of the misguided steps of the early Bush years before that administration adapted. Unlike Bush or Obama, Trump has appeared openly hostile even to attempting to address the socioeconomic and political conditions that enable jihadist groups to flourish. Instead, Trump has warmly embraced autocrats, sending the message that the United States condones, and perhaps even welcomes, their repressive activities.

The effects of his hypernationalist America First agenda on counterterrorism cooperation are also impossible to ignore. Normally, debates over whether to implement this or that counterterrorism-specific recommendation would occur within the traditional security paradigm that has shaped U.S. foreign policy for the past seventy years. However, it would be naïve to suggest that U.S. counterterrorism efforts and partnerships are not affected by the seismic shifts in America's approach to the world since Trump took the oath of office.

This makes it more challenging to present recommendations for how the United States might get more out of its partners and mitigate some of the negative side effects that come from working with them. Yet it is also the case that many policies are shaped and executed at the working level, and there are many policy makers and practitioners throughout the U.S. government who remain committed to a pragmatic and principled approach to counterterrorism. This probably helps explain why day-to-day cooperation with European allies and other partners has continued to function.

In a best-case scenario, the administration will rectify some of the most problematic elements of its foreign policy and evolving counterterrorism strategy. At the very least, what follows could offer guideposts for future administrations, which undoubtedly will continue to confront the challenges of working with difficult partners to combat nonstate terrorist groups. With this in mind, the next section sums up what the United States can expect from partner nations. The rest of the chapter presents ideas for how to consolidate counterterrorism cooperation where it is good, mitigate risks where it is bad, and get the most out of the trade space in between.

MANAGING EXPECTATIONS

The United States has sought more counterterrorism assistance from partner nations since 9/11 than it did beforehand. Cooperation could be direct or indirect, domestic or international, short-lived or sustained, and highly costly or relatively painless. Because counterterrorism has multiple elements, partner nations can directly and indirectly affect U.S. efforts in myriad ways. It is also important to be aware that the ability to secure cooperation or forge close partnerships does not always equate to success when it comes to achieving counterterrorism objectives. Most partner nations help and hinder U.S. efforts to achieve its objectives. In this book, I focused on jihadist groups that have preoccupied the United States since 9/11 and on partnerships with Muslim-majority countries where these actors developed and operated. The complexities of cooperation are especially acute with these states but many aspects of them are also found elsewhere. The cases selected also highlight the range of relationships that may exist between a partner nation and a targeted terrorist group.

The dynamics of traditional state-state alliances interact with terrorist-state relations to inform how a country helps or hinders U.S. counterterrorism efforts. Both sets of dynamics are shaped by a country's security paradigm, which is a function of its national interests, relevant domestic politics, strategic culture, and perceptions of its environment. Two factors determine terrorist-state relations. The first is whether and what type of utility a partner ascribes to the terrorist group or infrastructure that is the target of cooperation. A partner's threat perceptions are the second factor. As we have seen, threat perceptions include both a partner's understanding of the nature and causes of the terrorist threat and how it ranks that threat relative to others. Terrorist-state relations are the most important determinant regarding a partner's willingness to undertake domestic counterterrorism operations. They sometimes contribute to action or inaction when it comes to countering violent extremism. These dynamics also influence a partner's contributions on tactical and regional cooperation, although traditional alliance dynamics and instruments of statecraft are more salient here than for other types of cooperation. This is true in terms of whether a partner cooperates in these areas and also in terms of the type of actions it is willing to take.

Traditional alliances dynamics and instruments of statecraft are most salient for tactical and regional cooperation but are typically secondary to terrorist-state relations when it comes to domestic counterterrorism operations. Coercion may alter a country's strategic calculus in the short term. It worked with Pakistan and Yemen after 9/11, two cases where U.S. threats were credible and the potential costs to be imposed were high enough to yield the desired outcome. In both cases, the United States combined the threat of military force and international isolation with incentives to achieve stated objectives for cooperation. Yet neither country altered its security paradigm, and U.S. policy makers ultimately confronted one of the fundamental drawbacks of coercion: threats have a shelf life. They can only be made for so long before they must be carried out. Maintaining a coercive posture for an extended period of time is generally difficult. It is especially hard once a country has begun providing some cooperation, since carrying out ultimatums risks sacrificing tangible benefits from the partnership. This shortcoming does not only apply to military force. It is also true for threats to impose sanctions or cut off security assistance.

Good bilateral relations with a partner nation (or it desire for them) can act as a force multiplier when the United States and its partner share a threat and a similar perception of that threat. Where they do not share both, states rarely act against their own perceived interests simply because the United States asks them to. Stronger bilateral relations can help facilitate some aspects of regional cooperation and appear to be most useful when it comes to securing military access and for cooperation on intelligence or detainees. A long history of steady security cooperation helped pave the way for basing and transit rights in Egypt and Saudi Arabia. Robust intelligence-intelligence relationships also typically take time to develop and can be somewhat insulated from the vagaries of a partner's wider relationship with the United States. Yet there are limits. For example, the CIA and Pakistani ISI quickly rekindled their close working relationship after 9/11, but cooperation declined as U.S. and Pakistani interests diverged and the two countries became more antagonistic toward each other. Countries that have similar threat perceptions might find intelligence sharing difficult if their respective intelligence agencies do not have longstanding ties. For example, because the United States and Algeria did not have historically strong relations, cooperation on areas like intelligence sharing proved challenging despite their shared counterterrorism interests.[3]

U.S. policy makers have sometimes been overly optimistic about the influence that providing security and economic assistance brings, leading to considerable consternation when it fails to create sufficient leverage to shift a partner's behavior.[4] Given the large sums of money involved, the expectation that aid could be a lever makes sense. Yet the provision of assistance alone is rarely enough to change a partner's strategic calculus, alter how it views its threat environment, or promote domestic reforms. This does not mean assistance is worthless. Where the United States and its partners share similar objectives for how assistance will be used, it can make a partner force more effective at doing something it was already committed to doing. Even when this is not the case, security cooperation and assistance can help promote stronger relationships and build patterns of cooperation over time.[5] The provision of assistance sometimes incentivizes partners to take limited actions they otherwise would not. For example, countries may mount patrols or stage periodic raids in return for aid. These operations are unlikely to be comprehensive or consistent if done mainly to keep assistance flowing, but in some cases they will be enough to keep the threat at bay.

Using assistance as an incentive rather than as a mechanism for building capacity is more likely to be effective in terms of securing tactical cooperation, especially access. However, the longer security assistance is provided, the more likely the recipient country will view it less as an incentive than as an entitlement. Ongoing U.S. assistance and diplomatic support may also make a partner even more resistant to change in areas where that partner is already reluctant to reform because it defrays the costs of staying the course.[6] Because dependence is rarely a one-way street, the United States must weigh the potential leverage that comes with threatening to cut off assistance against the perceived costs of doing so. This calculus becomes even more complicated when assistance is intended to achieve multiple objectives, not all of which may relate to counterterrorism.

The conventional wisdom holds that partners play the counterterrorism card and exaggerate the terrorist threats in order to extract security assistance from the United States. This was true in some cases. Yemen, for example, had an incentive to maintain a terrorist threat in order to keep assistance flowing. But the reality is more complicated. For example, Mali welcomed U.S. aid but did not go out of its way to hype the terrorist threat. And Algeria downplayed it and evinced minimal interest in military aid, though the security forces did benefit from increased sales of nonlethal equipment after 9/11. The propensity to use terrorist threats as a way to extract assistance appears most likely in countries that face one or multiple other threats—interstate or internal—for which they require military aid the United States is unwilling to provide. Fears, which are not always unfounded, of U.S. abandonment once a terrorist threat is dealt with may reinforce a partner's predilection to engage in this behavior. In addition to using a terrorist threat to extract assistance, states such as Egypt have utilized it as a way to fend off U.S. pressure to make unwanted reforms.

Gaining traction on efforts to counter radicalization and recruitment has proved more challenging than on other areas of cooperation. Militarized approaches to counterterrorism are often ineffective and risk making the problem worse. Thus, it is impossible to ignore the need for noncoercive methods of reducing the pool of recruits for terrorist groups. Yet finding the right methods, adopting the patience necessary to see them through, and convincing partners to get on board has been difficult. The terrorism expert John Horgan compared the difficulties inherent in tackling radicalization to being shipwrecked with only a tiny rowboat for survival. "Once you realize that staying put is not a feasible option," he wrote, "it can be impossible to know in which direction you should row."[7] This is not a reason to stop rowing. The field of countering violent extremism is still in its infancy. Healthy skepticism about what can be accomplished is a good thing, provided it drives efforts to refine CVE efforts. The same goes for attempts to promote political reforms in partner nations. It is unrealistic to expect partners to make fundamental changes to their polities. However, even undemocratic regimes might be willing to make modest reforms if they can be convinced it will help them avoid or reduce threats.[8]

Any counterterrorism strategy must account for two immutable realities: cooperation from other countries is necessary to achieve many counterterrorism objectives, and most partners will both advance and impede U.S. efforts to achieve them. This book's conclusion presents ideas for how the United States might optimize its counterterrorism partnerships. These ideas focus on how to get the most out of partner nations, not work around them. The United States has made considerable strides in its ability to gather and synthesize intelligence, track and target terrorists, and use direct action to eliminate threats. It has also put in place a robust homeland security architecture that in concert with international protocols has helped prevent another centrally directed terrorist attack from overseas. These are important facets of counterterrorism in their own right and can reduce U.S. reliance on difficult partners in certain areas. There undoubtedly are ways these and other unilateral measures could be improved. However, because partnerships remain critical to so many aspects of counterterrorism, I zero in on how to make the most of cooperation. Some of the ideas that follow have applicability beyond counterterrorism partnerships but are especially relevant when working with weak or difficult countries to achieve counterterrorism objectives.

KNOW YOUR PARTNERS, NOT JUST YOUR ENEMIES

Partners are commonly thought of in the context of their relationship with the United States. As we have seen, it is also critical to distinguish them based on their threat perceptions and relationships with the terrorist group or infrastructure that is the target of counterterrorism cooperation. When a partner prioritizes a terrorist threat relative to other internal or external security challenges, it is likely to conduct counterterrorism operations of its own volition. Security assistance can be a force multiplier, but there is likely little need to expend leverage or attempt to incentivize actions a partner is already taking. American officials can focus on other issues such as capacity building or political reform without fear of jeopardizing counterterrorism efforts against the group in question. However, things become more complicated with states that simultaneously target some terrorist groups while supporting others or engaging in enabling behavior. As the number of divergences with the United States increases, so does the need for American officials to pick and choose where they exert limited leverage. And across the board, for all types of states, the desire for tactical cooperation can militate against exerting pressure on other issues.

Sometimes, a partner's deficiencies are so great that addressing them is simply unrealistic. In a world of such imperfect partners, securing limited military access, intelligence cooperation, or other ad hoc assistance taking the fight to the enemy is easier to achieve. These types of cooperation are also generally more concrete and easier to observe than progress on areas like governance or shifts in a partner's regional outlook. And in some cases, such cooperation can be enough to keep the homeland safe or protect U.S. civilians and interests overseas. It is also important to note that tactical cooperation can yield strategic effects, as was the case with the ability to conduct drone strikes against core al-Qaeda in Pakistan. However, this type of cooperation is typically insufficient for defeating terrorist groups *and* removing the conditions that might enable them to regenerate.

Eliminating risk is impossible. The key is to recognize potential costs, determine where to accept more risk, and then plan accordingly. For example, if the United States is going to sacrifice the pursuit of a partner nation's political reforms and prioritize short-term security objectives, then it should be prepared for terrorism to fester. America's reputation may also suffer if the partner engages in harsh repression and the United States is seen as enabling this behavior. The converse is equally true. Punishing partners for bad political behavior may strain the bilateral relationship and could place certain aspects of tactical cooperation at risk or reduce U.S. influence over how another country conducts its domestic counterterrorism operations. Even pushing a willing partner government to move too quickly on reforms may have negative consequences, by, for example, making reformists the target of competing power brokers whose positions or wealth is endangered.

If the threat has not yet manifested, then the United States may be able to focus more on promoting reforms and building capacity. Identifying willing or potentially necessary partners and investing early—that is, before a crisis—provides space to take a firmer line with partners. In other cases, America will need to work around its partners wherever possible. Finding alternatives in terms of access, intelligence, or other forms of cooperation can reduce U.S. reliance on a problematic partner and possibly enable the United States to make some gains on the margins. These alternatives are not always available, however, and often come with their own costs.

Sometimes, the United States will need to moderate its objectives at times or alter its strategy based on a partner's motivations, political makeup, and capacity. Knowing when to pursue maximalist objectives, put enough skin in the game to mobilize partners, deploy assistance or coercion, or settle for killing the enemy requires understanding as much about the partner in question as it does about the threat America is attempting to combat. Currently, the real or potential threat a terrorist group presents to the United States is the critical variable determining U.S. counterterrorism policy toward the country or region where that group is based. Once that policy is set, there is a shift toward implementation using whatever instruments are deemed necessary or available. This might become an iterative process that considers a partner's calculus along the way, but assessments of what the United States can expect from other countries still typically receive shorter thrift. Optimizing cooperation requires augmenting a threat-centric paradigm with a partner-centric one that dedicates sufficient time and resources to assessing what the United States can expect in the way of cooperation from other countries, and at what cost.

TOWARD A PARTNER-CENTRIC PARADIGM

U.S. threat assessments consider a range of factors to determine a terrorist group's intent and capability, which are the two key variables that inform the danger that organization poses to the United States. A similar set of indicators could help unpack the concepts of a partner nation's "will" and "capacity," enabling U.S. policy makers to get a better picture of what they can expect from these countries, and at what cost.

These indicators include where a partner ranks a specific terrorist threat relative to other threats; whether the partner in question is so preoccupied with another security challenge that it cannot provide the cooperation the United States needs or, worse, subverts U.S. objectives; if other U.S. foreign policy initiatives might enhance these other threats or otherwise impair cooperation; what assistance the partner might seek in terms of dealing with these other threats and whether the United States is prepared to service these requests; the potential utility and staying power of incentives or coercive measures to secure various forms of cooperation; clear-eyed assessments of the transactional benefits a specific bilateral relationship yields; whether aspects of cooperation are more static, such as longstanding access, or dynamic, like intelligence sharing or permission to launch drone strikes; the institutional capacity of a partner's military, law enforcement, and intelligence agencies; and the nature of a partner's civil-military dynamics.

Additionally, it is always important to evaluate not only how a partner can help or hurt directly but also how else it might indirectly enable or constrain U.S. counterterrorism efforts and why. This would help determine when America should wrap its efforts around shared interests with a partner and where it should not because of the potential negative externalities that could result. A partner-centric paradigm would also account for how the partner in question would respond to coercion, incentives, or the assignment of conditions to assistance. For example, which actors inside the partner nation would be empowered or undercut? How would these actions affect other U.S. objectives? Is the reward or punishment appropriately matched to the goal it is intended to achieve, and, if so, how does that goal advance U.S. counterterrorism efforts, and at what cost to the United States? This is not an exhaustive list, but it highlights the sorts of potential indicators that could help the United States optimize its partnerships and the types of questions policy makers and practitioners should ask when it comes to counterterrorism cooperation.

Efforts to augment a threat-based paradigm with a partner-centric one would benefit from reducing divisions between regional and counterterrorism officials in both the intelligence and policy making worlds. The United States made real strides breaking down barriers separating counterterrorism analysts across the intelligence community.[9] Yet counterterrorism and regional analysts are still not as integrated as they could be. The same is true on the policy side. Sometimes this is done to protect strictly compartmented information, because of turf battles, or simply as a result of normal bureaucratic silos. Barriers come down at higher levels in the policy making process, but much of the heavy lifting is done at the working level. This is also where officials with deep country expertise are most often found. These divisions and imbalances can make it more difficult to maximize the value of relationships with local partners and to situate counterterrorism efforts within the framework of broader U.S. policy.[10]

Policy makers must also task the intelligence community to focus more on partners' motivations and potential for cooperation. When it comes to understanding U.S. partners, policy makers' requests to the intelligence community typically focus on information about these countries' capabilities and absorption capacity. Turning out analytical products that provide a more holistic intelligence picture of U.S. partners requires a demand signal from policy makers. At the CIA in particular, this focus ideally would be part of a wider shift back toward the production of strategic analysis that is not exclusive to terrorism, even if it comes at the expense of the type of tactical intelligence that has enabled direct action against al-Qaeda and ISIS. Making assessments about partner nations also requires more intelligence about these countries. Because of the difficulties sometimes inherent in collecting on partners, the intelligence community could rely more on third parties, including independent research institutions, to supplement its own collection and analysis. As other scholars have observed, third parties can undertake these types of investigation with less risk of damaging the intelligence-intelligence relationship with a partner.[11] Finally, policy makers must not only signal interest in understanding U.S. partners. They also need to be prepared to accept and work within limitations where they exist.

EXPAND THE TOOLKIT FOR ENGAGEMENT

Combating terrorism does not lend itself to the use of instruments of statecraft the same way that competing with nation-states does. This extends to their utility for obtaining counterterrorism cooperation. Expanding the toolkit of engagement could help U.S. policy makers get more out of its partners.

WHAT'S IN YOUR WALLET?

Considering the limited options available to the United States, security assistance will remain a critical instrument for eliciting counterterrorism cooperation and building partners' capacity to provide it. To increase the efficacy of counterterrorism-related security assistance, the U.S. government should do three things: invest more in building civilian institutions, increase the use of regional programs, and put greater emphasis on assessing, evaluating, and monitoring assistance programs.

The first step the United States should take is to invest more in building civilian security-sector capacity. U.S. spending on military capacity building for counterterrorism is already considerably higher than on civilian security-sector reforms. Donald Trump's preference for military action as a standalone tool divorced from other instruments of national power would exacerbate this imbalance if it extends to the support the United States offers other countries. Yet law enforcement and domestic security services are often on the front lines against terrorism, or at least they should be. Even if the military does have to play the lead role, the aim should ultimately be to transition responsibility to law enforcement. This requires building the capacity of police forces, whether local or national, in the cases of countries with a gendarmerie or its equivalent. Failing to develop these forces risks creating conditions in which partner militaries either fill the void or hand off responsibility to civilian entities unable to sustain any gains made. Similarly, slashing development assistance, which the Trump administration has advocated, would make stabilizing conflict zones where terrorists operate more difficult. It also reinforces the message that the United States only cares about counterterrorism, which, as we have seen, can create perverse incentives for partners to ensure that a terrorist threat is never fully extinguished.

Programs targeted toward improving the security-sector capacity of partner nations are not only under-resourced. They also tend to focus on improving the technical capacity of security forces at the expense of building strong and accountable institutions.[12] The United States should be doing more across the security sector of partner nations, including building the institutional capacity of partners' ministries of the interior and professionalizing law enforcement and judicial personnel.[13] Stronger rule of law and higher bureaucratic capacity both correlate with lower instances of terrorism, and even military capacity building is likely to be more effective if the recipient practices good governance.[14]

Needs assessments that focus broadly on defense and law enforcement institutions rather than narrowly on technical proficiency can help partners make incremental progress improving governance while simultaneously fortifying them against terrorist threats. Institutional reform takes time. Tying this type of capacity building to more traditional training and assistance can help bridge the gap between short- and long-term requirements. Critically, the U.S. government also must recruit and retain experts who can implement these types of programs. The U.S. government previously created the Civilian Response Corps, which was a cadre of federal employees and volunteers from the private sector, state, and local governments who were prepared to deploy rapidly to provide reconstruction and stabilization assistance. The program did not survive budget cuts. Recreating and expanding this type of program would help fill an important gap when it comes to capacity building.

Second, jihadist groups don't recognize national borders, but many counterterrorism programs remain bound by them. The U.S. government should continue looking for ways to increase the use of regional programs and funds for security assistance and cooperation where appropriate. The overwhelming amount of assistance is still provided bilaterally to individual countries despite recognition that these efforts should be linked to a broader regional approach, including cross-border program coordination, support for regional organizations, and facilitation of linkages among partner countries. Seeking regionally appropriated funds would advance this cause. Because not all regional security organizations are similarly equipped, rigorous assessments would be needed to ensure that regional assistance is calibrated accordingly. This approach to capacity building would help situate specific initiatives within a broader context and facilitate coordination between partner countries. A regional outlook would also do more to account for states where jihadists are not currently active but that have neighbors where they are or where large outflows of foreign fighters might return home to wreak havoc.

Third, whether assistance is channeled to military or civilian entities bilaterally or regionally, U.S. agencies currently lack sophisticated frameworks for evaluating if the assistance accomplishes the objectives for which it is ostensibly provided. The specific outcomes that assistance is intended to achieve are rarely articulated. Metrics that exist typically focus mainly on investments, not results, and they often fail to account for higher-order issues such as a partner's threat perceptions, strategic interests, or internal political dynamics. The lack of effective monitoring and evaluation absolves policy makers from articulating how assistance advances U.S. objectives, which as we have seen do not always align with a partner's goals. Congress mandated that the Department of Defense, which dispenses a growing amount of security-assistance money, institute assessment, monitoring, and evaluation protocols for all security-cooperation programs. Development was still underway at the time this book went to press.

Any effort to develop better processes should account for the fact that effective evaluations do not begin once assistance has been disbursed. They start in the design phase of a program, with an articulation both of how assistance will be used to achieve measurable objectives in an identified timeframe and how achieving these objectives will advance U.S. national interests (in this case, related to counterterrorism). Conducting this exercise at the outset forces policy makers to wrestle with the art of the possible. There is sometimes a belief that if the United States does not achieve maximalist objectives, then the use of assistance was not worthwhile. In reality, attaining minimal but critical aims can have substantial benefits for U.S. counterterrorism efforts if they are identified and pursued effectively. Identifying objectives up front is also essential for reconciling disparate goals for security assistance and determining which of them takes precedence and why. For example, it is critical to be clear whether aid is intended to build capacity, secure access, offset asymmetric intelligence cooperation, or maintain the relationship in order to achieve other objectives. Sometimes assistance can help achieve many or even all of these goals. In other cases, pursuit of some objectives may hamper others.

An effective planning process must include a realistic assessment of the partner's strategic environment, including its threat perceptions, assistance needs, and how its different power centers will use the assistance. Evaluations also require the identification of milestones or benchmarks that can be used to track progress over time. This is especially important when undertaking longer-term and harder-to-measure efforts like institution building. Ideally, policy makers would develop a menu of common metrics to enable better coordination between different government agencies and devote 3 percent to 5 percent (the internationally accepted best practice) of any program budget for monitoring and evaluation.[15]

RETHINK CONDITIONALITY

No reasonable offers of assistance are likely to change a partner's strategic calculus or lead entrenched elites to act against their own interests. However, conditioning assistance more effectively could help mitigate some of the ways that partners hinder U.S. counterterrorism efforts and reinforce the more positive aspects of their cooperation. Research suggests conditionality works best when a donor does not have critical interests in the recipient country and the recipient's vulnerability based on its need for assistance is high. Conditionality is least successful in cases where the donor perceives its vulnerability to be high and the recipient is prepared to leave assistance on the table to secure other interests.[16] In practice, this means the costs for the partner of noncompliance must be higher than that of adherence, and the United States must be prepared to stand firm if conditions are not met. Yet once a recipient is providing cooperation that America is loath to lose, this makes it easier for that country to refuse entreaties on other issues and still keep U.S. assistance flowing.

The United States has not had much success attaining counterterrorism objectives using negative conditionality, which threatens to end, suspend, or reduce assistance if conditions are not met. Failed efforts, like the ones we saw with Egypt and Pakistan, often share one or more characteristics.

First, the United States almost always imposes conditions unilaterally and retroactively. The recipient may be forewarned that Congress plans to put conditions on existing aid packages, but the scope of these conditions is not subject to negotiation with the partner. Second, the perceived costs of acceding to U.S. demands may be disproportionately high relative to the costs of forgoing aid. Third, although the executive branch can place its own internal conditions on releasing assistance, it is Congress that can mandate by law whether money is spent. However, legislators are also often reluctant to tie the hands of the executive branch and so build in waivers on the conditions they devise. This creates situations in which Congress imposes conditions and the administration caves (and waives) when they are not met, thereby damaging U.S. credibility. There are fewer examples of Congress imposing conditions that cannot be waived, but even here the record is not promising, for similar reasons.

All of this suggests that policy makers should be more selective about when and where they employ negative conditionality. The optimal time to use it is when U.S. vulnerability is low and recipient vulnerability is high. For example, if the partner really requires assistance and the United States is mainly focused on longer-term objectives—because a threat has not yet manifested or if the partner is already conducting an effective domestic counterterrorism campaign and there is little need for tactical cooperation—using negative conditionality could be effective. Negative conditionality can also have value in cases where U.S. and partner vulnerability are both low. In these cases, even if cutting assistance does not immediately lead a partner to change its behavior, it can still have an important signaling effect. By setting clear expectations and then reducing assistance if they are not met, the United States can build credibility with the partner in question and send a message to other countries.[17] The key is that the U.S. government must be prepared to enforce any conditions it puts in place, hence the importance of choosing cases where the United States is prepared to risk the cooperation it receives.

What should the United States do if it has limited leverage and is at risk of caving? In these instances, policy makers should consider using positive conditionality. This form of conditionality, which has been used for years in the development world, promises assistance in return for "good behavior" defined in advance. Instead of authorizing aid and then withholding it, the United States would identify positive actions that a recipient is considering—or at least open to taking—and then incentivize them. Because of its potential benefits, policy makers might also consider using positive conditionality to supplement, rather than to supplant, negative conditionality in instances where the latter could still be effective.

Negotiating conditions in advance helps reduce the potential for mismanaged expectations on either side. It also gets the recipient more invested in the process, signaling that it is a partner and not merely a proxy benefiting from U.S. paternalism. Depending on the nature of the aid agreement, this might help ameliorate a partner's anxieties about abandonment as well. Where capacity building rather than cooperation or reform is the objective, positive conditionality can ensure that the partner is investing its own funds to support or sustain the capacity being built. Investing early—that is, before a crisis—provides additional space to take a firmer line with partner forces. This is not always possible. Where it is, the United States should seize these opportunities.

There are multiple ways in which the United States could implement this approach. None of them is likely to prompt major changes in a partner's calculus, but these options could promote tactical shifts in behavior or incremental steps toward reform that might have strategic effects over time.

First, draft a memorandum of understanding with the partner nation that articulates a roadmap for how assistance will be used.[18] Security assistance to U.S. foreign partners already carries conditions to ensure that the partner can absorb the assistance and that sustainment needs are met. However, there typically is no established policy framework for leveraging security assistance to achieve broader policy objectives. A roadmap that articulated the shared goals of U.S. assistance and the manner in which it would be used could help address this deficiency. The United States and its partner would also agree on metrics for success, methods of measurement, and the consequences if these metrics are not met and additional rewards that would accrue if they were.

Second, set aside a portion of the total amount authorized for security assistance to the partner for a grant program modeled on those administered by the Millennium Challenge Corp (MCC). In the MCC process, partner nations identify their priorities (for achieving sustainable economic growth and poverty reduction) and work with MCC teams to refine an assistance program. Countries must also meet certain criteria to qualify for MCC funds, the monitoring of which is typically rigorous and transparent. In a security-assistance model, partners could be rewarded for achieving counterterrorism goals, especially ones tied to sustainable governance, institution building, or other reforms that are notoriously difficult to achieve. Partners could "graduate" to more competitive grant levels once lower threshold goals are met.

Third, tie the ongoing provision of a certain piece of equipment or weapons system to its use for a specific, measurable purpose. For example, the United States would agree to provide specific munitions on the condition that the recipient takes certain actions with them that advance U.S. counterterrorism objectives.[19] A key to this type of conditionality lies in providing specific goods that other countries do not manufacture, thereby enabling the United States to control the flow of these goods based on a partner's behavior. These goods must also be consumable, unlike a weapons platform that can be reused and cannot easily be taken back.

GET A BETTER HAMMER

It may seem odd to discuss coercion in a book about partners until one recognizes that many of them hinder as well as help U.S. counterterrorism efforts. Fear of losing existing cooperation is what makes the use of coercive measures so challenging. There is no better example of this than Pakistan, where the need for ongoing cooperation has been a powerful check on impulses to designate it as a state sponsor of terrorism despite the fact that it clearly is one.[20] It can be equally difficult to coerce countries that ignore or enable terrorist groups or engage in other behaviors, such as human rights violations, that hinder U.S. counterterrorism efforts. Applying the normal tools of coercion—threats of military force, the imposition of sanctions, and international isolation—could be counterproductive in these cases.[21] This does not mean the United States must accept the status quo. The United States can use its political muscle and soft power to pressure partner nations. For example, America could begin to collaborate more closely with an unhelpful partner's regional rival or neglect to intervene on that partner's behalf with international institutions. In addition to these types of diplomatic maneuvers, there are policy tools the United States could consider developing and using.

For example, the U.S. government could create a counterterrorism grading system similar to the one used by the Financial Action Task Force (FATF) for money laundering and terrorist financing. The FATF identifies jurisdictions with weak measures to combat money laundering and terrorist financing and publicly identifies "Non-Cooperative Countries or Territories" in public documents. The FATF has reviewed over eighty countries and placed sixty-one of them on this "blacklist" since 2000. Of these countries, fifty-one had made the called-for reforms by 2017.[22] Creating a mechanism to assess counterterrorism efforts could have similar benefits. Even though it would be unilateral, a U.S. "counterterrorism blacklist" would have shaming and signaling aspects. The United States could develop releasable evidence of material support for or enabling of terrorist groups and publicize it when listing countries. This could help pressure countries that worry about the reputational costs of being included. Congress could also tie limited penalties to a blacklist while still allowing engagement. This step provides space for a partner to reform and thus remove itself from the blacklist. It also sends a message that the United States is building a case to end the partnership or take additional punitive actions if reforms are not forthcoming.

Whether to use coercion and which measures to apply will depend on various factors. The timeliness in terms of requests, on the one hand, and application of coercive measures, on the other, is critical to avoid perceptions that the United States is moving the goalposts or belatedly punishing a partner for past actions. In some cases, it might make sense to start smaller in order to enable space for escalation and deescalation depending on a partner's behavior, conditions on the ground, and evolving U.S. objectives. Escalating slowly also enables the United States to use the imposition of costs as a way of signaling potential future actions. Of course, using coercion is rarely without risk because countries on the receiving end may respond in kind. Thus, it is unwise to start down this path unless two endpoints have been established in advance: one where the United States has achieved a realistic objective and another where the risks to U.S. interests outweigh the damage to U.S. credibility if the United States blinks first.

REFINE, ADVISE, AND ASSIST

Building partners' military capacity through train-and-equip efforts remains a critical component of U.S. counterterrorism partnerships, but U.S. forces are increasingly engaged in advising, assisting, and accompanying friendly forces at the tactical level as well. This was most evident in the counter-ISIS campaign, where the role of U.S. special operations forces (SOF) expanded considerably after 2014. One expert, who embedded with these forces, identified three major developments that enabled their success to work "by, with, and through" partner forces in Iraq and Syria.[23] First, these forces were embedded in combat units and operated with indigenous forces closer to the front lines. As a result, they could observe operations directly and were in a better position to advise on tactics. Second, the number of forces—hovering around ten thousand as of 2017—was sufficient to enable this type of support across the relevant geography. Third, U.S. SOF played an increasingly large role in coordinating fire support. In layman's terms, this means they arranged and directed artillery fire and airstrikes against hostile targets that were in close proximity to friendly forces.

The counter-ISIS campaign in Iraq and Syria is an outlier in that the United States confronted a global terrorist organization that controlled a lot of territory and had considerable war-fighting capabilities. Nevertheless, early indications suggest the more hands-on approach used in Iraq and Syria could be considered for other terrorist-related conflicts.[24] A muscular advise-and-assist approach can bring real benefits in terms of enabling partner forces, but it also has significant requirements and risks.

SOF bring with them critical "operational enablers," which is the term for things like close air support to protect forces on the ground and airlifts to deploy, evacuate, and sustain them. It also includes the provision of intelligence, surveillance, and reconnaissance, often via unmanned drones, and other logistical support. When combined with the tactical advice SOF provides, these enablers can make partner forces much more effective. The presence of military advisors and access to operational enablers also can reassure friendly forces, providing them with greater confidence in terms of taking the fight to the enemy. Working closer to where battlefield operations are occurring and developing more intimate relationships with partner forces has other benefits as well. These include greater access to information about the partner and the operating environment and to intelligence on the enemy.

These benefits make a "by, with, and through" approach very appealing, but this approach is not without its risks. First, getting the most out of U.S. military advisers requires placing them close to operations, which increases the chance of casualties. Second, the special-operations community is relatively small, so another consequence of relying heavily on SOF is that it requires high deployment rates. There is a danger of overtaxing elite forces, which are not easily replaced. Third, the increasing use of SOF for advise-and-assist missions intended to accomplish counterterrorism objectives also reduces their availability for other missions, such as supporting European partners against Russian aggression. Fourth, partner forces may not share the U.S. military's commitment to the Law of Armed Conflict, which is intended to regulate the conduct of armed hostilities. This is not solely a values issue. There are real security risks to putting U.S. forces in a position where they are aware of or complicit in abuses that could stain America's reputation and provide terrorists with propaganda for recruitment. Finally, there is the perpetual risk of viewing military solutions as a panacea for terrorism problems that invariably have political, sociocultural, and economic components. Even at a purely military level, one must distinguish between advise-and-assist missions that temporarily make partners more effective and ones that actually turn partners into more effective fighting forces.

As using SOF for advise-and-assist missions becomes a bigger part of the U.S. approach to partnerships, there are several steps that could help optimize the benefits and mitigate potential costs. First, as with security assistance and all uses of military force, it is critical to determine the purpose of the mission. Is the United States propping up a partner or making it a more professional and effective force? The former may still be worth doing, depending on the nature of the threat and potential to alter conditions on the ground. But it is critical not to have any illusions about what the United States can accomplish. Second, and relatedly, policy makers must marry any military plans to a political strategy that accounts for other challenges, such as ones related to governance, rule of law, or regional competition. Third, the Department of Defense should develop requirements and protocols for embedded U.S. personnel to report suspected abuses or violations of the laws of war. As other experts have recommended, allowing collaboration to continue while investigations occur and taking a surgical approach to removing offending personnel instead of severing the relationship could help reduce the disincentives for reporting.[25] Fourth, U.S. SOF already receive a good deal of support from major allies such as Australia, Britain, and Canada. However, it is worth considering ways that America could do even more to leverage close allies.

LEVERAGE CLOSE ALLIES

To enable a more regionalized CT strategy that does not spread U.S. forces or resources too thin, Washington should do more to leverage its close allies (Australia, New Zealand, and NATO members) and the comparative advantages they offer. Obama encouraged greater counterterrorism cooperation—including robust law enforcement and intelligence cooperation—among democratic partners by better aligning U.S. actions and values with those of America's closest allies, especially in Europe. The fact that cooperation with these countries does not appear to have dropped off despite Trump's attempts to treat NATO like a de facto protection racket is a testament to the durability of these counterterrorism relationships. The United States should further insulate these relationships and harmonize its counterterrorism efforts even more closely with those of close Western allies where possible. There are several areas where policy makers and military planners could consider increasing cooperation.

First, as noted above, the United States should explore how to increase coordination when it comes to advise-and-assist efforts. Greater coherence of action would help the United States and its allies take a more comprehensive regional approach. This does not mean asking close allies to fight America's fights or fighting theirs for them, although it could require furnishing them with operational enablers in certain cases. The French intervention in Mali, where the United States provided aerial refueling and other types of support it is uniquely positioned to furnish, is a good example and could be a model for future cooperation with other countries. When other countries step up to take the lead, America should be prepared to contribute financially or in other ways to make them more effective and reinforce this type of burden sharing.

Second, coordinating more closely on capacity building would help Washington get a better return on its investment by avoiding duplicative efforts. It could also give the United States and its Western partners more leverage with recipient countries. Ensuring that recipients do not play donors off against one another is a critical step when it comes to providing counterterrorism assistance they actually *need* as opposed to the types of equipment they might *want*.

A truly coordinated approach would necessitate the United States cede a level of control to its allies and might require the creation of a shared architecture, such as a common platform for intelligence, surveillance, and reconnaissance. Alliance structures are already in place to facilitate these types of arrangements. Policy makers might also consider developing a lend-lease program for the twenty-first century in order to provide close allies with military platforms they might not otherwise develop.[26] The 2007 National Defense Authorization Act already permits the Defense Department to provide equipment, logistics support, and services to partner forces participating in combined operations with U.S. military.[27] A lend-lease program would go a step further and create a mechanism for providing military platforms to close counterterrorism allies even when not involved in combined operations. The U.S. government would provide this equipment via a loan or low-cost lease. Recipients would consent to use it in an agreed-upon manner to achieve shared objectives for a set period of time, after which they could purchase the equipment at a reduced cost. If this concept proved feasible with close allies, the United States could consider expanding it to other partner nations once a functional framework for assessment, monitoring, and evaluation has been established to track assistance more reliably.

SEE THE WHOLE BOARD

Counterterrorism should not be the sole animating principle of U.S. foreign policy. Terrorism in general and jihadists specifically will likely pose significant and persistent threats to the United States for the foreseeable future. From a traditional geostrategic perspective, a rising China and resurgent

Russia pose greater challenges to the United States. Climate change is a truly existential threat to America and the world. One of the major security challenges American policy makers face is how to balance combating the threats from al-Qaeda, ISIS, and other actors within the jihadist movement with the need to confront these other ones. Striking the right balance requires crafting a U.S. counterterrorism policy that is geopolitically, militarily, and financially sustainable. It also necessitates recognizing the tradeoffs that exist when working with counterterrorism partners, some of which are critically important to the success of other U.S. initiatives. Tradeoffs have always been necessary, but they have become starker since 9/11 because of the elevated threat that international jihadist terrorism poses to the United States.

Counterterrorism policies must be crafted with the recognition of other priorities that require time, attention, resources, and the use of limited influence. Not every country where jihadists operate is of equal importance to the United States, and not every jihadist group poses the same type or degree of threat to it. There will be cases where defeating a jihadist group might be achievable but is not necessary to secure vital or critical U.S. interests. Similarly, there may be countries where the United States could bring sufficient resources and pressure to force a shift in their security paradigm but where the effort is simply not worth the potential costs. Because America faces numerous challenges, in some cases it must be prepared to settle for making the most of minimal objectives rather than pursuing maximalist ones. In short, American policy makers need to take a two-level analysis, asking both "What works best to defeat the terrorists in question or counter the threats they pose?" and "What is feasible/sustainable given other priorities?" Failure to integrate counterterrorism efforts into broader U.S. foreign policy almost certainly ensures that the United States will confront unexpected costs on one or more fronts.

For the foreseeable future, any comprehensive counterterrorism approach will continue to require that the United States engage with an array of partner nations, especially in the Middle East, Africa, and South Asia, where many of the jihadist groups that threaten the United States are based. Some partners cooperate in certain areas while actively attempting to undermine U.S. interests in others. Others may simply be incapable of providing the cooperation the United States requires. Either way, the bottom line is that most partners both help and hinder the U.S. pursuit of counterterrorism objectives. As a result, counterterrorism cooperation can be difficult and unsatisfying. It is also almost always unavoidable. To paraphrase Winston Churchill's famous adage about going to war with allies, however, the only thing worse than trying to execute effective counterterrorism policies with partners is trying to do it without them.

Getting the most out of the countries America cooperates with, knowing when to shrink or sever partnerships, and recognizing countries worthy of greater investment requires that policy makers understand what to expect from U.S. partners. It is critical to comprehend the security paradigm that drives a partner's decision making, how relations with the terrorists that are the target of cooperation fit into that paradigm, and how U.S. policies influence the political and security challenges the partner faces. Only by doing so is it possible to assess clearly the costs and benefits of counterterrorism partnerships—for the United States and its partners—and to plan accordingly. To adapt Sun Tzu, the United States must know not only its enemies and itself, but also its partners.

APPENDIX

	PROGRAM	DEPARTMENT/AGENCY
Major CT-relevant security assistance and cooperation programs before 9/11	Antiterrorism Assistance (ATA) program	State Department
	International Narcotics Control and Law Enforcement (INCLE)	State Department
	Foreign Military Financing (FMF)	State Department
	Foreign Military Sales (FMS)	State Department
	International Military Education and Training (IMET)	State Department
	International Criminal Investigative Training Assistance (ICITAP)	DoJ program funded and authorized by interagency agreements with State, USAID, and DoD
	Peacekeeping Operations (PKO)	State Department

(*continued*)

	PROGRAM	DEPARTMENT/AGENCY
Major CT-relevant security assistance and cooperation programs created after 9/11	Coalition Support Funds (CSF)—technically a reimbursement and not assistance	Department of Defense
	Counterterrorism Partnerships Fund (CTPF)	Pooled State-DoD Fund
	Combating Terrorism Fellowship Program (CTFP)	Department of Defense
	Train and Equip (Section 1206) Reauthorized as Building Capacity of Foreign Security Forces (Section 2282)	Department of Defense
	Global Lift and Sustain	Department of Defense
	Support to Foreign Forces (Section 1208)	Department of Defense
	Logistics Support to Foreign Forces (Section 1210)	Department of Defense
	Ministry of Defense Advisors Program	Department of Defense
	Global Security Contingency Fund	Pooled State-DoD Fund
Major CT-relevant country- and region-specific security assistance and cooperation programs after 9/11	Pakistan Counterinsurgency Capability Fund (PCCF)	State Department
	Pakistan Counterinsurgency Fund (PCF)	Department of Defense
	Trans-Saharan Counterterrorism Partnership (TSCTP)	Pooled State-DoD-USAID Fund
	Afghanistan Security Forces Fund (ASFF)	Department of Defense
	Iraq Train and Equip Fund (ITEF)	Department of Defense
	Authority to Provide Assistance to the Vetted Syrian Opposition (Section 1209)	Department of Defense

NOTES

INTRODUCTION

1. Suzanne Goldenberg, "Bush Threatened to Bomb Pakistan, Says Musharraf," *Guardian*, September 22, 2006.
2. Paul R. Pillar, *Terrorism and U.S. Foreign Policy* (Washington, D.C.: Brookings Institution Press, 2003), 183–84.
3. National Commission on Terrorist Attacks Upon the United States, *The 9-11 Commission Report* (Washington, DC: Norton, 2004), 379.
4. The White House, *National Strategy for Counterterrorism* (Washington, DC: June 2011).
5. See, for example, Bruce Drake and Carroll Doherty, "Key Findings on How Americans View the U.S. Role in the World," *Pew Research Center*, May 5, 2016.
6. I use the terms "terrorism" and "counterterrorism" for the purposes of simplicity, but jihadist groups have also engaged in guerrilla warfare and even conventional combat. Bruce Hoffman defined terrorism as "the deliberate creation and exploitation of fear through violence or the threat of violence in the pursuit of political change." He observed that terrorism is conducted by subnational groups or other nonstate entities. This distinguishes it from violence executed by state agents. Bruce Hoffman, *Inside Terrorism* (New York: Columbia University Press, 2006), 40.
7. Daniel Byman, "Remaking Alliances for the War on Terrorism," *Journal of Strategic Studies* 29, no. 5 (October 2006): 767–811.
8. George W. Bush, "Address to a Joint Session of Congress and the American People," September 20, 2001.
9. Glenn H. Snyder, *Alliance Politics* (Ithaca, NY: Cornell University Press, 1997), 4.
10. Dan Reiter, *Crucible of Beliefs: Learning, Alliances, and World Wars* (Ithaca, NY: Cornell University Press, 1996), 58; Eric A. Miller and Arkady Toritsyn, "Bringing the Leader Back In: Internal Threats and Alignment Theory in the Commonwealth of Independent States," *Security Studies* 14, no. 2 (2004/2005): 325–63.

11. Stephen M. Walt, *The Origins of Alliance* (Ithaca, NY: Cornell University Press, 1987), 12.
12. Kurt M. Campbell, "The End of Alliances? Not so Fast," *Washington Quarterly* 27, no. 2 (2004): 151–63.
13. The United States has made de facto defense commitments to Israel and Saudi Arabia. However, these countries do not necessarily perceive themselves to enjoy the same level of security guarantees as formal treaty allies.
14. Other GCC members include Kuwait, the United Arab Emirates, Bahrain, Qatar, and Oman.
15. Pillar, *Terrorism and U.S. Foreign Policy*, chap. 4; Audrey Kurth Cronin, "Introduction: Meeting and Managing the Threat," in *Attacking Terrorism: Elements of a Grand Strategy*, ed. Audrey Kurth Cronin and James M. Ludes (Washington, DC: Georgetown University Press, 2004), 1–16; Nora Bensahel, "A Coalition of Coalitions: International Cooperation Against Terrorism," *Studies in Conflict and Terrorism* 29, no. 1 (2006): 35–49; Robert J. Art and Louise Richardson, "Introduction," in *Democracy and Counterterrorism: Lessons from the Past*, ed. Louise Richardson and Robert J. Art (Washington, DC: United States Institute of Peace Press, 2007), 1–24.
16. On U.S. counterterrorism objectives, see the White House, *National Strategy for Combating Terrorism* (Washington, DC: February 2003); White House, *National Strategy for Combating Terrorism* (Washington, DC: September 2006); White House, *National Strategy for Counterterrorism.*
17. There have been exceptions, including airstrikes and commando raids in Syria and Libya after both countries descended into civil war.
18. The Trump administration was considering renaming CVE as "Countering Radical Islamic Extremism" at the time of writing.
19. Peter Romaniuk, *Does CVE Work? Lessons Learned from the Global Effort to Counter Violent Extremism* (Goshen, IN: Global Center on Cooperative Security, 2015).
20. Interview with Luke Hartig, former NSC senior director for counterterrorism, March 14, 2017.
21. *Department of State and USAID Joint Strategy on Countering Violent Extremism* (Washington, DC: May 2016).
22. Patricia A. Weitsman, "Alliance Cohesion and Coalition Warfare," *Security Studies* 12, no. 3 (Spring 2003): 79–113.
23. Daniel Byman ("Remaking Alliances") drew a similar analogy.
24. Stephen M. Walt, "Alliances in a Unipolar World," *World Politics* 61, no. 1 (January 2009): 86–120.
25. Sameer Lalwani, "Geography, Identity, and Strategies of Counterinsurgency: Evidence from South Asia," unpublished manuscript, draft as of March 30, 2016.
26. For instance, the 2011 counterterrorism strategy asserts that "building strong enduring partnerships based on *shared understandings of the threat and common objectives* is essential to every one of our overarching CT objectives." White House, *National Strategy for Counterterrorism*, emphasis added. For another example, see White House, "Fact Sheet: Strategy to Counter the Islamic State of Iraq and the Levant (ISIL)," September 10, 2014.

27. Daniel Byman, *Deadly Connections: States That Sponsor Terrorism* (New York: Cambridge University Press, 2008), 36–50.
28. Byman, *Deadly Connections*, 59.
29. Pillar distinguishes "sponsors" from "enablers." Byman differentiates active and passive supporters of terrorism, although his latter category is closer to benign neglect. I draw on their definitions in presenting my own. Pillar, *Terrorism and U.S. Foreign Policy*, 179–185; Byman, *Deadly Connections*, 13–15, 222.
30. Paul Staniland, "States, Insurgents, and Wartime Political Orders," *Perspectives on Politics* 10, no. 2 (2012): 243–64.
31. On intelligence, see Jennifer E. Sims, "Foreign Intelligence Liaison: Devils, Deals, and Details," *International Journal of Intelligence and CounterIntelligence* 19, no. 2 (2006): 195–217.

1. COUNTERTERRORISM PARTNERSHIPS IN CONTEXT

1. Michael Mandelbaum, *Mission Failure: America and the World in the Post–Cold War Era* (Oxford: Oxford University Press, 2006), 4–5.
2. George Kennan, "The Chargé in the Soviet Union to the Secretary of State, 861.00/2–2246," telegram, February 22, 1946, from the National Security Archive at George Washington University.
3. Stephen Walt, *The Origins of Alliance* (Ithaca, NY: Cornell University Press, 1987), 4.
4. Kurt M. Campbell, "The End of Alliances? Not So Fast," *Washington Quarterly* 27, no. 2 (2004): 151–63.
5. This description is attributed to General Hastings Lionel Ismay.
6. Campbell, "The End of Alliances?"
7. Other countries in the extended family, according to Kurt Campbell, who proposed this formulation, included Singapore, Thailand, Indonesia, Taiwan, Colombia, and South Africa.
8. Greece, Portugal, and Spain were autocracies during periods of the Cold War.
9. Mandelbaum, *Mission Failure*, 249.
10. David C. Rapoport, "The Four Waves of Rebel Terror and September 11," *Anthropoetics* 8, no. 1 (Spring/Summer 2002).
11. Martin Klimke, *The Other Alliance: Student Protest in West Germany and the United States in the Global Sixties* (Princeton, NJ: Princeton University Press, 2010), 5.
12. Rapoport, "The Four Waves of Rebel Terror and September 11."
13. Rapoport, "The Four Waves of Rebel Terror and September 11."
14. Peter Romaniuk, *Multilateral Counter-Terrorism: The Global Politics of Cooperation and Contestation* (New York: Routledge, 2004), 38.
15. Christopher Andrew and Vasili Mitrokhin, *The Sword and the Shield: The Mitrokhin Archive and the Secret History of the KGB* (New York: Basic Books, 1999), 247–49; Yonah Alexander, "Introduction," in *Evolution of U.S. Counterterrorism Policy*, ed. Yonah Alexander and Michael B. Kraft (London: Praeger, 2008), 1:xxiv–xxvii.
16. Rapoport, "The Four Waves of Rebel Terror and September 11."
17. Bruce Hoffman, *Inside Terrorism* (New York: Columbia University Press, 2006), 158.

18. Brian Jenkins, "International Terrorism: A New Mode of Conflict," in *International Terrorism and World Security*, ed. David Carlton and Carlo Schaerf (London: Croom Helm, 1975), 15.
19. Michael B. Kraft, "Evolution of U.S. Counterterrorism Laws, Policies, and Programs," in *Evolution of U.S. Counterterrorism Policy*, ed. Yonah Alexander and Michael B. Kraft (London: Praeger, 2008), 1:2.
20. Kraft, "Evolution of U.S. Counterterrorism Laws, Policies, and Programs," 9.
21. Section 303 of the International Security Assistance and Arms Export Control Act of 1976, which created Sec. 620A of the Foreign Assistance Act (since modified in 2002), P.L. 107-115: Stat. 3147, 2153, 2155.
22. Export Administration Act, PL 96-72, 50 U.S.C. App § 2405 (6) (j) (1979).
23. Rapoport, "The Four Waves of Rebel Terror and September 11."
24. The 1988 bombing of Pan Am 103 is among the most notable examples.
25. U.S. Department of State, "Overview of State Sponsored Terrorism," *Patterns of Global Terrorism* (1990), http://fas.org/irp/threat/terror_90/sponsored.html.
26. Anti-Terrorism and Arms Export Amendments Act, PL 101-222, 22 U.S.C.A. §§ 1732, 2364, 3371, 2776, 2778, 2780 and 50 U.S.C.A § 2405 (1989).
27. Stephen Krasner, *Sovereignty: Organized Hypocrisy* (Princeton, NJ: Princeton University Press, 1999).
28. UN General Assembly Resolution, part A of General Assembly resolution 217 (III). International Bill of Human Rights, A/RES/3/217 A (December 10, 1948).
29. Derek Chollet and James Goldgeier, *America Between the Wars: From 11/9 to 9/11* (New York: Public Affairs, 2009), 3.
30. Chollet and Goldgeier, *America Between the Wars*, 5. See also James A. Baker III, *The Politics of Diplomacy* (New York: Putnam's, 1995), 430–35; Christian Alfonsi, *Circle in the Sand: Why We Went Back to Iraq* (New York: Doubleday, 2006), 218–34.
31. Chollet and Goldgeier, *America Between the Wars*, 32–42, 67–68.
32. Bruno Tertrais, "The Changing Nature of Military Alliances," *Washington Quarterly* 27, no. 2 (2004): 138; Stephanie Neuman, "Security Assistance and the New World Order," *Foreign Policy Interests* 23 (2001): 310; Campbell, "The End of Alliances?"; Daniel Byman, "Remaking Alliances for the War on Terrorism," *Journal of Strategic Studies* 29, no. 5 (October 2006), 767–811.
33. See, for example, Bill Clinton, "Remarks at the Pentagon," Washington, DC, February 17, 1998; Bill Clinton, "Speech by President Upon Being Presented the Charlemagne Prize 2000," Aachen, Germany, June 2, 2000; Sidney Blumenthal, *The Clinton Wars* (New York: Farrar, Straus and Giroux, 2003), 671.
34. Chollet and Goldgeier, *America Between the Wars*, 10–11.
35. Stephen M. Walt, "Alliances in a Unipolar World," *World Politics* 61, no. 1 (January 2009): 86–120; Stewart Patrick, "'The Mission Determines the Coalition': The United States and Multilateral Cooperation After 9/11," in *Cooperating for Peace and Security: Evolving Institutions and Arrangements in a Context of Changing U.S. Security Policy*, ed. Bruce D. Jones, Shepard Forman, and Richard Gowan (New York: Cambridge, 2009).
36. Islamists advance a framework in which Islam provides a complete system for all spheres of life and consider their religion to be a political ideology. Most Islamists are prepared to engage in politics and endorse jihad only under certain circumstances.

37. Revolutionary jihadists were not unconcerned with foreign policy or liberating Muslim lands occupied by infidels, but they believed the first step was to institute their interpretation of Islamic law at home.
38. Libya was another North African country that faced a jihadist insurgency, albeit of more limited duration, in the 1990s.
39. Mohammed M. Hafez and Quintan Wiktorowicz, "Violence as Contention in the Egyptian Islamic Movement," in *Islamic Activism: A Social Movement Theory Approach*, ed. Quintan Wiktorowicz (Bloomington: Indiana University Press, 2004), 66–70.
40. Pan-Islamism calls for solidarity among all Muslims to confront non-Muslim aggression. Participating in a pan-Islamist jihad does not necessarily make someone a jihadist. This classification is reserved those who believe jihad is an obligation for all able-bodied Muslims and must continue until all lands ever under Muslim control are liberated.
41. John Miller, "Declaration of War Against the Americans: Interview with Osama bin Laden," *ABC News*, May 1998.
42. "Letter from Abu Huthayfa to Abu Abdallah," Harmony Database, June 20, 2000, AFGP-2002-003251; Nasir al-Bahri, *Al-Quds Al-Arabi*, March 31, 2005.
43. White House, PDD-39 U.S. Policy on Counterterrorism, June 21, 1995, http://fas.org/irp/offdocs/pdd39.htm.
44. National Commission on Terrorist Attacks Upon the United States, *The 9-11 Commission Report* (Washington, DC: Norton, 2004), 100.
45. Antiterrorism and Effective Death Penalty Act of 1996, P.L. No. 104-132, 110 Stat.
46. Department of State, "Fact Sheet: Secretary of State Designates Foreign Terrorist Organizations (FTOs)," September 28, 2001.
47. Department of State, Office of the Coordinator for Counterterrorism, *Terrorist Exclusion List*, November 15, 2002
48. Keith Sutton and Ahmed Aghrout, "Multiparty Elections in Algeria," *Bulletin of Francophone Africa* 2 (1992).
49. This paragraph draws on Fawaz A. Gerges, *America and Political Islam: Clash of Cultures or Clash of Interests* (New York: Cambridge University Press, 1999), 179–80.
50. Mark Paris, "Update on the Crisis in Algeria," testimony before the House Foreign Affairs Committee, Subcommittee on Africa, March 22, 1994; Edward Djerejian, "Hearings and Recommendations for U.S. Foreign Assistance to Africa," testimony before the House Committee on Foreign Relations, Subcommittee on Africa, May 12, 1993. See also Gerges, *America and Political Islam*, 233.
51. For example, the United States helped the Algerian government reschedule its country's debts and provided it with hundreds of millions of dollars in agricultural credits. Gerges, *America and Political Islam*, 233.
52. Dirk Axtmann, "Algeria," in *Elections in Africa: A Data Handbook*, ed. Dieter Nohlen, Michael Krennerich, and Bernhard Thibaut (Oxford: Oxford University Press, 1999), 60.
53. Lawrence Wright, *The Looming Tower: Al-Qaeda and the Road to 9/11* (New York: Knopf Doubleday, 2006), 215; Blake Mobley, *Terrorism and Counterintelligence: How Terrorist Groups Elude Detection* (New York: Columbia University Press, 2012), 186.
54. Fawaz A. Gerges, *The Far Enemy: Why Jihad Went Global* (New York: Cambridge University Press, 2005), 169; Wright, *The Looming Tower*, 268.

55. Mustafa Hamid and Leah Farrall, *The Arabs at War in Afghanistan* (New York: Oxford University Press, 2015), 79–81.
56. Thomas Hegghammer, *Jihad in Saudi Arabia: Violence and Pan-Islamism Since 1979* (New York: Cambridge University Press, 2010), chap. 2.
57. Edmund J. Hull, *High-Value Target: Countering Al Qaeda in Yemen* (Washington, DC: Potomac Books, 2011), xxix; Ali Soufan, *The Black Banners: The Inside Story of 9/11 and the War Against al-Qaeda* (New York: Norton, 2011), 237, 256–57; Victoria Clark, *Yemen: Dancing on the Heads of Snakes* (New Haven, Conn.: Yale University Press, 2010), 170.
58. Laurent Bonnefoy, "Jihadi Violence in Yemen: Dealing with Local, Regional, and International Contingencies," in *Contextualising Jihadi Thought*, ed. Jeevan Deol and Zaheer Kazmi (London: Hurst and Co., 2012), 247; Jason Burke, *Al-Qaeda: The True Story of Radical Islam* (New York: I. B. Tauris, 2004), 141; Gregory D. Johnsen, *The Last Refuge: Yemen, Al-Qaeda, and America's War in Arabia* (New York: Norton, 2013), 48–51, 54, 58–59.
59. *The 9-11 Commission Report*, 60, 122; Rachel Bronson, *Thicker Than Oil: America's Uneasy Partnership with Saudi Arabia* (New York: Oxford University Press, 2006), 214–15.
60. John Roth, Douglas Greenburg, and Serena Wille, "Staff Report to the Commission: Monograph on Terrorist Financing," prepared for the National Commission on Terrorist Attacks Upon the United States, 39, http://www.9-11commission.gov/staff_statements/911_terrfin_monograph.pdf; Richard A. Clarke, *Against All Enemies: Inside America's War on Terror* (New York: Free Press, 2004), 194–96.
61. Soufan, *The Black Banners*, 176.
62. Laurence Pope, acting coordinator for counterterrorism, "Terrorism and America," testimony before the Senate Judiciary Committee, April 21–22, 1993.
63. The United States threatened to label Pakistan a state sponsor of terrorism in 1993. On Pakistan's support for terrorism, see chapter 4.
64. On Sudan, see Daniel Byman, *Deadly Connections: States That Sponsor Terrorism* (New York: Cambridge University Press, 2005), chap. 10; David Rose, "The Osama Files," *Vanity Fair*, January 2002. On Afghanistan, see Alex Strick Van Linschoten and Felix Kuehn, *An Enemy We Created: The Myth of the Taliban–Al Qaeda Merger in Afghanistan* (New York: Oxford University Press, 2012), chaps. 5–6.
65. Linschoten and Kuehn, *An Enemy We Created*, 288; Shuja Nawaz, *Crossed Swords: Pakistan, Its Army, and the Wars Within* (New York: Oxford University Press, 2008), 536–37.
66. *The 9-11 Commission Report*, 125, 138–39.
67. *The 9-11 Commission Report*, 110–13, 132.
68. *The 9-11 Commission Report*, 143.
69. *The 9-11 Commission Report*, 136–37.
70. *The 9-11 Commission Report*, 117.
71. *The 9-11 Commission Report*, 138–39.
72. White House, *The National Security Strategy of the United States of America* (Washington, DC: 2002).
73. Patrick, "'The Mission Determines the Coalition.'"
74. Department of Defense, "Briefing by Secretary of Defense Donald Rumsfeld," September 25, 2001. Transcript available at http://www.washingtonpost.com/wp-srv/nation/specials/attacked/transcripts/rumsfeld_092601.html.

75. I'm grateful to Nora Bensahel for this observation.
76. Paul Dibb, "The Future of International Coalitions: How Useful? How Manageable?" *Washington Quarterly* 25, no. 2 (2002): 131–44.
77. Nora Bensahel, "A Coalition of Coalitions: International Cooperation Against Terrorism," *Studies in Conflict and Terrorism* 29, no. 1 (2006): 35–49.
78. Byman, "Remaking Alliances for the War on Terrorism."
79. Because security guarantees could and did lead the United States to intervene on behalf of its clients, the relationship between alliance formation and the occurrence of interstate war also received considerable attention.
80. Steven R. David, *Choosing Sides: Alignment and Realignment in the Third World* (Baltimore, MD: Johns Hopkins University Press, 1991).
81. Walt, "Alliances in a Unipolar World."
82. Walt, *The Origins of Alliance*, 5.
83. Kenneth Waltz, *Theory of International Politics* (Reading, MA: Addison-Wesley, 1979), chap. 6; Hans J. Morgenthau, *Politics Among Nations: The Struggle for Power and Peace*, 7th ed., rev. by Kenneth W. Thompson and W. David Clinton (Boston: McGraw-Hill Higher Education, 2006), pt. 4.
84. Walt, *The Origins of Alliance*, 5–6.
85. On why states should be considered the main actors in international politics, see Waltz, *Theory of International Politics*, 93–95, n. 3.
86. Steven R. David, "Explaining Third World Alignment," *World Politics* 43, no. 2 (January 1991): 233–56.
87. Michael N. Barnett and Jack S. Levy, "Domestic Resources of Alignment: The Case of Egypt, 1962–73," *International Organization* 45, no. 3 (1991): 369–95.
88. David, *Choosing Sides.*
89. Walt, *The Origins of Alliance*, 221.
90. The pursuit of shared counterterrorism interests made strange bedfellows among geopolitical rivals. After 9/11, America engaged in ad hoc counterterrorism cooperation with Iran, Syria, Russia, and China at various times. None of these countries could be considered an ally or even a close partner.
91. Alastair Smith, "Alliance Formation and War," *International Studies Quarterly* 39, no. 4 (1995): 405–25.
92. See, for example, Paul R. Pillar, "Counterterrorism After Al Qaeda," *Washington Quarterly* 27, no. 3 (Summer 2004): 101–13.

2. AMERICA AND ITS PARTNERS IN THE WAR ON TERROR

1. Interview with Noman Benotman, the former head of the political and media committees for the Libyan Islamic Fighting Group, March 3, 2010; Peter Bergen and Paul Cruickshank, "The Unraveling," *New Republic*, June 11, 2008.
2. "Jihad Against Jews and Crusaders," World Islamic Front Statement, February 23, 1998.
3. National Commission on Terrorist Attacks Upon the United States, *The 9-11 Commission Report* (Washington, DC: Norton, 2004), 259.

4. Richard Clarke, *Against All Enemies: Inside America's War on Terror* (New York: Simon and Schuster, 2008), 225–26.
5. "Bin Laden Determined to Strike in U.S.," President's Daily Briefing, declassified and approved for release, April 10, 2004, http://nsarchive.gwu.edu/NSAEBB/NSAEBB116/pdb8-6-2001.pdf.
6. For a clear articulation of the incoming Bush administration's approach, see Condoleezza Rice, "Promoting the National Interest: Life After the Cold War," *Foreign Affairs* 79, no. 1 (2000): 45–62.
7. Paul Dibb, "The Future of International Coalitions: How Useful? How Manageable?" *Washington Quarterly* 25, no. 2 (2002): 131–144.
8. Bob Woodward, *Bush at War* (New York: Simon & Schuster, 2002), 39.
9. White House, *National Strategy for Combating Terrorism* (Washington, DC: February 2003).
10. George W. Bush, "Address to a Joint Session of Congress and the American People," September 20, 2001.
11. Joint Resolution to Authorize the Use of United States Armed Forces Against Those Responsible for the Recent Attacks Launched Against the United States, Pub. L. no. 107-40, 115 Stat. 224 (2001), http://www.gpo.gov/fdsys/pkg/PLAW-107publ40/html/PLAW-107publ40.htm.
12. James Mann, *Rise of the Vulcans: The History of Bush's War Cabinet* (New York: Viking, 2004), 317.
13. George W. Bush, *Decision Points* (New York: Broadway, 2011), 145. See also Audrey Kurth Cronin, "The 'War on Terrorism:' What Does It Mean to Win?" *Journal of Strategic Studies* 37, no. 2 (2014): 174–97.
14. Cronin, "The 'War on Terrorism,'" 174–97; Steven Metz and Raymond Millen, *Insurgency and Counterinsurgency in the Twenty-First Century: Reconceptualizing Threat and Response* (Carlisle, PA: U.S. Army War College, November 2004), 18.
15. *The 9-11 Commission Report*, 118.
16. On U.S. assessments, see Bush, *Decision Points*, 144–45, 153–54; Philip Mudd, *Takedown: Inside the Hunt for al-Qaeda* (Philadelphia: University of Pennsylvania Press, 2013), 54.
17. White House, *National Strategy for Combating Terrorism* (2003).
18. White House, *National Strategy for Combating Terrorism* (2003); White House, *The National Security Strategy of the United States of America* (Washington, DC: 2002).
19. Some Taliban leaders supported the idea of turning over bin Laden. Alex Strick van Linschoten, and Felix Kuehn, *An Enemy We Created: The Myth of the Taliban–Al Qaeda Merger in Afghanistan* (New York: Oxford University Press, 2012), 233.
20. Nora Bensahel, *The Counterterror Coalitions: Cooperation with Europe, NATO, and the European Union* (Arlington, VA: RAND Corporation, 2003), 11.
21. Bensahel, *The Counterterror Coalitions*, 15.
22. "NATO's role in Afghanistan," North Atlantic Treaty Organization Topics, April 9, 2009, http://www.nato.int/summit2009/topics_en/03-afghanistan.html#evolution.
23. Anand Gopal, *No Good Men Among the Living: America, the Taliban, and the War Through Afghan Eyes* (New York: Metropolitan, 2014), 47, 105, 195.
24. This assessment is a major theme of Gopal's *No Good Men Among the Living.*

25. Vanda Felbab-Brown, *Aspiration and Ambivalence: Strategies and Realities of Counterinsurgency and State Building in Afghanistan* (Washington, DC: Brookings Institution Press, 2013), 265; Carlotta Gall, *The Wrong Enemy: America in Afghanistan: 2001–2014* (New York: Houghton Mifflin Harcourt), 211–12.
26. Douglas J. Feith, *War and Decision: Inside the Pentagon at the Dawn of the War on Terrorism* (New York: Harper, 2008), 19, 56, 81.
27. Peter Baker, *Days of Fire: Bush and Cheney in the White House* (New York: Anchor Books, 2013), 191; Ron Suskind, *The One Percent Doctrine: Deep Inside America's Pursuit of Its Enemies Since 9/11* (New York: Simon and Schuster, 2006), 123.
28. Wyn Rees, *Transatlantic Counter-Terrorism Cooperation: The New Imperative* (New York: Taylor and Francis, 2007), 127.
29. The invasion also stoked Turkish fears about Kurdish nationalism.
30. Suzanne Maloney, "Tehran and Washington: A Motionless Relationship?" Brookings Institute, n.d.; James Dobbins, "Negotiating with Iran: Reflections from Personal Experience," *Washington Quarterly* 33, no. 1 (2010): 149–62.
31. See, for example, Glenn Kessler, "Kerry's Claim That Iran Offered Bush a Nuclear Deal in 2003," *Washington Post*, December 9, 2013.
32. John R. Bolton, "Beyond the Axis of Evil: Additional Threats from Weapons of Mass Destruction," Heritage Foundation, May 6, 2002.
33. Peter Neumann, "Suspects Into Collaborators," *London Review of Books* 36, no. 7 (April 2014).
34. Michael Slackman, "Wary of U.S., Syria and Iran Strengthen Ties," *New York Times*, June 25, 2006.
35. Iranian support to Shiite insurgent groups and militants was also a function of Tehran's longstanding religious, economic, and social ties to Iraqi Shiites. See, for example, Michael R. Gordan and Andrew W. Lehran, "Leaked Reports Detail Iran's Aid for Iraqi Militias," *New York Times*, October 22, 2010.
36. Dana Priest, "Foreign Network at Front of CIA's Terror Fight: Joint Facilities in Two Dozen Countries Account for Bulk of Agency's Post-9/11 Successes," *Washington Post*, November 18, 2005.
37. The United States also worked with partners in East Africa, where a small number of al-Qaeda operatives were based.
38. On OEF-Philippines, see Richard Swain, *Case Study: Operation Enduring Freedom Philippines* (Leavenworth: U.S. Army Counterinsurgency Center, 2010).
39. David Gordon and Samuel Lindo, *Jemaah Islamiyyah* (Washington, DC: Center for Strategic and International Studies, November 2011).
40. Sean Naylor, *Relentless Strike: The Secret History of Joint Special Operations Command* (New York: St. Martin's Press, 2015), 325–26.
41. The CIA oversaw this campaign from Addis Ababa in Ethiopia and then the Kenyan capital of Nairobi after 2003. Sean D. Naylor, "Years of Detective Work Led to al-Qaeda Target," *armytimes.com*, November 21, 2011.
42. Sean D. Naylor, "Lack of Human Intel Hampered AQ Hunt in Africa," *armytimes.com*, March 29, 2013.
43. On the campaign, see Naylor, "Years of Detective Work Led to al-Qaeda Target."

44. Al-Shabaab, "The Life of Aden Hashi Ayro, Part I"; and Al-Shabaab, "The Life of Aden Hashi Ayro, Part II," in Stig Jarle Hansen, *Al-Shabaab in Somalia: The History and Ideology of a Militant Islamist Group, 2005–2012* (New York: Oxford University Press, 2013).
45. Mark Mazzetti, *The Way of the Knife: The CIA, a Secret Army, and a War at the Ends of the Earth* (New York: Penguin, 2013), 142.
46. Mazzetti, *The Way of the Knife*, 149.
47. Roland Marchal, "Harakat Al-Shabaab Al Mujahedin," report for UK Foreign Office (London: March 2011); Ken Menkhaus, "A Country in Peril, a Policy Nightmare," *Enough Paper*, September 3, 2008.
48. J. M. Berger, "Al Qaeda's Merger," *Foreign Policy*, February 15, 2012.
49. Thomas Hegghammer, "The Ideological Hybridization of Jihadi Groups," *Current Trends in Islamist Ideology* 9 (November 2009).
50. Stephen Tankel, "Beyond FATA: Exploring the Punjabi Militant Threat to Pakistan," *Terrorism and Political Violence* 28, no. 1 (2016), 49–71.
51. "National Strategy for Combating Terrorism," 2006.
52. Leah Farrall, "How Al-Qaeda Works," *Foreign Affairs* 90, no. 2 (March/April 2011).
53. "Dots on the Letters, *as-Sahab*'s 2nd Interview with Sheikh Abu Yahya at-Libi, Two Years After His Deliverance from Bagram Prison," *as-Sahab*, September 9, 2007.
54. Bernard Haykel, "Al-Qa'ida and Shiism," in *Fault Lines in Global Jihad*, ed. Assaf Moghadam and Brian Fishman (London: Routledge, 2011), 194.
55. Seth G. Jones, *Hunting in the Shadows: The Pursuit of Al Qa'ida Since 9/11* (New York: Norton, 2012), 227.
56. Paul Cruickshank, *The Militant Pipeline: Between the Afghanistan-Pakistan Border Region and the West* (Washington, DC: New America Foundation, July 2011).
57. The North-West Frontier Province became Khyber Pakhtunkhwa Province in April 2010.
58. "Al-Qaeda in Yemen Claims Responsibility for the Suicide Car Bombings Targeting Western Oil Facilities in al-Dhabba and Safer in September 2006," SITE Intelligence Group Enterprise, November 7, 2006.
59. National Intelligence Council, "Trends in Global Terrorism: Implications for the United States" (Washington, DC: April 2006).
60. White House, *National Strategy for Combating Terrorism* (2003).
61. Quote from a former senior Defense Department official in Naylor, *Relentless Strike*, 165.
62. Robert D. Putnam, "Diplomacy and Domestic Politics: The Logic of Two-Level Games," *International Organization* 42 (1988).
63. Pillar, "Counterterrorism After al-Qaeda."
64. David Kilcullen, "Countering Global Insurgency," *Journal of Strategic Studies* 28, no. 4 (2005): 597–617.
65. Eric Schmitt and Thom Shanker, *Counterstrike: The Untold Story of America's Secret Campaign Against Al Qaeda* (New York: Henry Holt, 2011), 51, 62.
66. Al-Qaeda and its affiliates ultimately did more to undermine their own appeal than any U.S. effort could. Because these groups were based in Muslim countries, their attacks mainly killed Muslims. Indeed, bin Laden and other al-Qaeda leaders retrospectively questioned the logic of adding affiliates given the reputational costs incurred. Bin Laden's frustration with al-Qaeda affiliates, especially over their targeting of fellow

Muslims, is a common theme in some of the documents recovered from his compound in Abbottabad.

67. Interview with Juan Zarate, former deputy assistant to the president and deputy national security advisor for combating terrorism, September 17, 2015; Interview with Tricia Bacon, former State Department intelligence official, September 29, 2015.
68. White House, *The National Security Strategy of the United States of America* (Washington, DC: March 2006); Department of Defense, *National Implementation Plan for the War on Terror* (Washington, DC: 2006), http://nsp_ .golearnportal.org/lesson6/nat Implementation/.
69. Amy Belasco, *Troop Levels in the Afghan and Iraq Wars, FY2001–FY2012: Cost and Other Potential Issues* (Washington, DC: Congressional Research Service, July 2, 2009).
70. White House, *National Strategy for Combating Terrorism* (Washington, DC: 2006).
71. Michael E. O'Hanlon and Ian Livingston, "Iraq Index," Brookings Institution, January 31, 2012; Ian S. Livingston and Michael O'Hanlon, "Afghanistan Index," Brookings Institution, March 31, 2016.
72. John Pike, "U.S. Ground Forces End Strength," GlobalSecurity.org, http://www .globalsecurity.org/military/ops/iraq_orbat_es.htm.
73. Condoleezza Rice, *No Higher Honor: A Memoir of My Years in Washington* (New York: Crown, 2011), 694–95.
74. The United States of America and the Republic of Iraq, *Agreement Between the United States of America and the Republic of Iraq on the Withdrawal of United States Forces from Iraq and the Organization of Their Activities During Their Temporary Presence in Iraq*, November 17, 2008, https://www.state.gov/documents/organization/122074.pdf.
75. Interview with a former National Counterterrorism Center official, name withheld upon request, August 12, 2014.
76. White House, *National Security Strategy of the United States of America* (Washington, DC: May 2010).
77. White House, *National Security Strategy* (May 2010).
78. White House, *National Security Strategy* (May 2010); *National Strategy for Counterterrorism* (2011).
79. Barack Obama, speech at Woodrow Wilson International Center, Washington, DC, August 1, 2007.
80. "President Obama Delivers Remarks to State Department Employees," *Washington Post*, January 22, 2009.
81. White House, White Paper of the Interagency Policy Group's Report on U.S. Policy Towards Afghanistan and Pakistan, March 2009.
82. Chapter 4 explores these tradeoffs in detail.
83. Gall, *The Wrong Enemy*, 196.
84. Ronald E. Neumann, *Failed Relations Between Hamid Karzai and the United States: What Can We Learn?* (Washington, DC: USIP, 2015).
85. Eric Schmitt, "U.S. Envoy's Cables Show Worries on Afghan Plans," *New York Times*, January 24, 2010.
86. Belasco, *Troop Levels in the Afghan and Iraq Wars*.
87. Bob Woodward, *Obama's Wars* (New York: Simon & Schuster, 2010), 117–18.

88. Derek Chollet, *The Long Game: How Obama Defied Washington and Redefined America's Role in the World* (New York: Public Affairs, 2016), 68–69.
89. David E. Sanger, *Confront and Conceal: Obama's Secret Wars and Surprising Use of American Power* (New York: Random House, 2012), 19–20.
90. Jason Ukman, "Cost of Civilian 'Surge' in Afghanistan: $1.7 billion," *Washington Post*, September 8, 2011.
91. Rajiv Chandrasekaran, *Little America: The War Within the War for Afghanistan* (New York: Random House, 2012), part 2.
92. Ariella Viehe, Jasmine Afshar, and Tamana Heela, *Rethinking the Civilian Surge: Lessons from the Provincial Reconstruction Teams in Afghanistan* (Washington, DC: Center for American Progress, December 2015).
93. Peter Baker, "How Obama Came to Plan for 'Surge' in Afghanistan," *New York Times*, December 5, 2009.
94. Barack Obama, "Address to the Nation on the Way Forward in Afghanistan and Pakistan," West Point, NY, December 1, 2009. See also Barack Obama, "Remarks by the President on the Way Forward in Afghanistan," Washington, DC, June 22, 2011.
95. NATO member countries subsequently agreed to a full handover of responsibility to Afghan forces by the end of 2014. North Atlantic Council, "Lisbon Summit Declaration," November 20, 2010, http://www.nato.int/cps/en/natolive/official_texts_68828.htm.
96. Obama, "Address to the Nation on the Way Forward in Afghanistan and Pakistan," 2009.
97. Chollet, *The Long Game*, 71.
98. *National Strategy for Counterterrorism* (2011).
99. Woodward, *Obama's Wars*, 8.
100. David H. Ucko, "'Small Is Beautiful': El Salvador's Lessons and Non-Lessons for the Indirect Approach," *War on the Rocks*, May 15, 2014.
101. Chollet, *The Long Game*, 214–15.
102. Barack Obama, "Remarks at the National Defense University," Ft. McNair, Washington, DC, May 23, 2013; *National Strategy for Counterterrorism* (2011).
103. Barack Obama, "Remarks by the President at the United States Military Academy Commencement Ceremony," West Point, NY, May 28, 2014.
104. *National Strategy for Counterterrorism* (2011); U.S. Department of Defense, *Quadrennial Defense Review 2014* (Washington, DC, March 4, 2014), 16; White House, *National Security Strategy* (February 2015), 10–11; Obama, "Remarks by the President at the United States Military Academy Commencement Ceremony."
105. Barack Obama, *The Audacity of Hope* (New York: Vintage, 2006), 309–11.
106. Jeffrey Goldberg, "The Obama Doctrine," *Atlantic*, April 2016.
107. Barack Obama, "A New Beginning," *New York Times*, Cairo, June 4, 2009.
108. *National Strategy for Counterterrorism* (2011).
109. Andrea Elliott, "Charges Detail Road to Terror for 20 in U.S.," *New York Times*, November 23, 2009.
110. Clint Watts, a veteran counterterrorism practitioner, made this observation during a workshop organized to review a draft of this book.
111. *United States v. Umar Farouk Abdulmutallab*, Case 2:10-cr20005-NGE-DAS, no. 7 (U.S. District Court Eastern District of Michigan Southern Division).

112. Jeffrey D. Feltman and Robert F. Godec, "Yemen on the Brink: Implications for U.S. Policy," testimony before the House Committee on Foreign Affairs, Februrary 3, 2010.
113. Michael Morell, *The Great War of Our Time: The CIA's Fight Against Terrorism—From al Qa'ida to ISIS* (New York: Grand Central, 2015), 179.
114. Morell, *The Great War of Our Time*, 179; Ken Dilanian, "U.S. Intelligence Official Acknowledges Missed Arab Spring Signs," *Los Angeles Times*, July 19, 2012.
115. Morell, *The Great War of Our Time*, 179.
116. Dilanian, "U.S. Intelligence Official Acknowledges Missed Arab Spring Signs."
117. Ryan Lizza, "The Consequentialist," *New Yorker*, May 2, 2011; Mark Landler, "Secret Report Ordered by Obama Identified Potential Uprisings," *New York Times*, February 16, 2011.
118. Chollet, *The Long Game*, 93.
119. Interview with Steven Simon, former NSC senior director for the Middle East and North Africa, October 29, 2015; Goldberg, "The Obama Doctrine."
120. Marc Lynch, "Obama and the Middle East: Rightsizing the U.S. Role," *Foreign Affairs* 94, no. 5 (September/October 2015): 23.
121. Scott Wilson and Joby Warrick, "Obama's Shift Toward Military Action in Libya," *Washington Post*, March 19, 2011; UN Security Council Resolution 1973, S/RES/1973 (March 17, 2011), http://www.nato.int/nato_static/assets/pdf/pdf_2011_03/20110927_110311-UNSCR-1973.pdf.
122. Jo Becker and Scott Shane, "Hillary Clinton, 'Smart Power' and a Dictator's Fall," *New York Times*, February 27, 2016.
123. "NTC declares 'Liberation of Libya,'" *Al Jazeera*, October 24, 2011.
124. Goldberg, "The Obama Doctrine."
125. Scott Wilson and Joby Warrick, "Assad Must Go, Obama Says," *Washington Post*, August 18, 2011.
126. David S. Cloud and Raja Abdulrahim, "U.S. Has Secretly Provided Arms Training to Syria Rebels Since 2012," *Los Angeles Times*, June 21, 2003.
127. Joel Rayburn, *Iraq After America: Strongmen, Sectarians, Resistance* (Stanford, CA: Hoover Institution, 2014), 215.
128. Rayburn, *Iraq After America*, 214; Rice, *No Higher Honor*, 694–95.
129. Rayburn, *Iraq After America*, 217–19.
130. "Leon Panetta: How the White House Misplayed Iraqi Troop Talks," *Time*, October 1, 2014.
131. Jack Healy, Tim Arango, and Michael S. Schmidt, "Premier's Actions in Iraq Raise U.S. Concerns," *New York Times*, December 12, 2011.
132. Timothy Williams and Duraid Adnan, "Sunnis in Iraq Allied with U.S. Rejoin Rebels," *New York Times*, October 16, 2010.
133. Will McCants, *The ISIS Apocalypse: The History, Strategy, and Doomsday Vision of the Islamic State* (New York: St. Martin's, 2015), 81.
134. Martin Chulov, "Isis: The Inside Story," *Guardian*, December 11, 2014.
135. For example: Letter from 'Atiyya (aka Mahmud) to Bin Laden, June 19, 2010, Government Exhibit 421-10-CR-019-S-4-RJD (Abbottabad document released at trial of Abid Naseer).
136. Mark Mazzetti, "CIA Drone Is Said to Kill Al Qaeda's No. 2," *New York Times*, August 27, 2011.

137. Seth Jones, *A Persistent Threat: The Evolution of al Qa'ida and Other Salafi Jihadists* (Arlington, VA: RAND, 2014), x.
138. Letter to Atiyya (Sheikh Mahmud) from Osama bin Laden (Abu Abdullah), April 26, 2011, SOCOM-2012-0000010.
139. Daveed Gartenstein-Ross, "The Cuban in the Desert," *Foreign Policy*, August 13, 2013.
140. On Libya, see Mohammed Abbas, "Libya Prisoner Release Stokes Fears of Tribal Strife," *Reuters*, March 3, 2011. On Syria, see Michael Weiss and Hassan Hassan, *ISIS: Inside the Army of Terror* (New York: Simon and Schuster, 2015), 139.
141. Michael Totten, "Year Four: The Arab Spring Proved Everyone Wrong," *World Affairs Journal* 177, no. 2 (July/August 2014): 43–49.
142. George Packer, "Exporting Jihad," *New Yorker*, March 28, 2016.
143. Anne Barnard, "Death Toll from War in Syria Now 470,000, Group Finds," *New York Times*, February 11, 2016.
144. Eric Schmitt, "ISIS Fighters Are Not Flooding Back Home to Wreak Havoc as Feared," *New York Times*, October 22, 2017.
145. McCants, *The ISIS Apocalypse*, 85.
146. Cole Bunzel, *From Paper State to Caliphate: The Ideology of the Islamic State* (Washington, DC: Brookings Institution, 2014).
147. Weiss and Hassan, *ISIS: Inside the Army of Terror*, 99–111.
148. Abū Bakr al-Baghdādī, "Wa-bashshir al-mu'minīn," *Jihadology*, April 9, 2013, http://jihadology.net/2013/04/09/al-furqan-media-presents-a-new-audio-message-from-the-islamic-state-of-iraqs-shaykh-abu-bakr-al-%E1%B8%A5ussayni-al-qurayshi-al-baghdadi-announcement-of-the-islamic-state-of-iraq-an/.
149. Noman Benotman and Roisin Blake, "Jabhat al-Nusra: A Strategic Briefing," Qulliam Foundation, n.d.
150. David Kilcullen, *Blood Year: The Unraveling of Western Counterterrorism* (New York: Oxford University Press, 2016), 77.
151. Christoph Reuter, "The Terror Strategist: Secret Files Reveal the Structure of Islamic State," *Der Spiegel*, April 18, 2015.
152. "20,000 Foreign Fighters Flock to Syria, Iraq to Join Terrorists," *CBS News*, February 10, 2015.
153. ISIS claimed to have been independent from al-Qaeda since 2006, when AQI formally became the Islamic State of Iraq. See Bunzel, *From Paper State to Caliphate*. On al-Qaeda's disavowing ISIS, see Liz Sly, "Al-Qaeda Disavows Any Ties with Radical Islamist ISIS Group in Syria, Iraq," *Washington Post*, February 3, 2014.
154. Kenneth Katzman, *Iraq: Politics, Security, and U.S. Policy* (Washington, DC: Congressional Research Service, 2015).
155. Joshua Paltrow, "Maliki's Office Is Seen Behind Purge in Forces," *Washington Post*, April 30, 2007; Rayburn, *Iraq After America*, 59.
156. Karl Vick, "Iraq's Second Largest City Falls to Extremists," *Time*, June 10, 2014.
157. "Sunni Rebels Declare New Islamic Caliphate," *Al Jazeera*, June 30, 2014.
158. Anonymous letter (assessed to be either Osama bin Laden and/or 'Atiyya) to Abu Basir (Nasir al-Wuhayshi), written after October 2010, SOCOM-2012-0000016; Anonymous letter (assessed to be Osama bin Laden) to unknown, date unknown, SOCOM-2012-0000017.

159. Daveed Gartenstein-Ross and Madeleine Blackman, "ISIL's Virtual Planners: A Critical Terrorist Innovation," *War on the Rocks*, January 4, 2017.
160. White House, "Statement by the President on ISIL," September 10, 2014.
161. Kathleen J. McInnis, *Coalition Contributions to Countering the Islamic State*, (Washington, DC: Congressional Research Service, 2016).
162. "Joint Comprehensive Plan of Action," Vienna, July 14, 2015, http://www.state.gov/documents/organization/245317.pdf. See also Gary Samore, *The Iran Nuclear Deal: A Definitive Guide* (Cambridge: Belfer Center, 2015).
163. "Remarks by Secretary Hagel at the Manama Dialogue," Bahrain, December 7, 2013.
164. Kilcullen, *Blood Year*, 70.
165. Patrick Cockburn, "Whose Side Is Turkey on?" *London Review of Books*, November 6, 2014.
166. "Islamic State and the Crisis in Iraq and Syria in Maps," *BBC*, November 3, 2017.
167. Schmitt, "ISIS Fighters Are Not Flooding Back Home."
168. Priynanka Boghani, "Where the Black Flag of ISIS Flies," *Frontline*, May 13, 2016.
169. Goldberg, "The Obama Doctrine."

3. THE ELEMENTS OF COUNTERTERRORISM COOPERATION

1. Brian Michael Jenkins, *The Study of Terrorism: Definitional Problems* (Santa Monica, CA: RAND, 1980), 1.
2. Joseph Nye, *Bound to Lead: The Changing Nature of American Power* (New York: Basic Books, 1991).
3. The U.S. government does a poor job of tracking how money is spent, and there is no single official source for this data. I rely on the Security Assistance Monitor for data on assistance provided to partner nations. Unless otherwise indicated, amounts are for funding appropriated by the U.S. Congress. This money was not always obligated by federal agencies or spent.
4. Walter Ladwig, "Influencing Clients in Counterinsurgency: U.S. Involvement in El Salvador's Civil War, 1979–1992," *International Security* 41, no. 1 (Summer 2016): 99–146.
5. Daniel Byman, "Friends Like These: Counterinsurgency and the War on Terrorism," *International Security* 31, no. 2 (Fall 2006): 79–115.
6. White House, *National Strategy for Combating Terrorism* (Washington, DC: 2003); White House, *National Strategy for Combating Terrorism* (Washington, DC: 2006); White House, *National Strategy for Counterterrorism* (Washington, DC: 2011).
7. This paragraph and the next are drawn from Sameer Lalwani, "Geography, Identity, and Strategies of Counterinsurgency: Evidence from South Asia," unpublished manuscript, March 30, 2016.
8. Juan Zarate, *Treasury's War: The Unleashing of a New Era of Financial Warfare* (New York: Public Affairs, 2013), 41.
9. Zarate, *Treasury's War*, 21.
10. Jimmy Gurulé, "The Global Fight Against the Financing of Terror: Prevention—A New Paradigm," speech delivered to the Heritage Foundation, Washington, DC, June 26, 2002.

11. Zarate, *Treasury's War*, 8–10, 151.
12. Uniting and Strengthening America by Providing Appropriate Tools Required to Intercept and Obstruct Terrorism (USA PATRIOT Act) Act of 2001, Public Law 107-56 (2001).
13. Zarate, *Treasury's War*, 25.
14. UN Security Council, "S/RES 1373," September 28, 2001, http://www.un.org/en/sc/ctc/specialmeetings/2012/docs/United%20Nations%20Security%20Council%20Resolution%201373%20(2001).pdf.
15. Zarate, *Treasury's War*, 8.
16. "Full text: George Bush's Iraq speech," June 28, 2005, https://www.theguardian.com/world/2005/jun/29/iraq.usa.
17. Department of State, Bureau of Diplomatic Security, "Antiterrorism Assistance Program," http://www.state.gov/m/ds/protection/terrorism/c8583.htm.
18. Nina M. Serafino, *The Counterterrorism Partnerships Fund (CTPF) Proposal: Questions for Congress* (Washington, DC: Congressional Research Service, July 14, 2014); Janine Davidson and Emerson Brooking, "How the Overseas Contingency Operations Fund Works—and Why Congress Wants to Make It Bigger," in *Defense in Depth* (Washington, DC: Council on Foreign Relations, 2015).
19. Mara Karlin, *Building Militaries in Fragile States: Challenges for the United States* (Philadelphia: University of Pennsylvania Press, 2017).
20. On GVHR, support for remediation efforts for foreign military and security services is granted under Subsection (c) of 22 U.S.C. § 2378d, "Limitation on assistance to security forces." On coups, Subsection (b) of 22 U.S.C. § 8422 "restricts assistance to the government of any country whose duly elected head of government is deposed by military coup or decree."
21. Dafna Rand and Stephen Tankel, *Security Cooperation and Assistance: Rethinking the Return on Investment* (Washington, DC: Center for a New American Security, 2015).
22. Michael J. McNerney et al., *Assessing Security Cooperation as a Preventative Tool* (Arlington, VA: RAND, 2014); Christopher Paul et al., *What Works Best When Building Partner Capacity and Under What Circumstances?* (Arlington, VA: RAND, 2013).
23. Rose Jackson, *Untangling the Web: A Blueprint for Reforming American Security Sector Assistance* (Washington, DC: Open Society Foundations, January 2017).
24. White House, "Fact Sheet: U.S. Security Sector Assistance Policy," April 5, 2013.
25. Interview with Steven Simon, former NSC senior director for the Middle East and North Africa, October 29, 2015.
26. Jackson, *Untangling the Web.*
27. Christopher Paul et al., *What Works Best.*
28. Ladwig, "Influencing Clients in Counterinsurgency"; Douglas S. Blaufarb, *The Counterinsurgency Era: U.S. Doctrine and Performance, 1950 to the Present* (New York: Free Press, 1977); D. Michael Shafer, *Deadly Paradigms: The Failure of U.S. Counterinsurgency Policy* (Princeton, N.J.: Princeton University Press, 1988).
29. Karlin identifies this as a major impediment to success along with the failure to focus on organizational and personnel issues. Mara Karlin, "Why Military Assistance Programs Disappoint: Minor Tools Can't Solve Major Problems," *Foreign Affairs* 96, no. 6 (2017): 111–20.

30. Peter Baker, *Days of Fire: Bush and Cheney in the White House* (New York: Doubleday, 2013), 148.
31. Sean Naylor, *Relentless Strike: The Secret History of Joint Special Operations Command* (New York: St. Martin's Press, 2015), 169.
32. Naylor, *Relentless Strike*, 172; Jeremy Scahill, *Dirty Wars: The World Is a Battlefield* (New York: Nation Books, 2013), 388.
33. Joint Chiefs of Staff, *The National Military Strategy of the United States of America, 2011: Redefining America's Military Leadership* (Washington, DC: 2011); John T. Bennett, "U.S. Military Envisions More Bases Like Djibouti Facility," *U.S. News and World Report*, January 30, 2012.
34. Naylor, *Relentless Strike*, 329.
35. Charlie Savage, "How 4 Federal Lawyers Paved the Way to Kill Osama Bin Laden," *New York Times*, October 28, 2015.
36. National Commission on Terrorist Attacks Upon the United States, "Staff Statement No. 6: The Military," March 23, 2004, http://govinfo.library.unt.edu/911/archive/hearing8/9-11Commission_Hearing_2004-03-23.htm#statement6.
37. Micah Zenko, "Armed Drones and the Hunt for Bin Laden," *Politics, Power, and Preventive Action*, August 20, 2012.
38. "New America Foundation's Drones Database," *New America*, http://securitydata.newamerica.net/index.html.
39. The Trump administration has since loosened the rules of engagement and ordered a troop increase in Afghanistan. On the use of drone strikes in Afghanistan under Obama, see Josh Smith, "Exclusive: Afghan Drone War—Data Show Unmanned Flights Dominate Air Campaign," *Reuters*, April 20, 2016.
40. Chelsea J. Carter, Tom Cohen, and Barbara Starr, "U.S. Jet Fighters, Drones Strike Isis Fighters, Convoys in Iraq," *CNN*, August 9, 2014; Greg Miller, "U.S. Launches Secret Drone Campaign to Hunt Islamic State Leaders in Syria," *Washington Post*, September 1, 2015; Helene Cooper and Eric Schmitt, "U.S. Strikes Help Libyan Forces Against ISIS in Surt," *New York Times*, August 2, 2016.
41. Micah Zenko and Emma Welch, "Where the Drones Are," *Foreign Policy*, May 29, 2012.
42. Dana Priest and William Arkin, "A Hidden World, Growing Beyond Control," *Washington Post*, July 19, 2010.
43. Paul R. Pillar, "Intelligence," in *Attacking Terrorism: Elements of a Grand Strategy*, ed. Audrey Kurth Cronin and James M. Ludes (Washington, DC: Georgetown University Press, 2004), 115.
44. Daniel Byman, "The Intelligence War on Terrorism," *Intelligence and National Security* 29, no. 6 (2014): 853.
45. Dana Priest and William Arkin, *Top-Secret America: The Rise of the New American Security State* (New York: Little, Brown, 2011), 7.
46. Stéphane Lefebvre, "The Difficulties and Dilemmas of International Intelligence Cooperation," *International Journal of Intelligence and Counterintelligence* 16, no. 4 (2003): 527–42.
47. Jennifer E. Sims, "Foreign Intelligence Liaison: Devils, Deals, and Details," *International Journal of Intelligence and CounterIntelligence* 19, no. 2 (2006): 195–217.
48. Lefebvre, "The Difficulties and Dilemmas of International Intelligence Cooperation."

49. Dana Priest, "Foreign Network at Front of CIA's Terror Fight: Joint Facilities in Two Dozen Countries Account for Bulk of Agency's Post-9/11 Successes," *Washington Post*, November 18, 2005.
50. The intelligence alliance between Australia, Canada, New Zealand, the United Kingdom, and the United States, which dates back to 1948 and is commonly called the Five Eyes alliance, is an important exception to this rule. On bilateral cooperation, see Paul Pillar, *Terrorism and U.S. Foreign Policy* (Washington, DC: Brookings Institution Press, 2001), 75–76.
51. J. Paul de B. Taillon, *Hijacking and Hostages: Government Responses to Terrorism* (Westport, CT: Greenwood, 2002), 172.
52. Sims, "Foreign Intelligence Liaison."
53. Byman, "The Intelligence War on Terrorism."
54. Martin Rudner, "Hunters and Gatherers: The Intelligence Coalition Against Islamic Terrorism," *International Journal of Intelligence and Counterintelligence* 17, no. 2 (2004): 217.
55. Byman, "The Intelligence War on Terrorism."
56. Rudner, "Hunters and Gatherers."
57. Dana Priest, "Foreign Network at Front of CIA's Terror Fight," *Washington Post*, November 18, 2005.
58. Daniel Byman, *Going to War with the Allies You Have: Allies, Counterinsurgency, and the War on Terror* (Carlisle: Strategic Studies Institute, 2005), 9–10.
59. Sims, "Foreign Intelligence Liaison."
60. Sims, "Foreign Intelligence Liaison."
61. Sean McFate, *The Modern Mercenary: Private Armies and What They Mean for World Order* (New York: Oxford University Press, 2014), 56; Mark Mazzetti, *The Way of the Knife: The CIA, a Secret Army, and a War at the Ends of the Earth* (New York: Penguin, 2013), chaps. 10–11.
62. Greg Miller and Julie Tate, "CIA Shifts Focus to Killing Targets," *Washington Post*, September 1, 2011.
63. Edmund Clark and Crofton Black, *Negative Publicity: Artefacts of Extraordinary Rendition* (Italy: Aperture, 2016).
64. Jane Mayer, *The Dark Side: The Inside Story of How the War on Terror Turned Into a War on American Ideals* (New York: Doubleday, 2008), 108.
65. Michael F. Scheuer, former chief of the Bin Laden Unit, Central Intelligence Agency, "Extraordinary Rendition in U.S. Counterterrorism Policy: The Impact on Transatlantic Relations," testimony before House Committee on Foreign Affairs, the Subcommittee on International Organizations, Human Rights, and Oversight, and the Subcommittee on Europe, April 17, 2007. https://fas.org/irp/congress/2007_hr/rendition.pdf, 15.
66. Scheuer, "Extraordinary Rendition in U.S. Counterterrorism Policy"; Mayer, *The Dark Side*, 108.
67. George Tenet, CIA director, "Intelligence Policy and National Policy Coordination," testimony before National Commission on Terrorist Attacks Upon the United States, March 24, 2004, https://shareslide.org/9-11commission-hearing-2004-03-24.
68. Douglas Jehl and David Johnston, "Rule Change Lets CIA Freely Send Suspects Abroad to Jails," *New York Times*, March 6, 2005; Mayer, *The Dark Side*, 110; Jane Mayer,

"Outsourcing Torture," *New Yorker*, February 8, 2005; Dana Priest, "CIA Holds Terror Suspects in Secret Prisons: Debate Is Growing Within Agency About Legality and Morality of Overseas System Set Up After 9/11," *Washington Post*, November 2, 2005.

69. Sims, "Foreign Intelligence Liaison."
70. This paragraph is drawn from Priest, "CIA Holds Terror Suspects in Secret Prisons."
71. Mayer, *The Dark Side*, 299–300.
72. Bill Adair, "More Than 500 Guantanamo Detainees Were Released or Transferred Under Bush," *PolitiFact*, June 18, 2009.
73. Mark Mazzetti and William Glaberson, "Obama Issues Directive to Shut Down Guantánamo," *New York Times*, January 21, 2009.
74. See, for example, Chris McGreal, "Barack Obama Abandons Guantánamo Closure Plan After Congress Veto," *Guardian*, January 20, 2011.
75. Charlie Savage, "Administration Prepares to Lift Ban on New Guantánamo Cases," *New York Times*, January 19, 2011.
76. Jacqueline Klimas, "Many Released from Gitmo Will Resume Fight Against U.S.," *Washington Times*, March 8, 2015.
77. George W. Bush, "Second Inaugural Address," Washington, DC, January 20, 2005; White House, *National Strategy for Combating Terrorism* (2006). On Bush speeches in 2003, see, for example, George W. Bush, "The Future of Iraq," speech at American Enterprise Institute, Washington, DC, February 26, 2003; George W. Bush, "Freedom in Iraq and Middle East: Address at the 20th Anniversary of the National Endowment for Democracy," Washington, DC, November 6, 2003.
78. White House, *National Strategy for Combating Terrorism* (2006); Richard N. Haass, "Towards Greater Democracy in the Muslim World," speech to the Council on Foreign Relations, Washington, DC, December 4, 2002; White House, *National Strategy for Combating Terrorism* (2003).
79. On push and pull factors, see Magnus Ranstorp, "The Root Causes of Violent Extremism," RAN Issue Paper, January 4, 2016, https://ec.europa.eu/home-affairs/sites/home affairs/files/what-we-do/networks/radicalisation_awareness_network/ran-papers/docs /issue_paper_root-causes_jan2016_en.pdf.
80. Bush, "Second Inaugural Address."
81. Peter Romaniuk, *Does CVE Work? Lessons Learned from the Global Effort to Counter Violent Extremism* (New York: Global Center on Cooperative Security, September 2015).
82. CVE is an American term. Other countries refer to programs with similar objectives by different names. CVE is also sometimes used interchangeably with "preventing violent extremism" (PVE).
83. White House, "Fact Sheet: The White House Summit on Countering Violent Extremism," February 18, 2015.
84. Will McCants and Clinton Watts, "U.S. Strategy for Countering Violent Extremism: An Assessment," *Foreign Policy Research Institute E-Notes*, December 10, 2012, https://www .fpri.org/article/2012/12/u-s-strategy-for-countering-violent-extremism-an-assessment/.
85. Background briefings for the author by U.S. government officials. See also *Department of State and USAID Joint Strategy on Countering Violent Extremism* (Washington, DC: 2016); Romaniuk, *Does CVE Work?*
86. Andrew Glazzard and Eric Rosand, "Is It All Over for CVE?" *Lawfare*, June 11, 2017.

87. White House, "Executive Order 13584—Developing an Integrated Strategic Counterterrorism Communications Initiative," September 9, 2011.
88. Some of the local efforts built on preexisting initiatives, such as a USAID pilot program launched in 2006 to combat radicalization in the Sahel. See Jeffrey Swedberg and Steven Smith, "Mid-Term Evaluation of USAID's Counter-Extremism Programming in Africa," USAID, February 1, 2011.
89. Interview with Dan Benjamin, former U.S. ambassador-at-large and coordinator for counterterrorism at the U.S. State Department, November 13, 2015; Glazzard and Rosand, "Is It All Over for CVE?"
90. Hedayah Center, "About Us: History of Hedayah," http://www.hedayahcenter.org/about-us/177/history; Hedayah Center, "About Us: Global Counter Terrorism Forum," http://www.hedayahcenter.org/about-us/177/history/181/global-counter-terrorism-forum.
91. *Department of State and USAID Joint Strategy on Countering Violent Extremism.*
92. Will McCants, email with author, April 14, 2017.
93. Eric Rosand, *Communities First: A Blueprint for Organizing and Sustaining a Global Movement Against Violent Extremism* (Washington, DC: The Prevention Project—Organizing Against Violent Extremism, December 2016).
94. Ban Ki-moon, "Remarks at General Assembly Presentation of the Plan of Action to Prevent Violent Extremism," January 15, 2016, https://www.un.org/sg/en/content/sg/statement/2016-01-15/un-secretary-generals-remarks-general-assembly-presentation-plan; Nate Rosenblatt, "All Jihad Is Local: What ISIS's Files Tell Us About Its Fighters," *New America*, July 20, 2016; Rebecca Wagner and Julia Dankova, "The CSO's Shrinking and Closing Space Tendency—How EU Institutions Can Support CSOs Worldwide," *Heinrich Böll Stiftung*, April 7, 2016.
95. Scott N. McKay and David A. Webb, "Comparing Counterterrorism in Indonesia and the Philippines," *CTC Sentinel* 8, no. 2 (2015); Nicholas Grono, "Australia's Response to Terrorism," *Studies in Intelligence* 48, no. 1 (2007).
96. Interview with Juan Zarate, former deputy assistant to the president and deputy national security advisor for combating terrorism, September 17, 2015; Interview with Tricia Bacon, former State Department intelligence official, September 29, 2015.
97. Bronwyn Bruton and Paul D. Williams, "Counterinsurgency in Somalia: Lessons Learned from the African Union Mission in Somalia, 2007–2013," (Tampa: Joint Special Operations University, 2014).
98. Thomas Fessy, "Boko Haram: Can Regional Force Beat Nigeria's Militant Islamists?" *BBC News*, March 3, 2015.
99. Jeremy M. Sharp, *Jordan: Background and U.S. Relations* (Washington, DC: Congressional Research Service, January 27, 2016); Kenneth Katzman, *The United Arab Emirates (UAE): Issues for U.S. Policy* (Washington, DC: Congressional Research Service, August 16, 2016).
100. Catherine Lutz and Sujaya Desai, "U.S. Reconstruction Aid for Afghanistan: The Dollars and Sense," *Costs of War* (Occasional Papers Series), January 5, 2015.
101. See, for example, Barbara Slavin, "U.S. Builds War Coalition with Favors—and Money," *USA Today*, February 25, 2003; David E. Sanger, "President Rewards Like-Minded Leaders with State Visits," *New York Times*, May 27, 2003.

102. "Iraq Index: Tracking Variables of Reconstruction and Security in Post-Saddam Iraq," Brookings Institution, February 26, 2010, https://www.brookings.edu/iraq-index/. "Facts, Figures Related to the Iraq War," *Associated Press*, August 31, 2010.
103. U.S. Department of State, Special Presidential Envoy for the Global Coalition to Counter ISIL, http://www.state.gov/s/seci/.
104. White House, "Fact Sheet: Maintaining Momentum in the Fight Against ISIL," January 15, 2016.
105. Kathleen J. McInnis, *Coalition Contributions to Countering the Islamic State* (Washington, DC: Congressional Research Service, 2016).
106. See, for example, Aaron Stein, "The Awkward, Necessary U.S.-Turkey Relationship," *Atlantic*, August 23, 2017.

4. PAKISTAN: THE PARADOX

1. Jane Perlez, "Pakistani Army Chief Warns U.S. on Another Raid," *New York Times*, May 5, 2011.
2. *The Abbottabad Commission Report*, n.d., https://assets.documentcloud.org/documents/724833/aljazeera-bin-laden-dossier.pdf.
3. C. Christine Fair, *The Counterterrorism Coalitions: Cooperation with Pakistan and India* (Arlington, VA: RAND Corporation, 2004), n17.
4. Ahmed Rashid, *Descent Into Chaos: The U.S. and the Disaster in Pakistan, Afghanistan, and Central Asia* (New York: Penguin, 2008), 29.
5. Rizwan Hussein, *Pakistan and the Emergence of Islamic Militancy in Afghanistan* (Burlington, VT: Ashgate, 2005), chap. 2.
6. Barnett R. Rubin, *The Fragmentation of Afghanistan* (New Haven, CT: Yale University Press, 2002), 83–84.
7. Mohammad Yousaf and Mark Adkin, *The Bear Trap: The Defeat of a Superpower* (Havertown, PA: Casemate, 1992).
8. Steve Coll, *Ghost Wars: The Secret History of the CIA, Afghanistan, and Bin Laden, from the Soviet Invasion to September 10, 2001* (New York: Penguin, 2004), 202.
9. Seyyed Vali Reza Nasr, *The Islamic Leviathan: Islam and the Making of State Power* (Oxford: Oxford University Press, 2001), 62–63.
10. Nasr, *The Islamic Leviathan*, 24–25.
11. Arif Jamal, *Shadow War: The Untold Story of Jihad in Kashmir* (New York: Melville House, 2009), 109–10.
12. National Commission on Terrorist Attacks Upon the United States, *The 9-11 Commission Report* (Washington, DC: Norton, 2004), 157.
13. Ahmed Rashid, "Pakistan: Trouble Ahead, Trouble Behind," *Current History* 95, no. 600 (April 1996).
14. For example, see Anatol Lieven, *Pakistan: A Hard Country* (New York: Public Affairs, 2011), 465.
15. Pervez Musharraf, *In the Line of Fire: A Memoir* (New York: Free Press, 2006), 201–204.
16. *The 9-11 Commission Report*, 331; "Pakistan's Sanction Waivers: A Summary," Carnegie Endowment for International Peace, October 29, 2001.

17. Dan Balz, Bob Woodward, and Jeff Himmelman, "Afghan Campaign's Blueprint Emerges," *Washington Post*, January 29, 2002.
18. Asad Khan, "Pakistan—An Enduring Friend," *Marine Corps Gazette* 86, no. 6 (June 2002): 34–35; Department of Defense, "Fact Sheet: Coalition Contributions to the War on Terrorism," June 10, 2002.
19. "Tora Bora Revisited: How We Failed to Get Bin Laden and Why It Matters Today," report to the members of the Committee on Foreign Relations, U.S. Senate, November 30, 2009.
20. Rashid, *Descent Into Chaos*, 148.
21. Rashid, *Descent Into Chaos*, 91–93, 147, 240; Khalid Homayun Nadiri, "Old Habits, New Consequences: Pakistan's Posture Toward Afghanistan Since 2001," *International Security* 39, no. 2 (Fall 2014): 132–68.
22. World Bank Group, "Country Brief: Pakistan," August 2003.
23. Fair, *The Counterterrorism Coalitions*, 18.
24. Data on security and economic assistance from https://securityassistance.org/data/program/military/Pakistan/2002/2007/all/Global/; https://securityassistance.org/data/country/economic/country/2002/2007/all/South%20Asia/.
25. Susan B. Epstein and K. Alan Kronstadt, *Pakistan: U.S. Foreign Assistance* (Washington, DC: Congressional Research Service, July 1, 2013), 19, 25–26.
26. C. Christine Fair, "The U.S.-Pakistan Relations After a Decade of the War on Terror," *Contemporary South Asia* 20, no. 2 (2012): 243–53.
27. C. Christine Fair, "Under the Shrinking U.S. Security Umbrella: India's End Game in Afghanistan?" *Washington Quarterly* 34, no. 2 (2011): 179–92.
28. Seth G. Jones and C. Christine Fair, *Counterinsurgency in Pakistan* (Santa Monica, CA: RAND Corporation 2010), 45; Ashley Tellis, *Pakistan and the War on Terror: Conflicted Goals, Compromised Performance* (Washington, DC: Carnegie Endowment for International Peace, 2008).
29. Sameer Lalwani, "Geography, Identity, and Strategies of Counterinsurgency: Evidence from South Asia," unpublished manuscript, draft as of March 30, 2016.
30. Musharraf technically banned LeT, JeM, and HuM, along with various other groups, but they still operated and received varying degrees of state support.
31. Mark Mazzetti, *The Way of the Knife: The CIA, a Secret Army, and a War at the Ends of the Earth* (New York: Penguin, 2013), 34.
32. Shehzad H. Qazi, "Rebels of the Frontier: Origins, Organization, and Recruitment of the Pakistani Taliban," *Small Wars and Insurgencies* 22, no. 4 (2011): 574–602.
33. Mariam Abou Zahab, "Pashtun and Punjabi Taliban," in *Contextualising Jihadi Thought*, ed. Jeevan Deol and Zaheer Kazmi (London: Hurst and Co., 2011), 372–73.
34. Stephen Tankel, "Beyond FATA: Exploring the Punjabi Militant Threat to Pakistan," *Terrorism and Political Violence* 28. no. 1 (2016): 49–71.
35. David E. Sanger, *The Inheritance: The World Obama Confronts and the Challenges to American Power* (New York: Harmony, 2009), 137; Amir Mir, "Pak Tribals Warn of War Against U.S. Tribals," *Rediff*, May 23, 2002; Jones and Fair, *Counterinsurgency in Pakistan*, xiv.
36. Mazzetti, *Way of the Knife*, 38–39, 109; Fair, *The Counterterrorism Coalitions.*
37. Mazzetti, *Way of the Knife*, 169.

38. Fadil Harun, *al-Harb 'ala al-Islam: Qissat Fadil Harun* [The war against Islam: The story of Fadil Harun], 534–536, found in Nelly Lahoud, *Beware of Imitators: Al-Qa'ida Through the Lens of Its Confidential Secretary* (West Point, NY: Combating Terrorism Center, 2012), 105–8.
39. Central Intelligence Agency, "Detainee Reporting Pivotal for the War Against Al-Qa'ida," June 3, 2005; Peter L. Bergen, *Manhunt: The Ten-Year Search for Bin Laden from 9/11 to Abbottabad* (New York: Random House, 2012), 63–66.
40. C. Christine Fair, "The Militant Challenge in Pakistan," *Asia Policy* 11, no. 1 (2011): 105–37.
41. C. Christine Fair, "Why the Pakistan Army Is Here to Stay: Prospects for Civilian Governance," *International Affairs* 87, no. 3 (2011): 571–88.
42. Jones and Fair, *Counterinsurgency in Pakistan*, 54.
43. Iqbal Khattak, "I Did Not Surrender to the Military, Said Nek Mohammad," *Friday Times*, April 30–May 6, 2004.
44. Alex Strick van Linschoten and Felix Kuehn, *An Enemy We Created: The Myth of the Taliban–Al Qaeda Merger in Afghanistan* (New York: Oxford University Press, 2012), 252–53; Antonio Giustozzi, *Koran, Kalashnikov, and Laptop: The Neo-Taliban Insurgency in Afghanistan* (London: Hurst and Co., 2009), 34–40.
45. Michael Scheuer, *Imperial Hubris: Why the West Is Losing the War on Terrorism* (Washington, DC: Brassey's, 2004), 55.
46. Stephen Tankel, *Storming the World Stage* (New York: Columbia University Press, 2011), 114–15, 127–28, 136, 156–57, 176.
47. Sunni militants who targeted Pakistan's Shiite minority also took advantage of this infrastructure.
48. As of 2012, U.S. officials reportedly continued to alert Pakistan of where it would conduct strikes. Adam Entous, Siobhan Gorman, and Evan Perez, "U.S. Unease Over Drone Strikes," *Wall Street Journal*, September 26, 2012.
49. Information in this paragraph from Mazzetti, *The Way of the Knife*, 108–9.
50. Mark Mazzetti and Declan Walsh, "Pakistan Says U.S. Drone Killed Taliban Leader," *New York Times*, May 29, 2013.
51. Saba Imtiaz, "What Do Pakistanis Really Think About Drones?" in *Drone Wars: Transforming Conflict, Law, and Policy*, ed. Peter L. Bergen and Daniel Rothenberg (New York: Cambridge University Press), 90.
52. Tankel, *Storming the World Stage*, 162–63.
53. Raffaello Pantucci, "A Biography of Rashid Rauf: Al-Qa'ida's British Operative," *CTC Sentinel* 5, no. 7 (2012): 12–16.
54. National Intelligence Council, *National Intelligence Estimate: The Terrorist Threat to the Homeland* (Washington, DC: 2007), http://nsarchive.gwu.edu/nukevault/ebb270/18.pdf.
55. Bergen, *Manhunt*, 65; "Top Al Qaeda Suspect in U.S. Custody," *CBS News*, March 3, 2003.
56. Seth Jones, "The Future of al-Qa'ida," testimony before the House Foreign Affairs Committee, Subcommittee on Terrorism, Nonproliferation, and Trade, May 24, 2011, http://archives.republicans.foreignaffairs.house.gov/112/jon052411.pdf.
57. Daud Khattak, "Reviewing Pakistan's Peace Deals with the Taliban," *CTC Sentinel* 5, no. 9 (September 2012): 11–14.

58. The North-West Frontier Province was officially renamed Khyber Pakhtunkhwa in 2010.
59. Mazzetti, *The Way of the Knife*, 158.
60. Jones and Fair, *Counterinsurgency in Pakistan*, 36.
61. David Wood, "Commanders Seek More Forces in Afghanistan: Taliban Prepare Offensive Against U.S., NATO Troops," *Baltimore Sun*, January 8, 2007.
62. Sanger, *The Inheritance*, 154–55; Tellis, *Pakistan and the War on Terror.*
63. Nadiri, "Old Habits, New Consequences."
64. Pakistan and India launched a peace process in 2004, accompanied by backchannel negotiations over Kashmir, which contributed to Pakistani efforts to rein in state-allied groups. Tankel, *Storming the World Stage*, 176–77.
65. Jones and Fair, *Counterinsurgency in Pakistan*, 53–54.
66. Mazzetti, *The Way of the Knife*, 171–72.
67. Sanger, *The Inheritance*, 154–55, 240–51.
68. Bob Woodward, *Obama's Wars* (New York: Simon & Schuster, 2010), 3.
69. C. Christine Fair, "The U.S.-Pakistan F-16 Fiasco," *Foreign Policy*, February 3, 2011.
70. Barack Obama, "Address to the Nation on the Way Forward in Afghanistan and Pakistan," West Point, NY, December 1, 2009, https://obamawhitehouse.archives.gov/the-press-office/remarks-president-address-nation-way-forward-afghanistan-and-pakistan.
71. Although KLB authorized $1.5 billion a year, the United States only dispensed the full amount once (in FY2010). On average, Pakistan received approximately $1.15 billion annually, and some of that was spent on U.S. contractors to administer funded projects. U.S. Senate, Enhanced Partnership with Pakistan Act of 2009, S.1707, 111th Cong. (2009).
72. On the precise conditions, see Enhanced Partnership with Pakistan Act of 2009.
73. Atika Rehman, "Work Harder to 'Squeeze' Haqqanis, Clinton Tells Pakistan," *Express Tribune*, October 21, 2011.
74. Daniel Markey, *No Exit from Pakistan: America's Tortured Relationship with Islamabad* (New York: Cambridge University Press, 2013), 16–18.
75. Epstein and Kronstadt, *Pakistan: U.S. Foreign Assistance.*
76. Zahid Hussain, "Conspiratorial Paranoia," *Dawn*, August 28, 2012; Khaled Ahmed, "Our Pathology of Fear," *Express Tribune*, November 24, 2012.
77. Stephen Tankel, "Beyond the Double Game: Lessons from Pakistan's Approach to Islamist Militancy," *Journal of Strategic Studies*, June 16, 2016.
78. Qazi, "Rebels of the Frontier."
79. Hassan Abbas, "Defining the Punjabi Taliban Network," *CTC Sentinel* 2, no. 4 (2009): 1–4.
80. Tankel, "Beyond FATA."
81. "FATF Blacklists Eight Countries Including Pakistan," *Dunya News*, February 20, 2010; "Pakistan on Money-Laundering Blacklist," *Dawn*, February 16, 2012.
82. Letter From: 'Atiyya (aka Mahmud), To: Bin Laden, June 19, 2010, Government Exhibit 421-10-CR-019-S-4-RJD. Letter From: Atiyya (aka Mahmud), To: Bin Laden (aka Shaykhuna, i.e., "our shaykh"), Date: May 5, 2011, Government Exhibit 431-10-CR-019-S-4-RJD. Letter From: 'Atiyya (aka Mahmud), To: Bin Laden, April 5, 2011. Letter From: 'Atiyya (aka Mahmud), To: Bin Laden, June 19, 2010, Government Exhibit 421-10-CR-019-S-4-RJD.

83. Qazi, "Rebels of the Frontier."
84. On LeT's use against the TTP, see C. Christine Fair, "Lashkar-e-Tayiba and the Pakistani State," *Survival* 53, no. 4 (2011): 29–52; Stephen Tankel, *Domestic Barriers to Dismantling the Militant Infrastructure in Pakistan* (Washington, DC: US Institute of Peace, 2013). On LeT's use in Balochistan, see Tankel, "Beyond the Double Game."
85. Vahid Brown and Don Rassler, *Fountainhead of Jihad: The Haqqani Nexus, 1973–2012* (New York: Oxford University Press, 2013), 159–61.
86. Amir Mir, *Talibanization of Pakistan: From 9/11 to 26/11 and Beyond* (New Delhi: Pentagon, 2009), 108–9.
87. Brown and Rassler, *Fountainhead of Jihad*, 186.
88. Woodward, *Obama's Wars*, 4–5.
89. New America Foundation, "Drone Wars Pakistan: 2008," http://securitydata.newamerica.net/drones/overview.html?yr=2008&country=Pakistan.
90. Woodward, *Obama's Wars*, 4–5.
91. Mazzetti, *The Way of the Knife*, 109.
92. Woodward, *Obama's Wars*, 6.
93. New America Foundation, "Drone Wars Pakistan: Analysis," http://securitydata.newamerica.net/drones/pakistan-analysis.html.
94. Mazzetti, *The Way of the Knife*, 290.
95. New America Foundation, "Drone Wars Pakistan: Leaders Killed," http://securitydata.newamerica.net/drones/leaders-killed.html?country=Pakistan.
96. Letter From: 'Atiyya (akak Mahmud), To: Bin Laden, June 19, 2010, Government Exhibit 421-10-CR-019-S-4-RJD (Abbottabad document released at trial of Abid Naseer).
97. Letter From: 'Atiyya (akak Mahmud), To: Bin Laden, June 19, 2010.
98. Letter From: Bin Laden, To: Atiyya (aka Mahmud), August 7, 2010, Government Exhibit 425-10-CR-019-S-4-RJD.
99. "The Organization of al-Qaida in the Islamic Maghreb: From the Organization's Shura Council to Our Good Brothers in the Shura Council of the Masked Brigade," *Associated Press*, The al-Qaida Papers, http://hosted.ap.org/specials/interactives/_international/_pdfs/al-qaida-belmoktar-letter-english.pdf.
100. Javier Jordan, "The Effectiveness of the Drone Campaign Against al-Qaeda Central: A Case Study," *Journal of Strategic Studies* 37, no. 1 (2014): 4–29.
101. C. Christine Fair, Karl Kaltenthaler, and William Miller, "Pakistani Political Communication and Public Opinion on U.S. Drone Attacks," *Journal of Strategic Studies* 38, no. 6 (2015): 852–72.
102. Tom Coghlan, Zahid Hussain, and Jeremy Page, "Secrecy and Denial as Pakistan Lets CIA Use Airbase to Strike Militants," *Times* (London), February 17, 2009; "U.S. Forces Using Shamsi Airbase in Balochistan," *Dawn*, December 12, 2009. On Pakistani requests, see Mazzetti, *The Way of the Knife*, 227–28.
103. Omega teams comprising CIA personnel and U.S. special operations forces reportedly launched a limited number of incursions from Afghanistan into the FATA and Balochistan to pursue specific high-value targets. See Dan Lamothe, "SEAL Team 6, the CIA, and the Secret History of U.S. Kill Missions in Afghanistan," *Washington Post*,

June 6, 2015; Mark Mazzetti et al., "The Secret History of SEAL Team 6: Quiet Killings and Blurred Lines," *New York Times*, June 6, 2015.

104. Mark Mazzetti and Dexter Filkins, "U.S. Military Seeks to Expand Raids in Pakistan," *New York Times*, December 20, 2010.
105. Mazzetti, *The Way of the Knife*, 160–65; Woodward, *Obama's Wars*, 6.
106. "Haqqani Says [He] Facilitated Presence of CIA Men in Pakistan," *Pakistan Today*, March 12, 2017.
107. A U.S. embassy vehicle speeding to the scene killed a Pakistani bystander. See Mark Mazzetti, "How A Single Spy Helped Turn Pakistan Against the United States," *New York Times*, April 9, 2013.
108. Mark Mazzetti et al., "American Held in Pakistan Worked with CIA," *New York Times*, February 21, 2011.
109. Omar Waraich, "U.S. Diplomat Could Bring Down Pakistan Gov't," *Time*, February 9, 2011.
110. Mazzetti, "How a Single Spy."
111. *The Abbottabad Commission Report*, n.d., https://assets.documentcloud.org/documents/724833/aljazeera-bin-laden-dossier.pdf.
112. Adam Entous and Tom Wright, "U.S. Apologizes to Pakistan, Says Supply Routes to Reopen," *Wall Street Journal*, July 2, 2012.
113. Bradley Klapper, "U.S. Quietly Releasing $1.6B in Pakistan Assistance," *Associated Press*, October 19, 2013.
114. Matthew Rosenberg, "U.S. Disrupts Afghans' Tack on Militants," *New York Times*, October 28, 2013.
115. Ellen Barry, "Al Qaeda Opens New Branch on Indian Subcontinent," *New York Times*, September 4, 2014.
116. Stephen Tankel, "Destabilizing Elements: The Punjabi Militant Threat to Pakistan," in *Pakistan's Political Labyrinths: Military, Society, and Terror*, ed. Ravi Kalia (London: Routledge, 2015), 96–98.
117. ISKP also included some erstwhile Afghan Taliban fighters.
118. Saeed Shah, Safdar Dawar, and Adam Entous, "Militants Slip Away Before Pakistan Offensive," *Wall Street Journal*, July 17, 2014.
119. Pak Institute for Peace Studies, "Pakistan Security Report 2015" (Islamabad: 2016).
120. Institute of Economics and Peace, "Global Terrorism Index 2016: Measuring and Understanding the Impact of Terrorism," http://economicsandpeace.org/wp-content/uploads/2016/11/Global-Terrorism-Index-2016.2.pdf.
121. Pak Institute for Peace Studies, "Pakistan Security Report 2016" (Islamabad: 2017).
122. "Pakistan Security Report," *PIPS Research Journal Conflict and Peace Studies* 9, no.1 (Spring 2017): 11–20.
123. Sameer Lalwani, "Actually, Pakistan Is Winning Its War on Terror," *Foreign Policy*, December 10, 2015.
124. National Defense Authorization Act for Fiscal Year 2013, Public Law 112-239, January 2, 2013; Epstein and Kronstadt, *Pakistan: U.S. Foreign Assistance.*
125. National Defense Authorization Act for Fiscal Year 2015, Public Law 113-291, December 19, 2014.

126. National Defense Authorization Act for Fiscal Year 2016, Public Law 114-92, November 25, 2015.
127. Eric Schmitt, "Al Qaeda Turns to Syria, with a Plan to Challenge ISIS," *New York Times*, May 15, 2016; Eric Schmitt and David E. Sanger, "As U.S. Focuses on ISIS and the Taliban, Al Qaeda Reemerges," *New York Times*, December 29, 2015.
128. It is tough to determine how much U.S. assistance was related to CVE because disparate implementing agencies characterized CVE efforts differently.
129. On U.S. policies, see United States Agency for International Development, "USAID/Pakistan Interim Strategic Plan, May 2003–September 2006" (Islamabad: USAID, May 2003); United States Agency for International Development, "Pakistan-Political Transition Initiatives," https://www.usaid.gov/political-transition-initiatives/pakistan; "Enhanced Partnership with Pakistan Act of 2009." On research, see Graeme Blair, C. Christine Fair, Neil Malhotra, and Jacob N. Shapiro, "Poverty and Support for Militant Politics: Evidence from Pakistan," *American Journal of Political Science* 57, no. 1 (2013): 30–48.
130. "Madrassa Reforms in Tatters," *Dawn*, July 16, 2009; Secretariat Youth Parliament Pakistan, "Madrassa Education: 2014 Challenges, Reforms and Possibilities," Pakistan Institute of Legislative Development and Transparency, March 2015.
131. C. Christine Fair, "Militant Recruitment in Pakistan: A New Look at the Militancy-Madrasah Connection," *Asia Policy* 1, no. 4 (2007): 107–34.
132. Madiha Afzal, *Education and Attitudes in Pakistan: Understanding Perceptions of Terrorism* (Washington, DC: U.S. Institute of Peace, April 2015).
133. USAID, "Education," https://www.usaid.gov/pakistan/education; "New Pakistani Education Reforms will Reach Millions," British Council, December 3, 2015.
134. Gopal Ratnam, "Pakistan Public School Curriculum Distorts Views on Terrorism, Researcher Says," USIP, June 12, 2016.
135. Hedieh Mirahmadi, Waleed Ziad, Mehreen Farooq, and Robert D. Lamb, "Empowering Pakistan's Civil Society to Counter Global Violent Extremism," in *U.S.-Islamic World Forum Papers 2014* (Washington, DC: Brookings Institution, 2015).
136. "Grants Opportunities," Embassy of the United States, Pakistan, http://islamabad.usembassy.gov/pr_122712.grant.html.
137. Sebastian Abbot, "AP Exclusive: U.S. Ups Extremist Fight in Pakistan," *Associated Press*, December 31, 2011.
138. Mirahmadi et al., "Empowering Pakistan's Civil Society."
139. Author discussions with Pakistani journalists and members of civil society during visits to Pakistan and at international forums between 2008 and 2016.
140. Christine C. Fair, Neil Malhotra, and Jacob N. Shapiro, "The Roots of Militancy: Explaining Support for Political Violence in Pakistan," working paper, Princeton University, 2009.
141. Pew Global Attitudes Project, "Pakistani Public Opinion: Growing Concerns About Extremism, Continuing Discontent with U.S.," August 13, 2009, http://www.pewglobal.org/files/pdf/265.pdf.
142. Mirahmadi et al., "Empowering Pakistan's Civil Society."
143. "National Internal Security Policy—2014–18."

144. "20 Points of National Action Plan," All Parties Conference, http://infopak.gov.pk/InnerPage.aspx?Page_ID=46.
145. Lalwani, "Actually, Pakistan Is Winning Its War on Terror."
146. Zahid Gishkori, "102 Madrassas Sealed for Stoking Sectarianism," *Express Tribune*, November 12, 2015.
147. Hassan Abbas, "The Roots of Radicalization in Pakistan," *South Asia Journal* 9 (Summer 2013).
148. Faisal Ali Ghuman, "Deradicalization in Disarray," *Dawn*, October 24, 2014.
149. Interview with Swat deradicalization center administrator, name withheld upon request, July 2011.
150. Donald Trump, "Remarks on the Strategy in Afghanistan and South Asia," Washington, DC, August 21, 2017, https://www.whitehouse.gov/the-press-office/2017/08/21/remarks-president-trump-strategy-afghanistan-and-south-asia.
151. Background briefings provided to author by current and former U.S. officials.
152. Nadiri, "Old Habits, New Consequences"; Dean Nelson and Ben Farmer, "Hamid Karzai Held Secret Talks with Mullah Baradar in Afghanistan," *Telegraph*, March 16, 2010.
153. Mujib Mashal, "How Peace Between Afghanistan and the Taliban Foundered," *New York Times*, December 26, 2016.
154. Carlotta Gall, "Saudis Bankroll Taliban, Even as King Officially Supports Afghan Government," *New York Times*, December 6, 2016.
155. Carlotta Gall, "From Where Ex-Taliban Minister Sits, Demand Is Growing for Afghan Peace," *New York Times*, September 9, 2016.
156. Barnett Rubin, "Afghanistan and the Taliban Need Pakistan for Peace," *Al-Jazeera*, January 10, 2016.
157. This paragraph draws on Rubin, "Afghanistan and the Taliban Need Pakistan for Peace."
158. U.S. Department of State, "Joint Press Release of the Quadrilateral Coordination Group on Afghan Peace and Reconciliation," January 11, 2016, https://2009-2017.state.gov/r/pa/prs/ps/2016/01/251105.htm.
159. "Mullah Omar: Taliban Leader 'Died in Pakistan in 2013,'" *BBC News*, July 29, 2015.
160. Mujib Mashal, "Taliban Chief Targeted by Drone Strike in Pakistan, Signaling a U.S. Shift," *New York Times*, May 22, 2016.
161. Interviews with Afghan government officials, July 2017.
162. Mansour also raised funds from donors in Arab Gulf states and through dealings with Afghan drug lords.
163. This paragraph draws on Carlotta Gall and Ruhullah Khapalwak, "Taliban Leader Feared Pakistan Before He Was Killed," *New York Times*, August 9, 2017.

5. SAUDI ARABIA: ARSONIST AND FIREFIGHTER

1. Rachel Bronson, *Thicker Than Oil: America's Uneasy Partnership with Saudi Arabia* (New York: Oxford University Press, 2006), 238.
2. Policy making is the product of consensus building among senior members of the royal family.

3. Roel Meijer, "Introduction," in *Global Salafism: Islam's New Religious Movement*, ed. Roel Meijer (New York: Oxford University Press, 2009), 8.
4. Thomas Hegghammer, *Jihad in Saudi Arabia: Violence and Pan-Islamism Since 1979* (New York: Cambridge University Press, 2010), 17.
5. Despite its universal pretensions, interpretations of Salafism depend on local circumstances as well as global developments. It is also worth noting that Wahhabis often reject the term Wahhabism because it suggests they follow Ibn Wahhab, a person, rather than God, preferring the term Salafist. For more on Wahhabi doctrine, Salafism, and jihad, see Roel Meijer, "Introduction," in *Global Salafism*; Natana DeLong-Bas, *Wahhabi Islam: From Revival and Reform to Global Jihad* (Oxford: Oxford University Press, 2008), chaps. 5–6; Shiraz Maher, *Salafi-Jihadism: The History of an Idea* (New York: Oxford University Press, 2016).
6. Hegghammer, *Jihad in Saudi Arabia*, 17–19.
7. Toby Jones, "Rebellion on the Saudi Periphery: Modernity, Marginalization, and the Shi'a Uprising of 1979," *International Journal of Middle East Studies* 38, no. 2 (2006): 213–33.
8. Stéphane Lacroix, *Awakening Islam: The Politics of Religious Dissent in Contemporary Saudi Arabia* (Cambridge, MA: Harvard University Press, 2011), chap. 3.
9. Thomas Hegghammer, "Jihad, Yes, but Not Revolution: Explaining the Extroversion of Islamist Violence in Saudi Arabia," *British Journal of Middle Eastern Studies* 36, no. 3 (2009): 395–416.
10. Mustafa Hamid and Leah Farrall, *The Arabs at War in Afghanistan* (New York: Oxford University Press, 2015), 79–81; Hegghammer, *Jihad in Saudi Arabia*, 25–30.
11. Hegghammer, *Jihad in Saudi Arabia*, chap. 2.
12. For example, Government's Evidentiary Proffer Supporting the Admissibility of Co-Conspirator Statements' *United States of America v. Enaam M. Arnaout*, United States District Court Northern District of Illinois Eastern Division, Case #02 CR 892.3, February 2003.
13. Hamid and Farrall, *The Arabs at War in Afghanistan*, 170–173; Joas Wagemakers, *A Quietist Jihadi: The Ideology and Influence of Abu Mohammad al-Maqdisi* (New York: Cambridge University Press, 2012), 38, 71, 104–8.
14. Hamid and Farrall, *The Arabs at War in Afghanistan*, 243.
15. Hegghammer, *Jihad in Saudi Arabia*, 75.
16. Juan Zarate, *Treasury's War: The Unleashing of a New Era of Financial Warfare* (New York: Public Affairs, 2013), 69.
17. Hamid and Farrall, *The Arabs at War in Afghanistan*, 37, 280; National Commission on Terrorist Attacks Upon the United States, *The 9-11 Commission Report* (Washington, DC: Norton, 2004), 233.
18. On the anti-Soviet jihad, see Steve Coll, *Ghost Wars: The Secret History of the CIA, Afghanistan, and Bin Laden, from the Soviet Invasion to September 10, 2001* (New York: Penguin, 2004), part 1. On U.S. support for exporting Wahhabism, see Bronson, *Thicker Than Oil*, 233, 237, 241–42.
19. John Roth, Douglas Greenburg, and Serena Wille, "Staff Report to the Commission: Monograph on Terrorist Financing," prepared for the National Commission on Terrorist Attacks Upon the United States, in *The 9-11 Commission Report*, 122, fn 66.
20. *The 9-11 Commission Report*, 60, 122. Bronson, *Thicker Than Oil*, 214–15.

21. *The 9-11 Commission Report*, 122n67.
22. Dan Byman, "The Intelligence War on Terrorism," *Intelligence and National Security* 29, no. 6 (2014): 837–63.
23. Bronson, *Thicker Than Oil*, Loc. 217–18, 234–35.
24. As of 2002, the total value of U.S. arms sales to Saudi Arabia was close to $100 billion. Josh Pollack, "Saudi Arabia and the United States," *Middle East Review of International Affairs* 6, no. 3 (2002): 77–102.
25. National Commission on Terrorist Attacks Upon the United States, "Staff Statement No. 15: Overview of the Enemy," March 23, 2004, 10.
26. Zarate, *Treasury's War*, chap. 3.
27. Scott Shane, "Saudis and Extremism: 'Both the Arsonists and the Firefighters," *New York Times*, August 25, 2016.
28. F. Gregory Gause, III, "Be Careful What You Wish For: The Future of U.S.-Saudi Relations," *World Policy Journal* 19, no. 1 (2002): 37–50.
29. Daniel Byman, *Deadly Connections: States That Sponsor Terrorism* (New York: Cambridge University Press, 2008), 232.
30. Robert Lacey, *Inside the Kingdom: Kings, Clerics, Modernists, Terrorists, and the Struggle for Saudi Arabia* (New York: Viking, 2009), 228–31.
31. Lacey, *Inside the Kingdom*, 232–34.
32. Michael Scott Doran, "The Saudi Paradox," *Foreign Affairs* 83, no. 1 (2004).
33. For example, Alaa Shahine, "Saudi Interior Minister: Jews Were Behind September 11 Attacks," *Associated Press*, December 5, 2002.
34. Michael R. Gordon, "Saudis Warn Against Attack on Iraq by the United States," *New York Times*, March 17, 2002.
35. David Ottaway, *The King's Messenger: Prince Bandar bin Sultan and America's Tangled Relationship with Saudi Arabia* (New York: Walker and Co., 2008), 214.
36. Lacey, *Inside the Kingdom*, 287–291.
37. Bronson, *Thicker Than Oil*, 240.
38. Bronson, *Thicker Than Oil*, 253.
39. John Solomon, "Saudis Secretly Provided Extensive U.S. Help During Iraq War," *Associated Press*, April 24, 2004.
40. Gause, "Be Careful What You Wish For."
41. Lacey, *Inside the Kingdom*, 291.
42. Zarate, *Treasury's War*, 67.
43. Bootie Cosgrove-Mather, "Al-Qaeda Skimming Charity Money," *CBS News*, June 7, 2004.
44. Zarate, *Treasury's War*, 72–73.
45. Jamal Khashoggi, "Saudi Religious Establishment Has Its Wings Clipped," *Daily Star*, July 1, 2002.
46. Bronson, *Thicker Than Oil*, 241.
47. Joseph A. Kéchichian, "Testing the Saudi 'Will to Power': Challenges Confronting Prince Abdallah," *Middle East Policy* 10, no. 4 (2003): 100–115.
48. Doran, "The Saudi Paradox."
49. Pascal Menoret, "Riyadh Rage: Inside Saudi Arabia's Joyriding Craze," *Guardian*, June 22, 2014.

50. "Profile: Abdul Aziz al-Muqrin," *BBC*, June 19, 2004; Lawrence Joffe, "Abd al-Aziz al-Muqrin: Al-Qaida Mastermind Behind Saudi Killings," *Guardian*, June 20, 2004.
51. Hegghammer, *Jihad in Saudi Arabia*, 163–64.
52. Hegghammer, "Jihad, Yes, but Not Revolution."
53. Hegghammer, *Jihad in Saudi Arabia*, 156–57.
54. For different accounts, see Vahid Brown, *A Profile of Saif al-Adel* (West Point: Combating Terrorism Center, n.d.), 7; Ali Soufan, *The Black Banners: The Inside Story of 9/11 and the War Against al-Qaeda* (New York: Norton, 2011), 513–514; Ron Suskind, *The One Percent Doctrine: Deep Inside America's Pursuit of Its Enemies Since 9/11* (New York: Simon & Schuster, 2006), 146–47.
55. Thomas Hegghammer, "The Failure of Jihad in Saudi Arabia," Combating Terrorism Center Occasional Paper Series (2010), 14.
56. Neil MacFarquhar, "Among Saudis, Attack Has Soured Qaeda Supporters," *New York Times*, November 11, 2003.
57. Lacey, *Inside the Kingdom*, 248.
58. Nawaf Obaid, "Remnants of al-Qaeda in Saudi Arabia: Current Assessment," presentation at Council of Foreign Relations, New York, 2006.
59. Anthony H. Cordesman and Nawaf Obaid, *Saudi National Security: Military and Security Services—Challenges and Developments* (Washington, DC: Center for Strategic and International Studies, September 2004), 144–47; Roth, Greenburg, and Wille, "Staff Report to the Commission," 46.
60. Christopher M. Blanchard and Alfred B. Prados, *Saudi Arabia: Terrorist Financing Issues* (Washington, DC: Congressional Research Service, September 14, 2007), 22.
61. Bronson, *Thicker Than Oil*, 244.
62. Department of State, *Country Reports on Terrorism 2015* (Washington, DC: 2016), 337–39.
63. Lacey, *Inside the Kingdom*, 258.
64. On calls for dialogue, see Lacey, *Inside the Kingdom*, 297. On balancing, F. Gregory Gause, III, *Saudi Arabia in the New Middle East* (New York: Council on Foreign Relations, December 2011).
65. Angela Gendron, "Confronting Terrorism in Saudi Arabia," *International Journal of Intelligence and Counterintelligence* 23, no. 3 (2010): 487–508.
66. James Sturcke, "Nine Killed as U.S. Consulate in Jeddah Attacked," *Guardian*, December 6, 2004.
67. Wagemakers, *A Quietist Jihadi*, 129–30, 133; Joas Wagemakers, "Al-Qaida's Editor: Abu Jandal al-Azdi's Online Jihadi Activism," *Politics, Religion, and Ideology* 12, no. 4 (2011): 355–69.
68. Hegghammer, "Jihad, Yes, but Not Revolution."
69. Cordesman and Obaid, *Saudi National Security*; Roth, Greenburg, and Wille, "Staff Report to the Commission," 46.
70. Hegghammer, "The Failure of Jihad in Saudi Arabia," 19.
71. Hegghammer, *Jihad in Saudi Arabia*, 217.
72. Gendron, "Confronting Terrorism in Saudi Arabia."
73. Hegghammer, "The Failure of Jihad in Saudi Arabia," 19–20.

74. "Terrorists Offered Amnesty," *Arab News*, June 24, 2004.
75. On Saudi efforts, Hegghammer, *Jihad in Saudi Arabia*, 217–225.
76. Hegghammer, *Jihad in Saudi Arabia*, 222.
77. "The Fatwa of the 26 Clerics: 'Open Sermon to the Militant Iraqi People,'" *Frontline*, November 5, 2004.
78. Gendron, "Confronting Terrorism in Saudi Arabia."
79. Hegghammer, "Jihad, Yes, but Not Revolution."
80. Hegghammer, "The Failure of Jihad in Saudi Arabia," 23.
81. Thomas Hegghammer, *Saudi Militants in Iraq: Backgrounds and Recruitment Patterns* (Kjeller: Norwegian Defence Research Establishment, 2007), http://rapporter.ffi.no/rapporter/2006/03875.pdf.
82. Hegghammer, "The Failure of Jihad in Saudi Arabia," 19.
83. Martin Rudner, "Misuse of Passports: Identity Fraud, the Propensity to Travel, and International Terrorism," *Studies in Conflict and Terrorism* 31, no. 2 (2008): 95–110.
84. David Aufhause, "An Assessment of Current Efforts to Combat Terrorism," testimony before the Senate Committee on Governmental Affairs, June 15, 2004.
85. Thomas J. Harrington, "Saudi Arabia and the Fight Against Terrorism Financing," testimony before the House Committee on International Relations, Subcommittee on the Middle East and Central Asia, March 24, 2004; Juan C. Zarate, "Saudi Arabia and the Fight Against Terrorism Financing," testimony before the House Committee on International Relations, Subcommittee on the Middle East and Central Asia, March 24, 2004.
86. Susan Schmidt, "U.S. Officials Press Saudis on Aiding Terror," *Washington Post*, August 6, 2003.
87. A. S. M. Ali Ashraf, "Transnational Cooperation on Anti-Terrorism: A Comparative Case Study of Saudi Arabia and Indonesia," *Perceptions: Journal of International Affairs* 12, no. 2/3 (2007).
88. FATF, *Annual Report 2003–2004* (Paris: FATF Secretariat, 2004), annex C.
89. Zarate, *Treasury's War*, 76.
90. Zarate, "Saudi Arabia and the Fight Against Terrorism Financing"; Harrington, "Saudi Arabia and the Fight Against Terrorism Financing."
91. Harrington, "Saudi Arabia and the Fight Against Terrorism Financing."
92. Gause, *Saudi Arabia in the New Middle East*, 29.
93. Gendron, "Confronting Terrorism in Saudi Arabia."
94. Daniel L. Glaser, testimony before the Senate Committee on the Judiciary, November 8, 2005; Eric Lichtblau and Eric Schmitt, "Cash Flow to Terrorists Evades U.S. Efforts," *New York Times*, December 5, 2010.
95. Peter Bergen, "Secrets of the bin Laden Treasure-Trove," *CNN*, May 20, 2015.
96. Zarate, *Treasury's War*, 90; "Letter of Advice to UBL," SOCOM-2012-0000018, c. September 12–14, 2006.
97. Lichtblau and Schmitt, "Cash Flow to Terrorists."
98. Lichtblau and Schmitt, "Cash Flow to Terrorists"; Carlotta Gall, "Saudis Bankroll Taliban, Even as King Officially Supports Afghan Government," *New York Times*, December 6, 2016.
99. Zarate, *Treasury's War*, 78–79.

100. Stuart Levey, testimony before the Senate Committee on Banking, Housing, and Urban Affairs, July 13, 2005.
101. Gendron, "Confronting Terrorism in Saudi Arabia."
102. For example, see Gall, "Saudis Bankroll Taliban."
103. Zarate, *Treasury's War*, 71.
104. Gall, "Saudis Bankroll Taliban."
105. Lichtblau and Schmitt, "Cash Flow to Terrorists."
106. This paragraph draws from Christopher Boucek, *Saudi Arabia's "Soft" Counterterrorism Strategy: Prevention, Rehabilitation, and Aftercare* (Washington, DC: Carnegie Endowment for International Peace, 2008).
107. Boucek, *Saudi Arabia's "Soft" Counterterrorism Strategy.*
108. Lacey, *Inside the Kingdom*, 294; Janet Breslin Smith and Caryle Murphy, "The Struggle to Erase Saudi Extremism," *New York Times*, November 20, 2014.
109. Boucek, *Saudi Arabia's "Soft" Counterterrorism Strategy.*
110. Eleanor Doumato, "Manning the Barricades," *Middle East Journal* 57, no. 2 (2003): 233–38; Lisa Beyer et al., "Inside the Kingdom," *Time*, January 15, 2003.
111. Smith and Murphy, "The Struggle to Erase Saudi Extremism."
112. Daniel Byman, "Passive Sponsors of Terrorism," *Survival* 47, no. 4 (2005): 117–44.
113. Smith and Murphy, "The Struggle to Erase Saudi Extremism."
114. U.S. Commission on International Religious Freedom, *Annual Report 2013*, 142. Shane, "Saudis and Extremism."
115. Boucek, *Saudi Arabia's "Soft" Counterterrorism Strategy*; Ben Hubbard, "Inside Saudi Arabia's Re-education Prison for Jihadists," *New York Times*, April 29, 2016.
116. Lacey, *Inside the Kingdom*, 256–59.
117. Christopher Boucek, "Extremist Reeducation and Rehabilitation in Saudi Arabia," in *Leaving Terrorism Behind: Individual and Collective Disengagement*, ed. Tore Bjørgo and John Horgan (New York: Taylor and Francis, 2008), 217.
118. "Saudi Frees 1,500 Extremists Who Changed Course: Report," *Agence France Presse*, November 25, 2007.
119. Boucek, *Saudi Arabia's "Soft" Counterterrorism Strategy*; Abdullah F. Ansary, "Combating Extremism: A Brief Overview of Saudi Arabia's Approach," *Middle East Policy* 15, no. 2 (2008): 111–42.
120. This number excludes Guantanamo returnees who went through the program. See Angel Rabasa et al., *Deradicalizing Islamist Extremists* (Arlington, VA: RAND, 2010), 75.
121. This cohort included Said al-Shiri, who became the deputy leader of AQAP.
122. Michael J. Williams and Samuel C. Lindsey, "A Social Psychological Critique of the Saudi Terrorism Risk Reduction Initiative," *Psychology, Crime, and Law* 20, no. 2 (2014): 135–51.
123. Rabasa et al., *Deradicalizing Islamist Extremists*, 76.
124. Christopher Boucek, "The Saudi Process of Repatriating and Reintegrating Guantanamo Returnees," *CTC Sentinel* 1, no. 1 (December 2007): 10–12.
125. Lacey, *Inside the Kingdom*, 271.
126. Mark C. Thompson, *Saudi Arabia and the Path to Political Change: National Dialogue and Civil Society* (New York: I. B. Tauris, 2014), chap. 5.
127. U.S. Commission on International Religious Freedom, *Annual Report 2013*, 143–144.

128. Mansour al-Nogaidan, "Telling the Truth, Facing the Whip," *New York Times*, November 28, 2003.
129. Cole Bunzel, *The Kingdom and the Caliphate: Duel of the Islamic States* (Washington, DC: Carnegie Endowment for International Peace, February 2016), 20.
130. Shane, "Saudis and Extremism"; Carlotta Gall, "How Kosovo Was Turned Into Fertile Ground for ISIS," *New York Times*, May 21, 2016.
131. Bronson, *Thicker Than Oil*, 244.
132. Gendron, "Confronting Terrorism in Saudi Arabia."
133. Lichtblau and Schmitt, "Cash Flow to Terrorists."
134. Interview with Steven Simon, former NSC senior director for the Middle East and North Africa, October 29, 2015; interview with Dan Benjamin, former U.S. ambassador-at-large and coordinator for counterterrorism, November 13, 2015; Ellen Knickmeyer and Siobhan Gorman, "Behind Foiled Jet Plot, Stronger Saudi Ties," *Wall Street Journal*, May 9, 2012.
135. Knickmeyer and Gorman, "Behind Foiled Jet Plot, Stronger Saudi Ties"; Christopher Blanchard, *Saudi Arabia: Background and U.S. Relations* (Washington, DC: Congressional Research Service, November 27, 2012).
136. Mark Mazzeti, Robert Worth, and Eric Lipton, "Quick Response to Intelligence Foiled Bombers," *New York Times*, November 1, 2010.
137. Sudarsan Raghavan, Peter Finn, and Greg Miller, "In Foiled Bomb Plot, AQAP Took Bait Dangled by Saudi Informant," *Washington Post*, May 9, 2012.
138. Robert F. Worth, Mark Mazzetti, and Scott Shane, "Drone Strikes' Risks to Get Rare Moment in the Public Eye," *New York Times*, February 5, 2013.
139. Blanchard, *Saudi Arabia: Background and U.S. Relations*.
140. Bronson, *Thicker Than Oil*, 240.
141. Nawaf Obaid, "Amid the Arab Spring, a U.S.-Saudi Split," *Washington Post*, May 15, 2011.
142. Ben Hubbard and Nicholas Kulish, "Obama to Visit a Saudi Arabia Deep in Turmoil," *New York Times*, April 18, 2016.
143. Jeffrey Goldberg, "The Obama Doctrine," *Atlantic*, April 2016.
144. David E. Sanger, David D. Kirkpatrick, and Somini Sengupta, "Rancor Between Saudi Arabia and Iran Threatens Talks on Syria," *New York Times*, October 29, 2015.
145. Dafna Rand and Stephen Tankel, *Security Cooperation and Assistance: Rethinking the Return on Assistance* (Washington, DC: Center for a New American Security, 2015), n17.
146. Kenneth M. Pollack, "Regional Implications of a Nuclear Agreement with Iran," testimony before the House Committee on Foreign Affairs, July 9, 2015.
147. Ben Hubbard, "ISIS Turns Saudis Against the Kingdom and Families Against Their Own," *New York Times*, March 31, 2016.
148. ISIS also posed an ideological challenge to the kingdom because it presented its caliphate as the only genuine Wahhabi state. Bunzel, *The Kingdom and the Caliphate*.
149. Gregory D. Johnsen, *The Last Refuge: Yemen, Al-Qaeda, and America's War in Arabia* (New York: Norton, 2013), 284–86.
150. Angus McDowall, "Inside the Saudi Prison That's Home to New Wave of Jihadis," *Reuters*, July 6, 2015; Ahmed Al Omran, "Saudi Arabia Arrests 431 People with Suspected Islamic State Links," *Wall Street Journal*, July 18, 2015.
151. Blanchard, *Saudi Arabia: Background and U.S. Relations*.

152. McDowall, "Inside the Saudi Prison That's Home to New Wave of Jihadis."
153. Khaled al-Shayea, "Saudis Fighting with IS a 'Ticking Time Bomb,'" *Al-Araby al-Jadeed*, March 20, 2015.
154. Matthew Levitt, "The Islamic State Is Financially Self-Sufficient," Washington Institute for Near East Policy, December 19, 2015.
155. U.S. State Department, *2016 International Narcotics Control Strategy Report (INCSR)*, vol. 2: *Money Laundering and Financial Crimes Country Database*, July 2016.
156. U.S. State Department Bureau of Counterterrorism, *Country Reports on Terrorism 2015*.
157. Cole Bunzel, *From Paper State to Caliphate: The Ideology of the Islamic State* (Washington, DC: Brookings, 2015).
158. Bunzel, *From Paper State to Caliphate*.
159. Bunzel, *The Kingdom and the Caliphate*.
160. Shane, "Saudis and Extremism."
161. David D. Kirkpatrick, "ISIS's Harsh Brand of Islam Is Rooted in Austere Saudi Creed," *New York Times*, September 24, 2014.
162. Bunzel, *The Kingdom and the Caliphate*.
163. Blanchard, *Saudi Arabia: Background and U.S. Relations*.
164. Yaroslav Trofimov, "New Saudi Monarch Brings Major Change at Home," *Wall Street Journal*, April 29, 2015.
165. Smith and Murphy, "The Struggle to Erase Saudi Extremism."
166. Gause, *Saudi Arabia in the New Middle East*.
167. Alexandra Siegel, "Sectarian Twitter Wars: Sunni-Shia Conflict and Cooperation in the Digital Age," Carnegie Endowment for International Peace, December 20, 2015.
168. Aaron Y. Zelin and Phillip Smyth, "The Vocabulary of Sectarianism," *Foreign Policy*, January 29, 2014.
169. Department of Defense, "News Release: Operation Inherent Resolve Strikes Continue in Syria, Iraq," November 14, 2015, https://www.defense.gov/News/Article/Article/644277/operation-inherent-resolve-strikes-continue-in-syria-iraq/.
170. Mark Mazzetti and Matt Apuzzo, "U.S. Relies Heavily on Saudi Money to Support Syrian Rebels," *New York Times*, January 23, 2016.
171. Qatar and Turkey also provided bases. See Matt Spetalnick, Jeff Mason, and Julia Edwards, "Saudi Arabia Agrees to Host Training of Moderate Syria Rebels," *Reuters*, September 10, 2014.
172. Ben Hubbard, "In Syria, Potential Ally's Islamist Ties Challenge U.S.," *New York Times*, August 25, 2015.
173. Ilan Goldenberg, Nicholas A. Heras, and Paul Scharre, *Defeating the Islamic State: A Bottom-Up Approach* (Washington, DC: Center for a New American Security, June 2016), 32.
174. The Republic of Yemen was another co-chair.
175. "Financial support for Yemen," Foreign and Commonwealth Office and Department for International Development, February 1, 2013, https://www.gov.uk/government/news/financial-support-for-yemen.
176. Johnsen, *The Last Refuge*, 281–282.
177. The ten Sunni states were Saudi Arabia, United Arab Emirates, Bahrain, Kuwait, Qatar, Egypt, Jordan, Morocco, Senegal, and Sudan.

178. David D. Kirkpatrick, "Surprising Saudi Rises as a Prince Among Princes," *New York Times*, June 6, 2015.
179. David Ignatius, "A 30-Year-Old Saudi Prince Could Jump-Start the Kingdom—or Drive It Over a Cliff," *Washington Post*, June 28, 2016; "Saudi Arabia's Changing International Role," Carnegie Endowment for International Peace, April 18, 2016.
180. Andrew Exum, "What's Really at Stake for America in Yemen's Conflict," *Atlantic*, April 14, 2017.
181. Mark Mazzetti and Eric Schmitt, "Quiet Support for Saudis Entangles U.S. in Yemen," *New York Times*, March 13, 2016; Shadi Hamid, "Was the Iran Deal Worth It?" *Defense One*, July 17, 2015.
182. Andrea Shalal, "U.S. Approves $1.29 Billion Sale of Smart Bombs to Saudi Arabia," *Reuters*, November 16, 2015.
183. David D. Kirkpatrick, "Egypt Says It May Send Troops to Yemen to Fight Houthis," *New York Times*, March 26, 2015; Oriana Pawlyk, "2 Years Into Yemen War, U.S. Ramps Up Refueling of Saudi Jets," *Military Times*, February 15, 2017; Stephen Snyder, "U.S. Lawmakers Want to Stop Trump from Supporting Saudi Arabia's War in Yemen," Public Radio International, October 9, 2017.
184. UN Human Rights Office of the High Commissioner, "Press Briefing Notes on Yemen, Central African Republic and Escalating Tensions in East Jerusalem and West Bank," September 29, 2015, http://www.ohchr.org/EN/NewsEvents/Pages/DisplayNews.aspx?NewsID=16518&LangID=E.
185. Houthis were also responsible for gross violations of human rights. On Saudi air strikes, see Ewen MacAskill and Paul Torpey, "One in Three Saudi Air Raids on Yemen Hit Civilian Sites, Data Shows," *Guardian*, September 16, 2016.
186. Helene Cooper, "U.S. Blocks Arms Sale to Saudi Arabia Amid Concerns Over Yemen War," *New York Times*, December 13, 2016.
187. Shuaib Almosawa, Kareem Fahim, and Eric Schmitt, "Islamic State Gains Strength in Yemen, Challenging Al Qaeda," *New York Times*, December 14, 2015.
188. Maria Abi-Habib and Mohammed al-Kibsi, "Al Qaeda Fights on Same Side as Saudi-Backed Militias in Yemen," *Wall Street Journal*, July 16, 2015; "Yemen Conflict: Al-Qaeda Joins Coalition Battle for Taiz," *BBC*, February 22, 2016; David Ottaway, *Saudi Arabia's "Terrorist" Allies in Yemen* (Washington, DC: Woodrow Wilson International Center for Scholars, 2015); Joshua Koonz, "The End of AQAP's Last Refuge in Yemen?," *The Cipher Brief*, February 1, 2017; Bethan McKernan, "Al-Qaeda Claims It Is 'Fighting Alongside' U.S.-Backed Coalition Forces in Yemen," *The Independent*, May 2, 2017.
189. Daniel Benjamin, "The King and ISIS," *Foreign Policy*, September 10, 2015.
190. Ignatius, "A 30-Year-Old Saudi Prince."
191. Daniel R. Coats, "Statement for the Record: Worldwide Threat Assessment of the U.S. Intelligence Community," Senate Select Committee on Intelligence, May 11, 2017, https://www.dni.gov/files/documents/Newsroom/Testimonies/SSCI%20Unclassified%20SFR%20-%20Final.pdf. See also Yara Bayoumy, Noah Browning, and Mohammed Ghobari, "How Saudi Arabia's War in Yemen Has Made al-Qaeda Stronger and Richer," *Reuters*, April 8, 2016.
192. Donald Trump, "Speech to the Arab Islamic American Summit," Saudi Arabia, May 21, 2017.

193. In the spring of 2017, the United States and Saudi Arabia announced their intention to establish the Terrorist Financing Targeting Center to confront new threats from terrorist financing. It is too early to assess the efficacy of this effort. U.S. Treasury Department, "U.S. and Saudi Arabia to Co-Chair New Terrorist Financing Targeting Center," May 21, 2017, https://www.treasury.gov/press-center/press-releases/Pages/sm0092.aspx.
194. Mohammed bin Salman also took control of the kingdom's three main security forces and had a number of potential rivals arrested. Ben Hubbard, "Saudi Prince, Asserting Power, Brings Clerics to Heel," *New York Times*, November 5, 2017; Aya Batrawy, "Saudi Crown Prince's Arrests Are a Risky Gamble," *Associated Press*, November 6. 2017.
195. In October 2017, Trump disavowed the Iran nuclear deal and called on Congress to enact legislation that defined triggers for reimposing sanctions. Mark Landler and David E. Sanger, "Trump Disavows Nuclear Deal, but Doesn't Scrap It," *New York Times*, October 13, 2017.

6. YEMEN: AN UNSTABLE PARTNER

1. Laurent Bonnefoy, *Salafism in Yemen: Transnationalism and Religious Identity* (London: Hurst & Co., 2011), 23–26.
2. Jillian Schwedler, "The Islah Party in Yemen: Political Opportunities and Coalition Building in a Transitional Polity," in *Islamic Activism: A Social Movement Theory Approach*, ed. Quintan Wiktorowicz (Bloomington: Indiana University Press, 2003), 210–11.
3. Victoria Clark, *Yemen: Dancing on the Heads of Snakes* (New Haven, Conn.: Yale University Press, 2010), 104, 159.
4. Gregory Johnsen, *The Last Refuge: Yemen, Al-Qaeda, and America's War in Arabia* (New York: Norton, 2013), 7.
5. Johnsen, *The Last Refuge*, 7–8, 55; Clark, *Yemen*, 159.
6. Laurent Bonnefoy, "Jihadi Violence in Yemen: Dealing with Local, Regional,and International Contingencies," in *Contextualising Jihadi Thought*, ed. Jeevan Deol and Zaheer Kazmi (London: Hurst & Co., 2011), 247; Jason Burke, *Al-Qaeda: The True Story of Radical Islam* (New York: I. B. Tauris, 2003), 141; Johnsen, *The Last Refuge*, 48–51, 54.
7. Johnsen, *The Last Refuge*, 39, 58–59.
8. Edmund J. Hull, *High-Value Target: Countering al Qaeda in Yemen* (Washington, DC: Potomac Books, 2011), xxix.
9. U.S. Department of State, "Patterns of Global Terrorism 1996—Yemen," April 1, 1997.
10. Jeremy Scahill, *Dirty Wars: The World Is a Battlefield* (New York: Nation Books, 2013), 62.
11. Hull, *High-Value Target*, xxix; Ali Soufan, *The Black Banners: The Inside Story of 9/11 and the War Against al-Qaeda* (New York: Norton, 2011), 237, 256–57.
12. Clark, *Yemen*, 170.
13. Soufan, *The Black Banners*, 95, 154–58.
14. Raymond Bonner, "Long at Odds with the U.S., Yemen Is Now Cooperating to Fight Terror," *New York Times*, November 25, 2001.
15. Soufan, *The Black Banners*, 176.
16. Jeremy M. Sharp, *Yemen: Background and U.S. Relations* (Washington, DC: Congressional Research Service, January 13, 2010), 10; Scahill, *Dirty Wars*, 132.

17. Hull, *High-Value Target*, chap. 2; Patrick E. Tyler, "In Washington, a Struggle to Define the Next Fight," *New York Times*, December 2, 2001.
18. Dana Priest, "Foreign Network at Front of CIA's Terror Fight," *Washington Post*, November 18, 2005.
19. Patrick E. Tyler, "Threats and Responses: The Mideast; Yemen, an Uneasy Ally, Proves Adept at Playing Off Old Rivals," *New York Times*, December 19, 2002.
20. Interview with congressional staff member, name withheld upon request, July 8, 2015; interview with former State Department official, name withheld upon request, November 10, 2015; Robert D. Kaplan, *Imperial Grunts: On the Ground with the American Military, from Mongolia to the Philippines to Iraq and Beyond* (New York: Vintage, 2006), 23; Clark, *Yemen*, 159.
21. International Crisis Group, "Yemen's Military-Security Reform: Seeds of New Conflict?," Middle East/North Africa Report 139, April 4, 2013, https://www.crisisgroup.org/middle-east-north-africa/gulf-and-arabian-peninsula/yemen/yemen-s-military-security-reform-seeds-new-conflict.
22. "Response to Terror: U.S. to Train Yemeni Soldiers in Hunt for al-Qaeda Suspects," *Los Angeles Times*, February 12, 2002; Jeremy Sharp, *Yemen: Background and U.S. Relations*, (Washington, DC: Congressional Research Service, November 1, 2012), 14–20.
23. Johnsen, *The Last Refuge*, 90.
24. Johnsen, *The Last Refuge*, 70, 114; Andrew Higgins and Alan Cullison, "Friend or Foe: The Story Of a Traitor to al Qaeda," *Wall Street Journal*, December 20, 2002.
25. International Crisis Group, "Yemen's Military-Security Reform."
26. Data on security assistance from https://securityassistance.org/data/program/military/Yemen/2002/2004/all/Global/.
27. Clyde Mark, *Middle East: U.S. Foreign Assistance, FY2001, FY2002, and FY2003 Request* (Washington, DC: Congressional Research Service Report, 2002).
28. Priest, "Foreign Network at Front of CIA's Terror Fight."
29. This funding came from the U.S. Terrorist Interdiction Program.
30. Hull, *High-Value Target*, 102–3.
31. Data on economic assistance from https://securityassistance.org/data/country/economic/country/2002/2004/all/Middle%20East/.
32. Hull, *High-Value Target*, 103.
33. "Yemen Ex-Leader Saleh 'Amassed up to $60bn'—UN Probe," *BBC*, February 25, 2015.
34. Alfred B. Prados and Jeremy M. Sharp, *Yemen: Current Conditions and U.S. Relations* (Washington, DC: Congressional Research Service, January 2007).
35. Robin Allen, Farhan Bokhari, and Mark Huband, "U.S. 'Has Been Ready for Action Inside Yemen,'" *Financial Times*, September 19, 2002; Tyler, "Yemen, an Uneasy Ally."
36. Hull, *High-Value Target*, 24–25.
37. United Nations, "International Border Treaty Between the Republic of Yemen and the Kingdom of Saudi Arabia," June 12, 2000, http://peacemaker.un.org/saudiarabiayemen-bordertreaty2000.
38. "Sympathizers with Al Qaeda" claimed responsibility for the bombings and demanded the release over 170 imprisoned mujahedeen. "Statement by the Sympathizers with Al Qaeda," April 10, 2002.
39. Hull, *High-Value Target*, 55–56.

40. Robert Chesney, "Military Commission Charges Sworn Against al Nashiri," *Lawfare*, April 20, 2011.
41. Hull, *High-Value Target*, 57; Jonathan Schanzer, "Yemen's War on Terror," *Orbis* 43, no. 3 (2004): 526.
42. *Terror in Yemen: Where To?* (Sanaa: 26th September Publications, 2002), 18–19.
43. Sean Naylor, *Relentless Strike: The Secret History of Joint Special Operations Command* (New York: St. Martin's, 2015), 332.
44. Johnsen, *The Last Refuge*, 90, 111.
45. Hull, *High-Value Target*, 79–80.
46. Naylor, *Relentless Strike*, 331–32. James Bamford, "He's In the Backseat," *Atlantic*, April 2006.
47. Hull, *High-Value Target*, 79–80.
48. Naylor, *Relentless Strike*, 332.
49. Bamford, "He's in the Backseat."
50. Johnsen, *The Last Refuge*, 123.
51. Evan Thomas and Mark Hosenball, "The Opening Shot," *Newsweek*, November 17, 2002.
52. *Terror in Yemen*, 76–77.
53. "U.S.: Top al-Qaeda Operative Arrested," *CNN*, November 22, 2002.
54. Tyler, "Threats and Responses."
55. Prados and Sharp, *Yemen*.
56. Johnsen, *The Last Refuge*, 143.
57. Laurent Bonnefoy, "Violence in Contemporary Yemen: State, Society, and Salafis," *Muslim World* 101, no. 2 (2011): 324–46; W. Andrew Terrill, *The Struggle for Yemen and the Challenge of al-Qaeda in the Arabian Peninsula* (Carlisle, PA: U.S. Army War College Press, 2013), 25.
58. Johnsen, *The Last Refuge*, 164.
59. Hull, *High-Value Target*, 84–85.
60. U.S. Department of State, *Country Reports on Terrorism 2004*, 69.
61. Gregory D. Johnsen, "Yemen: Confronting al-Qaeda, Preventing State Failure," testimony before the Senate Committee on Foreign Relations, January 20, 2010.
62. Gabriel Koehler-Derrick, ed., *A False Foundation? AQAP, Tribes, and Ungoverned Spaces in Yemen* (West Point, NY: Combating Terrorism Center at West Point, 2011), 35.
63. Andrew McGregor, "Prosecuting Terrorism: Yemen's War on Islamist Militancy," *Terrorism Monitor* 4, no. 9 (May 4, 2006).
64. Johnsen, *The Last Refuge*, 135–36.
65. On the contours of the program and prisoner release, see Johnsen, *The Last Refuge*, 141; Kathy Gannon, "Yemen Employs New Terror Approach," *Washington Post*, July 4, 2007.
66. Gregory D. Johnsen, "The Expansion Strategy of Al-Qa'ida in the Arabian Peninsula," *CTC Sentinel* 2, no. 9 (2009): 8–11.
67. Hull, *High-Value Target*, 116–17.
68. Johnsen, *The Last Refuge*, 160–63, 143.
69. Michael Scheuer, "Yemen's Role in al-Qaeda's Strategy"; and Gregory D. Johnsen, "Yemen Attack Reveals Struggle Among al-Qaeda's Ranks," both in *The Battle for Yemen:*

Al-Qaeda and the Struggle for Stability, ed. Ramzy Mardini (Washington, DC: Jamestown Foundation, 2011).

70. Khaled al-Hammadi, "Yemeni Sources Report Failure of Dialogue," *al-Quds al-Arabi*, December 10, 2005.
71. Christopher Boucek, *War in Saada: From Local Insurrection to National Challenge* (Washington, DC: Carnegie Endowment for International Peace, April 2010).
72. The group was formally called Ansar Allah.
73. This paragraph draws from Stephen W. Day, *Regionalism and Rebellion in Yemen: A Troubled National Union* (New York: Cambridge University Press, 2012), 6–14.
74. B. A. Salmoni, B. Loidolt, and M. Wells, *Regime and Periphery in Northern Yemen: The Huthi Phenomenon* (Santa Monica, CA: RAND, 2010), chap. 4.
75. Salmoni, Loidolt, and Wells, *Regime and Periphery in Northern Yemen*, chap. 5; Boucek, *War in Saada*; Johnsen, *The Last Refuge*, 148–53.
76. Johnsen, *The Last Refuge*, 184.
77. Johnsen, *The Last Refuge*.
78. Interview with former State Department official; Ellen Knickmeyer, "Yemen's Double Game," *Foreign Policy*, December 7, 2010.
79. Sarah Phillips, *Yemen and the Politics of Permanent Crisis* (New York: International Institute for Strategic Studies and Routledge, 2011), 42.
80. Andrew McGregor, "Yemen Convicts PSO Members Involved in February's Great Escape," in *The Battle for Yemen*, 87.
81. Johnsen, *The Last Refuge*, 208.
82. Johnsen, "The Expansion Strategy of Al-Qa'ida in the Arabian Peninsula."
83. Johnsen, "The Expansion Strategy of Al-Qa'ida in the Arabian Peninsula"; Johnsen, "Yemen Attack Reveals Struggle Among al-Qaeda's Ranks."
84. "A Commander of al-Qaeda in Yemen Urges Through an Audio Speech the Mujahideen to Refrain from Negotiating with the Enemy," via SITE Intelligence Group Enterprise, June 20, 2007.
85. Jeremy Sharp, "Where Is the Tipping Point for Yemeni Stability?" Carnegie Endowment for International Peace, August 8, 2008; Scahill, *Dirty Wars*, 212; Hull, *High-Value Target*, 117.
86. Johnsen, *The Last Refuge*, 222–23; Scahill, *Dirty Wars*, 213.
87. Barton Gellman, "Is the FBI Up to the Job 10 Years After 9/11? Inside Bob Mueller's 10-Year Campaign to Fix the FBI," *Time*, May 12, 2011.
88. Hull, *High-Value Target*, 115–16.
89. "Al-Qaeda in Yemen Claims Responsibility for the Suicide Car Bombings Targeting Western Oil Facilities in al-Dhabba and Safer in September 2006," via SITE Intelligence Group Enterprise, November 7, 2006.
90. Ahmed al-Hajj, "Suicide Attacker Kills 9 at Yemen Temple," *Washington Post*, July 2, 2007.
91. Jeremy M. Sharp, *Yemen: Background and U.S. Relations* (Washington, DC: Congressional Research Service, January 13, 2010), 10–11.
92. Johnsen, *The Last Refuge*, 225; Day, *Regionalism and Rebellion in Yemen*, 243.
93. Johnsen, *The Last Refuge*, 231.
94. Scahill, *Dirty Wars*, 236.

95. "African Militants Learn from Al Qaeda in Yemen," *PRI*, September 10, 2012; Maseh Zarif, "Terror Partnership: AQAP and Shabaab," American Enterprise Institute, July 2, 2011.
96. Hull, *High-Value Target*, 117–18; Sharp, *Yemen* (2010), 10.
97. Data from https://securityassistance.org/data/program/military/Yemen/2008/2009/all /Global/.
98. Scahill, *Dirty Wars*, 256.
99. Shihri fled to Yemen following his release from the Saudi rehabilitation program.
100. Andrew Higgins and Maia de la Baume, "Two Brothers Suspected in Killings Were Known to French Intelligence Services," *New York Times*, January 8, 2015.
101. Scott Shane, *Objective Troy: A Terrorist, a President, and the Rise of the Drone* (New York: Penguin, 2015), 4, 244.
102. Scott Shane, "Qaeda Branch Aimed for Broad Damage at Low Cost," *New York Times*, November 20, 2010.
103. Scott Shane, "Born in U.S., a Radical Cleric Inspires Terror," *New York Times*, November 18, 2009.
104. Scott Shane, Richard Pérez-Peña, and Aurelien Breeden, "'In-Betweeners' Are Part of a Rich Recruiting Pool for Jihadists," *New York Times*, September 22, 2016.
105. Marc Ambinder, "Al-Qaeda's First English-Language Magazine Is Here," *Atlantic*, June 30, 2010.
106. Michael Isikoff, Pete Williams, and Erin McClam, "Search of Tsarnaevs' Phones, Computers Finds No Indication of Accomplice, Source Says," *NBC News*, April 23, 2013.
107. Abu Zubayr Adel al-Abab, "Online Question and Answer Session with Abu Zubayr Adel al-Abab, Shariah Official for al-Qaeda in the Arabian Peninsula," trans. Amany Soliman, International Centre for the Study of Radicalisation and Political Violence, April 18, 2011, available at *Jihadology*, http://azelin.files.wordpress.com/2011/04/ghorfah -minbar-al-ane1b9a3c481r-presents-a-new-audio-message-from-al-qc481_idah-in-the -arabian-peninsulas-shaykh-abc5ab-zc5abbayr-adc4abl-bc4abn-abdullah-al-abc481b -en.pdf.
108. Christopher Swift, "Arc of Convergence: AQAP, Ansar al-Sharia, and the Struggle for Yemen," *CTC Sentinel* 5, no. 6 (2012): 1–6.
109. Johnsen, *The Last Refuge*, 209, 266.
110. Ambassador Robert F. Godec and Jeffrey D. Feltman, "Yemen on the Brink: Implications for U.S. Policy," testimony before the House Committee on Foreign Affairs, February 3, 2010; Barack Obama, President's Weekly Address, January 2, 2010.
111. Greg Miller, "CIA Sees Increased Threat in Yemen," *Washington Post*, August 25, 2010.
112. Jack Freeman, "The al-Houthi Insurgency in the North of Yemen: An Analysis of the Shabab al Moumineen," *Studies in Conflict and Terrorism* 32, no. 11 (2009): 1008–19.
113. International Crisis Group, "Yemen's Southern Question: Avoiding a Breakdown," Middle East/North Africa Report 145, September 25, 2013, https://www.crisisgroup.org/middle -east-north-africa/gulf-and-arabian-peninsula/yemen/yemen-s-southern-question -avoiding-breakdown.
114. Scahill, *Dirty Wars*, 280.
115. Scahill, *Dirty Wars*, 280.
116. "Interview with al Qaeda Information Officer," *Al Wasat*, January 31, 2008.

117. Scahill, *Dirty Wars*, 131.
118. Eugenio Lilli, *New Beginning in U.S.-Muslim Relations: President Obama and the Arab Awakening* (New York: Palgrave Macmillan, 2016), 145.
119. Interview with Steven Simon, former NSC senior director for the Middle East and North Africa, October 29, 2015; interview with Dan Benjamin, former U.S. ambassador-at-large and coordinator for counterterrorism, November 13, 2015; interview with former State Department official. See also Johnsen, "The Expansion Strategy of Al-Qa'ida in the Arabian Peninsula."
120. Scahill, *Dirty Wars*, 211; Sam Kimball, "Whose Side Is Yemen On?" *Foreign Policy*, August 29, 2012; "America's Dangerous Game," *Al-Jazeera*, March 8, 2012; Robert F. Worth, "Wanted by FBI but Walking Out of a Yemen Hearing," *New York Times*, March 1, 2008.
121. Interview with Luke Hartig, former NSC senior director for counterterrorism, March 14, 2017.
122. Interview with congressional staff member.
123. This paragraph draws on Johnsen, *The Last Refuge*, 216, 225–26.
124. Scahill, *Dirty Wars*, 387–89.
125. Data from https://securityassistance.org/data/country/economic/country/2002/2010/all/Middle%20East/.
126. "Friends of Yemen: Questions and Answers," Foreign & Commonwealth Office and Department for International Development, February 1, 2013.
127. Jeni Klugman, "The Real Wealth of Nations: Pathways to Human Development," in *Human Development Report 2010* (New York: Palgrave Macmillan, 2010). On corruption, see "Corruption Perceptions Index 2010," October 2010, http://www.transparency.org/cpi2010/results.
128. Interview with Luke Hartig.
129. Joseph Trevithick, "Thanks to American Help, Yemen's Commandos Aren't Half Bad," *War Is Boring*, December 9, 2014.
130. Data from https://securityassistance.org/data/program/military/Yemen/2009/2010/all/Global/.
131. Interview with congressional staff member; Interview with former State Department official; Scahill, *Dirty Wars*, 131.
132. Scahill, *Dirty Wars*, 258, 262.
133. Scahill, *Dirty Wars*, 262.
134. Scahill, *Dirty Wars*, 280–81.
135. Naylor, *Relentless Strike*, 416.
136. Found in Scahill, *Dirty Wars*, 236–37.
137. Scott Shane, Mark Mazzetti, and Robert F. Worth, "Secret Assault on Terrorism Widens on Two Continents," *New York Times*, August 14, 2010.
138. Brian Ross, Richard Esposito, Matthew Cole, Luis Martinez, and Kirit Radia, "Obama Ordered U.S. Military Strike on Yemen Terrorists," *ABC News*, December 18, 2009.
139. Richard Spencer, "U.S. Cluster Bombs 'Killed 35 Women and Children,'" *Telegraph*, June 7, 2010; Dexter Filkins, "What We Don't Know About Drones," *New Yorker*, February 6, 2013.

140. Scahill, *Dirty Wars*, 322; Johnsen, *The Last Refuge*, 261.
141. Bill Roggio and Bob Barry, "Charting the Data for U.S. Air Strikes in Yemen, 2002–2016," *Long War Journal*, http://www.longwarjournal.org/multimedia/Yemen/code/Yemen-strike.php.
142. Adam Entous, Julian Barnes, and Margaret Coker, "U.S. Doubts Intelligence That Led to Yemen Strike," *Wall Street Journal*, December 29, 2011.
143. Interviews with two former U.S. officials, both of whom requested anonymity.
144. Letta Tayler, *No Direction Home: Returns from Guantanamo to Yemen* (Washington, DC: Human Rights Watch, 2009).
145. Scahill, *Dirty Wars*, 257.
146. "U.S. Halting Transfer of Guantanamo Detainees to Yemen," *CNN*, January 5, 2010.
147. "Arab Uprising: Country by Country—Yemen," *BBC*, December 16, 2013.
148. Katherine Zimmerman, "Al Qaeda in Yemen: Countering the Threat from the Arabian Peninsula," American Enterprise Institute, October 19, 2012.
149. Military assistance dropped from $175 million in FY2010 to $31 million in FY2011. Department of State, "Fact Sheet: U.S. Government Assistance to Yemen," September 27, 2012.
150. Laura Kasinof and David E. Sanger, "U.S. Shifts to Seek Removal of Yemen's Leader, an Ally," *New York Times*, April 3, 2011.
151. Erica Gaston, *Process Lessons Learned in Yemen's National Dialogue* (Washington, DC: U.S. Institute of Peace, February 2014). "Agreement on the Implementation Mechanism for the Transition in Yemen Pursuant to the GCC Initiative," Lauterpacht Centre for International Law, November 21, 2011.
152. On drone strikes, see "Drone Wars Yemen: 2011," http://securitydata.newamerica.net/drones/overview.html?yr=2011&country=Yemen.
153. "Second Letter from Abu Basir to Emir of Al-Qaida in the Islamic Maghreb," August 6, 2012, https://cryptome.org/2013/11/aqp-win-friends.pdf.
154. Christopher Swift, "To Defeat Al-Qaeda, Win in Yemen," *Bloomberg View*, June 21, 2012.
155. Michael Horton, "Fighting the Long War: The Evolution of Al-Qa'ida in the Arabian Peninsula," *CTC Sentinel* 10, no. 1 (2017): 17–23.
156. "First Letter from Abu Basir to Emir of Al-Qaida in the Islamic Maghreb," May 21, 2012, https://cryptome.org/2013/11/aqp-win-friends.pdf; Aaron Zelin, "Al-Qaeda in Syria: A Closer Look at ISIS," Washington Institute for Near East Policy, September 11, 2013.
157. Interview with congressional staff member; interview with Luke Hartig; Eric Schmitt, "U.S. Teaming with New Yemen Government on Strategy to Combat Al-Qaeda," *New York Times*, February 26, 2012; Johnsen, *The Last Refuge*, 286.
158. Zelin, "Al-Qaeda in Syria"; Peter Bergen and Jennifer Rowland, "Obama Ramps up Covert War in Yemen," *CNN*, June 12, 2012.
159. Interview with congressional staff member; Schmitt, "U.S. Teaming with New Yemen Government"; Johnsen, *The Last Refuge*, 286.
160. The strike that targeted Awlaki also killed Samir Khan, who oversaw AQAP's English-language magazine. See "Drone Wars Yemen: 2011."

161. "Second Letter from Abu Basir to Emir of Al-Qaida in the Islamic Maghreb."
162. Gregory D. Johnsen, "How We Lost Yemen," *Foreign Policy*, August 6, 2013.
163. Interview with former National Counterterrorism Center official, name withheld upon request, August 12, 2014; Sudarsan Raghavan, "In Yemen, U.S. Airstrikes Breed Anger, and Sympathy for al-Qaeda," *Washington Post*, May 29, 2012.
164. Interview with congressional staff member; interview with Luke Hartig.
165. "President Hadi Announces Sweeping Reforms to Yemeni Military," Project on Middle East Democracy; "Yemeni President Abolishes Two Major Military Units," *Reuters*, December 19, 2012.
166. Interview with congressional staff member.
167. April Longley Alley, "Yemen Changes Everything . . . and Nothing," *Journal of Democracy* 24, no. 4 (2013): 74–85; Day, *Regionalism and Rebellion in Yemen*, 298; International Crisis Group, "The Huthis: From Saada to Sanaa," Middle East/North Africa Report 154, June 10, 2014, 2.
168. Lucas Winter, "Yemen's Houthi Movement in the Wake of the Arab Spring," *CTC Sentinel* 5, no. 8 (2012): 13–17.
169. Interview with Luke Hartig.
170. Laura Kasinof, "How the Houthis Did It," *Foreign Policy*, January 23, 2015.
171. Mareike Transfeld, "Houthis on the Rise in Yemen," Carnegie Endowment for International Peace, October 31, 2014.
172. "Yemen: The Peace and National Partnership Agreement," September 21, 2014, http://www.jadaliyya.com/pages/index/19341/yemen_the-peace-and-national-partnership-agreement.
173. Robin Simcox, "AQAP's Ideological Battles at Home and Abroad," Hudson Institute, January 20, 2015; Abdul-Ghani al-Iryani, "Fast-Tracking the Arab Spring in Yemen," Washington Institute for Near East Policy, October 9, 2014.
174. David D. Kirkpatrick, "Yemeni Fighters Close In on President's Refuge Amid Reports He Has Fled," *New York Times*, March 25, 2015.
175. Jay Solomon, Dion Nissenbaum, and Asa Fitch, "In Strategic Shift, U.S. Draws Closer to Yemeni Rebels," *Wall Street Journal*, January 29, 2015.
176. Stephen W. Day, "What's Behind Yemen's Recent Political Turmoil," *Washington Post*, February 23, 2015.
177. David Hearst, "Blowback in Yemen: Houthi Advance Is a Saudi Nightmare," *Huffington Post*, October 20, 2014.
178. Greg Miller and Hugh Naylor, "CIA Scales Back Presence and Operations in Yemen, Home of Potent al-Qaeda Affiliate," *Washington Post*, February 11, 2014.
179. Mark Mazzetti and David Kirkpatrick, "A Policy Puzzle of U.S. Goals and Alliances in the Middle East," *New York Times*, March 26, 2015.
180. "Yemen al-Qaeda Chief al-Wuhayshi Killed in U.S. Strike," *BBC*, June 16, 2015.
181. Adam Baron, "Mapping the Yemen conflict," European Council on Foreign Relations, 2016.
182. International Crisis Group, "Yemen's al-Qaeda: Expanding the Base," Middle East/North Africa Report 174, February 2, 2017, https://www.crisisgroup.org/middle-east-north-africa/gulf-and-arabian-peninsula/yemen/174-yemen-s-al-qaeda-expanding-base.

183. See, for example, Nasser bin Ali al-Ansi, "A Call to Confront the Crusader-Safavid Campaign," al-Malahem Media Foundation, September 30, 2014.
184. Tim Lister and Paul Cruickshank, "Al-Qaeda Resurgent in Yemen Amid Political Turmoil," *CNN*, October 18, 2014.
185. Joshua Koonz, "The End of AQAP's Last Refuge in Yemen?," *Cipher Brief*, February 1, 2017; Bethan McKernan, "Al-Qaeda Claims It Is 'Fighting Alongside' U.S.-Backed Coalition Forces in Yemen," *Independent*, May 2, 2017; Maria Abi-Habib and Mohammed al-Kibsi, "Al-Qaeda Fights on Same Side as Saudi-Backed Militias in Yemen," *Wall Street Journal*, July 16, 2015; "Yemen Conflict: Al-Qaeda Joins Coalition Battle for Taiz," *BBC*, February 22, 2016; David Ottaway, *Saudi Arabia's "Terrorist" Allies in Yemen* (Washington, DC: Woodrow Wilson International Center for Scholars, 2015).
186. Thomas Gibbons-Neff and Missy Ryan, "In Deadly Yemen Raid, a Lesson for Trump's National Security Team," *Washington Post*, January 31, 2017.
187. Eric Schmitt and David E. Sanger, "Raid in Yemen: Risky from the Start and Costly in the End," *New York Times*, February 1, 2017.
188. Yara Bayoumy, Noah Browning, and Mohammed Ghobari, "How Saudi Arabia's War in Yemen Has Made al-Qaeda Stronger and Richer," *Reuters*, April 8, 2016.
189. Jon Finer, "From SEALs to All-Out War: Why Rushing Into Yemen Is a Dangerous Idea," *Foreign Policy*, February 9, 2017; Maggie Michael and Ahmed al-Haj, "Saudi Barred Yemeni President from Going Home, Officials Say," *Washington Post*, November 6, 2017.
190. Schmitt and Sanger, "Raid in Yemen."
191. Ryan Browne, "Daughter of Anwar Al-Awlaki Reported Killed in Yemen Raid," *CNN*, February 1, 2017.
192. Alexa Liautaud, "The Forgotten War," *Vice News*, June 8, 2017.
193. Stephen Snyder, "U.S. Lawmakers Want to Stop Trump from Supporting Saudi Arabia's War in Yemen," *PRI*, October 9, 2017.
194. Jack Moore, "Trump Targets ISIS in Yemen for First Time with Strikes on Training Camps," *Newsweek*, October 17, 2017.
195. Courtney Kube, "U.S. Officials: Iran Supplying Weapons to Yemen's Houthi Rebels," *NBC News*, October 27, 2016.
196. Andrew Exum, "What's Really at Stake for America in Yemen's Conflict," *Atlantic*, April 14, 2017.
197. Sam LaGrone, "*USS Mason* Fired 3 Missiles to Defend from Yemen Cruise Missile Attack," *USNI News*, October 11, 2016.
198. Snyder, "U.S. Lawmakers Want to Stop Trump."

7. MALI: THE WEAKEST LINK

1. Lianne Kennedy-Boudali, "Examining U.S. Counterterrorism Priorities and Strategy Across Africa's Sahel Region," testimony before the Senate Committee on Foreign Relations, Subcommittee on African Affairs, November 17, 2009.
2. Interview with Mounir Boudjemaa, assistant editor at *Liberté*, May 12, 2010; Ali Oussi, "Fight Against Terror," *L'Expression*, March 29, 2004.

3. Craig S. Smith, "U.S. Training African Forces to Uproot Terrorists," *New York Times*, May 11, 2004.
4. Interview with Tricia Bacon, former State Department intelligence official, September 29, 2015.
5. Smith, "U.S. Training African Forces to Uproot Terrorists."
6. Smith, "U.S. Training African Forces to Uproot Terrorists"; interview with Tricia Bacon.
7. Robert Windrem, "U.S. Had Mali Terror in Crosshairs Before Siege," *NBC News*, November 20, 2015.
8. Anneli Botha, *Terrorism in the Maghreb: The Transnationalisation of Domestic Terrorism*, ISS Monograph Series, June 2008; Muhammad Mokaddem, "Algerian Armed Organization Transfers Battlefield to French Territories With al-Qaeda's Support," *Al-Hayah*, October 2, 2006.
9. Interview with former U.S. intelligence official, name and date withheld upon request.
10. Craig Whitlock, "U.S. Counterterrorism Effort in North Africa Defined by Decade of Missteps," *Washington Post*, February 4, 2013.
11. Botha, *Terrorism in the Maghreb*, 50.
12. Whitlock, "U.S. Counterterrorism Effort in North Africa."
13. Stephen A. Harmon, *Terror and Insurgency in the Sahara-Sahel Region* (New York: Routledge, 2016), 71.
14. "Mali," Human Development Reports: UN Development Programme, http://hdr.undp.org/en/countries/profiles/MLI.
15. Kalifa Keita, "Conflict and Conflict Resolution in the Sahel: The Tuareg Insurgency in Mali," *Small Wars and Insurgencies* 9, no. 3 (1998): 105.
16. The Songhay are also present in the government and have played key security roles.
17. Jennifer Seely, "A Political Analysis of Decentralisation: Coopting the Tuareg Threat in Mali," *Journal of Modern African Studies* 39, no. 3 (2001): 499–524.
18. William Farrell and Carla Komich, "USAID/DCHA/CMM Assessment: Northern Mali," prepared by Management Systems International for the USAID Office of Conflict Management and Mitigation, June 17, 2004, 6.
19. Angel Rabasa et al., *From Insurgency to Stability* (Arlington, VA: RAND, 2011), 121–23.
20. Baz Lecocq, *Disputed Desert: Decolonisation, Competing Nationalisms, and Tuareg Rebellions in Northern Mali* (London: Brill, 2010), 304–5.
21. "National Pact Concluded Between the Government of Mali and the Unified Movements and Fronts of Azawad Giving Expression to the Special Status of Northern Mali," April 11, 1992, https://peaceaccords.nd.edu/sites/default/files/accords/Mali_Peace_Accord-proof.pdf.
22. International Crisis Group, "Islamist Terrorism in the Sahel: Fact or Fiction?" *Africa Report* 92, March 31, 2005; Transparency International, "Corruption Perceptions Index 2003," http://www.transparency.org/research/cpi/cpi_2003/0/.
23. Nicholas Van de Walle, "Working Paper no. 2012/6, Foreign Aid in Dangerous Places: Donors and Mali's Democracy," World Institute for Development Economics Research, United Nations University, July 2012, 12.
24. "Algiers Accord," signed July 4, 2006, http://saadlounes.unblog.fr/files/2010/05/accordsdalgerjuillet2006.pdf.

25. On the 2006–2009 rebellion, see Alexander Thurston and Andrew Lebovich, "A Handbook on Mali's 2012–2013 Crisis," Institute for the Study of Islamic Thought in Africa (ISITA) Working Paper Series 13-001, September 2013, 24–25.
26. Alexis Arieff and Kelly Johnson, *Crisis in Mali* (Washington, DC: Congressional Research Service, August 16, 2012); International Crisis Group, "Islamist Terrorism in the Sahel: Fact or Fiction?"
27. Interview with former Defense Department official, name withheld upon request, March 3, 2016; interview with Tricia Bacon; Simon J. Powelson, *Enduring Engagement Yes, Episodic Engagement No: Lessons for SOF from Mali* (Monterey, CA: Naval Postgraduate School, 2013), 9–10.
28. Powelson, *Enduring Engagement Yes, Episodic Engagement No*, 9–10.
29. Interview with Tricia Bacon.
30. Mark Moyar, *Countering Violent Extremism in Mali* (Tampa: Joint Special Operations University, 2015), 22.
31. Harmon, *Terror and Insurgency in the Sahara-Sahel Region*, 93, 187.
32. Lesley Anne Warner, "Catch-22 in the Sahel: America's Fight Against Terror in West Africa—and Its Shortcomings," *National Interest*, April 3, 2014.
33. Walter Pincus, "Mali Insurgency Followed 10 Years of U.S. Counterterrorism Programs," *Washington Post*, January 16, 2013.
34. Amounts are for funds distributed, not obligated. U.S. Government Accountability Office, "Combating Terrorism: Actions Needed to Enhance Implementation of Trans-Sahara Counterterrorism Partnership," GAO-08-860, July 31, 2008; U.S. Government Accountability Office, "Combating Terrorism: U.S. Efforts in Northwest Africa Would Be Strengthened by Enhanced Program Management," GAO-14-518, June 2014.
35. Warner, "Catch-22 in the Sahel"; Tawfiq al-Madini, "America and Al-Qaeda Are 'Competing' for North Africa," *Al-Hayah*, February 23, 2007; Donna Miles, "New Counterterrorism Initiative to Focus on Saharan Africa," *American Forces Press Service*, May 16, 2005.
36. Jeffrey Swedberg and Steven Smith, "Midterm Evaluation of USAID's Counterextremism Programming in Africa," USAID, February 1, 2011, 7.
37. Lesley Anne Warner, *The Trans-Sahara Counter Terrorism Partnership: Building Partner Capacity to Counter Terrorism and Violent Extremism* (Arlington: Center for Naval Analysis, April 2014), 56.
38. As quoted in Warner, *The Trans-Sahara Counter Terrorism Partnership*, 65.
39. "Country Overview: Mali," World Bank, May 3, 2016, http://www.worldbank.org/en/country/mali/overview.
40. Data on economic and security assistance: https://securityassistance.org/data/program/military/Mali/2001/2011/all/Global/; https://securityassistance.org/data/country/economic/country/2001/2011/all/West%20Africa/.
41. Moyar, *Countering Violent Extremism in Mali*, 21.
42. "Mali," Human Development Reports.
43. Warner, *The Trans-Sahara Counter Terrorism Partnership*, 45–51.
44. Johnnie Carson, "Opening Remarks for Hearing on Counterterrorism in Africa (Sahel Region)," testimony before the Senate Committee on Foreign Relations, Subcommittee

on African Affairs, November 17, 2009; Earl Gast, "Mali: Current Threats to Development Gains and the Way Forward," testimony before the Senate Committee on Foreign Relations, Subcommittee on African Affairs, December 5, 2012.

45. Moyar, *Countering Violent Extremism in Mali*, 15.
46. Marietou Macalou, "The Politicization of the Malian Civil Service in the Context of Democratization," PhD diss., University of Pittsburgh, 2010, 163.
47. Isaline Bergamaschi, "Mali: How to Avoid Making the Same Mistakes," *Good Governance Africa*, April 1, 2013.
48. Bruce Whitehouse, "The Malian Government's Challenge to Restore Order in the North," *CTC Sentinel* 7, no. 2 (2014): 12–14.
49. Wolfram Lacher, *Organized Crime and Conflict in the Sahel-Sahara Region* (Washington, DC: Carnegie Endowment for International Peace, September 2012).
50. Powelson, *Enduring Engagement Yes, Episodic Engagement No*, 11.
51. Interview with U.S. intelligence official, name and date withheld upon request; interview with Tricia Bacon.
52. Interview with Marc-André Boisvert, researcher specializing in civil-military relations in West Africa, November 4, 2016.
53. Stew Magnuson, "Mali Crisis Offers Lessons for Special Operations Command," *National Defense*, May 2013.
54. U.S. Department of State, "Foreign Policy Objectives—Africa Region," *Foreign Military Training: Joint Report to Congress, Fiscal Years 2003 and 2004* (June 2004).
55. International Crisis Group, "Islamist Terrorism in the Sahel: Fact or Fiction?"
56. Moyar, *Countering Violent Extremism in Mali*, 14.
57. $5 million of the $7.15 million Mali received in 2007 came from Section 1207 funding. The Section 1207 authority was created in FY 2006 and authorized the transfer of up to $100 million in 2006 and 2007 from the secretary of defense to the secretary of state for programs that support security, reconstruction, or stabilization. Data from https://securityassistance.org/data/program/military/Mali/2002/2007/all/Global/.
58. UN Security Council, Report of the Secretary-General on the Situation in Mali, S/2012/894, November 29, 2012, 4; Moyar, *Countering Violent Extremism in Mali*, 14.
59. Powelson, *Enduring Engagement Yes, Episodic Engagement No*, 26–28.
60. Karolina MacLachlan, *Security Assistance, Corruption, and Fragile Environments: Exploring the Case of Mali, 2001–2012* (London: Transparency International, August 2015), 28.
61. Carter Ham, "TRANSCRIPT: Presentation on the Role and Mission of United States Africa Command," U.S. AFRICOM, January 27, 2013.
62. U.S. Agency for International Development, "Counter Extremism and Development in Mali," October 2009.
63. Morten Bøås, "Guns, Money, and Prayers: AQIM's Blueprint for Securing Control of Northern Mali," *CTC Sentinel* 7, no. 4 (2014): 1–6.
64. Mohammed Mahmoud Abu al-Ma'ali, *Al-Qaeda and Its Allies in the Sahel and the Sahara* (Doha: Al-Jazeera Center for Studies, May 1, 2012).
65. Ricardo René Larémont, "Al Qaeda in the Islamic Maghreb: Terrorism and Counterterrorism in the Sahel," *African Security* 4, no. 4 (2011): 242–68.
66. Lacher, *Organized Crime and Conflict in the Sahel-Sahara Region*.

67. Carson, "Opening Remarks"; Thurston and Lebovich, *A Handbook on Mali's 2012–2013 Crisis*.
68. Lacher, *Organized Crime and Conflict in the Sahel-Sahara Region*.
69. MacLachlan, *Security Assistance, Corruption, and Fragile Environments*, 25.
70. Salima Tlemcani, "Claim of Responsibility for the Attack on a Barracks in Mauritania," *El Watan*, September 14, 2006.
71. Jean-Pierre Filiu, *Could Al-Qaeda Turn African in the Sahel?* (Washington, DC: Carnegie Endowment for International Peace, June 2010).
72. Jean-Pierre Filiu, "The Local and Global Jihad of al Qa'ida in the Islamic Maghrib," *Middle East Journal* 63, no. 2 (2009): 213–26.
73. Rukmini Callimachi, "Paying Ransoms, Europe Bankrolls Qaeda Terror," *New York Times*, July 29, 2014.
74. Julian Borger and Helen Pidd, "Al-Qaida Murders British Tourist Seized in Mali," *Guardian*, June 3, 2009.
75. Daniel Benjamin, "LRA, Boko Haram, Al-Shabaab, AQIM, and Other Sources of Instability in Africa," testimony before the House Committee on Foreign Affairs, April 25, 2012.
76. Department of State, *Country Reports on Terrorism 2012* (Washington, DC: 2013), 8–9, 21–23.
77. Interview with Tricia Bacon; Christopher S. Chivvas and Andrew Liepman, *North Africa's Menace: AQIM's Evolution and the U.S. Policy Response* (Arlington, VA: RAND, 2013); Andre Le Sage, "The Evolving Threat of al Qaeda in the Islamic Maghreb," *Strategic Forum* (Washington, DC: NDU, July 2011).
78. Interview with French intelligence officials, March 2010; interview with Algeria-based Western intelligence official, May 2010.
79. Interview with Algeria-based Western intelligence official.
80. Powelson, *Enduring Engagement Yes, Episodic Engagement No*, 9.
81. Interview with Marc-André Boisvert.
82. Modibo Goita, "West Africa's Growing Terrorist Threat: Confronting AQIM's Sahelian Strategy," *Africa Security Brief* 11 (2011): 4.
83. Powelson, *Enduring Engagement Yes, Episodic Engagement No*, 9.
84. Thurston and Lebovich, *A Handbook on Mali's 2012–2013 Crisis*, 25.
85. Powelson, *Enduring Engagement Yes, Episodic Engagement No*, 9–12.
86. Steven Edwards, "Al-Qaeda Want Prisoner Exchange for Canadian Diplomats," *Canwest News Service*, February 17, 2009.
87. Matthew Weaver, "British Hostage Edwin Dyer 'Killed by al-Qaida,'" *Guardian*, June 3, 2009.
88. Jean-Pierre Filiu, "On Al Qaeda in North Africa and the Sahel," presented at the conference Al-Qaeda and Its Affiliates, New America Foundation, April 27, 2010.
89. Filiu, "Could Al-Qaeda Turn African in the Sahel?"
90. Lacher, *Organized Crime and Conflict in the Sahel-Sahara Region*.
91. MacLachlan, *Security Assistance, Corruption, and Fragile Environments*, 25.
92. Lacher, *Organized Crime and Conflict in the Sahel-Sahara Region*, 13.
93. I'm grateful to Andrew Lebovich for highlighting this fact for me.

94. Powelson, *Enduring Engagement Yes, Episodic Engagement No*, 11.
95. This paragraph drawn from Powelson, *Enduring Engagement Yes, Episodic Engagement No*, 13–14.
96. Media Committee of al-Qa'ida in the Lands of the Islamic Maghreb, Al-Fajr Media, July 9, 2009.
97. Powelson, *Enduring Engagement Yes, Episodic Engagement No*, 14.
98. Larémont, "Al Qaeda in the Islamic Maghreb."
99. International Crisis Group, "Mali: Avoiding Escalation," *Africa Report* 189, July 18, 2012.
100. Anouar Boukhars, *The Paranoid Neighbor: Algeria and the Conflict in Mali* (Washington, DC: Carnegie Endowment for International Peace, October 2012).
101. Lacher, *Organized Crime and Conflict in the Sahel-Sahara Region*.
102. Lacher, *Organized Crime and Conflict in the Sahel-Sahara Region*; Boukhars, *The Paranoid Neighbor*.
103. Andrew Lebovich, a researcher who has conducted extensive fieldwork in Mali, heard this from UN officials in Dakar and then from additional sources in Mali. A former U.S. official independently confirmed this to the author.
104. Lamine Chikhi, "Algeria Recalls Envoy from Mali Over Qaeda Row," *Reuters*, February 23, 2010; "Mauritania Recalls Ambassador to Mali in al-Qaeda Row," *Reuters*, February 23, 2010.
105. "Mauritania's Goals in Its Struggle Against al-Qaeda," Al Jazeera Center for Studies, July 25, 2011.
106. Lacher, *Organized Crime and Conflict in the Sahel-Sahara Region*; International Crisis Group, "Mali: Avoiding Escalation."
107. Moyar, *Countering Violent Extremism in Mali*, 17.
108. Description of training from Powelson, *Enduring Engagement Yes, Episodic Engagement No*, 29–34, 64.
109. Moyar, *Countering Violent Extremism in Mali*, 18–19.
110. Powelson, *Enduring Engagement Yes, Episodic Engagement No*, 34–35.
111. David Pugliese, "Canadian Special Forces Mentor Mali's Military," *National Post*, March 12, 2011.
112. Interview with Marc-André Boisvert.
113. Powelson, *Enduring Engagement Yes, Episodic Engagement No*, 41.
114. Adam Nossiter, "Qaddafi's Weapons, Taken by Old Allies, Reinvigorate an Insurgent Army in Mali," *New York Times*, February 6, 2012.
115. Thurston and Lebovich, *A Handbook on Mali's 2012–2013 Crisis*, 21–25.
116. Adam Nossiter and Neil MacFarquhar, "Algeria Sowed Seeds of Hostage Crisis as It Nurtured Warlord," *New York Times*, February 1, 2013.
117. Andy Morgan, "The Causes of the Uprising in Northern Mali," *Think Africa Press*, February 6, 2012; Serge Daniel, "Mali Rebel Iyad Ag Ghaly: Inscrutable Master of the Desert," *Agence France-Presse*, April 5, 2012.
118. UN Security Council, "QE.A.135.13. ANSAR EDDINE," March 20, 2013, http://www.un.org/sc/committees/1267/NSQE13513E.shtml; Andrew Lebovich, "AQIM and Its Allies in Mali," Washington Institute for Near East Policy, February 5, 2013.

119. Thurston and Lebovich, *Handbook on Mali's 2012–2013 Crisis*, 26; Jessica M. Huckabey, "Al-Qaeda in Mali: The Defection Connections," *Orbis* 57, no. 3 (2013): 467–484.
120. Peter Tinti, "The Jihadi from the Block," *Foreign Policy*, March 19, 2013.
121. Windrem, "U.S. Had Mali Terror in Crosshairs."
122. Thurston and Lebovich, *Handbook on Mali's 2012–2013 Crisis*, 5.
123. As quoted in International Crisis Group, "Mali: Avoiding Escalation," 8.
124. Rukmini Callimachi, "In Timbuktu, al-Qaida Left Behind a Manifesto," *Associated Press*, February 14, 2013.
125. Adam Entous and Drew Hinshaw, "U.S. Sets Sights On Al Qaeda in Mali," *Wall Street Journal*, July 27, 2012; Eric Schmitt, "American Commander Details Al Qaeda's Strength In Mali," *New York Times*, December 4, 2012; "Insight: Islamist Inroads in Mali May Undo French War on Al Qaeda," *Reuters*, March 13, 2013.
126. Sudarsan Raghavan, "Nigerian Militants Return from Mali with New Weapons," *Washington Post*, June 1, 2013.
127. Callimachi, "In Timbuktu"; "Mali Al-Qaida's Sahara Playbook" (confidential letter from AQIM amir Abdelmalek Droukdel to his fighters in Mali), n.d. (but likely sent around June 2012), recovered by the Associated Press, http://hosted.ap.org/specials/interactives/_international/_pdfs/al-qaida-manifesto.pdf.
128. "First Letter from Abu Basir to Emir of Al-Qaida in the Islamic Maghreb," May 21, 2012, https://cryptome.org/2013/11/aqp-win-friends.pdf; "Second Letter from Abu Basir to Emir of Al-Qaida in the Islamic Maghreb," August 6, 2012, https://cryptome.org/2013/11/aqp-win-friends.pdf.
129. Charles Lister, *The Syrian Jihad: Al-Qaeda, the Islamic State, and the Evolution of an Insurgency* (New York: Oxford University Press, 2016), 67.
130. "Mali-al-Qaida's Sahara Playbook."
131. The SOF team reportedly was not allowed to interact with the Malian military after the coup. Amanda Dory, testimony before the Senate Committee on Foreign Relations, Subcommittee on African Affairs, December 5, 2012.
132. Gast, "Mali: Current Threats to Development Gains and the Way Forward."
133. Adam Nossiter, Eric Schmitt, and Mark Mazzetti, "French Strikes in Mali Supplant Caution of U.S.," *New York Times*, January 13, 2013.
134. Michael Shurkin, *France's War in Mali: Lessons for an Expeditionary Army* (Santa Monica, CA: RAND, 2014), 8.
135. Adam Entous, David Gauthier-Villars, and Drew Hinshaw, "U.S. Boosts War Role in Africa," *Wall Street Journal*, March 4, 2013; Eric Schmitt, "Terror Haven in Mali Feared After French Leave," *New York Times*, March 18, 2013.
136. Siobhan Gorman and Adam Entous, "U.S. Moving to Broaden African Presence," *Wall Street Journal*, January 28, 2013.
137. Adam Entous and Julian E. Barnes, "Mali Exposes Flaws in West's Security Plans," *Wall Street Journal*, January 24, 2013.
138. Michael A. Sheehan and Geoff D. Porter, "The Future Role of U.S. Counterterrorism Operations in Africa," *CTC Sentinel* 7, no. 2 (2014): 1–3; Ernesto Londono, "U.S. Broadens Aid to France in Mali," *Washington Post*, January 27, 2013.
139. Gabe Starosta, "Mission to Mali," *Air Force Magazine*, November 2013.

140. Craig Whitlock, "U.S. Sends a Handful of Troops to Mali," *Washington Post*, May 1, 2013.
141. Craig Whitlock, "Drone Base in Niger Is Key Asset," *Washington Post*, March 22, 2013.
142. "Background: United Nations Stabilization Mission in Mali," *MINUSMA*, http://www.un.org/en/peacekeeping/missions/minusma/background.shtml.
143. Moyar, *Countering Violent Extremism in Mali*, 44.
144. Margaret Besheer, "UN: Recent Security Incidents in Mali 'Wake-up Call,'" *Voice of America*, October 16, 2013.
145. John Irish, "French Soldier Dies in Mali as Paris Readings Counter-Insurgency Plan," *Reuters*, May 8, 2014.
146. Michael Shurkin, Stephanie Pezard, and S. Rebecca Zimmerman, *Mali's Next Battle: Improving Counterterrorism Capabilities* (Arlington, VA: RAND Corporation, 2017), 88–92.
147. Kevin Seiff, "The World's Most Dangerous UN Mission," *Washington Post*, February 17, 2017.
148. Andrew Lebovich, "The Hotel Attacks and Militant Realignment in the Sahara-Sahel Region," *CTC Sentinel* 9, no. 1 (2016): 22–28.
149. Serge Daniel and Sebastien Rieussec, "Mali hunts suspects after deadly hotel siege," *AFP*, November 21, 2015.
150. Windrem, "U.S. Had Mali terror in Crosshairs."
151. Conor Gaffey, "African Jihadi Groups United and Pledge Allegiance to Al Qaeda," *Newsweek*, March 3, 2017.
152. Siobhan O'Grady, "What the Hell Happened in Niger?" *Atlantic*, October 20, 2017.
153. Colum Lynch, "With the World's Gaze Fixed on the Islamic State, Mali's Jihadists Return," *Foreign Policy*, October 14, 2014.
154. United Nations, "Security Council Welcomes Deployment of Joint Force to Combat Terrorism Threat, Transnational Crime in Sahel, Unanimously Adopting Resolution 2359," June 21, 2017, https://www.un.org/press/en/2017/sc12881.doc.htm.
155. Sheehan and Porter, "The Future Role of U.S. Counterterrorism Operations in Africa."
156. Eric Schmitt and Thomas Gibbons-Neff, "Deadly Ambush of Green Berets in Niger Belies a 'Low Risk' Mission," *New York Times*, October 5, 2017; Eric Schmitt, "2 Navy SEALs Under Suspicion in Strangling of Green Beret in Mali," *New York Times*, October 29, 2017.
157. Samantha Power, "Remarks at a Ministerial Meeting on Implementation of the Agreement for Peace and Reconciliation for Mali," United Nations, September 23, 2016.
158. Interview with Andrew Lebovich, researcher specializing in West Africa, November 2, 2016; interview with Marc-André Boisvert; Shurkin, Pezard, and Zimmerman, *Mali's Next Battle*, 27, 45–47, 57.
159. Army Sgt. 1st Class Tyrone C. Marshall Jr., "AFRICOM Commander Addresses Concerns, Potential Solutions in Mali," *American Forces Press Service*, January 24, 2013.
160. As quoted in Warner, *The Trans-Sahara Counter Terrorism Partnership*, 68.
161. Moyar, *Countering Violent Extremism in Mali*, 56.
162. Lacher, *Organized Crime and Conflict in the Sahel-Sahara Region.*
163. Vicki Huddleston, "Why We Must Help Save Mali," *New York Times*, January 14, 2013; Pincus, "Mali Insurgency Followed 10 Years of U.S. Counterterrorism Programs."

164. Powelson, *Enduring Engagement Yes, Episodic Engagement No*, 53–54; Magnuson, "Mali Crisis Officer Lessons for Special Operations Command."

8. EGYPT AND ALGERIA: THE REVOLUTIONARY HEARTLAND

1. Mary Anne Weaver, "The Battle for Cairo," *New Yorker*, January 30, 1995.
2. Jihan al-Husseini and Ishraf al-Fiqi, "Mubarak: The Terrorists in Britain and No Dialogue with Them Because It Strengthens Them," *Al-Hayat*, November 24, 1997.
3. "Egypt Is Upset by Britain's Noncooperation in Combating Terrorism," *Al-Hayat*, November 30, 1997; Douglas Jehl, "Islamic Militants' War on Egypt: Going International," *New York Times*, November 20, 1995.
4. Jeremy Sharp, *Egypt: Background and U.S. Relations* (Washington, DC: Congressional Research Service, July 24, 2015).
5. International Crisis Group, "Algeria and Its Neighbours," Middle East/North Africa Report 164, October 12, 2015.
6. William B. Quandt, "U.S. and Algeria: Just Flirting," *Le Monde Diplomatique*, July 2002.
7. 98 percent of voters endorsed the referendum. International Crisis Group, "The Civil Concord: A Peace Initiative Wasted," Africa Report 31, July 9, 2001.
8. Ahmed Abou-el-Wafa, "Egypt," in *Counterterrorism Strategies: Successes and Failures of Six Nations*, ed. Yonah Alexander (Washington, DC: Potomac, 2006), 133–34.
9. Human Rights Watch, "Egypt," in *World Report 2002* (New York: Human Rights Watch, 2002), 414–423.
10. Department of State, *Country Reports on Terrorism 2009* (Washington, DC: 2010), 118–19.
11. Niveen Wahish and Sherine Abdel-Razek, "The Guessing Game," *Al-Ahram Weekly*, April 27–May 3, 2006.
12. International Crisis Group, "Egypt's Sinai Question," Middle East/North Africa Report 61, January 30, 2007.
13. Holly L. McCarthy and Ami Pedahzur, "The Sinai Terrorist Attacks," in *The Evolution of the Global Terrorist Threat: From 9/11 to Osama bin Laden's Death*, ed. Bruce Hoffman and Fernando Reinares (New York: Columbia University Press, 2014).
14. International Crisis Group, "Egypt's Sinai Question."
15. International Crisis Group, "Egypt's Sinai Question."
16. Lina Attalah, "In Sinai, the Tribe Comes Before the State, the State Before Islamists," *Egypt Independent*, June 11, 2012.
17. Joshua Gleis, "Trafficking and the Role of the Sinai Bedouin," *Jamestown Terrorism Monitor* 5, no. 12 (June 2017).
18. International Crisis Group, "Egypt's Sinai Question."
19. Serene Assir, "Law of the Land," *Al-Ahram Weekly*, December 29, 2005–January 4, 2006; International Crisis Group, "Egypt's Sinai Question."
20. Interview with Juan Zarate, former deputy assistant to the president and deputy national security advisor for combating terrorism, September 17, 2015.
21. Steven A. Cook, "How to Get Egypt's Generals Back on Our Side," *Foreign Policy*, January 5, 2015.

22. George W. Bush, "Address at Whitehall Palace," London, UK, November 19, 2003, http://www.foxnews.com/story/2003/11/19/raw-data-bush-speech-at-whitehall-palace.html.
23. George W. Bush, "Freedom in Iraq and Middle East: Address at the 20th Anniversary of the National Endowment for Democracy," Washington, DC, November 6, 2003, https://www.ned.org/remarks-by-president-george-w-bush-at-the-20th-anniversary/.
24. David Remnick, "Going Nowhere," *New Yorker*, July 24, 2004; Jeremy Sharp, (Washington, DC: Congressional Research Service, 2008).
25. Jeremy Sharp, *Egypt: 2005 Presidential and Parliamentary Elections* (Washington, DC: Congressional Research Service, September 21, 2005).
26. Maamoun Youset, "Egypt's Muslim Brotherhood Leader Says Arrests of Members of Attempt to Intimidate Votes," *Associated Press*, November 29, 2005.
27. Jeremy Sharp, *Egypt: Background and U.S. Relations* (Washington, DC: Congressional Research Service, 2007).
28. "Egypt: Proposed Constitutional Amendments Greatest Erosion of Human Rights in 26 Years," *Amnesty International*, March 18, 2007.
29. Sharp, *Egypt* (2007).
30. Sharp, *Egypt* (2007).
31. An Act Making Appropriations for the Department of State, Foreign Operations, and Related Programs for the Fiscal Year Ending September 30, 2008, and for Other Purposes, Public Law 110-161, 121 Stat. 2364, Section 690(a).
32. U.S. Department of State, Public Notice 6139, "Determination and Waiver of Section 690(a) of the Department of State, Foreign Operations, and Related Programs Appropriations Act, 2008 (Div. J, P.L. 110-161) Relating to Assistance for Egypt, February 29, 2008," *Federal Register* 73, no. 55 (March 20, 2008): 15041.
33. "Mubarak Warns of '100 Bin Ladens,'" *Reuters*, March 31, 2003.
34. U.S. Government Accountability Office, "Security Assistance: State and DOD Need to Assess How the Foreign Military Financing Program for Egypt Achieves U.S. Foreign Policy and Security Goals," GAO-06-437, April 2006, 17.
35. Mary Beth Sheridan and Joby Warrick, "Mubarak Resignation Throws Into Question U.S.-Egyptian Counterterrorism Work," *Washington Post*, February 13, 2011.
36. Interview with Steven Simon, former NSC senior director for the Middle East and North Africa, October 29, 2015.
37. Daniel Byman, "Extraordinary Rendition, Extraterritorial Detention, and Treatment of Detainees: Restoring Our Moral Credibility and Strengthening Our Diplomatic Standing," testimony before the Senate Committee on Foreign Relations, July 26, 2007.
38. Department of State, *Country Reports on Terrorism 2009* (Washington, DC: August 2010), 119.
39. Amnesty International, "USA Below the Radar: Secret Flights to Torture and 'Disappearance,'" April 5, 2006, https://www.amnesty.org/en/documents/AMR51/051/2006/en/.
40. Johnsen, *The Last Refuge*, 70, 114; Andrew Higgins and Alan Cullison, "Friend or Foe: The Story Of a Traitor to al Qaeda," *Wall Street Journal*, December 20, 2002.
41. Interviews with Juan Zarate and Steven Simon.
42. Barack Obama, "A New Beginning," Cairo, Egypt, June 4, 2009, https://obamawhitehouse.archives.gov/the-press-office/remarks-president-cairo-university-6-04-09.

43. Jeremy Sharp, *Egypt: Background and U.S. Relations* (Washington, DC: Congressional Research Service, 2011).
44. "Cairo: Security Vacuum as Police Vanish," *CBS News*, January 29, 2011; Rania Abouzeid, "Did Prison Breakout Reveal a Plan to Sow Chaos in Egypt?" *Time*, March 16, 2011.
45. Zack Gold, *Security in the Sinai: Present and Future* (The Hague: International Centre for Counter-Terrorism, March 2014).
46. Jeremy Sharp, *Egypt: Background and U.S. Relations* (Washington, DC: Congressional Research Service, 2014).
47. Bruce Riedel, "Al-Qaeda Grows in Sinai," *National Interest*, February 10, 2012.
48. Gold, *Security in the Sinai*; Salah ElBoluk, "Army Tanks in N. Sinai for First Time Since Israeli Peace Treaty," *Egypt Independent*, August 14, 2011.
49. Gold, *Security in the Sinai*.
50. Colin Dueck, *The Obama Doctrine: American Grand Strategy Today* (New York: Oxford University Press, 2015), 78.
51. Interview with Steven Simon; Michael *Morell, The Great War of Our Time: The CIA's Fight Against Terrorism—From al Qa'ida to ISIS* (New York: Grand Central, 2015), 186.
52. Ahmed Eleiba, "Egypt's 'Operation Eagle' Sinai Campaign Draws Mixed Reviews," *Ahram Online*, September 4, 2012.
53. "The Root of Egypt's Coup: Morsi Giving Free Hand to Sinai Islamists," *Associated Press*, July 18, 2013; Sharp, *Egypt* (2014).
54. Christopher M. Blanchard, *Recent Protests in Muslim Countries: Background and Issues for Congress* (Washington, DC: Congressional Research Service, September 20, 2012).
55. Helene Cooper and Mark Landler, "Egypt May Be Bigger Concern Than Libya for White House," *New York Times*, September 13, 2012.
56. Interview with Steven Simon.
57. Jeremy Sharp, *Egypt: Background and U.S. Relations* (Washington, DC: Congressional Research Service, 2012); Jean-Pierre Filiu, *From Deep State to Islamic State: The Arab Counter-Revolution and Its Jihadi Legacy* (New York: Oxford University Press, 2015), 176–77.
58. See, for example, David Kirkpatrick, "Recordings Suggest Emirates and Egyptian Military Pushed Ousting of Morsi," *New York Times*, March 1, 2015.
59. Stephen Tankel, "The Egypt Aid Dilemma," *National Interest*, August 23, 2013.
60. Declan Walsh, "Why Was an Italian Graduate Student Tortured and Murdered in Egypt?" *New York Times*, August 15, 2017.
61. Vivian Salama, "What's Behind the Wave of Terror in the Sinai?" *Atlantic*, November 22, 2013.
62. Asma Al Sharif and Maggie Fick, "Bombing Wave Hits Egypt Amid Fear of More Violence," *Reuters*, January 24, 2014.
63. Al-Anani, "ISIS Enters Egypt," *Foreign Affairs*, December 4, 2014.
64. Patrick Kingsley, Martin Chulov, and Lotfy Salman, "Egyptian Jihadis Pledge Allegiance to Isis," *Guardian*, November 10, 2014.
65. David Kirkpatrick, "ISIS Ally in Egypt Emerges as Key Suspect in Russian Jet Crash," *New York Times*, November 9, 2015.

66. Seth G. Jones et al., *Rolling Back the Islamic State* (Arlington, VA: RAND Corporation, 2017), 139–40.
67. Shadi Hamid, "Sisi's Regime Is a Gift to the Islamic State," Brookings Institution, August 7, 2015.
68. Gold, *Security in the Sinai*; Sharp, *Egypt* (2014).
69. David Kirkpatrick, "31 Egyptian Soldiers Are Killed as Militants Attack in Sinai," *New York Times*, October 24, 2014; David Kirkpatrick, "Militant Group in Egypt Vows Loyalty to ISIS," *New York Times*, November 10, 2014.
70. Mohamed Elmenshawy, "Egypt's War on Terror: ISIS, President Sisi, and the U.S.-led Coalition," *Middle East Institute*, November 6, 2014.
71. Al-Anani, "ISIS Enters Egypt."
72. Gold, *Security in the Sinai.*
73. Sharp, *Egypt* (2015); "Egyptian Army Exercises Self-Restraint in Sinai: Spokesman," *Ahram Online*, August 6, 2013.
74. Allison L. McManus, *Egypt's Security: Threat and Response* (Washington, DC: The Tahrir Institute for Middle East Policy, 2014).
75. McManus, *Egypt's Security: Threat and Response*; Nancy Youssef, "For 3 Egyptian Islamists, Violence Is the Only Way to Respond to Police Crackdown," *McClatchy*, March 11, 2014.
76. Since FY1986, the "coup" limitation has been found in annual appropriations law.
77. Author's observations working for the Ibn Khaldun Center for Development Studies in Cairo, 2004–2005; Nadine Sika, "Civil Society and Democratization in Egypt: The Road Not yet Traveled," *Democracy and Society* 9, no. 2 (2012): 29.
78. Peter Beaumont and Paul Harris, "U.S. 'Deeply Concerned' After Egyptian Forces Raid NGO Offices in Cairo," *Guardian*, December 29, 2011, https://www.theguardian.com/world/2011/dec/29/us-egyptian-forces-raid-cairo.
79. "Defendants' Names in NGO Funding Case Revealed as U.S. Warns Egypt," *Egypt Independent*, February 6, 2012, http://www.egyptindependent.com/news/defendants-names-ngo-funding-case-revealed-us-warns-egypt.
80. Sarah el-Sirgany, "Politicized Verdict May Sway Brotherhood on Egypt NGO Law," *Al-Monitor*, June 13, 2013, http://www.al-monitor.com/pulse/originals/2013/06/egypt-ngo-law-muslim-brotherhood.html; "The Muslim Brotherhood on the State of Civil Society and Civil Society Law in Post-Mubarak Egypt," *International Journal of Not-for-Profit Law* 4, no. 1 (April 2013).
81. Saskia Brechenmacher, *Civil Society Under Assault: Repression and Responses in Russia, Egypt, and Ethiopia* (Washington, DC: Carnegie Endowment for International Peace, 2017).
82. Sharp, *Egypt* (2015).
83. "Egypt's Constitution of 2014," https://www.constituteproject.org/constitution/Egypt_2014.pdf.
84. Walsh, "Why Was an Italian Graduate Student Tortured and Murdered in Egypt?"; Eric Trager, "Egypt Renews Its Crackdown on NGOs," Washington Institute for Near East Policy, March 24, 2016.
85. On the provision of support, see A. Amer, "Cairo Backs Libyan Stance," *Al-Ahram Weekly*, September 21, 2016. On U.S. policy, see Christopher M. Blanchard, *Libya:*

Transition and U.S. Policy (Washington, DC: Congressional Research Service, 2017). On the dynamics of the conflict, see Frederick Wehrey, "Whoever Controls Benghazi Controls Libya," *Atlantic*, July 1, 2017; Karim Mezran and Elissa Miller, *Libya: From Intervention to Proxy War* (Washington, DC: Atlantic Council, 2017).

86. Sharp, *Egypt* (2014).
87. The law restricted the use of additional aid unless the secretary of state certified that Egypt had met democracy benchmarks.
88. William Wan and Ernesto Londono, "Egypt's Aid from U.S. in Peril Amid Crackdown on Prodemocracy Groups," *Washington Post*, February 4, 2012.
89. "U.S. to Cut Military and Economic Aid to Egypt in Shift of Policy After 'Coup,'" *Guardian*, October 9, 2013.
90. Department of State, "Press Statement: U.S. Assistance to Egypt," October 9, 2013, https://2009-2017.state.gov/r/pa/prs/ps/2013/10/215258.htm.
91. Sharp, *Egypt* (2015); Stephen McInerney and Cole Bockenfeld, "The Federal Budget and Appropriations for Fiscal Year 2016: Democracy, Governance, and Human Rights in the Middle East and North Africa," Project on Middle East Democracy, May 2015, http://pomed.org/wp-content/uploads/2015/05/FY2016-Budget-Report.pdf.
92. White House, *National Security Strategy* (Washington, DC: 2015) 26.
93. Oren Dorell, "Egypt Slams U.S. Aid Cut; Allies Concerned," *USA Today*, October 11, 2013.
94. Marcia Recio, "Rep. Granger Urges Obama to Send Arms Owed to Egypt," *McClatchy*, February 23, 2015; Dafna Rand and Stephen Tankel, *Security Cooperation and Assistance: Rethinking the Return on Assistance* (Washington, DC: Center for a New American Security, 2015).
95. "U.S. Unlocks Military Aid to Egypt, Backing President Sisi," *BBC*, June 22, 2014, http://www.bbc.com/news/world-middle-east-27961933.
96. The Obama administration announced it was discontinuing Egypt's use of cash flow financing (CFF), which is a mechanism that enabled Egypt to purchase equipment on credit. Ending CFF gave the United States more flexibility to tailor security assistance to conditions on the ground in Egypt. On the release of the weapons, see White House, "Readout of the President's Call with President al-Sisi Egypt," press release, March 31, 2015. On CFF, see Derek Chollet, "The Part of Obama's Arms-to-Egypt Deal That Matters," *Defense One*, April 2, 2015. On the release of aid, see Krishnadev Calamur, "Obama Releases Frozen Military Aid to Egypt," *NPR*, March 31, 2015; Sharp, *Egypt* (2015); U.S. Government Accountability Office, "Security Assistance: State and DOD Need to Assess How the Foreign Military Financing Program for Egypt Achieves U.S. Foreign Policy and Security Goals," GAO-06-437, April 2006.
97. White House, "Readout of the President's Call with President al-Sisi Egypt," March 31, 2015.
98. Barack Obama "Address to the United Nations General Assembly," New York, NY, September 24, 2013.
99. Arms sales were authorized soon after 9/11, but according to publicly available data deliveries did not begin until later in the decade.
100. Data on security assistance: https://securityassistance.org/data/program/military/Algeria/2001/2011/all/Global/.

101. Interview with Tricia Bacon, former State Department intelligence official, September 29, 2015; interview with Dan Benjamin, ambassador-at-large and coordinator for counterterrorism at the U.S. State Department, November 13, 2015; interview with U.S. intelligence official, name and date withheld upon request; interview with Juan Zarate.
102. This amnesty was connected to the Civil Concord approved in 1999.
103. Hanna Rogan, "Violent Patterns: A Quantitative Study of al-Qaida in the Islamic Maghreb," in *Understanding Jihadism: Origins, Evolution, and Future Perspectives* (Oslo: March 19–21, 2009).
104. Anneli Botha, *Terrorism in the Maghreb: The Transnationalisation of Domestic Terrorist* (Pretoria: Institute for Security Studies, 2008), 189–90.
105. Interview with French intelligence officials, March 9, 2010; interview with Algeria-based Western intelligence official, name withheld upon request, May 16, 2010.
106. Souad Mekhennet et al., "A Threat Renewed: Ragtag Insurgency Gains a Lifeline from Al Qaeda," *New York Times*, July 1, 2008.
107. This led some analysts to conclude the charter was a mechanism for President Bouteflika to retire a cadre of senior military officers. See Rafael Bustos, "The Algerian National Reconciliation Referendum of 2005," *Mediterranean Politics* (2006): 119–21; James D. Le Sueur, *Algeria Since 1989: Between Terror and Democracy* (London: Zed, 2013), 90.
108. Faycal Oukaci, "The Road to Baghdad," *L'Expression*, January 17, 2007.
109. Alexis Arieff, *Algeria: Current Issues* (Washington, DC: Congressional Research Service, November 18, 2013).
110. Interview with Mounir Boudjemaa, assistant editor at *Liberté*, Algeria, May 12, 2010; interview with Dris Cherif, professor at Université d'Alger, Algeria, May 10, 2010.
111. Emily Hunt, *Islamist Terrorism in Northwestern Africa: A "Thorn in the Neck" of the United States?* (Washington, DC: Washington Institute for Near East Policy, February 2007).
112. Jean-Pierre Filiu, "The Local and Global Jihad of al-Qaida in the Islamic Maghreb," *Middle East Journal* 63, no. 2 (2009): 213–26.
113. Jean-Pierre Filiu, *Al-Qaeda in the Islamic Maghreb: Algerian Challenge or Global Threat?* (Washington, DC: Carnegie Endowment for International Peace, 2009); Camille Tawil, "New Strategies in al-Qaeda's Battle for Algeria," *Jamestown Foundation Terrorism Monitor* 7, no. 2 (2009): 53.
114. Filiu, "Al-Qaeda in the Islamic Maghreb"; Petter Nesser, "Chronology of Jihadism in Western Europe, 1994–2007: Planned, Prepared, and Executed Terrorist Attacks," *Studies in Conflict and Terrorism* 31, no. 10 (2008): 924–46.
115. "The Second *As-Sahab* Interview with Dr. Ayman al-Zawahiri," September 11, 2006; Abdelmalek Droukdel, "Salafist Group for Preaching and Combat Announces Its New Name as al-Qaeda Organization in the Islamic Maghreb," January 24, 2007.
116. Camille Tawil, *Brothers in Arms: The Story of Al-Qa'ida and the Arab Jihadists* (London: Saqi Books, 2010), 195.
117. Interview with Tricia Bacon.
118. "Al Qaeda in 2008: The Struggle for Relevance," *Stratfor Global Intelligence Security Weekly*, December 19, 2007.
119. Department of State, *Country Reports on Terrorism 2008* (Washington, DC: 2009), 111–113.
120. Rogan, "Violent Patterns."

121. Information on homeland security measures based on interviews with Western security officials in Algiers in May 2010.
122. Department of State, *Country Reports on Terrorism 2008*, 112.
123. Hanna Rogan, "Al-Qaida in the Islamic Maghreb Strikes Again," *Perspectives on Terrorism* 2, no. 8 (2008): 23–28.
124. Interview with Idriss Lallali, head of Alert and Prevention Unit at the African Centre for the Study and Research of Terrorism (African Union), May 18, 2010; Botha, *Terrorism in the Maghreb*, 80–81.
125. Jacques Roussellier, *Terrorism in North Africa and the Sahel: Al-Qa'ida's Franchise or Freelance?* (Washington, DC: Middle East Institute, 2011).
126. Jolyon Ford, Beyond the *'War on Terror': A Study of Criminal Justice Responses to Terrorism in the Maghreb* (Pretoria: Institute for Security Studies, 2009), 52.
127. Floor Janssen and Bertus Hendriks, "Algeria's Counter-Terrorism Strategy: Radicalism and Terrorist Activity Within the Framework of National Reconciliation," in *Counter-Terrorism Strategies in Indonesia, Algeria, and Saudi Arabia*, ed. Roel Meijer (The Hague: Netherlands Institute of International Relations, 2012), 100.
128. Interview with Mohamad Hemur, BBC journalist, May 5, 2010; interview with Salima Tlemcani, journalist with *El Watan*, May 4, 2010.
129. Robert P. Parks, "An Unexpected Mandate? The April 8, 2004, Algerian Presidential Elections," *Middle East Journal* 59, no. 1 (2005): 98–106.
130. Carol Migdalovitz, *Algeria: Current Issues* (Washington, DC: Congressional Research Service, February 16, 2005), 6.
131. John P. Entelis, "Algeria, Revolutionary in Name Only," *Foreign Policy*, September 7, 2011; John P. Entelis, "Algerian Crisis: The Primacy of Le Pouvoir," *Cairo Review of Global Affairs*, January 28, 2013.
132. George Joffé, "Political Dynamics in North Africa," *International Affairs* 85, no. 5 (2009): 931–49.
133. Amel Boubekeur, "Political Islam in Algeria" Working Document 268, Centre for European Policy Studies, May 2007; Noura Hamladji, "Co-optation, Repression, and Authoritarian Regime's Survival: The Case of the Islamist MSP-Hamas in Algeria," Working Paper SPS no. 2002/7, European University Institute, Florence, August 2002.
134. Migdalovitz, *Algeria* (2005).
135. Migdalovitz, *Algeria* (2005).
136. "Corruption Perception Index 2005," Transparency International, http://www.transparency.org/research/cpi/cpi_2005/0/.
137. Amel Boubekeur, *Salafism and Radical Politics in Postconflict Algeria* (Washington, DC: Carnegie Endowment for International Peace, 2008).
138. "Algerian Mosques 'Declare War' on Extremism," *BBC*, November 7, 2007; Botha, *Terrorism in the Maghreb*, 187.
139. Janssen and Hendriks, "Algeria's Counter-Terrorism Strategy," 98.
140. "Révélations de Mossaab Abou Daoud. Désarroi des groupes armés," *L'Expression*, August 15, 2007.
141. Andrew Black, "The Ideological Struggle over al-Qaeda's Suicide Tactics in Algeria," *Jamestown Foundation Terrorism Monitor* 6, no. 3 (February 2008); Tawil, "New Strategies in al-Qaeda's Battle for Algeria."

142. Interviews with Lallali and Boudjemaa.
143. Arieff, *Algeria* (2013); U.S. Embassy Algiers, "Bilateral Counterterrorism Contact Group Launched," March 2011.
144. Interview with Dan Benjamin.
145. "Desert Shadows," *Africa Confidential* 45, no. 4 (February 10, 2004): 8; Migdalovitz, *Algeria* (2005).
146. Carol Migdalovitz, *Algeria: Current Issues* (Washington, DC: Congressional Research Service, 2010).
147. Migdalovitz, *Algeria* (2005).
148. The current and former intelligence officials who provided this assessment requested anonymity.
149. Interviews with Tricia Bacon and Juan Zarate.
150. Numerous interlocutors, including current and former U.S. officials, Algerian interlocutors, and African Union officials provided an assessment along these lines during interviews in Washington and Algiers. See also Lawrence Aida Ammour, "Regional Security Cooperation in the Maghreb and Sahel: Algeria's Pivotal Ambivalence," *Africa Security Brief* 18 (February 2012).
151. Migdalovitz, *Algeria* (2010).
152. Geoff D. Porter, "Challenges to Algeria's Non-Interventionist Stance Seen Through a Regional Lens," *Politique Étrangère* 3 (2015).
153. Constitution of the People's Democratic Republic of Algeria, http://confinder.richmond.edu/admin/docs/local_algeria.pdf.
154. Porter, "Challenges to Algeria's Non-Interventionist Stance."
155. Ammour, "Regional Security Cooperation in the Maghreb and Sahel."
156. Anouar Boukhars, *The Paranoid Neighbor: Algeria and the Conflict in Mali* (Washington, DC: Carnegie Endowment for International Peace, 2012).
157. This was the consensus of local and Western interlocutors in Algeria during interviews conducted in May 2010.
158. Migdalovitz, *Algeria* (2010).
159. General David M. Rodriguez, U.S. Army Nominee for Commander, U.S. Africa Command, advance policy questions for confirmation hearing before the Senate Committee on Armed Services, February 14, 2013.
160. International Crisis Group, "Algeria and Its Neighbours."
161. Carol Migdalovitz, *Algeria: Current Issues* (Washington, DC: Congressional Research Service, 2011).
162. International Crisis Group, "Algeria and Its Neighbours."
163. Carlotta Gall, "Who Runs Algeria? Many Doubt It's Ailing President Abdelaziz Bouteflika," *New York Times*, December 23, 2015.
164. "Algeria's Bouteflika Replaces Head of DRS Military Intelligence—Sources, State Media," *Reuters*, September 13, 2015.
165. Andrew Lebovich, *Deciphering Algeria: The Stirrings of Reform* (European Council on Foreign Relations, December 2015).
166. "The In Amenas Attack: Report of the Investigation Into the Terrorist Attack on In Amenas," prepared for Statoil ASA's board of directors, *Statoil ASA* (2013), 37, http://www.statoil.com/en/NewsAndMedia/News/2013/Downloads/In%20Amenas%20report.pdf.

167. Louise Loveluck, "Planting the Seeds of Tunisia's Ansar al-Sharia," *Foreign Policy*, September 27, 2012.
168. Said Ferjani, an Ennahda leader who evolved from participating in youthful militancy to peaceful politics, acknowledged that his party put too much hope in winning over young extremists and too little emphasis on security measures to control them. See David D. Kirkpatrick, "New Freedoms in Tunisia Drive Support for ISIS," *New York Times*, October 21, 2014; Aaron Y. Zelin and Vish Sakthivel, "Tunisia Designates Ansar al-Sharia," Washington Institute for Near East Policy, August 28, 2013.
169. Carlotta Gall, "Change in Militant Tactics Puts Tunisians on Edge," *New York Times*, August 9, 2015.
170. Aaron Y. Zelin, Andrew Lebovich, and Daveed Gartenstein-Ross, "Al-Qaida in the Islamic Maghreb's Tunisia Strategy," *CTC Sentinel* 6, no. 7 (2013).
171. Porter, "Challenges to Algeria's Non-Interventionist Stance"; Andrew Lebovich and Aaron Y. Zelin, "Assessing Al-Qaida's Presence in the New Libya," *CTC Sentinel* 5, no. 3 (2012): 21–25.
172. On the decline, see Roussellier, *Terrorism in North Africa and the Sahel*. On the surge, see Andrew Lebovich, "AQIM Returns in Force in Northern Algeria," *CTC Sentinel* 4, no. 9 (2011).
173. International Crisis Group, "Algeria and Its Neighbours."
174. "The In Amenas Attack." See also Salim Tamani, "Beyond the Terrorist Attack of Ain Amenas," *Aspen Institute*, January 2, 2013, https://www.aspeninstitute.it/aspenia-online/article/beyond-terrorist-attack-ain-amenas.
175. On the merger, see Thomas Joscelyn, "Al-Qaeda Groups Reorganize in West Africa," *Long War Journal*, March 13, 2017. On Ansar Dine, see Adam Nossiter and Neil MacFarquhar, "Algeria Sowed Seeds of Hostage Crisis as It Nurtured Warlord," *New York Times*, February 1, 2013; Boukhars, *The Paranoid Neighbor*.
176. Two additional groups in Algeria subsequently pledged allegiance to ISIS. On Jund-al-Khilafah, see "Jund al-Khilafah in Algeria Releases Video Reiterating Pledge to IS," SITE Intel Group, September 30, 2014.
177. Porter, "Challenges to Algeria's Non-Interventionist Stance."
178. International Crisis Group, "Algeria and Its Neighbours."
179. Lebovich, "AQIM Returns in Force in Northern Algeria."
180. "Algerian Army 'Kills Jihadist Behind Herve Gourdel Beheading,'" *BBC*, December 23, 2014.
181. Lebovich, *Deciphering Algeria*.
182. Mohamed Ben Ahmad, "Algeria Closes Most of Its Land Borders," *El Khabar*, May 22, 2014.
183. "Algeria Raises Alert Level Along Border with Libya," *Middle East Monitor*, June 4, 2015; International Crisis Group, "Algeria and Its Neighbours."
184. Lebovich, *Deciphering Algeria*.
185. Ismael Aidara, "Mali, Alger sort le grand jeu dans le dialogue inter-malien," *Les Afriques*, February 8, 2015.
186. Not all of the substate Malian groups signed at once. See Adama Diarra and Tiemoko Diallo, "Malian Rebel Alliance Signs Peace Deal with Government," *Reuters*, June 20, 2015.

187. International Crisis Group, "Algeria and Its Neighbours."
188. Lebovich, *Deciphering Algeria.*
189. Porter, "Challenges to Algeria's Non-Interventionist Stance."
190. "Tunisia Islamists Face Army Attack in Chaambi Mountains," *BBC*, August 2, 2013.
191. Kal Ben Khalid, "Evolving Approaches in Algerian Security Cooperation," *CTC Sentinel* 8, no. 6 (2015): 15–20.
192. Khalid, "Evolving Approaches in Algerian Security Cooperation"; Fouad Harit, "Terrorisme: l'armée algérienne débarque en Tunisie," *Afrik.com*, August 5, 2014; "L'engagement de l'armée algérienne," *El Watan*, August 4, 2014.
193. International Crisis Group, "Algeria and Its Neighbours"; Porter, "Challenges to Algeria's Non-Interventionist Stance."
194. Demetri Sevstopulo and Hebah Saleh, "Trump Signals New Approach to Egypt in Sisi Meeting," *Financial Times*, April 3, 2017.
195. Senior officials in the Trump administration have exhibited a more ambivalent attitude toward Egypt. In August 2017, the State Department withheld $195 million in FY 2016 FMF pending Egyptian improvement on its human rights and democracy record and also reprogrammed another $65.7 million in FY 2017 FMF and $30 million in FY 2016 Economic Support Funds. Arshad Mohammed and Warren Strobel, "U.S. to Withhold up to $290 Million in Egypt Aid," *Reuters*, August 22, 2017.

CONCLUSION

1. Lisa O. Monaco, "Evolving to Meet the New Terrorist Threat," speech at the Council on Foreign Relations, March 7, 2016, https://obamawhitehouse.archives.gov/the-press-office/2016/03/07/remarks-lisa-o-monaco-council-foreign-relations-kenneth-moskow-memorial.
2. Monaco reiterated the importance of local partners in an article for *Foreign Affairs* written after she left government. Lisa O. Monaco, "Preventing the Next Attack: A Strategy for the War on Terrorism," *Foreign Affairs* 96, no. 6 (2017): 23–29.
3. The Algerian security establishment is extremely guarded, which could make this case an outlier. However, the United States encountered similar problems with Tunisia after the Arab uprisings because the two countries did not have a shared history of cooperation. Interview with Steven Simon, former NSC senior director for the Middle East and North Africa, October 29, 2015. The literature also suggests that closer bilateral relations can enhance intelligence cooperation. See Jennifer E. Sims, "Foreign Intelligence Liaison: Devils, Deals, and Details," *International Journal of Intelligence and CounterIntelligence* 19, no. 2 (2006): 195–217.
4. Dafna Rand and Stephen Tankel, *Security Cooperation and Assistance: Rethinking the Return on Assistance* (Washington, DC: Center for a New American Security, 2015).
5. Christopher Paul et al., *What Works Best When Building Partner Capacity and Under What Circumstances?* (Arlington, VA: RAND Corporation, 2013).
6. Daniel Byman, "Friends Like These: Counterinsurgency and the War on Terrorism," *International Security* 31, no. 2 (Fall 2006): 79–115; Steven Metz and Raymond Millen, *Insurgency and Counterinsurgency in the Twenty-First Century: Reconceptualizing Threat*

and Response (Carlisle, PA: Strategic Studies Institute, U.S. Army War College, November 2004), 19.

7. John Horgan, "Theory vs. Practice," *United States Institute of Peace Insights* 1 (Spring 2014).
8. For example, efforts to promote security-sector reform in Algeria led it to welcome training and assistance intended to advance the rule of law.
9. Under Director John Brennan, the CIA also created functional centers that comingled case officers and analysts.
10. Information in this paragraph and the next is based on interviews with four U.S. intelligence analysts—two focused on regional issues and two focused on terrorism/counterterrorism—from three different agencies. All interviewees requested anonymity.
11. Byman, "Friends Like These."
12. Daniel L. Byman, "The Limits of Counterterrorism," *Lawfare*, August 4, 2015.
13. Defense institution building and professionalizing military personnel remained important, too. These issues were receiving more attention by the time of writing. Mara Karlin, *Building Militaries in Fragile States Challenges for the United States* (Philadelphia: University of Pennsylvania Press, 2017); Alexandra Kerr and Michael Miklaucic, eds., *Effective Legitimate Secure: Insights for Defense Institution Building* (Washington, DC: National Defense University, 2017).
14. On the correlation of terrorism to rule of law and bureaucracy, see Seung-Whan Choi, "Fighting Terrorism Through the Rule of Law?" *Journal of Conflict Resolution* 54, no. 6 (2010): 940–66; Michael G. Findley and Joseph K. Young, "Terrorism, Democracy, and Credible Commitments," *International Studies Quarterly* 55, no. 2 (2011): 357–78; C. S. Hendrix and J. K. Young, "State Capacity and Terrorism: A Two-Dimensional Approach," *Security Studies* 23, no. 2 (2014): 329–63. On the impact of governance on BPC, see Paul et al., *What Works Best.*
15. These recommendations are drawn from a study the author contributed to on evaluating counterterrorism assistance. See Ilan Goldenberg, Alice Hunt Friend, Stephen Tankel, and Nicholas A. Heras, *Remodeling Partner Capacity: Maximizing the Effectiveness of U.S. Counterterrorism Security Assistance* (Washington, DC: Center for a New American Security, November 2016), 30–32.
16. Melissa G. Dalton, *Smart Conditions: A Strategic Framework for Leveraging Security Assistance* (Washington, DC: Center for Strategic and International Studies, July 2016).
17. Dalton, *Smart Conditions.*
18. Such a document should be kept classified or in sensitive channels.
19. These types of conditions would be more expansive than current end-use monitoring, which mainly aims to ensure that arms and equipment are not misused.
20. U.S. policy makers also fear rupturing a relationship with a nuclear-armed state.
21. Daniel Byman, *Deadly Connections: States That Sponsor Terrorism* (New York: Cambridge University Press, 2008), 300.
22. "Topic: High-Risk and Noncooperative Jurisdictions," FATF website, http://www.fatf-gafi.org/publications/high-riskandnon-cooperativejurisdictions/.
23. Linda Robinson, "SOF's Evolving Role: Warfare 'by, with, and Through' Local Forces," *Cypher Brief*, May 9, 2017.

24. Author discussions with members of the U.S. special operations forces community. See also Robinson, "SOF's Evolving Role"; Michèle Flournoy and Richard Fontaine, "The Afghan War Is Not Lost," *National Interest*, July 11, 2017; Luke Hartig, "Reported Emirati Abuse of Detainees and the Perils of U.S. Partnerships," *Just Security*, June 22, 2017.
25. Ryan Goodman and Luke Hartig, "U.S.-UAE Partnership and Alleged Torture: Recommended Next Steps for the Administration and Congress," *Just Security*, July 5, 2017.
26. The original Lend-Lease Act was passed before the United States entered World War II and authorized the president to "lend" supplies to countries opposing Nazi Germany with repayment deferred.
27. John Warner National Defense Authorization Act for FY2007.

INDEX

Page numbers in italics indicate tables or figures.

COLUMBIA STUDIES IN TERRORISM AND IRREGULAR WARFARE

Bruce Hoffman, Series Editor

Michael W. S. Ryan, *Decoding Al-Qaeda's Strategy: The Deep Battle Against America*

David H. Ucko and Robert Egnell, *Counterinsurgency in Crisis: Britain and the Challenges of Modern Warfare*

Bruce Hoffman and Fernando Reinares, editors, *The Evolution of the Global Terrorist Threat: From 9/11 to Osama bin Laden's Death*

Boaz Ganor, *Global Alert: The Rationality of Modern Islamist Terrorism and the Challenge to the Liberal Democratic World*

M. L. R. Smith and David Martin Jones, *The Political Impossibility of Modern Counterinsurgency: Strategic Problems, Puzzles, and Paradoxes*

Elizabeth Grimm Arsenault, *How the Gloves Came Off: Lawyers, Policy Makers, and Norms in the Debate on Torture*

Assaf Moghadam, *Nexus of Global Jihad: Understanding Cooperation Among Terrorist Actor*

Bruce Hoffman, *Inside Terrorism*, 3rd edition